GUERRILLA WARFARE

A Historical, Biographical, and Bibliographical Sourcebook

Anthony James Joes

Robin Higham, Advisory Editor

GREENWOOD PRESS
Westport, Connecticut • London

Library of Congress Cataloging-in-Publication Data

Joes, Anthony James.
   Guerrilla warfare : a historical, biographical, and bibliographical
   sourcebook / Anthony James Joes.
      p.   cm.
   Includes bibliographical references and index.
   ISBN 0–313–29252–3 (alk. paper)
   1. Guerrilla warfare—History.   2. Guerrilla warfare—
Bibliography.   I. Title.
U240.J58   1996
355.4'25'09—dc20   95–52710

British Library Cataloguing in Publication Data is available.

Library of Congress Catalog Card Number: 95–52710
ISBN: 0–313–29252–3

First published in 1996

Greenwood Press, 88 Post Road West, Westport, CT 06881
An imprint of Greenwood Publishing Group, Inc.

Printed in the United States of America

The paper used in this book complies with the
Permanent Paper Standard issued by the National
Information Standards Organization (Z39.48–1984).

10 9 8 7 6 5 4 3 2 1

Contents

Preface

In the last paragraph of his massive volume on the Viet Nam wars, Philip Davidson made this stark statement: "Our involvement in Viet Nam has taught us nothing."[1] Many would agree with that ominous view, at least to some extent. In light of such sentiments, any effort to illuminate the subject of guerrilla war, however inadequate, can only be worthwhile. This book provides a three-part consideration of the subject: Part I, History and Analysis; Part II, Biographical Profiles; and Part III, Bibliographical Essays.

Part I surveys and analyzes guerrilla warfare from the American Revolution to twentieth-century post-colonial conflicts. Rather than exhaustively cataloging guerrilla conflicts, it gives a broad survey of all the major occurrences plus many less well-known wars, sufficient in number, variety, and scope to suggest important points and raise important questions. The emphasis falls not so much on presentation of historical facts as on analysis of causes and effects. In part for that reason, I have tried to keep distracting footnotes to a minimum (an endeavor that some readers may decide was not as successful as it might have been).

The general approach is to look for answers to fundamental questions: What is the genesis and context of this particular guerrilla insurgency? What identifiable factors contributed to the victory or defeat of these guerrillas (or the side they supported)? Which of these factors are common to guerrilla conflict, and which are unique to a particular case?

Following the example of Walter Laqueur,[2] among others, I draw a fundamental distinction between guerrilla warfare and terrorism, addressing the former and excluding the latter. Political violence in itself, however spectacular or destructive, and especially that type of violence that many would find hard to distinguish from mere criminality, does not establish any persons or groups as "guerrillas." I believe the tendency currently fashionable in some circles to lump together guerrillas and terrorists is extremely regrettable, retarding rather than advancing the process of analysis.

Part II includes alphabetically arranged profiles of individuals who are important to the subject. They include guerrilla chieftains, military commanders, government officials, party leaders, theorists, and instructors or people representing any combination of these, who exerted notable influence. Some subjects are included because they illustrate important points in the conflicts discussed in Part I.

Part III surveys the major English-language literature on guerrilla warfare, including works from several foreign languages when available. It provides a wide-ranging, representative, and intensive collection of works on the origins, context, and consequence of guerrilla conflicts.

NOTES

1. Philip B. Davidson, *Viet Nam at War: The History, 1946–1975* (Novato, CA: Presidio, 1988).

2. Walter Laqueur, *Guerrilla: A Political and Military History* (Boston: Little, Brown, 1976).

PART I
History and Analysis

Introduction: The Nature of Guerrilla War

In the latter half of the twentieth century many Americans came to associate the term "guerrilla" with communist revolutionary movements. Certainly, Communists directed many of the most notable instances of guerrilla warfare, such as those in China, Greece, Viet Nam, and Nicaragua. But in the Ukraine, Tibet, Eritrea, and most spectacularly in Afghanistan, guerrillas fought *against* Communist regimes; in these cases, as well as other major instances, such as the Vendean resistance to the French Revolution and the Spanish insurgency against Napoleon (where the word "guerrilla" comes from), guerrilla war has been the instrument of conservative, religious, or nationalist popular movements.

HOW GUERRILLAS FIGHT

Guerrilla war is also far from being a modern phenomenon. Five hundred years before the Christian Era, the hit-and-run tactics of the nomadic Scythians frustrated the efforts of Darius I to conquer them. Three and a half centuries later, Judas Maccabeus led successful guerrilla campaigns against the Syrians. In Wales, final establishment of English control in 1282 came only after two hundred years of bitter fighting, in which encastellation—covering the country with small strongholds—foreshadowed the blockhouse systems of later counterinsurgencies.

In Spain, the Romans needed centuries to overcome the guerrilla tactics of the Lusitanians and Celtiberians. During the second century B.C. Viriathus, the most famous of the Iberian resistance leaders (flourished 147–139 B.C.), employed tactics against the Romans remarkably similar to those used in Spain against Napoleon nearly two millennia later. In turn, Roman counterinsurgency efforts bore most of the stigmata of similar efforts in our own era. For example, Roman atrocities against civilian populations enflamed popular resistance. Overconfidence, poor intelligence, and inappropriately conventional tactics characterized many Roman efforts; Appian writes that "the weight of their armor, the ignorance of the roads, and the inferiority of their horses" greatly hampered the Romans, operating in a hostile country in which large armies could not find sufficient sustenance and small armies were subject to attack. (Later on, Scipio Aemilianus would drastically simplify the Roman supply system.) Spanish guerrillas tied up large numbers of troops and thus weakened Rome on other fronts. Under these circumstances Roman forces suffered several serious defeats. In the end victory came to the Romans not because of superiority in skill and leadership but by a policy of exhaustion: they killed or enslaved captives by the thousands and assassinated rebel leaders through perfidy. And the Romans won also because they learned to take advantage of tribal rivalries in Spain and recruit thousands of soldiers from the local population.

Thus, guerrilla war is not the hallmark of any particular ideology, century, or culture. What defines guerrillas is not why they fight, nor when, nor where, but *how*: guerrilla war is a set of *tactics*. Guerrilla tactics are an effort to answer the question: *How can the weak make war against the strong?*

Since guerrillas are by definition the weaker side, their first duty is to survive. Their second duty is to alter the odds. Out of these exigencies evolve the classic method of the guerrilla: surprise the adversary by concentrating strength against weakness. Strategically—looking at the war as a whole—the guerrillas are inferior to their enemy in numbers, equipment, and training; that is why they fight as guerrillas rather than march out to meet the enemy head to head. But tactically—at the specific place where they make their attack—the guerrillas can be overwhelmingly more numerous and thus win a particular engagement. As Mao wrote, "The strategy of guerrilla war is to pit one man against ten, but the tactic is to pit ten men against one." To have constant tactical superiority the guerrillas must be able to assemble quickly (to achieve surprise) and disperse quickly (to get away from regular troops coming to the rescue). Secrecy and deception must be their sharpest tools. Thus guerrillas attack small enemy posts or detachments at night, or in the rain, or when the troops are eating or have just completed a march. "Guerrilla warfare means constant fighting rather than big battles. It is not spectacular victories and territories that count, but the annihilation of small units and the preservation of one's own vital force."[1] To this end the great Prussian military theorist Karl von Clausewitz advised guerrillas to fight far from the population centers, in rough terrain, forests, or marshes; here their light armament and scanty supplies will be a positive advantage, whereas the heavy equipment of conventional armies slows them down. (The revealing Roman word for the baggage that regular armies drag around with them is *impedimenta*.)[2]

That is why the favorite operation of guerrilla units is to ambush convoys and, in modern times, mine highways and railroads, especially those leading into guerrilla-dominated territory. Guerrillas attack the rear of the enemy army and in effect its psyche, inflicting casualties, making nighttime movements too dangerous. By enticing their enemies into constant, fruitless pursuit (sometimes ending in a well-prepared ambush), guerrillas undermine their opponents' strength, both physical and moral. They are especially keen to interrupt their enemies' food and water supplies: however unromantic this may sound, it is of the essence of war—even the bravest and most disciplined of soldiers cannot go three days without water. Further, well-led guerrillas operating in support of their own side's conventional army will cause the enemy to divert many soldiers from the struggle with that army; that is a major reason why the Duke of Wellington, for example, was able to win battles in Spain against a numerically superior French occupation force. Indeed, to be most effective guerrillas need to operate in tandem with regular units. The presence of such units prevents the counterinsurgency army from breaking down into small groups, whereas large formations cannot harass the guerrillas or occupy the land and control the population. This situation—guerrillas and conventional forces operating together—presents the gravest challenge to any counterinsurgency campaign.

Clearly, however, guerrillas can win, or at least survive, even if they are not supported by regular troops, as Castro demonstrated in Cuba, as well as the Khmer Rouge in Cambodia and the mujahideen in Afghanistan. If unsupported by conventional units, the guerrillas must be able to do more damage to the enemy than the enemy does to them. If they cannot, the guerrillas will not win.

WHAT GUERRILLAS NEED

To *survive*, guerrillas need intelligence (i.e., good information about their environment), high morale, and ideally a secure base. To *win*, they need help from outside the country. Good intelligence is of primary and decisive importance. Well-led guerrillas assemble rapidly in numbers superior to their opponents and then disperse quickly. To do this they must have accurate information on the location, numbers, equipment, morale, and intentions of the enemy. This intelligence must come from the civilian population (normally peasants and small merchants) of the area in which the guerrillas operate. Mao's famous dictum that "the guerrilla moves among the people as the fish through the water" has several meanings; one of them is that since accurate intelligence from civilians enables the guerrillas to win and even to exist, the guerrillas absolutely must have good relations with the peasantry. One reliable way to ensure exemplary behavior by the guerrillas toward the peasants is to recruit locally. During the Greek Civil War the Communist-led guerrillas systematically violated this principle of good civilian relations, to their great cost.

Closely related to the treatment of civilians, from an intelligence viewpoint, is the treatment of prisoners. Mao advised guerrillas to feed their prisoners, give them a political lecture, and then release them. The return of prisoners unharmed to their comrades teaches the latter that they need not fear capture and hence need not go down fighting when the guerrillas are upon them. In these circumstances, not only are guerrilla casualties lowered but it becomes much easier for the guerrillas to take prisoners, and from prisoners can come precious nuggets of intelligence.

Guerrillas need, secondly, high morale; to fight their kind of war, to live their kind of life, is very hard. The existence of the guerrillas is not romantic—quite the contrary. Cut off from normal pleasures and concerns, guerrillas must be prepared to take human life and destroy human dwellings; hunted men and women, they live always with the prospect of capture and in the presence of death. Food is often scarce, cleanliness is often impossible. Consider this passage from the memoirs of a Filipino guerrilla: "Sickness was our worst enemy and accounted for many times the casualties inflicted by the Japanese and puppets. It was the one problem we were never quite able to overcome. Malaria was the worst cause of death. Our squadrons were often forced to live in the swamps, which were thickly infested by malarial mosquitos. . . . Dysentery and stomach ulcers from inadequate food were other serious afflictions."[3]

Clearly, with the first flush of glamour and excitement worn off, few guerrillas would be willing to continue that life unless their morale sustained them. Besides constant victories, nothing builds and maintains morale like belief that the cause for which one is fighting is both just and destined to triumph. Thus Maoists and other well-led guerrillas place great stress on political education. Effective indoctrination sustains high morale, which in turn contributes to proper treatment of civilians and thus the maintainance of reliable intelligence sources.

A third fundamental need of guerrillas is a base area, a place the government forces cannot reach in strength or at least not without the guerrillas knowing about it in plenty of time. Thus a guerrilla base will usually be located in the mountains or the jungle, preferably near an international frontier. In such a place the guerrillas can train and indoctrinate their members, nurse their wounded, and store their supplies. Ideally the guerrillas will establish several such bases, which will grow in size and eventually connect with one another until they effectively cover a large area of the country.

Lastly, whether or not the guerrillas have a safe base, they will find it very difficult to carry on successfully without a sanctuary—a neighboring country across whose border they can seek temporary shelter and from which they can bring in vital supplies, especially weapons. The ultimate aim of guerrillas is to develop into conventional forces powerful enough to face and defeat the conventional forces of the government. It will be close to impossible for guerrillas to obtain the quality and quantity of weapons needed unless they can get them from outside.

In summary, guerrillas are insurgents who seek to fight against superior forces by waging a hit-and-run war of lightning attacks against vulnerable targets, a war sustained by good intelligence, high morale, secure bases, and outside assistance. If it is done well, guerrilla warfare is a very cheap form of war. On one side of the ledger is a relatively small number of lightly armed guerrillas. On the other side are the possible results: the disruption of important areas of economic life, the destruction of the regular army's prestige and self-confidence, and the discrediting of the government.

NOTES

1. Milovan Djilas, *Wartime: With Tito and the Partisans*, trans. Michael B. Petrovich (London: Martin Secker and Warburg, 1977), 32.

2. Karl von Clausewitz, *On War*, ed. and trans. Michael Howard and Peter Paret (Princeton, NJ: Princeton University, 1976), 480.

3. Luis Taruc, *Born of the People* (Westport, CT: Greenwood, 1973), 139.

Section I: From Carolina to Castile

As the eighteenth century gave way to the nineteenth, four guerrilla conflicts exerted profound effects on the world scene.

In the American Revolution, guerrilla forces played a little-known but essential role in the drama leading to the surrender at Yorktown and American independence.

In the Vendée, the French Revolutionary regime waged a campaign of extermination chillingly suggestive of events to follow in Nazi-occupied Europe. Through reasonable compromise, a wise young military commander brought the open conflict there to an end; nevertheless, the final bill for the Vendean atrocities would be presented at Waterloo.

In Spain, Napoleon and his marshals met a strategic setback as disastrous as it was unexpected. The Spanish conflict was the true locus of Napoleon's undoing; thus it produced incalculable effects on the politics of Europe and the whole world for generations to come.

In Haiti, Napoleon's forces suffered another severe, if much less-known, reverse at the hands of guerrillas. One result of the stubborn and successful Haitian resistance would be the expansion of the United States across the Mississippi to the Rockies.

1
The American Revolution

Every American schoolchild used to know that in October 1781 the last great battle of the American Revolution took place at Yorktown, Virginia, where General Cornwallis surrendered his British army to his American and French opponents. In the events leading up to that historic surrender, American guerrillas played a major part. In fact, their contribution to the final achievement of the independence of the United States was as profoundly important as it has been widely ignored.

The American War of Independence had of course many roots, but a chief factor was the final defeat and removal of French power in North America. This vast strategic change took place as a result of the Seven Years War (1756–1763), called on this side of the Atlantic the French and Indian War. Freed from the menace of French intrigue and invasion from Canada, the American colonists became ever more restless under the control of the government in London. At the same time, the desire of the French monarchy to avenge the destruction of its North American empire was to exert a decisive effect on the outcome of the American struggle for independence. Indeed, for the French, the American Revolution was but one more chapter in a global contest for empire with the British that extended from the War of the Grand Alliance (1688–1697) to Waterloo (1815).

ENGLAND'S MILITARY PROBLEMS

In 1775, as relations between the British government and its thirteen American colonies moved inexorably toward armed confrontation, the Cabinet in London faced a strategic situation of much complexity. Although the thirteen colonies had a good deal less than four million inhabitants, their suppression by force would constitute an undertaking of gigantic proportions. The mere physical extent of the colonies was daunting: Boston was as far from Savannah as London was from Budapest; South Carolina was as large as all Ireland. Strategic parsimony would have dictated an attempt to capture the American capital city, the brain and nerve-center of this sprawling empire, but there was no such thing; the largest city in North America was Philadelphia, with a population of only twenty-nine thousand and its capture would have little material or even psychological effect on the rebellion. To achieve lasting success, therefore, the British army would have to corner and dismantle any conventional American armed forces and simultaneously smother guerrillas—who would be operating in ideal guerrilla country.

But the regular British army was small, and the ruling classes in England had no desire to pay for a big war. In addition, it was advisable (and after 1778 essential) to maintain a large body of troops at home against a possible French invasion attempt. As late as 1781, on the eve of Yorktown, the British had only fifty-six thousand troops in all North America, including the West Indies. Thus the Cabinet felt compelled to hire and deploy Hessian mercenaries, an act that only inflamed revolutionary opinion in America (and aroused deep misgivings among many Englishmen as well).

Britain's wealth and industrial development did not translate into a decisive advantage over the Americans in terms of military technology. The British infantryman carried as his main weapon the musket, with an optimal range of only forty yards. The men of Washington's army had the same weapon. Remarkably, the situation on the high seas was hardly better; although the British faced responsibilities and challenges on a global scale, they had allowed their navy to deteriorate since the Seven Years War. Thus the French navy, though smaller and with a less glorious tradition, could at certain times achieve actual superiority in North American waters.

The logistical aspects of a British effort to subdue their colonies constituted a true nightmare. Every British soldier in America needed half a ton of food a year; the four thousand British army horses in America needed fourteen thousand tons of hay and six thousand tons of oats annually. Only a very small proportion of these supplies could, for various reasons, be obtained in America; it was thus necessary to bring over most of the British army's necessities by ship. Consequently, if British military units in America went very far from the seacoast they risked having their supply lines cut, and it is not always easy to tell the difference between a hungry army and a mob. Their seaborne supply system itself, employing primitive techniques of food preservation, stretched across the grim and threatening North Atlantic; crossings could take two months, and ships bound for Boston might end up in Charleston or as French prizes of war. Also, the logistical services in charge of overcoming these challenges were rife with amateurism and corruption. The problem of getting enough food for British man and beast, serious enough in the best of times, was to offer American guerrillas an opportunity that they were to exploit to the full.

Finally, there was from the beginning much unease in England about employing force against British subjects, however obstreperous and unreasonable, on British-American soil. If the campaign of suppression was not quickly won, this unease might develop into serious opposition.

PRELUDE TO THE CAROLINA CAMPAIGN

Aware of the inadequate numbers of their troops, in the fall of 1777 the British sought to execute a master plan. According to it, British forces would first divide the colonies into two parts and then subdue one part at a time, effectively doubling the power of the available British forces. Three columns of troops, one proceeding up the Hudson, another marching east through the Mohawk Valley, and the third and principal force under General John Burgoyne moving south from Montreal, would converge near Albany. The intention behind these maneuvers was to isolate New England, rightly viewed in London as the main center of the rebellion, from Pennsylvania and the South. The consequence of this plan was the Battle of Saratoga (October 1777), in which Burgoyne, after a campaign full of hardship, surrendered his force of 3,500 (out of an original 8,200) to the American general, Horatio Gates. Saratoga was one of the most important battles in the history of the world. One of its effects was to convince the French government that the American rebellion was indeed a serious affair, one in which British power could suffer a severe reverse. French gold and arms began to flow toward the Americans, and eventually France entered the war on a full-scale basis, bringing in Spain as well. Another consequence of Saratoga was that the British shifted their strategic focus from isolating New England to subduing the southern colonies. Both of these effects—French intervention and southern concentration—led eventually to Yorktown.

Failure in the North turned British eyes to the South, where the climate was supposed to be mild and the fields bountiful. Above all, there was a widespread view in London that the southern colonies were full of loyal subjects just waiting for assistance to free themselves from the oppression of the disloyal minority. This belief in great numbers of southern loyalists appealed simultaneously to British vanity and British niggardliness—let the loyalists fight the war and thereby keep taxes down in Britain. This chimera was to bring their whole war effort to ultimate disaster.

In May 1780 Sir Henry Clinton arrived by sea with a large force off Charleston, South Carolina. The fall of that city and the capture of its American garrison was the most notable American defeat of the entire war. Clinton soon sailed back to New York, leaving General Sir Charles Cornwallis in charge. A few months later, at Camden, South Carolina, Lord Cornwallis defeated the last regular American force remaining in the entire South.

THE AMERICAN PARTISANS

Now began the guerrilla warfare that was to play so fateful a role in the American Revolution. Partisan units emerged under the command of Thomas Sumter, Andrew Pickens, and perhaps the most famous of the guerrilla chieftains in the Carolina campaign, Francis Marion, the "Swamp Fox." Forty-eight years old in 1780, before the Revolution Marion had served in the South Carolina Provincial Congress and was later a colonel of state troops. Leading bands varying in size from fifty to 250, Marion prevented the British from gathering supplies, pushed in small outposts, harassed the string of small forts between Charleston and Camden, and eventually rendered reliable communications between those two centers precarious if not impossible. "Fertile in Strategem, he struck unperceived."[1] That sentence encapsulates the consummate guerrilla chief. His men were well-mounted and thus highly mobile. In December 1780 Cornwallis wrote to Clinton that Marion had "carried terror to the gates of Charleston." Marion was also very careful of the lives of his men. In contrast, Thomas Sumter, called "The Gamecock," was heedless of the cost of victory. Born in 1734, Sumter had been a small plantation owner, a member of the South Carolina Provincial Congress, and both an Episcopalian and a Baptist (simultaneously!).

The partisan war in Carolina was all too frequently marked by the burning of property and the stealing of slaves. Sumter, known as "The Gamecock," adopted the practice of paying his men with slaves confiscated from the plantations of loyalists. In contrast to Marion, he was heedless of the lives of his men. Bands of freebooters plagued the country, posing as partisans of one side or the other but actually interested in getting whatever they could for themselves. British and loyalist units burned churches, especially Presbyterian ones, which they looked upon as particular centers of sedition. On several occasions men who had surrendered in battle were killed in hot blood. Such acts of vandalism and slaughter were not confined to one side, but they cost the British and loyalists more dearly, since it was after all they who claimed to be the legitimate government and thus should have been the strict upholders of law and defenders of order. In July 1781 they put the entire community of Georgetown, South Carolina, to the torch. Marion and his followers, however, were almost completely innocent of such grisly acts. A deeply religious man, Marion forbade house burning and was in general "void of ruthlessness or cruelty to his victims,"[2] a quality attested to by his enemies.

THE AMERICANS: TACTICAL DEFEAT, STRATEGIC VICTORY

Cornwallis came to believe that the partisans who so tormented him in South Carolina were receiving recruits and supplies from North Carolina. Therefore in October 1780 he led an invasion of that colony. This was the first time that a major British force had ventured so far from the sea since the disaster of Saratoga. Hardly had he established his base in North Carolina than Cornwallis learned of the disaster of the Battle of King's Mountain, in which swarms of hastily gathered American militia achieved a total victory over British forces.

Previously, General George Washington had appointed Nathanael Greene to command a small army of American regulars (around three thousand) to harass Cornwallis. To chase away this rebel force was another reason why Cornwallis had invaded North Carolina. To this end, he had detached part of his command to operate independently, and these elements suffered disaster at the Battle of the Cowpens (January 1781). Cowpens was one of the clearest victories of American forces over the British in the entire war. When Cornwallis received the shocking news of Cowpens, he set out in pursuit of Greene's army. Eager to increase the pace of his march, overestimating both the number of loyalists and the availability of food in North Carolina, and underestimating the numbers of the guerrillas and their resourcefulness, he set fire to all his supply wagons and plunged into the unknown North Carolina countryside. In March, Cornwallis finally caught up with Greene's army at Guilford Court House. At battle's end, Greene's troops retired from the field, giving Cornwallis's better equipped and trained troops a technical victory; but Cornwallis had suffered many casualties, five hundred out of his force of 1,900, and they were all but irreplaceable.

After the Pyrrhic victory at Guilford Court House, Cornwallis should have gone back to his base in South Carolina, but he did not. Instead he retreated in April to Wilmington, North Carolina, and the next month he abandoned the Carolinas altogether and led his diminished force into Virginia. General Greene, on the other hand, plunged back into South Carolina and gobbled up one after another all the little forts Cornwallis had established in a vain attempt to hold the southern colony in his absence. Soon British control extended no farther than the outskirts of Charleston itself, and so the troops left behind by Cornwallis were of no benefit whatsoever to the British cause.

The Carolina partisans and General Greene's regulars operated in a powerfully symbiotic relationship. Cornwallis was unable to deal successfully with the guerrillas: in order to do that he needed to break down his army into much smaller ''hunter'' groups, but such detachments would have been easy prey for Greene's forces. On the other hand, during the pursuit of Greene and his small army the guerrillas helped prevent the British from concentrating properly against him, as well as from gathering adequate supplies. The partisan bands under Sumter and Marion furnished Greene with intelligence and food, and acted as a tactical screen for his movements. They forced Cornwallis to tire his soldiers in tedious and dangerous convoy protection and to detach men from his main force in order to strengthen isolated posts. Constant depletion of his forces, endless anxiety over supplies, wearisome marches and countermarches and alarms: all these results of guerrilla activities wore Cornwallis and his men to exhaustion. In truth, ''Greene could hardly have kept the field without the aid of Marion, Sumter, Pickens, and the partisans.''[3] So it was that from South Carolina to North Carolina and then to Virginia, Cornwallis trod his appointed path to his destiny at Yorktown, where he hoped for succour from a British fleet that arrived just days too late to save him.

NOTES

1. Henry Lee, *Memoirs of the War in the Southern Department of the United States*, ed. Robert E. Lee (New York: Arno, 1969 [orig. 1869]), 174.

2. Christopher Ward, *The War of the Revolution* (New York: Macmillan, 1952), vol. 2, 661.

3. John Richard Alden, *The South in the Revolution, 1763–1789* (Baton Rouge, LA: Louisiana State University, 1957), 267.

2
The Vendée

In the spring of 1793 the French Revolution entered its most radical and terroristic phase. During this period, popular risings against the Revolutionary dictatorship in Paris flared in many parts of France. One of the most notorious occurred along the Atlantic coast in the province of the Vendée, an area about half the size of the state of Connecticut, with a population at that time of 800,000. "To this day the history of the Vendée [revolt] is capable of polarizing French historians and readers more than almost any other event of the Revolution."[1]

The many causes of that series of convulsions and bloodlettings known as the French Revolution included conflicts over the national debt, defeats in foreign wars, and the general spirit of the age. But it was the so-called Civil Constitution of the Clergy that prepared the ground for the Vendean uprising. That document sought to make the Catholic Church thoroughly subordinate to the revolutionary state; predictably, leaders of the Church both in Rome and in France rejected it. Thus "a powerful and conservative group of Catholics was forced irrevocably into opposition" to the Revolution.[2] That opposition was at first peaceful. Then, in what has been called "certainly the [Revolutionary] Constituent Assembly's most serious mistake," the government demanded that all clergymen swear a public oath of submission to the civil constitution.[3] Almost all the bishops and a majority of the parish priests refused the oath. They did so at great personal danger; the Revolutionary government began to authorize the looting and closing of churches and the jailing of priests. In this way the state created "the sine qua non of any peasant rebellion: an overwhelming conviction that the government, its officials, and friends were manifestly unjust."[4]

Persecution of their religion turned millions of peasants all over France into potential rebels. The torch was set to the combustible situation by the Paris regime's conscription decree of March 1793, calling for 300,000 draftees. From the effects of this measure the middle class largely exempted itself; the burden of revolutionary draft and revolutionary war was therefore to fall on the peasants. The enforcement of this conscription was in the hands of the very elements that had already antagonized the peasantry over the religious question. Within days resistance flared over western France and elsewhere. This rebellion, which began as a movement in defense of the traditional Church, was eventually to turn into a rejection of the revolutionary state.

Throughout the conflict the rebels were poorly armed and received almost no help at all from foreign sources. On the other hand, the revolutionary government (often called after its ruling body, the "Convention") had involved itself in war against all the powers of Europe and thus was unable to devote full attention to the uprisings in the West. The Vendean rebels took the towns of Cholet and Chalonnes in March, 1793, seizing much-needed munitions left behind by the fleeing republican soldiers. By the beginning of August eighty thousand republican troops were in the Vendée, against whom the rebels would eventually mobilize close to 120,000 men—and women. The Vendeans, fighting in defense of their homes against invaders, often employed guerrilla tactics; against them the republican troops used conventional tactics which proved disastrously inappropriate.[5]

The principal weaknesses of the Vendeans were those of all popular armed movements: no firm command structure, a pronounced tendency toward localism, a disinclination of individual leaders to follow central direction. Guerrillas would rally to repel an attack and then return to their homes. Clearly, under these conditions there was no possibility of a sustained strategic assault against their enemies. In June 1793 the Vendeans took the key city of Saumur. At that point, as Napoleon later wrote, there was nothing to stop them from marching to Paris and "flying the white flag [of the monarchy] from the towers of Notre Dame before it was possible for the armies on the Rhine to come to the aid of the government."[6] But the Vendeans did not march to Paris; instead they turned to attack Nantes, a siege well beyond their capabilities. As an increasing number of troops invaded the Vendée, about sixty-five thousand rebels, men, women, and children, crossed the Loire trying to get to a seaport. Had they attacked Cherbourg they might well have taken that city; instead they wandered aimlessly until December 12, when the republican armies caught them near Le Mans. In the words of the republican commander, "women, priests, monks, children, all have been put to death. I have spared nobody."[7] A week later, several thousands who had managed to survive that slaughter were massacred at Savenay, near Nantes.

Having beaten the revolt, the revolutionary republic next undertook to destroy the Vendée.

GENOCIDE

In the early months of 1794 thousands of Vendeans who had received amnesty were nevertheless rounded up and executed. Many were forced to dig their own burial pits and were shot beside them; some were buried alive. The republican troops gathered large numbers of women together, raped them en masse, and then killed them, along with their children, by sabre thrusts rather than gunfire in order to conserve ammunition.[8] Officers wrote home of seeing the naked bodies of young girls hanging from trees with their hands tied behind their backs. Meanwhile, mounted troops called "infernal columns" rode about setting fire to countless dwellings. Looting, rape, arson, and murder got so far out of hand that even the homes and persons of loyal republicans were not spared.

Eventually the government forces found themselves with too many prisoners to kill and dispose of efficiently. Hence they turned to drowning—the notorious *noyades*. Women, children, youths, and priests, were tied up and pushed out into the River Loire aboard boats which were then sunk. Cloaked at first by the darkness of the night, these drownings were eventually carried on in broad daylight. Perhaps 4,800 Vendean civilians suffered execution in this manner. Agents of the Paris regime also undertook to poison peasant wells; they even engaged in imaginative experiments with deadly gases, but the results proved disappointing. All this pushed the Vendeans into renewed rebellion.[9]

How could such practices exist under a government whose watchwords were "Liberty, Equality, Fraternity"? The Convention, the government that carried out the rape of the Vendée, had been elected in 1792 in a small turnout by a restricted electorate voting orally in the presence of government officials. The regime largely depended not on the citizenry but on the army. Warfare against all Europe on the one hand, and on the other, extermination of all domestic enemies, actual, suspected, or potential—these policies came to be mutually supporting, mutually necessary.

Desperate rebellion, bloody repression, and mass execution devastated many provinces of France, not just the Vendée. For example, in neighboring Brittany there flourished the guerrilla movement known as the Chouannerie, which grew out of the defeat of a popular rising in that province of March 1793. The Chouannerie was a textbook example of a spontaneous revolt by ordinary folk. By mid-May 1794, perhaps twenty-two thousand armed Chouans were in the field. Theirs were the standard tactics of guerrillas: they cut bridges, interfered with tax collections, assassinated government agents, attacked convoys, ambushed small bodies of troops, and sometimes even besieged towns. By October 1794, 130,000 republican troops were engaged in suppressing rebellion in Brittany and the Vendée, leaving only 180,000 soldiers to fight France's European enemies on the eastern and northern fronts.[10] The most serious handicap of

Chouannerie was the lack of serviceable weapons. The British would not risk sending proper arms unless the Chouans captured a good port, but of course the Chouans could not capture a good port because they lacked proper arms.

In July 1794 Maximilien Robespierre, the genius of the Terror, fell from power and went to his death. The following month, General Louis-Lazare Hoche arrived in the West to take command of counterguerrilla operations. Hoche drew up and put into operation a sound plan for pacifying the territory. He took steps to prevent any British assistance reaching the rebels and to cut off communication between the Vendée and Brittany. He caused the construction of strongpoints all along the Vendean borders, with frequent patrols between them, thus penning in the insurgents. To the west of this line he conducted heavy patrols and raids. Hoche moved the fortified line ever westward, thoroughly clearing one district at a time and steadily reducing the area in which the guerrillas could operate. To disarm the rebellion he levied a tax of weapons on each parish, so many guns each, taking hostages until the inhabitants turned in what was required. Most important of all, however, Hoche decreed tolerance for religious practice and sought to punish his own pillaging troops. The latter policy proved very difficult to implement, because the morale of the republican troops had been thoroughly debased by so much criminality in the years before. Nevertheless, in February 1795 a truce brought most of the fighting to an end.

But in June 1795 came the landing at Quiberon: there British vessels disembarked a small army of French royalists equipped with British weapons. The purpose of the landing was to re-ignite rebellion throughout the West. About 4,500 royalists came ashore; soon fifteen thousand Chouans joined them. The expected Austrian offensive in the East did not develop, however, and thus the Paris government was able to rush troops to the area and confine the rebels to the Quiberon peninsula. A massive republican attack on July 21 resulted in a general massacre of royalists and Chouans, from which British ships were able to save but 2,500.

Peace eventually returned to the Vendée because of the exhaustion of its civilian inhabitants, the reluctance of the English to send any more help, the abundance of troops at the disposal of the republicans, and the wisdom of Hoche's policy of religious pacification. Hoche then turned to Brittany, smothering it under a force of 140,000—one soldier for every seven inhabitants. A truce went into effect in that province on June 21, 1796.

The suppression of insurgency in the West cost 150,000 lives, more than the number of Frenchmen who perished in Napoleon's Russian campaign. Nevertheless, the Vendée was to have its revenge on the Revolution and those who served it. In May 1815, after Napoleon had returned from Elba, marched on Paris, and chased away the king, the Vendeans once again rose in rebellion. Napoleon had to send in thirty thousand troops. Those soldiers, had they been present, would almost certainly have changed the outcome of the battle of Waterloo.[11]

NOTES

1. Simon Schama, *Citizens: A Chronicle of the French Revolution* (New York: Alfred A. Knopf, 1989), 693.

2. Crane Brinton, *Anatomy of Revolution* (New York: Vintage, 1965 [orig. 1938]). 143.

3. William Doyle, *The Oxford History of the French Revolution* (Oxford, UK: Oxford University, 1989), 144.

4. Donald Sutherland, *The Chouans: The Social Origins of Popular Counterrevolution in Upper Brittany, 1770–1798* (Oxford, UK: Oxford University, 1982), 256.

5. Peter Paret, *Internal War and Pacification: The Vendée 1789–1796* (Princeton, NJ: Princeton University), 1961.

6. André Montagnon, *Une guerre subversive: La guerre de Vendée* (Paris: La Colombe, 1959), 66.

7. Doyle, *Oxford History*, 256.

8. Jean-Clement Martin, *La Vendée et la France* (Paris: Seuil, 1987), 232; see also Reynald Secher, *Le genocide franco-français: La Vendée-Vengé* (Paris: Presses universitaires de France, 1988, 2d ed.).

9. Louis Adolphe Thiers, *The History of the French Revolution* (Philadelphia: Lippincott, 1894), vol. 3, 453; Schama, *Citizens*, 789–90.

10. Ramsay Phipps, *The Armies of the First French Republic* (Westport, CT: Greenwood, 1980), 5.

11. Georges Lefebvre, *Napoleon from Tilsit to Waterloo*, trans. J. E. Anderson (New York: Columbia University, 1969), 363. Napoleon commanded an army of only seventy-two thousand at Waterloo.

3
Haiti

The present Republic of Haiti, about the size of the state of Maryland, occupies the western part (eleven thousand square miles) of the island of Hispaniola; the eastern part (nineteen thousand square miles) comprises the Dominican Republic.

THE NAPOLEONIC INVASION

In 1789, the population of Haiti included twenty-four thousand whites, twenty thousand mulattoes, and 400,00 blacks, both slave and free. The example set by the French Revolution, as well as the disorganization resulting from it, kindled a successful rebellion by the oppressed blacks. When Napoleon came to power, he at first adopted a conciliatory policy toward Haiti, mainly because, owing to his war with Britain and her navy, he could do little else. Indeed he officially recognized the black leader, Toussaint L'Ouverture, as commander in chief of the "Army of Saint-Domingue." But in October 1800 Napoleon obtained from Spain the retrocession of Louisiana, intending that this vast territory become the seat of renewed French power on the North American continent. As base for his grandiose plans, Napoleon needed a subdued Hispaniola. Accordingly, on January 29, 1802, a French armada carrying twelve thousand troops under the command of General Charles Leclerc anchored in Samana Bay on the east coast of the island. Napoleon was confident that these French soldiers would sweep aside black resistance in a matter of weeks. Further, he rejected all evidence that even first-class white troops would suffer inordinately from the climate and from yellow fever. Also, true to his usual practice, Napoleon made no adequate provision for the proper supply of the army. This underestimation of the difficulty of the reconquest of Haiti was the fundamental mistake of the entire enterprise.

The Haitian commander Henri Christophe burned Le Cap François (today called Cap-Haitien), a city of fifty thousand, before abandoning it to the French in February 1802. French troops, though they suffered numerous casualties, defeated their opponents in pitched battles. Continual defections by local black commanders also badly damaged Toussaint's cause. Besides, he had received news of the peace between Britain and France, which had been signed in March. Hence Toussaint surrendered to Leclerc on May 6, 1802, in return for his personal freedom, a guarantee that slavery would not be reimposed, and acceptance of his officers, with their rank, into the French army. Shortly thereafter the French arrested Toussaint, a piece of treachery in which they were supported by Christophe and Jean-Jacques Dessalines. Toussaint died in France less than a year later.

The French undertook to disarm the blacks, a move which convinced the Haitians that reenslavement was on the way. After the surrender of Toussaint several lesser black leaders had continued guerrilla warfare, and now many joined them in the mountains of the interior. Leclerc then adopted policies bordering on genocide: the French began to kill all black troops suspected of disloyalty, after first making them witness the executions of their wives.[1] Dessalines and Christophe still remained loyal to the French, but eventually they too rejoined the rebellion and claimed leadership of the guerrilla forces. Meanwhile hundreds of French troops were dying each month of yellow fever; Leclerc too was to succumb to the mysterious malady. Two Swiss brigades mutinied at Toulon rather than be sent into the hell of the West Indies. By November 1802 ten thousand Haitian insurgents were besieging Le Cap François, with its garrison of two thousand French troops.

In March 1803, Napoleon sent fifteen thousand reinforcements to General Donatien Rochambeau, Leclerc's successor. Rochambeau[2] launched a program of extermination. The French imported hundreds of killer dogs from Cuba trained to attack and devour blacks.[3] By May, however, Britain and France were again at war. A British fleet bombarded French strongholds in Haiti, and British arms and supplies reached the rebels. Finally, in November, the French in Haiti made arrangements with the British to carry them to Cuba. British vessels took aboard eighteen thousand refugees at Le Cap François, of which eight thousand were all that remained of Rochambeau's army.

The French lost thousands of soldiers in Haiti, many of them veterans of the conquest of Italy and Germany. One author has justly observed that "if Bonaparte's military reputation had rested upon his invasion of Saint-Domingue, he would be remembered quite differently today."[4]

THE MARINE OCCUPATION

In the first decade of the twentieth century, the beginning of the construction of the Panama Canal and the simultaneous German naval buildup under Kaiser Wilhelm II greatly increased the interest of the United States in events in the Caribbean. Inevitably Haiti attracted the attention of Americans in charge of foreign policy and national defense.

During the six decades preceding the outbreak of World War I, Haiti had presented a spectacle of almost unrelieved misery, violence, and chaos. Its indebtedness to foreign countries increased as its economy deteriorated. Political mismanagement and instability reached remarkable proportions: for instance, between 1908 and 1915 no less than seven men occupied the presidency of the republic. The poor peasants, who composed the great bulk of the inhabitants, were at the mercy of the so-called Cacos, semiprofessional brigands living in the upland interior who sold their services to competing aspirants for the presidential office. From time to time the Cacos descended from their strongholds to loot, rape, and murder. In January 1914 conditions in the large cities were so bad that elements of the British, French, and German navies landed marines to protect their nationals and embassies. Such occurrences alarmed Washington, and in July 1915 U.S. Marines landed in Cap-Haitien. By the end of that year there were approximately 1,950 Marines in Haiti, and by the end of 1916 less than 1,000 (the population of Haiti at this time being perhaps 1,500,000).

The looming threat of U.S. naval guns maintained order in the cities, while in the hinterland Marines dispersed the Cacos by the use of harassing patrols, and airplanes for spotting and even dive-bombing. The Marines also offered amnesty, payment for surrendered arms, medical care, and promises of government employment.

But the most ambitious effort of the Marines to silence the Cacos and establish lasting peace in Haiti was the building of a new Haitian Gendarmerie. This body was eventually to number 2,500, and its members proved to have, almost without exception, unswerving loyalty to their Marine trainers and officers. Recruiting for the new organization went slowly at first but accelerated rapidly when it was discovered that the members of the Gendarmerie would actually receive the wages that had been promised them. More than nine out of ten recruits needed immediate treatment for syphilis; many suffered from hookworm and other debilitating diseases. Within a short time Marine doctors were able to improve greatly the health and stamina of the Gendarmes. Aside from chasing Cacos and occupying strategic points, the Gendarmes also cleaned the filthy streets and prisons, built schools, and strung telegraph lines. By 1924 one-quarter of the officers of the Gendarmerie were Haitians; this proportion increased to two-fifths by 1930 and three-quarters by 1933.

The Marines and their Gendarmerie were effective in restoring order to the disturbed country. The last great Caco uprising, in which perhaps two thousand insurgents lost their lives, took place in 1919–1920. Peace was the rule after that, and the number of Marines in Haiti steadily declined until 1934, when the last were withdrawn. By then the Garde d'Haiti (as the Gendarmerie was known after 1928) numbered 2,800 officers and enlisted men. In 1949 the Garde d'Haiti changed its name to Armée d'Haiti.

A few broad observations on the U.S. occupation of Haiti suggest themselves. First, the contrast between the substantial armed forces of the Napoleonic French and the few companies of U.S. Marines is most striking. Not only was the amount of fighting incomparably less in the American intervention than in the French, but the American occupation force carried out many financial, sanitary, and transportation projects, which all acknowledged were of benefit to the Haitian people. Nevertheless, many Haitians simply did not believe that these improvements by the Americans justified the occupation of their country by foreign soldiers, however well-meaning or well-doing. Second, when the Americans left Haiti they had had the supervision of the country in their hands for nearly two decades; yet the island quickly slipped back into its old ways of corruption and bloodshed. Finally, one completely unexpected result of the United States occupation and its progressive policies was that the population of Haiti greatly increased, a phenomenon that would have a negative impact on the country's many problems. Today Haiti has the heaviest density of population, and the worst economy, in all of Latin America.

NOTES

1. Thomas O. Ott, *The Haitian Revolution 1789–1804* (Knoxville, TN: University of Tennessee, 1973), 175.
2. Lived 1750–1813; the son of the General Rochambeau of American Revolutionary War fame.
3. Ott, *Haitian Revolution*, 179.
4. Ibid., 146.

4
Spain

Napoleon sent his army into Spain in 1808. By this act he provoked a guerrilla conflict that tied up French resources, opened a continental front to the British, provided a training field for Wellington, cost Imperial armies tens of thousands of casualties, and perhaps most importantly, undermined the myth of Napoleonic invincibility and inevitability that had been for years such a potent weapon in the hands of the French.

In 1808 France had a population of thirty million and was incomparably Europe's greatest military power. Spain, with its population of eleven million, while still ruling tentatively over a vast empire in the New World, was a former great power that had gradually declined to the second rank at best. But while Spain could be no match at all for Napoleonic France in terms of conventional military power, it proved to be an ideal setting for fierce guerrilla resistance. Spain was more than six times the size of the Swamp Fox's South Carolina; Paris was farther from Cadiz than it was from Warsaw; the Iberian peninsula was crossed east to west by several mountain chains and rivers; and the road system was mostly primitive. Important military messages from Paris could require two weeks to arrive at Madrid—if they arrived at all. The interior of the country was poor, very difficult for invading troops to live in. If to these conditions one added an aroused population, then Spain would meet all the requirements that Clausewitz had laid down for the successful waging of a ''people's war''; in fact Spain would become the very model for such a war.

A major contributing factor to Napoleon's decision to subjugate Spain was the Battle of Trafalgar, the greatest sea battle of the entire age of sail and one of the most far-reaching contests in world history. The destruction of the combined Franco-Spanish fleet by the great Horatio Nelson drowned French hopes of an invasion of Britain. Thereafter to defeat Britain Napoleon sought to ruin its economy, by closing every European country to its exports. More effective enforcement of this Continental blockade was the principal reason why Napoleon invaded Spain and placed his brother Joseph on the throne. In a sense, Trafalgar was the European Saratoga: it led the country that lost the battle to enmesh itself in a devastating guerrilla war.

THE FIRST GUERRILLA

After the French violently suppressed a rising in Madrid (events immortalized by Goya), a Spanish provisional government of national resistance was established at Cadiz under the protection of the British navy. Napoleon, in response, made the mistake of sending inexperienced soldiers under General Pierre Dupont, who, after savagely looting the city of Cordoba, found himself cornered deep inside Andalucia by a Spanish regular army and swarms of guerrillas. At the town of Bailén his army of twenty thousand capitulated, and in consequence King Joseph had to evacuate Madrid. "Bailén created a sensation throughout Europe."[1] Two weeks after Bailén, Arthur Wellesley, the future Duke of Wellington,[2] landed in Portugal at the head of a small British force. Alarmed by these reverses, Napoleon himself stormed into Spain with his most famous commanders and 250,000 veteran imperial troops. After defeating a Spanish army in front of Burgos and then pillaging the city, the Emperor left Spain in January 1809 to deal with pressing central European problems, never to see Spain again—but it would never be far from his thoughts.

Even in the darkest days of Napoleonic conquest, the Spanish managed to keep a regular army in the field. Consequently the French were never able to launch a proper campaign of counterinsurgency, because they could not safely split up their forces into small units to pursue guerrillas. In the early days Spanish guerrillas (called *partidas*) made the grave mistake of fighting to hold particular places, but their tactics improved greatly with time. The partidas were capable of very rapid movement: some groups could cover eighty-five kilometers a day. They also enjoyed the overwhelming support of the civil population and thus could always obtain good intelligence about the movements of French and other Imperial troops. The guerrillas were "always beaten, never conquered."[3]

ARAGON

Directly across the line of communication between Paris and Madrid lay the province of Aragon. Napoleon's soldiers soon stripped the whole area clean of meat, and the French had to haul supplies for their armies across long routes constantly harassed by thousand of guerrillas. Aragon was the home base of perhaps the "greatest guerrilla warrior of them all," Francisco Espoz y Mina; by the spring of 1812 he was commanding ten thousand guerrillas. Across the peninsula, in the area between the Bay of Biscay and Madrid, close to twenty thousand guerrillas were operating by 1810. They did enormous damage to French communications and mauled even sizeable columns of troops. Communications grew so bad that Madrid was often isolated from outlying military units for weeks at a time; Paris frequently had little or no accurate knowledge of what was going on in Spain.

Eventually guerrilla attacks on French food supplies came very close to producing a serious crisis. In previous campaigns Napoleonic armies had lived off the countryside, and Napoleon had greatly overestimated Spanish wealth and productivity. The French were forced to protect their food and mail convoys with escorts of eight hundred men. Such operations were expensive and exhausting, and often even these large bodies were not immune from attack. French cavalry mounts, underfed and overworked, died by the hundreds. Finally, darting around the circumference of this scene of furious battle was the British navy, providing food, weapons, ammunition, money, and even evacuation when necessary. Without British seapower and the assistance it brought the French would probably have defeated—though only eventually and at great cost—both the guerrillas and the regular Spanish forces. The omnipresence of British seapower was of course another of the effects of Trafalgar.

From his Spanish experiences the influential Franco-Swiss strategist A.-H. Jomini developed a formula for successful counterinsurgency. Jomini's first requirement was that the counterguerrilla power employ troops sufficient in number both to garrison all major places securely and hunt guerrilla bands vigorously. But he also prescribed a politically sagacious policy of justice and gentleness toward the civilian inhabitants. If his formula is a valid benchmark, French counterinsurgency in Spain was a miserable failure right from the beginning. Early in the war the French concentrated on eliminating Spanish regular forces, which gave the guerrillas time to organize. The French military ethos rewarded bravery and improvisation, not that patient attention to planning which is needed to beat guerrillas. The French constantly used sweep tactics; because of Spain's poor communications and the hostility of the population, these sweeps almost always failed. Even the occasional successful operation bore no fruit, because the French would soon leave the swept area and the guerrillas would return. The French ratio of force to space was too low; hence they had to consolidate their smaller garrisons into ever larger ones, abandoning more and more of the countryside to the enemy. Even some of the larger cities suffered blockade and actual siege by thousands of guerrillas. As time went on the French lost even their tactical superiority over the guerrillas, whose skills improved constantly.

In these circumstances of inadequate numbers wedded to inadequate concepts, the best French approach would have been one of accommodation. However,

French failure here was even more obvious than in the strictly military realm. Joseph Bonaparte, placed on the throne of Spain by his brother, had from 1806 to 1808 been King of Naples, where he had introduced many reforms, including vaccination against smallpox. In Madrid he tried to be a true king: he learned Spanish, cared for the poor of the capital, and sought to ingratiate himself with the Church. But whatever his benevolent intentions or good works, everyone knew that Joseph was maintained on his throne by the presence of a truly hated foreign army. Besides, Napoleon's Spanish policy aimed at the annexation of Catalonia and perhaps Aragon, that is, destruction of the fruits of the Reconquista—the expulsion of the Moors and the unification of Spain—and so undermined King Joseph even with those groups who might have wished to support him.

In any case, the true face of the French occupation was presented not by King Joseph but by the armies of the French and their allies. These forces executed prisoners who could not pay bribes. They hanged hostages. They refused to recognize any distinction between rebels and peaceful civilians, so that many peasants found it safer to join the guerrillas than to remain quietly at home. Rape was everywhere, falling upon women of all conditions, including minors, nuns, and expectant mothers, provoking even high-ranking French officers to protest. Perhaps most self-destructive for the Imperial cause, the occupation forces looted and burned churches and cathedrals, murdered priests, and committed public sacrileges as a matter of policy. Consequently the Spanish resistance took on the aspect of a religious rising of the common people, a characteristic that helps account for the peasants' ferocity toward the French and Imperial forces.

By the beginning of 1812 partidas operating in the general vicinity of the Ebro River numbered around twenty-four thousand.[4] French convoys now required escorts of two thousand men; yet even these were often attacked and badly hurt by guerrillas. Preparations for the invasion of Russia began to drain troops and supplies from Spain; thus Salamanca fell to Wellington's army in June 1812. The 230,000 French and Imperial soldiers in Spain could no longer garrison even important posts, because there were not enough troops for mobile relief columns to assist such posts in case of attack. In June 1813 Wellington defeated King Joseph's army at Vitoria; this was the end of Napoleonic Spain. The role of the guerrillas in assisting Wellington's progress across Spain had been incalculable, and they now prevented many Imperial units from going to the aid of Joseph's army. When Wellington crossed the Pyrenees into southern France, General Soult advised the Emperor that the area should be defended by guerrilla tactics!

CONTINENTAL CONSEQUENCES

To win in Spain, or even to hold on there, the French needed to accomplish at least three tasks: isolate the Cadiz government from British aid, send enough troops to garrison the country effectively, and improve their treatment of the population. British seapower made the first objective impossible. The second escaped fulfillment because of constant demands for troops from other parts of the empire. As to the third, it was perhaps not reasonable to expect French forces to exhibit conduct in Spain superior to the barbarism they had displayed against their own countrymen in the Vendée.

In the face of British assistance and popular fury, the French and their allies never came close to having enough manpower in Spain. Wellington commanded sixty thousand Anglo-Portuguese regulars, and a very conservative estimate of guerrilla strength in 1812 would be thirty-five thousand. Using the commonly accepted ten-to-one ratio of soldiers to guerrillas for successful counterinsurgency, French and Imperial forces would have had to number 350,000 to combat and hunt the guerrillas, plus at least seventy-five thousand to contain Wellington and another fifty thousand to besiege Cadiz. This comes to a total of 475,000 men. In fact the French usually had only between 230,000 and 300,000 troops in Spain.[5] If, however, one accepts a higher estimate of guerrilla numbers, around seventy thousand, then the French would have needed 825,000 men. It would have been utterly impossible to approach such a figure, even using scores of thousands of allied troops from Italy and Poland, and of course the Russian campaign drained men from Spain by the regiment. The only way out of this manpower predicament for the French would have been to decrease the numbers of Spaniards determined to be guerrillas and to increase those willing to serve as Imperial troops; but this solution in turn would have required the most profound improvement in the conduct of French troops in Spain, a policy that was beyond the comprehension of most French leaders.

Besides, it is not clear that even substantial increases in French occupation forces would have sufficed, because of the poor command system of their forces in Spain. Each one of Napoleon's commanders exercised independent control over his assigned region, impeding cooperation against the guerrillas, whose most effective weapon was mobility. The generals were jealous of one another, ignored or insulted King Joseph, and continuously fed the fires of rebellion with their rapacity.

The fundamental Napoleonic error was invading Spain in the first place. He himself had said, "I am the heir of Charlemagne, not Louis XIV," meaning that he was aware that the destiny of his empire would be decided across the Rhine, not across the Pyrenees. The Spanish invasion did not increase Napoleon's security but decreased it, by exposing the myth of French invincibility and providing a continental foothold for the British enemy. Napoleon aimed for possession of the Spanish colonies; he got an invasion of southern France instead. If the initial mistake was geopolitical—going into Spain at all—others were added on. Neither Napoleon nor his marshals had any clear doctrine for successful counterinsurgency; they had learned nothing from their experience in Haiti. From this ignorance in turn grew the fatal policy of permitting French and Imperial troops to treat the Spanish population in such a way as to make inevitable a furious and permanent national resistance.

While the Spanish adventure was failing disastrously, Napoleon followed his fatal star into Russia. The wintry debacle there cost Napoleon over 200,000 French troops in one way or another, a figure that does not include losses among Imperial allies, such as the Poles.[6] In comparison, estimates of French and Imperial casualties in Spain run between 200,000 and 300,000; guerrillas may have inflicted at least half of them.[7] Those troops lost in Spain would have been of incalculable service to Napoleon in his desperate efforts to stave off disaster in 1813. All this was certainly a high price to pay for what was in essence "a strategically irrelevant diversion of effort."[8] The Spanish invasion surely ranks as the "most disastrous blunder of Napoleon's career."[9]

NOTES

1. Georges Lefebvre, *Napoleon* (translated by Henry F. Stockhold; New York: Columbia University, 1969 [orig. 1936]). vol. 2, 23.

2. To avoid confusion, he will be referred to hereafter as Wellington.

3. Gabriel Lovett, *Napoleon and the Birth of Modern Spain* (New York: New York University, 1965), 680.

4. Don W. Alexander, *Rod of Iron: French Counterinsurgency Policy in Aragon during the Peninsular War* (Wilmington, DE: Scholarly Resources, 1985), 162.

5. David Chandler, Foreword, in J. Tranie and J.-C. Carmigniani, *Napoleon's War in Spain* (tran. Janet Mallender and J. Clements) (London: Arms and Armour, 1982), 10.

6. Owen Connelly, *Blundering to Glory: Napoleon's Military Campaigns* (Wilmington, DE: Scholarly Resources), 181.

7. Tranie and Carmigniani, *Napoleon's War*, 10; Connelly, *Blundering to Glory*, 112n; Lovett, *Napoleon and the Birth of Modern Spain*, 683.

8. John Keegan, *The Price of Admiralty* (New York: Viking, 1989), 93.

9. Connelly, *Blundering to Glory*, 117.

Section II: From Waterloo through World War I

Although guerrilla conflict flared during the American Civil War, especially in Missouri, perhaps the most interesting question concerning guerrilla war in this period is: Why did a major insurgency not break out after the surrender of conventional Confederate forces?

As the nineteenth century gave way to the twentieth, the defeat of regular native forces in South Africa and the Philippines was followed by the eruption of guerrilla resistance. To defeat the Boer guerrillas the British empire had to wage its largest land campaign of the century, larger than its effort against Napoleon. On the other hand, in the Philippines, inexperienced U.S. forces, far from home and bolstered by neither aircraft nor overwhelming numbers, defeated indigenous guerrillas by a combination of sound military tactics and a sagacious political program.

The First World War produced one of the most famous guerrilla leaders of all times, Lawrence of Arabia, the scholarly Englishman who while still in his twenties achieved leadership of an Arab revolt. Notwithstanding, and with all due respect for Lawrence's personal qualities, his success clearly depended upon British naval power and Turkish military weakness.

In the post–world war period came the protracted U.S. occupation of Haiti and the suppression of a brief but significant guerrilla resistance there. Despite their undoubted good intentions, after nearly two decades the Americans were totally unsuccessful in building either an effective state or a politically neutral national army, a frustrating experience that would be repeated in Nicaragua (see Chapters 3 and 19).

5
The American Civil War

One often reads that the victory of the Union in the American War of Secession was "inevitable." What that seems to mean is that the Union could not help but win, because it was richer and more populous than its opponent. If such are the sole determinants of victory, however, why did the United States not obtain its goals in Viet Nam, goals for which it sacrificed nearly sixty thousand of its young people, many scores of billions of dollars, and much else besides? If Union victory was indeed inevitable, what was wrong with the leaders of secession and their followers? Were they crazed fanatics, or merely stupid? Ultimate Union victory did not appear inevitable to the Confederate leaders, or to the principal statesmen of Europe, and most certainly not to President Abraham Lincoln.

THE STRATEGIC SITUATION

To the contrary, several indicators pointed impressively to an eventual Confederate success. First, there were deep divisions within the Union states: Lincoln had received less than 40 percent of the popular vote in the 1860 election, and large strata of northern[1] opinion, especially in the Democratic Party, opposed a war of conquest of the seceded states. Only when Confederate forces committed the incredible blunder of firing on Fort Sumter was Lincoln able to mobilize public opinion behind a war to reestablish the country's unity. Even then it was unclear: If victory did not come soon, if the conflict proved protracted and bloody, would the will of loyal Unionists remain firm?

For that matter, what in fact did "victory" mean? For the Confederacy, it meant mere survival: resisting conquest until northern society tired of the struggle. For the Union, victory could mean nothing less than the total conquest and occupation of the Confederate states. But in the 1860s, as in most periods, weapon systems and fortifications favored the defensive, which was the strategic posture of the Confederacy.

"Conquest and occupation" of the Confederate states meant that Union forces would have to subdue an area as large as today's France, Spain, Italy, Switzerland, Germany, and Poland combined. This vast empire of seceding states had only a sketchy railway network and inadequate highways. The forces available to Lincoln with which to undertake this mighty task were in the beginning grotesquely inadequate. Even at the height of the war, the Union never mustered more than a million men at any one time, while Confederate forces peaked at 600,000, giving the Union a ratio of only five to three against an opponent operating along interior lines. Surely, it seemed long before such a colossal conquest could near completion, the Confederacy's great trump card, foreign intervention, would come into play: Britain and France would recognize the independence of the Confederacy and insist that the fighting cease—that the Union be sundered.

GUERRILLAS IN VIRGINIA

As Confederate forces slowly retreated, their supply lines grew shorter; as Federal forces painfully advanced, their supply lines grew longer, and thus more exposed to guerrilla attack. General William T. Sherman uttered the complaint of all who have marched through hostile territory: "Though our armies pass across and through the land, the war closes in behind and leaves the same enemy behind."[2] Besieging Vicksburg, Mississippi, in the summer of 1863, General Ulysses S. Grant had sixty thousand of his troops at the battlefront; fully another forty thousand were busy coping with guerrillas and raiders.

One of the most famous and successful Confederate guerrilla leaders was John S. Mosby, of Mosby's Rangers. He and his men operated in northwestern Virginia, an area well-suited to guerrilla war. In January 1863 he began activities with fifteen men; by war's end almost two thousand had served with him at one time or another, although he hardly ever deployed more than three hundred men for a given operation. Mosby's Rangers were mostly in their teens or early twenties (Mosby himself was twenty-nine when the war began), an age when men "haven't the sense to know danger when they see it."[3] Mosby had a clear strategy: "In general it was my purpose to threaten and harass the enemy on the border and in this way compel him to withdraw troops from his front to guard the lines of the Potomac and Washington. This would greatly diminish his offensive power."[4] His tactics were classically simple. For instance, the

Rangers derailed and looted trains and confiscated hundreds of thousands of dollars from Federal pay wagons. They were very aggressive for guerrillas. Well-mounted, armed with two revolvers each, the Rangers would charge Union formations even when outnumbered. Perhaps their most famous coup was the capture of Brigadier General Edwin H. Stoughton in a nighttime raid near Fairfax Court House in March 1863.

Mosby always obtained good intelligence, but Federal retaliation against suspected civilian sympathizers turned many inhabitants of northern Virginia against the guerrillas. Believing the Rangers to be no better than common bandits, Grant ordered General Philip Sheridan to hang any of Mosby's men he laid hands on (though Sheridan did not always enforce this order). Mosby retaliated against Federal prisoners for any executions of his men, and in November 1864 he and Sheridan formally agreed not to kill prisoners.

Mosby's men often slept in bed in the homes of their relatives and supporters. In just such a situation Mosby himself was nearly captured and suffered a serious wound. Many Confederate officers, including Robert E. Lee, disapproved of Mosby's Rangers and of guerrillas in general, seeing them as undisciplined at best, often criminal, and potentially destructive of the morale of regular soldiers. But Mosby always believed the activities of his unit prolonged the life of the Confederacy, a position that is still debated among students of the war. After peace was restored, Mosby became a supporter of President Grant and joined the Republican Party.

GUERRILLAS IN MISSOURI

Missouri entered the Union as a slave state in 1820, but on the eve of the Civil War the overwhelming majority of its inhabitants were small farmers. Blacks, slaves or free, constituted less than 10 percent of the population of 1.2 million. In March 1861, of the delegates who had been elected to a state convention to decide on the issue of secession, three-quarters declared for the Union. Nevertheless a very considerable proportion of the inhabitants were of southern origin and sympathy. Thus Missouri soon became a battleground between Federal troops and secessionist guerrillas. The guerrillas tore up railroad tracks, burned bridges, and ambushed small Federal patrols, and by the summer of 1864 they had halted all river traffic in the state. Thousands of Unionist soldiers had to carry on the struggle against these insurgents instead of participating in the regular war in Tennessee or Virginia.

The conflict that flamed across Missouri had a long fuse, one that reached back into the grim struggle over "Bleeding Kansas" during the 1850s. The Civil War provided an opportunity to settle or reopen accounts from that murderous episode. Thus unfortunate Missouri found itself the stage not for a contest between gallant cavaliers but for a war of "ten thousand nasty incidents": the nighttime burning of lonely farmhouses, the shooting down of all the men in a family in ruthless reprisal or random terror. Almost from the beginning Federal troops hanged any apprehended guerrillas, or suspected guerrillas, on the spot. As the remorseless fighting raged on, many Union soldiers, feeling themselves continually surrounded by malign observers, became more and more vengeful and undisciplined. Reprisal provoked counterreprisal; the state and its inhabitants were dragged down into an incomprehensible and accelerating whirlpool of vengeance. Across its formerly complacent counties raged "the worst guerrilla war in American history."[5] By 1864 most rural Missourians had become refugees, either inside or outside the state,[6] and land values fell precipitously.

In such circumstances of social disintegration psychopathic personalities find at last their proper arena. Many Missouri guerrillas wore human scalps or other body parts on their belts. The most notorious of these men of blood was William Clarke Quantrill, born in Ohio in 1837. He often led as many as several hundred men on raids, carrying Colt revolvers, far superior to the single-shot muskets of their Unionist opponents.

On August 21, 1863, Quantrill wrote his name ineradicably across the scarlet page of Civil War history. Quantrill led five hundred men (including Frank James) forty miles across the Kansas border to the town of Lawrence. There they rounded up 180 civilian men and boys, and gunned them all down. After that they put the town to the torch. Apparently only one guerrilla was killed in that raid. Even more remarkably, especially in contrast to the experiences of the Vendée and Spain, it is close to certain that not a single woman was killed or even seriously harmed in this attack that "shocked the whole nation." In retaliation, Union General Thomas Ewing ordered the complete evacuation of all civilians from Jackson, Bates, Cass, and most of Vernon counties, Missouri, the general vicinity from which Quantrill recruited his men and obtained their horses. Soon the population of Cass county sank from over ten thousand to only six hundred—and this in what was, after all, a Union state.

Quantrill's raid on Lawrence turned many Confederates against him, especially officers of the regular army. He found his way to Texas and in January 1865 attacked Danville, Kentucky. In May 1865 (after Lee's surrender) he was grievously wounded and captured in Spencer County, Kentucky. Just before he died he received Baptism into the Catholic Church, and left his girlfriend enough money to open up a brothel in St. Louis. In September 1864, before this surreal denouement, Confederate General Sterling Price rode up from Arkansas leading his long-anticipated invasion of Missouri. Price called upon the people of the blighted state, of which he had been governor before the war, to rise up; he urged new guerrilla bands to create havoc all across northern Missouri. Only five thousand responded to his call, and the invasion sputtered out.

Union forces eventually stationed garrisons in every county seat and sizeable town, put a blockhouse on every railroad bridge, and combed the state with patrols. Even all this was not enough: the guerrilla war in Missouri did not cease until the larger struggle in the East had ended. Many guerrillas had lost their lives. Those who survived "went back to the farm, raised corn and children, and attended the Methodist Church on Sundays."[7]

WHY DID THE GUNS FALL SILENT?

After Lee surrendered his army at Appomatox, nearly 100,000 Confederate troops still remained under arms. These would have been more than sufficient to launch a gigantic guerrilla war against the Union occupation forces. President Lincoln always feared such a development, and so did General Grant, and with good reason: ''To overcome a truly popular, national resistance in a vast territory without the employment of truly overwhelming force is probably impossible.'' The Union had no plans to cope with such an eventuality. But such a conflict did not break out. The American Civil War ended suddenly and completely in the spring of 1865 with a total victory for the Union. Why did the Confederates give up all at once the fight in which they had poured out their blood and treasure for almost four years? Why did the Confederates, after defeat in the conventional field, not continue the struggle, like their Carolina ancestors in the American Revolution or the Boers in southern Africa? Why, in a word, was there no post-Appomatox guerrilla insurgency?

The reasons were several and diverse. In the first place, within the South itself secession had provoked great opposition and deep misgivings. In the presidential contest of 1860, pro-Union candidates John Bell and Stephen Douglas had won a clear majority of the vote in Tennessee, Virginia, Georgia, and Louisiana, and half the vote in North Carolina. Nor did states rush into secession. South Carolina seceded in December 1860, Jefferson Davis took the oath as provisional Confederate President in February 1861, and Fort Sumter fell in April 1861. But even then, North Carolina did not secede until late May, and Tennessee not until early June, almost *half a year* after South Carolina. Robert E. Lee did not resign from the U.S. Army until his home state of Virginia seceded, and from eastern Tennessee alone at least 30,000 men were to serve in the Union ranks, a number greater than Lee commanded when he surrendered at Appomatox.

Many misgivings about the wisdom of secession were suppressed temporarily by the southern confidence that if war came it would be brief and victorious. Fashionable society in Charleston turned out as if for a picnic to watch the bombardment of Fort Sumter; the victory at Bull Run was deceptively encouraging. Besides, if the struggle ever did become really serious, England and France would intervene. In fact, however, Fort Sumter and Bull Run awakened Unionist opinion to the magnitude of the task ahead. Soon enough, ominous shadows began falling across the South: in February 1862 Nashville became the first Confederate capital to fall; New Orleans, the South's largest city and biggest port, was lost the following April; two months later Federal troops occupied Memphis. Meanwhile the Union naval blockade grew ever more effective, leading to inflation and serious shortages; bread riots broke out in Richmond itself as early as spring 1863. After Gettysburg (July 1863), desertion rates in the Confederate armies rose alarmingly.

As the war grew longer and bloodier, voluntary enlistments proved inadequate to fill the Confederate ranks. In April 1862 the Confederate Congress passed a conscription act, a year before the Union did. But national and state officials, as well as certain occupational categories, received exemptions. So did owners of twenty or more slaves: slaveless whites had to bear the burden of a war to preserve slavery. Men began to roam the South, because one could be drafted only in one's home state. Many Confederate politicians, including Vice President Alexander H. Stephens and several governors, bitterly opposed the draft; "conscription was the most unpopular act of the Confederate government."[8] Also, to keep the Confederate armies functioning, requisitions of food, livestock, and other items were required. All this fell upon the civilian population, often accompanied by corruption and enforced by brutality. These cruel blows would undoubtedly have been easier to bear if victory had been visible, however far away; but with each passing month the war news became more grim.

Within the Confederacy new divisions flared up: growing misgivings about secession, festering class resentments, disputes over military strategy, and constitutional squabbles between the Richmond government and various states. President Davis, a conservative ill-cast in the role of a revolutionary, indulged in debilitating public clashes with the Confederate Congress, key governors, and even his own generals. "One who delves deeply into the literature of the period may easily conclude that Southerners hated each other more than they did the Yankees."[9]

The spreading conviction that the war was almost certainly going to be lost increased the attractiveness of President Lincoln's amnesty proclamations, which would at war's end permit most Confederates to return peacefully to Federal allegiance and normal existence.

The real cause of secession had, of course, been slavery, even though a mere 6 percent of white Southerners owned any slaves at all, and even though many Southerners, from Washington and Madison to Robert E. Lee, had been deeply troubled by slavery. The issue of slavery delayed British intervention, and after the Emancipation Proclamation the British Cabinet believed that intervention had become politically impossible.

As the war ground on, the Federal government's search for more manpower inevitably led to the enlistment of emancipated slaves; eventually 180,000 wore the Federal uniform. The Confederacy was even more desperate for soldiers, but it drafted only free whites, not black slaves. As the tide of war turned more decisively against the South, demands became irresistible that everything must be cast into the furnace to keep the engine of war going—everything including slavery itself. Lee had favored arming the slaves after Gettysburg, and eventually President Davis himself embraced the idea. Of course the very concept of arming slaves to fight for the Confederate cause aroused ferocious opposition; as Major General (and former U.S. congressman) Howell Cobb declared, "If slaves make good soldiers then our whole theory of slavery is wrong."[10] Nevertheless, in March 1865—too late—the Confederate Congress, by a narrow vote in both houses, authorized the enlistment of up to 300,000 slaves. Four years previously the secessionists had started the war to continue slavery; now they would end slavery to continue the war. Truly, war is revolution.

Meanwhile, Sherman's march across Georgia to the sea was showing Southerners how incapable the Confederate government was of protecting them, and the fate that awaited those who would not read the writing on the wall. Finally, Lincoln's reelection destroyed any last hope for a negotiated peace based on northern acceptance of secession.

Thus, it is no mystery why the Confederate armies that surrendered in the spring of 1865 were exhausted morally as well as physically. They lacked the stamina, in every sense, to continue a conventional war; the prospects of guerrilla resistance were more than they could face.

Even if a guerrilla struggle were possible, against what enemy must such a fearsome fight be waged? The Federal armies were composed not of foreign invaders but of young men from Pennsylvania and Iowa and New Hampshire. If protracted guerrilla conflict did erupt, would not the Union counterinsurgency enroll more and more black troops, former slaves? Would these not then become politically dominant as well as legally emancipated? All this to save slavery? Slavery was dead; the Confederate Congress itself had signed its death warrant. Or to escape what terrible fate? Mass executions, sweeping confiscations, collective expulsions? On the contrary, Abraham Lincoln offered easy reconstruction, "with malice toward none"; Grant extended generous surrender terms to Lee's men at Appomatox, and a few days afterward Sherman did the same to Joseph E. Johnston's army.

Last but not least, after Appomatox Confederate guerrillas would have had to operate not only without the support of regular armies but also without assistance from foreign powers. If the French and the British had declined to help the Confederacy when it was in full flower, would they try to succor a beaten remnant reduced to guerrilla tactics? In such circumstances a guerrilla Confederacy would not be the Spain of 1812 but the Vendée of 1793. Thus Lee, embodiment of Southern fortitude, urged acceptance of the outcome of the war. Almost every single former supporter of the Confederacy, male and female, followed his counsel.

The Civil War cost 600,000 American lives, including Abraham Lincoln's, more than World War I, World War II and Korea *combined*. The Federal government had spent billions on the war, enough to have purchased at market prices the freedom of every single slave—but it had preserved the Union and freed the slaves. The nation had passed safely through its fiery trial.

NOTES

1. Throughout this chapter it will be convenient to refer to Unionist or Federal forces or states as "northern" and Confederate forces or states as "southern," despite the very important fact that both "North" and "South" were deeply divided by the issues of secession and war.

2. Herman Hattaway and Archer Jones, *How the North Won* (Urbana, IL: University of Illinois, 1991), 250.

3. Jeffrey D. Wert, *Mosby's Rangers* (New York: Simon and Schuster, 1990), 75.

4. John S. Mosby, *Memoirs of Colonel John S. Mosby* (New York: Kraus Reprint Co., 1969), 149–50.

5. Michael Fellman, *Inside War: The Guerrilla Conflict in Missouri during the American Civil War* (New York: Oxford University, 1989), xvi.

6. Ibid., 49.

7. Ibid., 142.

8. James M. McPherson, *Battle Cry of Freedom* (New York: Oxford University, 1988), 432.

9. Bell Wiley, *The Road to Appomatox* (New York: Atheneum, 1983 [orig. 1956]), 78.

10. Charles H. Wesley, *The Collapse of the Confederacy* (New York: Russell and Russell, 1937), 160.

6
The Boer War

In the South African War of 1899–1902—the "Boer War"—Great Britain mounted a military effort larger than any of her nineteenth-century conflicts, including those with Napoleon. This effort turned into the "longest, costliest, bloodiest and most humiliating" of Britain's wars between 1815 and 1914.[1]

The term "Boer" usually referred to the inhabitants of the two independent republics north of Britain's Cape Colony: the Transvaal, with an area of 110,000 square miles containing the cities of Pretoria and Johannesburg, and the Orange Free State, with forty-nine thousand square miles. The two Boer republics together were the size of Kansas and Nebraska combined. The Boers were overwhelmingly the descendants of Dutch (and some German) Protestant immigrants, some of whom had arrived in southern Africa as early as the middle of the seventeenth century. The Boers had pushed farther and farther north toward the interior of Africa, mainly to get away from the British on the Cape; nevertheless, by 1899 the Boer states were almost completely surrounded by British imperial territories. More ominously, the discovery of gold in Transvaal in 1886 had brought in a flood of immigrants, many English-speaking. Eventually these "outlanders" made up half the population of Transvaal and paid most of the taxes, but they were allowed no rights of citizenship.

In December 1895 several hundred armed men from British Rhodesia invaded Transvaal with the intent of overthrowing the Boer government. This was the notorious Jameson Raid. Though they easily defeated the raiders, the Boers took great alarm; war between their states and the British Empire seemed unavoidable. Eventually the Transvaal government issued an ultimatum to the British in Cape Colony regarding the landing and movement of British troops; failing to receive a reply, in October 1899 Transvaal and the Orange Free State declared war and launched invasions of Cape Colony and Natal.

THE CONVENTIONAL PHASE

At the outbreak of war the Transvaal fielded twenty-five thousand men and the Orange Free State another fifteen thousand. These forces composed the most potent army in Africa at the time; to resist them the British had only ten thousand soldiers on hand. During its early months the war developed along conventional lines, army against army. The Boers, who were fighting for their homes and their independence, enjoyed superior mobility and marksmanship. They also understood the importance of trenchworks; British forces would attack prepared Boer positions and suffer costly and embarrassing defeats. The fact that the Boers were of European origin evoked sympathy from many countries, especially Germany, which sent good artillery and some instructors to the embattled republics. In this South African contest the British found themselves dangerously isolated. There was also much opposition to the war in England itself, with the Liberal politician David Lloyd George taking a vociferously pro-Boer stance.

Nevertheless the Boers were predominantly a simple rural folk, and they often employed poor tactics in pursuit of poor strategy. For example, they wasted time and manpower in hopeless sieges that they lacked the skill and means to carry through; they besieged Mafeking for seven months until British forces relieved it. Nor did the Boers devote sufficient effort to the invasion of Cape Colony. They mobilized a total of around eighty-seven thousand men, of whom no more than fifty thousand were under arms at any one time. Meanwhile the British used their command of the seas to send into the contest ever-increasing numbers of men from many parts of their empire. All told, no less than 450,000 troops served on the British side, including seventeen thousand Australians,[2] an incredibly large force in view of the size of the Boer population. The British also employed fifty-three thousand white South Africans, mainly English-speakers; thus the struggle gained some aspects of a civil war. British seapower not only transported these forces in safety and kept them supplied but also cut the Boers off from the outside world.

The outcome of the conventional war was no surprise: British forces occupied Johannesburg in May and Pretoria in June 1900. Soon the two states were annexed to the British imperial system. The defeat of the Boer armies and the occupation of the Boer capitals, however, did not bring peace. Instead the war entered into a new guerrilla phase, which would become "the greatest nineteenth century partisan war."[3]

THE GUERRILLA STRUGGLE

Vast stretches of the Boer republics were level and treeless, excellent territory for mounted guerrillas in a pre-aircraft age. The Boers organized themselves into units called commandos and found leaders of previously unsuspected guerrilla talents, such as Jan Smuts and Louis Botha. But the command structure of the guerrillas resembled that of Boer civilian society, rather loose and uncoordinated, which made effective cooperation and concentration against the enemy more difficult.

The Imperial forces were under the command of General Horatio Kitchener who had defeated the Mahdists in the Sudan in the 1880s and 1890s. Kitchener had 250,000 men under his authority, but only 140,000 were regulars, and out of that number a mere twenty-two thousand represented mobile forces actually able to hunt guerrillas rather than occupy towns and forts. Kitchener had the assistance of at least two thousand National Scouts: these were Boers who, convinced that the struggle was hopeless, had surrendered and then volunteered to work against the guerrillas in order to hasten the coming of peace. One of these National Scouts was the younger brother of the famed guerrilla leader Christian De Wet.

During the conventional phase of the war both the Boers and the British had generally treated their prisoners well. But during the guerrilla phase the killing of prisoners by both sides became more common, partly out of vengeance, partly out of the inability of lightly armed and widely ranging mounted forces to transport and maintain prisoners.

Sir Alfred Milner, High Commissioner for South Africa, opposed the campaign of endless sweeps and farm burning that characterized early British counterinsurgency operations. He wanted a policy that today would be called clearing-and-holding: moving outward from secure populated bases, pushing the guerrillas slowly and methodically into marginal areas and wastelands, and letting the conflict wither at the cost of relatively little bloodshed or destruction of civilian property. General Kitchener soon enough came to see the inadequacy of sweep operations over the broad veldt. In January 1901 he inaugurated his blockhouse strategy, a variant of clear-and-hold: great grids of barbed wire covered the open country, guarded by chains of small forts of simple construction—blockhouses—close enough to each other to cover the intervals with searchlights and rifle fire. Eventually there were eight thousand blockhouses, each occupied by from eleven to thirty soldiers, connected by five thousand miles of wire. Chopping up the open veldt in this way greatly impeded the movement of mounted Boer guerrillas. It also made it easy for British mounted patrols to scour the areas between the blockhouse lines.

Kitchener directed several great drives of mounted troops, one man on a horse every ten yards, sometimes stretching fifty miles across.[4] Of course guerrillas sometimes cut through the wire at night or even broke through the line of mounted troops. But the blockhouse-and-drive system wore them down, and they lost many cattle and horses. Behind the blockhouse lines the Imperial forces built efficient police systems and helped in the reconstruction of normal economic activities. As the war ground on, independently operating, mobile strike columns were increasingly able to locate Boer encampments beyond the blockhouse lines, thanks in large part to improved intelligence, much of which came from native African scouts and spies.

Perhaps the most notorious feature of the British counterinsurgency effort was the erection of camps in which to concentrate the civilian population of contested areas. These ''concentration camps'' were intended to serve several purposes. One obviously was to deprive the guerrillas of food and intelligence; another was to provide shelter to families whose farms had been burned. A third was to give protection to Boers and native Africans who had accepted British rule and taken an oath of neutrality: Smuts and other guerrilla leaders often drove from their homes the families of surrendered guerrillas. In the early months of the camps thousands of their civilian inmates, mainly women and children, died of typhoid fever. Unhealthful conditions in the camps generally resulted from incompetence, not cruelty; nevertheless, revelations about the high death rates caused a worldwide scandal. Henry Campbell-Bannerman, leader of the opposition Liberal party, declared that British forces were employing ''methods of barbarism.''

PEACE

At the beginning of 1902 perhaps twenty thousand Boers were still under arms. Even at that late date they were able to win some notable victories against sizeable British units, but the Boers could not turn these tactical successes into strategic advances. They were hopelessly outnumbered; there was by then no prospect of foreign intervention; and relations with several African tribes had badly deteriorated, threatening the Boers with new dangers. On the other hand, the British were offering amnesty to all except war criminals and promising self-government in the near future, along with indemnities for damage to civilian property. Under these circumstances the guerrilla leaders voted to submit, and the peace was signed in May 1902. Imperial losses from battle and disease totalled over twenty-two thousand; seven thousand Boers died from combat, and thousands more perished in the camps. Many of those who would be Britain's principal commanders in World War I, including Edmund Allenby, Douglas Haig, John French, and of course Kitchener himself, saw service in the Boer War.

NOTES

1. Thomas Pakenham, *The Boer War* (New York: Random House, 1979), xix.
2. One of whom was ''Breaker'' Morant, executed for war crimes.
3. Lewis H. Gann, *Guerrillas in History* (Stanford, CA: Hoover Institution, 1971), 36.
4. Many years later the Indonesian army in East Timor would use a roughly similar tactic, forcing long chains of civilians to move toward each other on foot from extended distances.

7
The Americans and Aguinaldo

Many of the cases of guerrilla war in this book recount disasters suffered by major powers in their encounters with irregular forces. In contrast, the American experience with guerrillas in the post-1898 Philippines is an example of a complete victory of the major power—a victory, moreover, after which all sides were able to live with each other and with themselves.

SPANISH RULE AND THE SPANISH-AMERICAN WAR

The Philippine archipelago in which American troops fought between 1898 and 1902 has an area of 116,000 square miles, about the size of Arizona. There are seven thousand islands, less than half of which have names. Magellan the Circumnavigator met his violent death here in 1521. The Spanish named the islands after the man who ruled one of history's most extensive empires, Philip II, he who launched the misnamed Invincible Armada.

Spain imposed political unity on the islands for the first time in their history. Spain also brought the foundations of cultural unity, in the form of Roman Catholicism; to this day the Philippines are the sole Christian nation in Asia. As in Latin America, however, Spanish rule in the islands promoted neither economic development nor self-government; instead, local figures who considered themselves the natural leaders of their society were largely excluded from office and even from consultation.

In 1896 a major rebellion against Spanish rule broke out, organized by a secret society called the Katipunan. This rebellion was still unresolved when the United States and Spain went to war and Commodore George Dewey won his overwhelming victory against the Spanish fleet in Manila Bay (May 1, 1898). Shortly after Dewey's triumph, Emilio Aguinaldo, the thirty-year-old leader of the Katipunan, who had been brought home from exile by Dewey, proclaimed himself provisional dictator of an independent Philippine Republic. Apparently Aguinaldo expected the Americans to recognize his government; at any rate, the Spanish land forces in the islands still had to be dealt with. American troops captured Manila on August 13; Spain and the United States signed a peace treaty shortly afterward.

Although the outbreak of the Spanish-American war had had nothing to do with the Philippines, President McKinley now had to decide the fate of the islands. To hand them back to the Spanish seemed to him dishonorable, yet the islands could hardly preserve their independence in the face of Japanese and German expansionism in the Pacific. Hence the Americans chose to retain control in the Philippines for the indefinite future. Clashes between US forces and Aguinaldo's troops began on February 4, 1899.

GUERRILLA TACTICS

Aguinaldo at first intended to confront the Americans in conventional military style, but he soon became convinced that only guerrilla war had any chance of success. Aguinaldo's men employed the age-old tactics of the guerrilla. They dug pits with sharpened spears at the bottom and set booby-traps with poisoned arrows. They tended to avoid combat except where they had overwhelming numerical superiority. In between actions they dressed as civilians and hid themselves among the villagers. At the same time, American forces were not numerous enough to garrison simultaneously all the main towns and pursue the guerrillas, and in the tropical climate illnesses became widespread among them.

The guerrilla practice of hiding among peaceful villagers, the racial differences between the two sides, and the inability of most American troops to speak any Filipino languages created the classic environment for abuses of civilians and for war crimes. There were instances in which an American unit, in retaliation for some sanguinary act, set aflame the village within whose territory the act occurred. There were also complaints of the looting of churches by Americans. Of course the insurgents committed crimes as well: reports of robbery and rape were common, and the guerrillas sought to kill all local officials who cooperated in any degree with the Americans. On the whole, however, and considering how many opportunities were open to both sides, the cases of verifiable criminality remained remarkably few.

AMERICAN PREEMPTION AND VICTORY

Although the American forces in the Philippines were never numerically adequate, they had a powerful weapon, a vigorous policy of preemption: the Americans set out to win the Filipinos by good works. Almost immediately they began to open free schools, often with officers as instructors; they attacked the truly deplorable sanitation problems in Manila and outlying areas; they reformed the atrocious penal system; the U.S. Army provided free inoculations against the scourge of smallpox and waged a largely successful campaign against malaria. Despite Aguinaldo's dire warnings that the Americans had come to enslave the Filipinos and destroy Catholicism, it was clear to all that the rule of the Americans was, at the very least, an immeasurable improvement on that of the Spanish.

Of at least equal importance, as early as March 1899, President McKinley sent civilian commissioners, headed by the president of Cornell University, to pledge that the United States recognized the ultimate right of the Filipinos to independence and would work toward that goal; the representatives of the American president repeated that pledge frequently during the hostilities.

With respect to the purely military factors in the American victory, the American counterinsurgency in the Philippines provides an excellent illustration of the influence, even the decisive importance, of geography. Fighting as they were in an archipelago, Aguinaldo's guerrillas had no sanctuary, no international border to cross in times of difficulty. The guerrillas received no offer of assistance from any third power (although elements in the Japanese military strongly expressed their conviction that such aid should be sent), and in any event the U.S. Navy would have stopped or seriously hindered any efforts toward such assistance. Against guerrillas lacking both protective borders and outside aid, even the most uninspired counterinsurgency tactics would have been effective, over time. But in fact American tactics, first under General E. S. Otis and then General Arthur MacArthur, were generally sound. Rather than merely trying to kill guerrillas, American units concentrated on holding territory and creating local zones of safety, often with the help of the inhabitants. In some areas of high guerrilla activity, the rural population were gathered together into the nearest town. The American army also carried on programs whereby any Filipino who turned in a gun could receive either a cash bounty or the release of a prisoner of war, no questions asked. These tactics had the long-term effect of isolating the guerrillas and making their cause seem hopeless.[1] Also, they provided time for American political efforts against the guerrillas to take effect.

Four principal political factors were influential in deciding the final outcome of the struggle. First, many Filipinos felt that American preemptive policies in education and health were powerful arguments in favor of at least a temporary accommodation with their occupation. Second, Aguinaldo was unable to mobilize the power of Philippine nationalism, because for the most part it did not exist; regional, ethnic, linguistic, and religious divisions among the Filipinos undercut the potential for a truly national uprising, and indeed the Americans soon found it was easy to recruit scouts and even troops from among the minority peoples of Luzon and other areas. Third, whereas a potentially powerful card in the hands of the rebels was an appeal to social revolution, the conservative Aguinaldo rejected such a course; even so, the upper classes of Philippine society generally supported the Americans as the best guarantors of social order. Fourth, Aguinaldo claimed that he was fighting for the independence of the Philippines, but the Americans had pledged themselves, in writing, to that goal; a devastating war over the mere timing of that independence was unappealing to many Filipinos.

A SUMMING-UP

More Americans (4,200) lost their lives in repressing the Aguinaldo insurgency than in fighting the Spanish-American War. The American troops were culturally alien, far from their native land, less plentiful than they needed to be, and without imperial experience to guide them. They were on the guerrillas' home turf. There existed no tanks to deploy and no air force to call upon. In spite of all these handicaps (or more likely *because* of some of them) they were completely victorious. Not only that, but the victory over the guerrillas was won in such a way as to lay the basis for lasting cooperation and friendship between the Filipinos and the Americans; even Aguinaldo himself eventually became reconciled to American tutelage.[2] Yet it is not clear that the Americans studied the lessons of their success very assiduously. What is clear is that they took little notice of these lessons when they found themselves involved in counterinsurgency in another Southeast Asian country six decades later.

NOTES

1. John Morgan Gates, *Schoolbooks and Krags: The United States Army in the Philippines 1898–1902* (Westport, CT: Greenwood, 1973).

2. Emilio Aguinaldo, *A Second Look at America* (New York: Robert Speller, 1957).

8
Lawrence of Arabia

The story of Lawrence of Arabia constitutes an extraordinary and romantic chapter in the lengthy annals of guerrilla warfare. A scholarly young Englishman so assimilated himself to the Arabs of the desert that he was able to assume direction of an Arab trans-tribal uprising against the Ottoman Empire during a world war. Yet Lawrence's war was a small affair, and one critic has tartly commented that "seldom in history has so much been written about so little." [1]

BACKGROUND

The Arab Revolt, in which Lawrence of Arabia played such a dramatic role, developed in support of Britain's efforts in the Middle East during World War I. From the British point of view, the strategic situation in that part of the world at the outbreak of the war was as straightforward as it was troubling. The once-powerful Ottoman Empire had been for decades the "Sick Man of Europe," and in 1908 the original "Young Turks" seized power with an ambitious program of reform, stressing military modernization. But the reformers did not have sufficient time to implement their ideas, being instead swept up in the rising tide of European militarism. Italy successfully invaded Turkish Libya in 1911; the following year, the First Balkan War stripped Turkey of almost all of her remaining territories in Europe.

At the same time the Turks had fallen completely within the orbit of Wilhelmine Germany. The basis of this relationship was that since Russia was

Turkey's main enemy, and Britain and Russia were friends, Turkey was obliged to look for protection to the enemies of Russia, and thus to the enemies of Britain. German General Liman von Sanders arrived to supervise the Turkish army. Shortly after the outbreak of fighting in 1914, Russia declared war on Turkey. The Turks closed the Dardanelles to the British Royal Navy, thereby breaking the vital Mediterranean supply route from the Western allies to Russia and placing the latter in mortal danger. Consequently the British decided to mount a major attack on Turkey in order to take pressure from their hard-pressed czarist ally and reopen the water route to Russia; out of this plan came the British disaster in the notorious Gallipoli Campaign (April 1915–January 1916).

The costly failure of this amphibious attack upon the Turks set the stage for a thrust against them from some other quarter, and onto this stage strode the diminutive figure of Thomas Edward Lawrence. An Oxford-educated archaeologist and a frequent traveler in the Middle East, Lawrence received assignment as a British army intelligence officer because of his fluency in colloquial Arabic. By 1916 he had attached himself to anti-Turkish Arab rebels under Faisal, soon becoming Faisal's close adviser and confidant.[2]

WAR IN THE DESERT

Lawrence discovered that many Arab leaders wanted to be rid of the Turks but were unable to accept significant casualties among their own followers. Nor could they observe the hallowed European military principle of concentration of force, because the various tribes could not enter each other's territory. On the other hand, Lawrence estimated that to retain their grip on the Arab lands the Turks would need a force of 600,000, an impossibly large number to mobilize and maintain.[3] Besides, with their undeveloped economic base, "things" meant more to the Turks than men. Therefore, the best course for the insurgents would be to attack not troops but installations, bridges, and especially the railway that linked Damascus to Medina.[4] The clear course for Lawrence and his Arab allies was to wage a guerrilla war, which they proceeded to do, mounted on camels and carrying light automatic weapons and explosives. British gold bought recruits for the rebellion against the Turkish Sultan. After Lawrence and his guerrillas captured the little port of Aqaba (July 1917), not only gold but also food and ammunition flowed in to the rebels. (There were, however, no heavy weapons: the British were looking ahead toward the postwar situation.)

In his struggle Lawrence had three main advantages: he was operating in the midst of a mainly friendly civilian population; he was in terrain where his enemies' superior weapons availed them little; and he possessed a secure base always conveniently at hand, namely the coast of the Red Sea and the Royal Navy that dominated it. The Turks, for their part, were not prepared to cope with an ethnically based guerrilla conflict. Their superiority in conventional weapons and tactics was of no use to them in the sandy wastes into which the guerrillas retreated. Had their forces been equipped with ground-attack aircraft and armored cars, the Turks could have destroyed their enemies on the open desert in short order, but they had neither of those things. Thus Lawrence tied down great numbers of Turkish troops and even inflicted thirty-five thousand casualties on them. All this helped to relieve the pressure on the Russians, though they collapsed anyway in October 1917.

In November 1917, having entered in disguise the Turkish-held town of Dara, Lawrence was recognized, imprisoned, and brutalized. Escaping from his tormentors, he accompanied British and Arab forces in their triumphal entry into Jerusalem in December. This event "for me was the supreme moment of the war."[5] Not until October 1918, however, did Allied forces capture Damascus; within a month Turkey quit the war, and Germany itself imploded.

NOTES

1. Walter Laqueur, *Guerrilla: A Historical and Critical Study* (Boston: Little, Brown, 1976).

2. After the war the British established Faeisal (1885–1933) as first king of Iraq.

3. T. E. Lawrence, *Seven Pillars of Wisdom: A Triumph* (Garden City, NY: Doubleday, 1936), 192.

4. Ibid., 194.

5. Ibid., 453.

Section III: World War II in Europe

During World War II, perhaps the best-known guerrilla resistance to German occupation took place in Yugoslavia. Guerrilla conflict in that country had many aspects of a civil war. Out of the maelstrom emerged the dictator Josip Tito, helped along to victory by mountainous terrain, a national tradition of guerrilla resistance, German atrocities, British supplies, Soviet strategic pressures, and the abandonment of non-communist guerrilla forces by the Churchill cabinet.

The contrast between Yugoslavia and Poland was dramatic. Polish guerrilla forces were numerous and determined but, operating in unfavorable terrain, cut off from the Western Allies, and betrayed by Stalin, they perished in fire and blood.

In Italy and France, guerrilla movements (as distinguished from organized sabotage) went into operation when massive Allied armies were already on the territory of their countries. Their principle concern was with the politics of the postwar period, and the exact value of their contribution to final victory is in dispute.

9
Guerrillas against Hitler and Stalin

POLAND

In September 1939, the republic of Poland was invaded and overrun from the west by Nazi Germany and from the east by Stalinist Russia. A Polish government-in-exile established itself in London, supported by all of Poland's major non-communist parties. The western powers recognized it as the legitimate representative of the suffering people of Poland. At the behest and under the leadership of this government, all but a few underground resistance groups operating inside Poland, gathered within an organization called the Home Army (AK). Command of the AK eventually devolved upon General Tadeusz Komorowski, whose codename was ''Bor.'' Unlike the situation in France or Italy, therefore, Polish resistance had real cohesion from the beginning.

The Polish government-in-exile saw the principal task of the Home Army as the preparation of a general uprising. Such an uprising could and should occur only when it became clear that Germany was not far from final defeat. Until that time, the AK engaged in acts of sabotage: during the German occupation the AK damaged seven thousand locomotives, blew up thirty-eight railway bridges, and destroyed or damaged 4,300 military vehicles. It carried out reprisals against individuals or groups, killing several thousand Gestapo agents and collaborators. The AK also gathered intelligence, published and circulated underground newspapers, trained its members, stockpiled arms, and maintained liaison both among its various branches and with the government-in-exile.

In April and May 1943, in response to the now-patent Nazi intention to kill every Jew in Poland, the Warsaw Ghetto burst into hopeless revolt. Many Warsaw Jews opposed such an enterprise for strategic reasons and refused to join it: of perhaps seventy thousand inhabitants of the Ghetto, less than two thousand participated in the struggle. But even had every Jew of the Ghetto joined in and fought like a lion, any uprising that sought merely to defend the boundaries of the Ghetto was doomed to failure. Although the AK rendered some assistance to the Ghetto rising, its leaders judged that the hour was far too premature; a general AK revolt could not be ready for more than a year, finally beginning when the fighting on the Russian front had clearly turned against the Germans.

The London government-in-exile and indeed almost the entire Polish nation viewed Joseph Stalin's USSR as quite as much the national enemy as Hitler's Germany. During the war Stalin refused to organize the Polish prisoners of war his soldiers had taken in 1939 into an anti-German force. Then in April 1943 the graves of almost fifteen thousand Polish officers were discovered in the Katyn Forest, victims of a mass execution. The Polish government in London requested the International Red Cross to investigate the massacre; Stalin (who of course knew who had perpetrated this slaughter) used the request as an excuse to break off relations with the Polish government. Stalin then set up his own puppet Polish government and a Polish communist army of sorts. At the Teheran Conference in November–December 1943 President Franklin D. Roosevelt implicitly accepted Stalin's postwar plans for Poland. As the Red Army approached Warsaw, therefore, the AK set its plans for revolt in motion. Russian radio broadcasts during July 1944 urged the Poles and especially the inhabitants of Warsaw to rise against the Germans. All Warsaw knew that the Germans were about to draft every young man remaining in the city for forced labor, with the aim of turning Warsaw into a second Stalingrad. Accordingly, the long-awaited rising of the Polish Home Army began on August 1, 1944.

Of the forty-six thousand insurgents, less than half had guns, and the AK had stocks of ammunition for only ten days' fighting. Nevertheless, hundreds of young men and women armed with Molotov cocktails and determined to sell their lives at a high price in Warsaw's narrow streets destroyed close to three hundred German tanks. The Luftwaffe staged massive raids, many incendiary; eventually it seemed as if the whole city was in flames. The task of repressing the revolt fell largely to savage SS units, because many German Army officers were repelled by such duty.

When the revolt began the Red Army was only six miles from Warsaw, having covered almost four hundred miles in the previous six weeks. But now, while the Nazis were systematically destroying the city, the Soviet forces remained immobile on the right bank of Vistula. Stalin even refused to allow Allied aircraft flying supplies to the burning capital to land in the Soviet zone of control. Under these conditions British and Polish pilots of the Royal Air Force took great risks to drop munitions into Warsaw, and many scores perished.

Resistance in the city continued hopelessly until October 2, when General

Bor and several hundred exhausted and weaponless AK members surrendered after receiving a promise from the Germans that they would be treated as prisoners of war. The ceasefire required that all civilians leave the city. Amid the smoking rubble of Warsaw scores of thousands were dead, including ten thousand AK fighters, both men and women, and soon the Nazis would deport hundreds of thousands more. Those areas of the city that had not already suffered destruction in the fighting were systematically blown up by the Germans: Hitler had ordered that Warsaw be obliterated from the earth. The destruction of the Home Army left Poland utterly defenseless against Stalinization after 1945. After the Soviets had clamped their power on the country, several of the surviving leaders of the Home Army died in the prisons of the NKVD—the People's Committee of Internal Affairs, the political secret police.

THE UKRAINE

The Republic of Ukraine today is 232,000 square miles in extent, about the size of Minnesota, Iowa, Illinois, and Indiana. Of its fifty million inhabitants, approximately one-fourth are non-Ukrainian. On the eve of World War II, the Soviet Ukraine was considerably smaller: 172,000 square miles, about the size of Indiana, Illinois, and Iowa. Until the Afghanistan war of the 1980s, the Ukrainian resistance to restalinization after 1944 was probably the most important example of a sustained anticommunist insurgency, though certainly it cannot compare in dramatic power to the Budapest Rising of 1956.

V. I. Lenin and Leon Trotsky gave up claims to control of the Ukraine by the Brest-Litovsk Treaty of 1918. The first Ukrainian republic struggled for independence (or a possible federation with newly resurrected Poland) until 1922, but it finally suffered conquest by the armies of Bolshevik Russia. The savagery of Stalinist collectivization fell with special severity on the Ukrainians, millions of whom died of starvation or in slave labor camps. In 1929 the anti-Soviet Organization of Ukrainian Nationalists (OUN) held its founding meeting in Vienna; the OUN was to become the parent group of the Ukrainian Insurgent Army, the UPA. Predictably, a very high proportion of the leadership of OUN was drawn from the educated middle class, especially writers and teachers.

The German invasion of the USSR that began on June 22, 1941 as a surprise to no one except the leaders inside the Kremlin, presented Ukrainian nationalists—who hated the Nazis but hated their communist overlords more—with their main chance. Many Ukrainian nationalists hoped for a protracted struggle between Germany and the USSR that would leave both exhausted. They also had some hopes from the August 1941 Atlantic Charter, which proclaimed that among Allied war aims was freedom for oppressed peoples. But unlike Tito's Yugoslavia, the Ukraine lay well within the area conceded to Stalin's control at the Yalta Conference of February 1945. For its part, the German occupation was deeply ambivalent toward Ukrainian nationalism, on one hand wishing to employ Ukrainians against the Red Army but on the other hesitating to arm "racially inferior" and hence politically unreliable Slavs.

During the winter of 1943–1944, the Red Army reconquered almost all of pre-1939 Soviet Ukraine. The returning communist rulers decreed a universal draft, to include even fifteen-year-old boys, many of whom were sent to the battlefront with little training, as mere cannon fodder. To escape this fate youths sought shelter with units of the Ukrainian Insurgent Army. Many UPA guerrilla groups were made up of former German-organized military or police units that had turned against the Germans; the relative ineffectiveness of German occupation in the Ukraine had given the UPA precious opportunities to organize itself. (In his so-called Secret Speech to the Twentieth Party Congress in 1956, Khrushchev stated that Stalin actually contemplated the removal of the entire Ukrainian population after the war as punishment for their anti-Soviet activities.)

After the departure of the Germans, Ukrainian resistance to communist control centered mainly in those Ukrainian areas formerly under the rule of Poland, and especially in Galicia. Never before having been occupied by the Red Army, "cleansed" by the NKVD, or subjected to collectivization, Galicia was a fertile recruiting ground for the UPA. Its location along the Carpathian mountains and its large and nationalistic peasant population made it an ideal area for guerrilla campaigning. After 1945 approximately six thousand members of the UPA were operating on the new Polish-Soviet frontier.

The NKVD (later known as the KGB, the Committee of State Security) was in charge of exterminating nationalist resistance. Soviet anti-UPA tactics included: threatening members of an entire family with removal to Siberia if a missing member or members did not return; committing outrages against civilians while wearing UPA uniforms; and repopulating entire villages with new settlers from distant parts of the USSR. In spite of these draconian measures, Poland, Czechoslovakia and the USSR found it necessary in May 1947 to enter into an agreement to increase their cooperation against the ferociously resisting UPA. Even as late as December 1949, the Ukrainian Ministry of the Interior was issuing proclamations of amnesty to UPA members who would lay down their arms. On March 5, 1950, the KGB apparently killed the last supreme commander of the UPA in a village near Lvov; after that, most resistance came to an end.

The UPA enjoyed the advantages of favorable terrain, a long period of preparation, an integrated organizational structure, a sense of aggrieved nationalism widespread among a large population, and at least in the first years some assistance from outside the Ukraine.[1] Overbalancing these plusses, the UPA found itself without a sanctuary, confronting the limitless resources of a ruthless police state, and written off and eventually forgotten by the outside world, Some of those who survived the suppression of the Ukrainian Insurgent Army lived to see the reemergence of an independent Ukrainian Republic in 1991.

YUGOSLAVIA

Out of the collapse of the Habsburg and Ottoman empires at the end of World War I emerged the new kingdom of Yugoslavia. It was put together from several different states and fragments of states. Within it, many ethnic and religious groups lived together uncomfortably, representing diverse and often hostile traditions and languages: Orthodox Serbs, Catholic Slovens and Croats, Muslims, Albanians, Macedonians, Hungarians, and yet others. During World War I the Croats and many Muslims had fought for the Habsburgs against the Serbs. From the beginning, the Serbian royal house and Serbian army dominated the new state; it soon began to appear to the other elements, especially the Croats, that the new Yugoslavia was hardly more than an expanded Serbia. The presence of increasingly disenchanted minority groups in border areas added to the tensions. Finally, in 1934 a Croatian separatist organization, the Ustasha, assassinated King Alexander of Yugoslavia in Marseilles.

The German Invasion

In March 1941 a coup in Belgrade brought to power a cabinet distinctly hostile to Nazi Germany. Yugoslavia, however, was Germany's geographical link with Greece and Bulgaria, ultimately with the Middle East and North Africa; the Germans therefore responded to the coup with a massive invasion in April. Many today believe that this invasion, because it delayed Hitler's attack on the Soviet Union by at least a month, was the real turning point of World War II; in any event, the Royal Yugoslav Army quickly collapsed. German, Italian, Hungarian, Bulgarian, and Rumanian forces occupied and partitioned the country. The rapid defeat at the hands of the Germans stunned many Yugoslavians. Open resistance organized slowly, and when it emerged it took the form not only of guerrilla warfare against the Axis invaders but of civil war among the country's ethnic minorities.

Among the resistance forces, the paladin of the royal house and the old Serbia was Draza Mihailovich, a colonel of the general staff; he took to the mountains and summoned all who could to come to him. Most of his original comrades were Serbian officers, who called themselves "Chetniks," a name redolent of countless wars against Turkish invaders. From London the Royal Yugoslav government-in-exile soon named Mihailovich the Minister of the Armed Forces and recognized him as the legitimate leader of all resistance groups, a recognition seconded by the Churchill cabinet.

In August 1941 the Yugoslav government broadcast over the BBC an appeal to its citizens not to endanger the survival of the country by premature uprising. Cut off from help and sometimes even from contact with the outside world, aware that the war would be long, and convinced that the Germans would lose, Mihailovich sought to conserve his forces and the lives of his countrymen for a better day. The Germans committed savagely disproportionate and indiscriminate reprisals against the defenseless civilian population for any acts of resistance from any quarter; acutely conscious of the devastating population losses in Serbia during World War I, the Chetniks wished to wait until Allied forces were close to Yugoslavia before launching a major uprising. Mihailovich further believed that after the inevitable German evacuation of Yugoslavia, the Communists would try to impose themselves on the country by force; to prevent this new catastrophe became his overriding concern and policy.

Opposing Mihailovich and the Chetniks were the communist-organized "Partisans," grouped around the Croat-Slovenian Josip Broz Tito, a devout Party member since 1917. When World War II broke out the Yugoslavian Communist Party loyally parroted the Comintern line that the struggle between Germany and Britain was merely a fight between imperialists. Yugoslavia's Communists did not undertake armed attacks on the Germans occupying their country until after invasion of the USSR in June 1941. Tito insisted that all command positions among the Partisans, even at low levels, be held by Party members.

Once they undertook to fight the Germans, Tito's Partisans did not worry about the inevitable reprisals against civilians. Indeed they deliberately drew down German punishments on the populace in order to obtain more recruits; besides, arousing Nazi destructiveness suited Tito's purpose of dismantling the old social bases of South Slav society. The price peaceful peasants had to pay for all this remains incalculable. Soon Tito was commanding thousands of guerrillas; they and to a lesser extent the Chetniks tied up numerous German units that could have been useful elsewhere, especially on the Russian front.

The German army in Yugoslavia mounted several encirclement operations and annihilation campaigns against the Partisans; one of them involved 120,000 German and Axis troops. None were as successful as the Germans hoped and planned. Nevertheless, in mid-1942 the Partisans were forced into Montenegro and Herzegovina, areas too poor to sustain them; in May 1943 Axis forces drove the Partisans out of Montenegro. In the latter campaign several thousand Partisans perished, indeed the whole movement came close to being snuffed out, and Tito himself suffered wounds. Compensating for this was the surrender of Italian forces in Yugoslavia in the fall of 1943, from which the Partisans were able to acquire great quantities of good weapons and ammunition.

As 1943 drew to a close there were several hundred thousand German and perhaps 200,000 Axis (excluding Italian) troops in Yugoslavia. Tito's admirers inside and outside the country claimed that he commanded about ninety thousand Partisans. Meanwhile the Chetniks, attacked by both the Axis and the Partisans, were a diminishing force. In May 1944 a German airborne attack on his headquarters at Drvar forced Tito to evacuate the area, eventually abandoning the mainland entirely and seeking refuge among the offshore islands in the Adriatic, where the Germans, because of their naval weakness, could not follow. By this time, however, the British had abandoned the Chetniks and switched their supply and intelligence efforts entirely to the Partisans, thus ensuring postwar control of the country by the communists.[2] Partisan forces accompanied Russian armored units entering Belgrade in October 1944; the Germans left Sarajevo in April 1945. By that date the Partisans claimed to have 400,000 fighters, a figure that may have been exaggerated to impress the British. The Partisans had also benefited from staff advice, instructions, and arms from the advancing Soviet armies.

Close to two million Yugoslavs, out of a prewar population of sixteen million, died at the hands of the Axis forces or each other during and soon after the war. Mihailovich himself, captured by the Partisans, endured a communist political show trial in July 1946; after his execution he was buried in a secret grave.

Why the Partisans Won

Tito and his Partisans emerged in control of Yugoslavia at the end of the war because of the nature of the country in which they waged their struggle, because both their German and Chetnik opponents carried certain handicaps, and because the Partisans enjoyed peculiar advantages of their own.

Yugoslavia was a close-to-ideal setting for guerrilla war, with a population inured to hardship and combat, having a tradition of resistance to invaders, living in a land of rugged mountains, wild ravines, and thick forests, and with few rail lines or good roads. These austere circumstances both inhibited the mobility of the German army and negated the value of much of its equipment. In addition, because of the inexorable demands of the Russian front, most of the German troops in the country were not of the best quality. Coordination among the multinational Axis occupation forces in Yugoslavia was poor, and their numbers were inadequate to control the countryside and carry out really effective clearing operations. As a result, the Partisans always managed to escape from or break through encircling movements, although they suffered many casualties in these episodes, including the sacrifice of their rear guards. Also, of course, the occupation played into the hands of the Partisans by its appalling brutality toward the population.

As for the Chetniks, they were the representatives of the old Serbian establishment—dynasty, army, church, politicians—which had been seriously discredited by its sudden collapse in 1941 and its impotence during the war. The Chetniks embodied Serb domination of Yugoslavia, while the collaborationist Croatian Ustasha stood for the breakup of the country; only Tito's Partisans flew the banner of a united Yugoslavia within which all ethnic groups might find equality.

Tito never allowed himself to be deterred by German atrocities against civilians in retaliation for Partisan actions; on the contrary, he welcomed them. Accordingly Tito acquired a reputation with the British as a fighter (as contrasted to the cautious Mihailovich) and therefore a valuable ally. It was for this reason, and apparently because British communist agents helped to convince Churchill that Mihailovich was actively collaborating with the Germans, that the British decided to abandon the Chetniks and help the Partisans exclusively.[3] This decision had decisive effects when the Allies obtained air bases in Italy in 1943; from them the Partisans obtained fifty thousand machineguns and submachineguns to add to all the equipment that had fallen into their hands when Italian forces surrendered in 1943. Tito now had a sanctuary in Italy, where many wounded Partisans obtained hospital treatment.

All these factors help explain why as the end of the war approached the Partisans were strong, much stronger than the Chetniks. But it was the inexorable advance of the Soviet army into the Balkans which made it certain that when the Germans left Yugoslavia Tito's Communist Party would pick up the pieces.

FRANCE

After France's humiliating defeat in 1940, General Charles de Gaulle established his Free French organization in Britain. With British help he soon had control over much of France's overseas empire. Considerable numbers of French officers joined him, first in England and then in Algeria, to prepare the day of liberation.

Within occupied France, early resistance groups were largely composed of draft-evaders, who gathered in the mountainous areas of the south where the German presence was slight. Here were the origins of the famous maquis. In the course of time no less than eight resistance groups arose, all with their own paramilitary forces, representing different political parties. The large communist contingent usually kept aloof from the others. The divergent groups pursued divergent ends: assassination and sabotage, or preparation for the inevitable allied invasion. Internecine violence flared; many old scores were settled, many lives were taken with an eye to the postwar political struggle. Betrayals to the Germans were frequent.

A National Resistance Council of all groups came into existence in May 1943, and the French Forces of the Interior (FFI) appeared in February 1944. Beginning with D-Day, French resistance manifested itself mainly in sabotage; for instance, on the night of D-Day itself (June 6, 1944), saboteurs disabled fifty-two locomotives in the Bellegarde depot. The railwaymen went out on strike on August 10. Guerrilla forces harassed German units heading into Normandy, and the Allies parachuted hundreds of tons of supplies to various resistance groups.

A German garrison of seventeen thousand held Paris. Original Allied plans did not call for the liberation of Paris, but at de Gaulle's insistence the Americans sent General Jacques Leclerc's Free French division toward the capital. In the revolutionary tradition, a National Resistance Council set itself up in the Hôtel de Ville. On August 25, two French armored divisions entered Paris; de Gaulle and Leclerc walked in triumph down the Champs Élysées even as fighting still went on in certain sections of the city.

ITALY

The regime of Benito Mussolini from 1922 to 1943 had been remarkably bloodless, even without comparison to Stalin and Hitler. But the post-1943 Nazi occupation of northern and central Italy unleashed ferocious combat between the German army and Mussolini's die-hard supporters on one hand, and guerrillas, called partisans and usually dominated by communists, on the other. Responsibility for dealing with the partisan bands fell mainly to the Italians.

The first notable groups of partisans appeared in opposition to German requisitioning, in the central regions of Abruzzi, Tuscany, and the Marches, and along the Apennines. In the northern regions of Liguria and Piedmont the partisans grew very numerous, but the Germans kept a tight grip on Lombardy and Venetia, which were their links with Austria and home. In the Alps and the Po Valley, communists took the lead, and general communist prominence among the partisan leadership aroused the lasting distrust of Churchill. By spring 1945 perhaps 200,000 partisans were active, and forty-five thousand died in action against Germans and Fascists. The high casualty figures resulted mainly from partisan units making the fatal error of establishing and defending "liberated areas" while German power was still unbroken.

In August 1944 Florence suffered a destructive liberation after bitter fighting between Germans and Allied troops and partisans. By the following April, German units in northern Italian cities found themselves caught between the advancing Allied armies and partisans coming down from the mountains. The Germans abandoned Milan after an agreement with the partisans that the city would be spared; in Turin, armed clashes flared, and at Genoa nine thousand Germans surrendered to partisan forces after destructive fighting. Mussolini himself, trying to escape into Switzerland under the protection of retreating German forces, fell into the hands of communist partisans; they executed him, contrary to explicit Allied orders, on 27 April. Serious combat was still going on in northern Italy when Hitler committed suicide.

What was the general impact on the war of guerrilla activities (as opposed to sabotage) in France and Italy? On the whole, not very great: "As the German position [in these countries] deteriorated, the German military leaders were totally preoccupied with the regular forces facing them."[4] In France, Italy, and elsewhere in western Europe, anti-German guerrillas "were less effective than widespread passive resistance—and brought far more harm to the people of their own country. They provoked reprisals much more severe than the injury inflicted on the enemy."[5]

NOTES

1. John A. Armstrong, *Ukrainian Nationalism* (New York: Columbia University, 1963), 301. See also Yaroslav Bilinsky, *The Second Soviet Republic: The Ukraine after World War II* (New Brunswick, NJ: Rutgers University, 1964).

2. See Churchill's expurgated account of all this in the fifth volume of his history of the Second World War, *Closing the Ring* (Boston: Houghton Mifflin, 1951), 461–79.

3. "Without British help, Tito could hardly have survived during World War II." Lewis G. Gann, *Guerrillas in History* (Stanford, CA-Hoover Institution, 1971), 92. Today the contention is becoming widespread that misrepresentations of conditions in Yugoslavia by British communist agents played a large role in Churchill's switch of support from Mihailovich to Tito. Michael Lees passionately presents this view in *The Rape of Serbia: The British Role in Tito's Grab for Power 1943–1944* (New York: Harcourt Brace Jovanovich, 1990).

4. Walter Laqueuer, *Guerrilla* (London: Weidenfeld and Nicolson, 1977), 237.

5. B. H. Liddell Hart, *Strategy* (New York: Signet, 1967), 368.

Section IV: The Cold War

The Cold War first turned hot in Greece. In that country, communist guerrillas committed every major error guerrillas can commit; accordingly, instead of imposing Stalinism on the birthplace of democracy, the guerrillas experienced an unambiguous defeat. The Greek example never received its due attention, being overshadowed by the thunderclouds of Maoist triumph in China. Here was the birthplace and proving ground, many supposed, of an undefeatable guerrilla strategy: revolutionary war, or people's war. Subsequently, in neighboring Viet Nam, the validity of the revolutionary guerrilla war strategy appeared to receive confirmation, despite the inadequate numbers and inappropriate strategy the French deployed against the insurgents. Simultaneously with these well-publicized Chinese and Indochinese dramas, Malaya and the Philippines witnessed the defeat of communist guerrillas by governments that combined good military tactics with intelligent political programs.

In addition to the definite vincibility of Maoist-inspired insurgency, several other lessons, old and new, about guerrilla warfare came to the surface during the Cold War. Geography was clearly a decisive asset for the guerrillas in both French Indochina and South Viet Nam, but it worked powerfully against them in Greece, Malaya, and the Philippines—mainly because outside assistance was able to reach the former but not the latter. In Algeria and in South Viet Nam the guerrillas experienced military defeat but nevertheless achieved political victory. In Afghanistan and Cambodia, the Cold War tables were turned, as powerful communist conventional armies grappled bitterly and fruitlessly with determined guerrilla forces.

10
Greece

The Greek Civil War was the first armed confrontation between the emerging Western and communist blocs. It called forth the proclamation of the Truman Doctrine and thus set the stage for the Cold War and the policy of containment.

THE GERMANS AND ELAS

With an area of fifty-one thousand square miles, present-day Greece is the size of Virginia and Maryland combined, although much of its territory was incorporated into the country only after 1912 or even 1919. The population of the Greek state at the outbreak of the civil war was approximately seven million.

Before World War II the Greek Communist Party was numerically tiny and intellectually sterile; even in the Depression-gloomed 1930s there were only about two hundred party members in Athens, and a few hundred elsewhere. In the first week of April 1941, while Hitler and Stalin were still allies, German troops stormed into Yugoslavia and Greece. Because it postponed for several crucial weeks the Nazi assault on the Soviet Union, this invasion possibly saved the Stalinist regime. It certainly transformed the Greek communists into a force capable of attempting an armed revolution, and it opened a long chapter of physical destruction and moral agony for the Greek people. The Greek army was quickly overwhelmed, and its remnants fled with the royal family to British protection in Egypt. For the next several years the Germans and their Axis partners maintained 180,000 troops in Greece, because the country was a strategic conduit of supplies to German forces in North Africa.

After Hitler invaded the Soviet Union (June 22, 1941), it again became permissible for good communists to oppose Nazism (as they could not after the Non-Aggression Pact of August 1939). Accordingly, the Greek Party organized the National Liberation Front (EAM), but not until December 1942 did it create an armed guerrilla force, the ELAS. Covered with mountains, crossed by few highways, and possessed of a long tradition of resistance to foreign invaders, Greece was an excellent country for guerrilla warfare. Nevertheless, the ELAS did little fighting against the Germans, preferring to undermine its domestic enemies and conserve its strength in preparation for the postwar period. For their part the German occupiers wished only to safeguard the main north-south passage through Greece; thus they did not pursue a very vigorous counterinsurgency campaign. ELAS did, however, carry out raids against the Germans in the expectation that severe reprisals against civilians would follow. ELAS was also busy executing its known and suspected political enemies. Many Greek villages, to prevent communists from provoking German reprisals, and also to beat off ELAS requisitions, kidnappings, and killings, organized home defense units. Meanwhile, the British government, blithely unconcerned with postwar considerations, lavished diplomatic and material support upon ELAS, even though there were noncommunist guerrilla forces in the country, notably EDES, that were literally dying for lack of weapons. ELAS also obtained great quantities of guns and munitions when Italian forces surrendered in the fall of 1943. In 1944 the German army began to evacuate Greece, not because of guerrilla activities but to avoid being cut off by developments elsewhere in Europe. As the Germans retreated out of Greece they left behind much equipment and ammunition that ELAS would use later against the British.

THE CIVIL WAR

Close on the heels of the retreating Germans, small British and Royal Greek Army elements began landing in the Athens area. In December 1944, ELAS attempted to seize Athens by force and attacked British positions there; it also destroyed most of the poorly armed EDES formations in the country. Hundreds of British troops in the Athens area were killed and wounded in the fighting, many undoubtedly with weapons that the British cabinet had previously supplied to ELAS units. Ultimately seventy-five thousand British soldiers were defending the Greek capital, and Prime Minister Churchill himself spent Christmas Day in the city. Realizing it could not win, ELAS (soon to call itself the Democratic Army) agreed to a truce in February 1945; at the same time it began executing thousands of hostages, including socialist politicians and labor leaders. This bloody episode accounts for the profound hostility in Athens toward the communists during subsequent phases of the civil war. In March 1946 national elections for a new parliament took place in the presence of hundreds of foreign journalists and observers. The communists boycotted these elections and embarked upon guerrilla war.

The ranks of the insurgents consisted predominantly of four groups: old-time Communist Party members, ex-ELAS guerrillas from the German occupation days, Macedonian separatists (probably few of whom were communists), and forced recruits and abductees, including teenaged girls, held in line by threats against their families.

The revolutionaries had some big cards to play. Greece historically and topographically was good country for guerrilla war. Underdeveloped and overcrowded, it had never been a prosperous country to begin with and, in contrast to the grim postwar desolation, the communists promised a Bright New Greece of Stalinist progress in which all would share. The communists enjoyed a certain prestige from having been leaders in the anti-German resistance, and they were allied with the mighty Soviets, who were close by and powerful. Very importantly, all three of Greece's northern neighbors were communist dictatorships. They provided the Democratic Army with not only munitions and camps for training and rest but most of all with invaluable sanctuaries: hard-pressed guerrilla units could easily escape Greek army forces by slipping across any of several international borders. Finally, the Greek government and army were in deep disarray. Reconstruction after the devastation of the war seemed beyond the capability of the politicians in Athens, who preferred to spend their time pursuing the debilitating prewar vendetta between republicans and royalists, just as if a national guerrilla emergency did not exist. The army lacked modern equipment. Its morale and effectiveness suffered severely from political interference in the appointment of officers and location of units, fruitless tactics of static defense, penetration by communist agents, and the ability of cornered guerrilla units to escape across the various borders. By spring 1947 belief in a government victory was visibly evaporating.

COMMUNIST DEFEAT

Clearly the communist-led guerrillas had many advantages, especially in the first years of the struggle. Why then did they lose? One might begin with "Che" Guevara's dictum that one cannot make a revolution against a democratic or even a quasi-democratic government, and the Greece of the late 1940s, with its parliament and its multiparty system, was at least the latter. However that may be, four factors specific and crucial to the defeat of the communists in this conflict stand out conspicuously.

First, American material assistance. Just when victory for the Greek communists appeared all but inevitable, the Truman administration concluded that the fall of Greece would have disastrous effects in Western Europe and elsewhere. Accordingly, in March 1947 President Truman told Congress: "I believe that it must be the policy of the United States to support free peoples who are resisting attempted subjugation by armed minorities or by outside pressures."

This was the Truman Doctrine, under which the United States would render economic assistance to Greece and other countries. Assistance, but not combat troops: the State Department feared that American fighting units in Greece might offer Stalin an excuse to move into Yugoslavia. Besides, the U.S. Army viewed Greece as a "strategic mousetrap" from which it might be difficult to extricate its forces in case of a Soviet invasion. During the course of the conflict several hundred American officers served as advisers to the Greek army, of whom three lost their lives.

Help from the United States allowed the Greek government to increase the size of its army and equip it properly without unduly disrupting the national economy, and American political and military advisers were able to pressure the Greek army to improve its practices and operations. Most Greeks warmly welcomed American help. On the other hand, the guerrillas were associated with Macedonian separatism and with countries (such as Bulgaria) that many Greeks looked upon as their traditional enemies.

Second, the loss of the Yugoslavian sanctuary. In July 1949 Tito closed the Yugoslavian frontier. This action not only trapped thousands of guerrillas inside Yugoslavia but also isolated several thousand more in Thrace (the far northeast of Greece), because they could no longer pass from there through Yugoslavia to get to western Greece. To appreciate the full meaning of this event, imagine the effects on the communist forces in South Viet Nam if the frontiers of Laos had been suddenly and effectively sealed in 1967, or even 1973.

Third, the premature adoption of conventional war by the communists. This fatal step had its foreshadowings in May and in December 1947, when massed guerrillas tried twice to capture a sizable town to serve as the capital of a "Free Greece." Both attempts failed, with heavy casualties for the guerrillas. In December 1948, the communist leadership definitely chose the path of conventional operations. They thereby gave up mobility and surprise and exposed the insurgents to attack by the Greek air force and to encirclement by the army. At that very moment, internal reforms and United States assistance were making the Greek army a much more effective force. At the dawn of 1949 the Greek regular army had 150,000 men, supplemented by fifty thousand militia and a paramilitary gendarmerie of twenty-five thousand. All of these were henceforth under the supreme command of the able General Alexander Papagos. The guerrillas counted about twenty-five thousand, of whom the majority were Macedonians; many were forced recruits. Usually only half this number were in Greece at any one time. In the summer of 1949, pursuing their new strategy of conventional warfare, the communists conveniently assembled fully twelve thousand fighters in the Grammos mountain area for the Greek army to attack; the insurgents lost at least two thousand and the remainder scuttled across the Albanian border.

Fourth, and most of all, communist alienation of the peasantry. Greek mountain folk had been willing enough to help guerrillas against German invaders, but not against fellow Greeks. At the same time, because they were receiving supplies from across the borders, the communists did not feel a great need for peasant support. The communists were overwhelmingly petit bourgeois intellectuals, or else social marginals like students, tobacco farmers, and seamen, many from territories only recently acquired; thus they were unrepresentative of the social sector among which they were forced to operate. More importantly, the hard-core party leaders were contemptuous, even ashamed, of the Greek peasantry; in their brave new world, peasants would not exist. As civil war waxed, communist policy toward the peasantry hardened, with executions, seizures of foodstuffs and hostages, and destruction of villages to create refugees that the hard-pressed Greek government would have to care for. In addition, the party forcibly sent twenty-eight thousand children to communist states in Eastern Europe. Thus the guerrillas themselves poisoned the waters in which they had to swim. At the same time, the Party had notable support neither in Athens nor in the Peloponnesus, where monarchist sentiment was strong.

As a consequence, with an ever-dwindling base of support inside the country, the communists became almost totally dependent on outside help. That help began to dry up; when the Yugoslavian border was sealed, so was their fate.

Thus the Greek communists lost because *they deliberately violated the two most fundamental rules* of guerrilla warfare: do not engage in combat unless certain to win, and make friends with the rural folk.

In November 1949, President Truman informed Congress that the civil war was over. The Greek armed forces in all branches had suffered seventeen thousand killed and forty thousand wounded or unaccounted for; the guerrillas had executed at least four thousand civilians and burned twelve thousand homes. Government forces had killed thirty-seven thousand guerrillas and captured another twenty thousand.

11
China

On October 1, 1949, before a mass audience in Peking, Mao Tse-tung proclaimed the birth of the People's Republic of China. This event marked the
culmination of more than twenty years of civil war between his Chinese Communist Party and the Kuomintang, under the leadership of Chiang Kai-shek.
During that long struggle the Chinese communists abandoned the orthodox Leninist model of revolution and created their own pattern, which achieved resounding success in China and found imitators, and would-be imitators, in many other
areas of the world.

THE KUOMINTANG

Modern Chinese politics began with the Revolution of 1911, which overthrew
the Ching dynasty and brought thousands of years of imperial rule to an end.
The subsequent struggle for political power and the anarchy that often accompanied that struggle is the matrix out of which the civil war and the victory of
the communists emerged. Among the many factors that led to the more or less
unexpected downfall of the ancient monarchical system, none was more important than the increasingly obvious inability of the central government to protect
China from foreign humiliation. From the outbreak of the Opium War of 1839
to the siege and occupation of Peking by a multinational army in 1900, the
Chinese had gradually lost control over large areas of their national life and

territory to militarily more powerful Europeans and Japanese, who treated the Chinese as inferiors and worse.

It proved far easier to overthrow the imperial government than to construct a replacement for it. The revolution of 1911 unleashed powerful centrifugal forces, which reached their zenith during the 1920s, the decade of the warlords. China appeared to be in danger of permanently disintegrating into its regional and provincial subdivisions. In these grave circumstances the twin desires to modernize China and to expel the barbarian invaders came to dominate the thinking of all but the most remote sectors of Chinese society. Several leaders and parties claimed to know how to accomplish these goals. Out of this competition for the leadership of the renewal process developed the epic struggle between the Nationalists of the Kuomintang (National People's Party, or KMT) and the Chinese Communist Party (CCP). Sun Yat-sen had founded the KMT in 1912. Watching the breakdown of order and the emergence of the warlords, KMT leaders became convinced that China could be reunified only through military means, and thus the party began to build its own armed forces. Based in Canton, the KMT eventually felt strong enough to undertake the military reconquest of all China. It launched the Northern Expedition in July 1926, led by Sun Yat-sen's principal adviser, the young Japanese-trained Chiang Kai-shek. After defeating or coopting most of the warlord forces in its way, the Northern Expedition entered Peking in June 1928. Chiang and Sun established their capital at Nanking, whence the KMT was to pursue the unification and modernization of China for the next ten years.

During this so-called Nanking Decade (1928–1937), the KMT program for modernization faced grave challenges: monetary chaos, rural overpopulation, backward agricultural techniques, a poor transportation system, little industry, and party factionalism. The KMT drew its supporters overwhelmingly from the middle classes of the great coastal cities; thus it was largely ignorant of the problems and aspirations of the peasantry, which constituted the vast majority of the population. Nevertheless, the Nanking regime made significant progress, building up the country's transportation infrastructure, extending the educational system, and promoting the emancipation of women. Had the KMT been granted one more decade of peace, its programs might well have produced results that would have been irreversible, in which case China would have been spared the ravages of civil war and the disasters that followed upon it. But the Nanking regime did not get its additional decade: Instead, in 1937, the Japanese launched a full-scale invasion of China, aiming at the total subordination of the country. That invasion was the real beginning of World War II. The Japanese war put a halt to KMT reforms and reversed or destroyed much of what had already been accomplished.

THE RISE OF MAO

The Leninist model of revolution derived from the events of October 1917 in Petrograd (the once and present St. Petersburg), interpreted by Lenin and his entourage. In that model, one makes revolution (1) in the great cities, the nerve centers of the society, (2) by the armed vanguard of the working class, (3) after some great crisis has undermined the state's ability to protect itself—in the 1917 case, the destruction of the Russian national army in the Great War. During the 1920s Moscow imposed this model on all communist parties: every true communist was expected to imitate it. Turning the peculiar conditions of 1917 Russia into an iron template applicable to all times and places of course produced many disasters; among them was the massacre of thousands of communists in Shanghai by Chiang's triumphant forces during the Northern Expedition.

In the wake of that disaster, Mao Tse-tung began to develop his own plan of revolution, quite different from the Leninist model and more appropriate to the kind of country China was. Mao placed at the center of his strategy the sound, if hardly surprising, idea that a revolution in a peasant country would have to be based on the peasantry. Thus the communists would have to go to the peasants and learn of and from them. In a large, impoverished country, with a rudimentary transportation system, revolution could not be made along the lines of the 1917 Petrograd coup; it required instead a protracted armed struggle. This Maoist insight was the seed of later success, and also of the subsequent hostility and mutual excommunication of Peking and Moscow.

During the 1930s, however, Mao and the CCP were having a very rough time. The Nationalist armies of the KMT waged several campaigns of extermination against the communists; while no single one of these campaigns ever quite succeeded, the Party was reeling under their cumulative damage. Finally, in late 1934, in a desperate effort to save what could be saved, Mao led the remnants of the Party on the Long March. This anabasis has gone down in history as if it were some great triumph, but at the time it was seen accurately as a desperate flight from the enveloping armies of the KMT.

THE JAPANESE WAR

Ruling circles in Japan had long contemplated expansion onto the mainland, at least since their victory in the Sino-Japanese War of 1894–1895. In 1931 the Japanese tore Manchuria from Chinese control and set up a puppet state, called Manchukuo. Six years later they began a full-scale invasion of China proper, the savagery of which shocked the world and reached its epitome (or nadir) in the aptly named Rape of Nanking. Japan lacked the human and material resources necessary to totally defeat and permanently subjugate all of China, especially after the tactical triumph and strategic disaster of Pearl Harbor. But the Japanese attempt had major effects within China that would last for decades and alter the shape of world politics in the second half of the twentieth century.

One of those effects was the doom of the KMT. Unable to confront the mighty Japanese war machine, Chiang's KMT government slowly retreated into China's mountainous and inaccessible southwestern provinces, finally setting up its capital in remote Chungking. In this way the KMT regime became separated from its natural constituency—the middle classes of the coastal cities—and was forced to rely for support on reactionary rural landlords. Its frantic efforts to pay for the war led to the almost unrestricted printing of money; the consequent rampant inflation struck hardest at the urban middle classes. Meanwhile the KMT army took a severe mauling from the better-equipped Japanese. It suffered especially serious losses among young officers, the backbone of the army and hence of the KMT party and regime. Most of all, the KMT experienced a drastic decline of prestige because of its inability to protect China from the rampaging foreigner, the very stigma that had helped bring the old imperial system to collapse three decades previously.

Japanese administration in the cities was harsh, but their behavior in rural areas was truly dreadful. Communist guerrillas often attacked Japanese garrisons in the hope, always fulfilled, that the Japanese would react with fury upon any available Chinese. The Japanese named one of their largest antiguerrilla campaigns the "Three Alls": *Kill all, burn all, destroy all*. Appalled at the obliteration of their way of life and unable to find security in neutrality or even in cooperation with the invader, thousands of peasants, especially in the northern provinces, had no choice but to join the nearest guerrilla band, which was almost always led by communists. In this struggle the guerrillas under control of the Communist Party grew into a formidable force.

MAO'S GUERRILLAS

During the anti-Japanese struggle Mao worked out those basic principles of guerrilla warfare that he would apply later with good effect against the KMT. Mao summarized his approach in the following passage: "The principal object of the action of a guerrilla unit lies in dealing the enemy the strongest possible blows to his morale, and in creating disorder and agitation in his rear, in drawing off his principal forces to the flanks or to the rear, in stopping or slowing down his operations, and ultimately in dissipating his fighting strength so that the enemy's units are crushed one by one and he is precipitated into a situation where, even by rapid and deceptive actions, he can neither advance nor retreat."[1]

One way for guerrillas to attack the enemy's morale is to treat prisoners well and then release them. Once it becomes known to the soldiers of the enemy that they need not fear the consequences of being taken prisoner, the fighting quality of their units cannot remain unaffected.

The best way, however, to attack enemy morale is to lead them to think that the guerrillas are invincible. Therefore Mao wrote: "If we do not have a 100 per cent guarantee of victory, we should not fight a battle."[2] Such an approach is also good for the morale of the guerrillas: nothing so stimulates the devotion of a fighter to the cause as the conviction that the cause will win. The "guarantee of victory" for guerrillas arises from refusal to enter into combat without a great preponderance of force at the scene of action: three to one, even five to one. To accomplish this quintessential act of the guerrillas—assemble, strike hard, and then disappear before superior enemy forces arrive—nothing is more important than mobility: "The great superiority of a small guerrilla unit lies in its mobility." The mobility that permits the rapid assembly of overwhelming numbers also creates "the peculiar quality of the operations of a guerrilla unit [which] lies in taking the enemy by surprise." To maintain the priceless advantage of surprise, guerrillas must guard against becoming stereotyped in their actions: hence "the sole habitual tactic of a guerrilla unit is the ambush."

In addition to constant small victories, the morale of guerrillas must rest on their conviction both that their cause is just and that it will eventually triumph. Insurgents therefore need continuous political education. "The fighting capacity of a guerrilla unit is not determined exclusively by military arts, but depends above all on political consciousness." Mao ceaselessly stressed the need for his followers to understand that they were fighting for the liberation of the peasantry and that they must have good relations with them: "The guerrillas move among the people as fish move through the water." Such an approach to the peasants could not have been in more dramatic contrast with the behavior of traditional Chinese armies, including the KMT, let alone the Japanese. If the guerrillas had good relations with the peasants among whom they operated, they would obtain that intelligence—where is the enemy, in what strength, with what morale—on which was based their ability to move safely and quickly with superior numbers to the point of attack. In essence, guerrilla victories depend on their mobility and numerical superiority, made possible by timely intelligence, which derives in turn from good relations with the peasants.

Finally, besides mobility, high morale, and political awareness, Mao wanted his guerrillas to have secure bases from which to operate, bases which, even if discovered by the enemy, would be too difficult to attack. In the China of the 1930s and 1940s, with its great distances, mountain chains, and primitive roads, such bases were fairly easy to develop. His concern for secure bases led Mao to doubt that successful guerrilla war would be possible in a small country.

Armed with these concepts, Mao was able to pursue his basic strategic aim of undermining enemy morale and energy: "When the enemy advances, we retreat. . . . When the enemy retreats, we pursue. . . . When the enemy halts, we harass." This precept may not be very profound, but it is a roughly adequate description of what actually now happened.

THE CIVIL WAR

In August 1945 came the unexpectedly sudden surrender of Japan, following the atomic obliteration of two of its cities. The KMT, headed by Chiang, who had become one of the "big four" statesmen of the world along with Roosevelt, Churchill, and Stalin, had apparently triumphed. But the KMT would soon commit many grievous errors, political and military. Returning to the eastern cities, its troops displayed contempt toward those Chinese who had remained behind in Japanese-occupied territory during the war. A great deal of looting and extortion followed, often striking at the natural constituency of the KMT. Little attention was paid to severe problems of postwar economic adjustment, and inflation continued to bring the KMT's middle-class followers to despair.

In addition, Chiang was determined, against American advice, to reoccupy all of China as soon as possible, without regard to the imperatives of strategy or the matching of ends to means. The simultaneous occupation of all China's great cities and the dispatch of a large force into remote Manchuria (Manchukuo) gravely overextended KMT forces. Mao and his newly named People's Liberation Army (PLA), who had been preparing for this showdown for years, had only followed their favorite and well-developed tactic of concentrating against one enemy unit at a time; this meant that the communist forces, which were smaller in 1945 than those of the KMT overall, always achieved their much-desired preponderance of numbers at the actual site of battle. The overextension of Chiang's forces was made worse by the sudden demobilization, as an economy measure, of almost one-and-a-half million KMT troops; in the chaotic economic conditions of post-surrender China, this drastic reduction of the army produced many embittered recruits for the PLA.[3]

By 1948 the civil war had evolved from a largely guerrilla to a mainly conventional conflict. Mao had always viewed guerrilla warfare as the prelude to the development of regular revolutionary military forces. From out of his guerrilla units, plus defecting puppet troops in Manchukuo and disgruntled former elements of the KMT, Mao fashioned conventional armies of considerable size.

The nucleus of Chiang Kai-shek's armed forces were the original leaders of the KMT army formed in the 1920s. During the Northern Expedition that army had been enlarged—but not strengthened—by the opportunistic accession to the KMT of many warlords, who chose accommodation rather than confrontation. During World War II a number of these warlords, and other elements in the KMT armies, had gone over to the Japanese at crucial points, and such defections continued during the struggle with the communists. Dismayed by such betrayals, during the civil war Chiang appointed army commanders more on the basis of political reliability than military competence. Personal and political ties often cut across proper lines of command.

The seriousness of these conditions became evident in the battle for Manchuria. This contest exposed all the weaknesses of the Nationalist armies and became the graveyard of KMT power. Despite the commitment of many resources to Manchuria, the KMT fought a defensive and stationary war in the face of communist tactics of rapid concentration. The PLA entered Mukden, the regional capital, on November 1, 1948; the KMT had lost an army of over 400,000.

In Washington, the Truman administration watched developments in China with distracted anxiety. The Americans did not wish to see a communist triumph in China and the disappearance of their difficult, but familiar, ally Chiang Kai-shek; in the immediate aftermath of the surrender of Japan, American troops had been deployed to hold certain coastal cities until Chiang's forces could arrive. The United States, however, was preoccupied with the fighting in Greece, the launching of the Marshall Plan, and the founding of NATO. It therefore devoted most of its efforts during the ever more massive Chinese conflict to diplomatic maneuvers aimed at bringing about a coalition between Chiang's declining Nationalists and Mao's rising communists. Since neither party in China desired such a coalition, the efforts came to nothing.[4]

In April 1949, in part by bribing key KMT commanders, the PLA crossed the Yangtze River; it soon occupied Nanking, former capital of the KMT regime. Shanghai fell to their advance in May. Success followed success until on October 1, 1949, Mao proclaimed the People's Republic, the triumph of rural China over urban China.

In summary, the disastrous Japanese war severely weakened both the Kuomintang's military power and its political prestige. At war's end the restored KMT regime seemed to have nothing to offer badly battered China but corruption and inflation. Chiang's army was a relic of the discredited past, ill-trained, ill-fed conscripts who abused civilians at every turn. In addition, he and his generals had a fatal talent for almost always making the worst possible military decision. Thus in the eyes of politically concerned Chinese, Chiang and the KMT had had their chance and had failed; they had lost the Mandate of Heaven. It was necessary to give some other party, some other leader, the opportunity to resurrect China. In contrast, Mao and his communists were held blameless for either the wartime disasters or postwar confusion. Consequently they could offer to all discontented and disillusioned elements the hope of a brave new China. Above all else, they had fashioned for themselves a regular army of superior organization, led by competent officers who pursued sound tactics.

REFLECTION

The triumph of Mao and his communist party and army thundered throughout the world. During the 1960s and 1970s many would seek to discern the essence of his victory and erect it into a universal and invincible model of revolution. Such an approach to the Maoist revolution was of course fatally inappropriate, because it ignored at least three supremely important factors in Mao's victory that were not—to say the least—producible on demand. First, the Japanese had played an essential role in weakening the KMT militarily and morally, and in turning peasants into recruits for Mao's guerrilla bands. Second, the collapse of Japan had been the work not of Maoist guerrilla warfare but of American naval power, in another theater. Third, Mao's great victories in 1948 and 1949 over the armies of the KMT were won not with partisan bands but, on the contrary, by large conventional armies equipped with modern Soviet, Japanese, and American weapons.

NOTES

1. Mao Tse-tung, *Basic Tactics*, trans. Stuart Schram (New York: Praeger, 1966, orig. 1938), 81. See also Mao Tse-tung, *Selected Military Writings* (Peking: Foreign Languages Press, 1966).

2. This and the next several quotations are from *Basic Tactics*.

3. James E. Sheridan, *China in Disintegration: The Republican Era in China 1912–1949* (New York: Free Press, 1975); Suzanne Pepper, *Civil War in China: The Political Struggle* (Berkeley, CA: University of California, 1978).

4. Tang Tsou, *America's Failure in China, 1941–1950* (Chicago: University of Chicago, 1963); U.S. Department of State, *United States Relations with China, with Special Reference to the Period 1944–1949* (Washington, DC: Government Printing Office, 1949).

12
Malaya

In the decade after the end of World War II, Malaya was the scene of a completely successful and relatively inexpensive counterinsurgency in which foreign forces (British and Commonwealth) defeated a communist-organized uprising while simultaneously guiding the country toward independence.

WARTIME ORIGINS

The Malay Peninsula is about the size of Alabama, or Czechoslovakia. Mountains run down its center and make east-west travel difficult. The British began to establish their presence in the area in 1786 and had complete control over present-day Malaya and its predominantly Muslim population by 1909.

During the 1930s the British actively impeded the growth of the Malayan Communist Party by deporting alien communists; the party had less than ten thousand members by 1939. But then World War II swept away colonial regimes that had seemed destined to last forever. All across Southeast Asia native populations saw the Japanese defeat their European overlords—and, though they later witnessed local surrenders, they did not see the final and utter defeat of the Japanese. In Malayan eyes the war was a series of British defeats culminating at Singapore, the greatest British disaster since the Battle of Hastings. It would be impossible to overemphasize how the war humiliated the British, as well as devastated the Malayan economy.

During the war the Malayan Communist Party constituted the principal organized anti-Japanese resistance, forming guerrilla units called the Malayan People's Anti-Japanese Army. The Japanese never solved the problem of the Malayan guerrillas. Four-fifths of the country was jungle-covered; Japanese troops in Malaya were not of the best fighting quality; and the guerrillas received supplies from the British and others. Nevertheless the MPAJA accomplished little: approximately 2,300 Japanese lost their lives in Malaya from 1942 to 1945, less than two per day. The guerrillas actually killed more anticommunist Chinese civilians than Japanese soldiers. In December 1945 the MPAJA had about ten thousand members; many of them were well-armed with weapons obtained from the defeated Japanese and also from the Japanese-sponsored "Indian National Army." Thus World War II removed British power, broke British prestige, allowed the communists to organize, and provided them with weapons.

The Japanese surrendered in August 1945, but the main British liberation force did not reach Singapore until September 5. In contrast to their counterparts in Hanoi, the Malayan communists did not seize power in the interval and probably lost thereby their only real opportunity to take over the country. In fact, open insurgency did not break out until much later, just before the British authorities, following the murder of three European civilians, proclaimed an "Emergency" on June 18, 1948. The timing of the revolt is notable: the British were pulling out of Burma and having a very bad time in Palestine; the communist war in Greece seemed to be going well; Ho Chi Minh was tying up substantial French forces in Viet Nam; and Mao's armies were headed for total victory. At the same time communist-led insurgencies were breaking out in Indonesia, Burma, and India. In open imitation of the Maoists, the Malayan communists changed the name of their forces to the Malayan People's Liberation Army (later the Malayan Races Liberation Army).

The MRLA engaged in standard guerrilla tactics. It attacked small police posts (often unsuccessfully) and staged ambushes of civilian vehicles, sometimes also ambushing the rescue force. It practiced economic warfare as well, damaging bridges and machinery, slashing rubber trees, and burning the huts of rubberworkers. Such tactics inflicted real hardship on many poor laborers. Notably, the guerrillas ignored Mao's teachings about the treatment of prisoners: they killed every European they captured. They also killed their Malayan and Chinese prisoners, after torturing them.

THE BRIGGS PLAN

Outside Singapore, which remained mostly quiet throughout the Emergency, the population of Malaya (1951) consisted of 2.7 million Malays, two million Chinese, and about 700,000 others, mainly Indians. These ethnic communities lived in isolation from each other. Since the MRLA was almost exclusively Chinese, the British automatically had the support of the Malay half of the population, living under their traditional leaders whose authority the British had preserved. The Chinese population felt vulnerable both to the guerrillas and to pressures from their homeland: what would happen to them if Mao came to power in China and the British pulled out of Malaya? The British military and political establishment employed very few Chinese speakers, and in the early period of the Emergency the British tended to treat all Chinese as the enemy. On the other hand, by far most of those killed by the MRLA were Chinese, and the MRLA platform—drive the British out—held little appeal to the Chinese, many of whom did not consider themselves permanent residents of Malaya.

Beginning in the early summer of 1950, Malaya's military chief, General Sir Harold Briggs, put into operation the "Briggs Plan." Its principal elements were: (1) clearing the country of guerrillas methodically from south to north, (2) resettling the numerous Chinese squatters, the principal source of food for the guerrillas, into secure villages, (3) uprooting the guerrilla infrastructure inside the cleared areas, and (4) closely coordinating civil and military activities. Briggs also pressed for a great increase in the number of troops and police on hand, not to fight guerrillas but rather to encourage friends and convert doubters. The British authorities received their best intelligence in areas where troops were visible and permanent.

The centerpiece of the counterinsurgency was the resettlement of vulnerable Chinese squatters. By early 1952 so-called "new villages" had grouped together 400,000 such people, up to 570,000 by 1954. Squatters received title to their land in these villages. The enterprise stood Mao on his head, draining away the water in which the guerrilla "fish" had been swimming. The resettlement was one component of a general food denial program: controls were placed on all food bought and sold, and rice convoys went heavily guarded. Simply getting enough food to stay alive became the major problem of the guerrillas; they relied more and more on extortion from local peasants. By June 1954 the combination of resettlement and general food denial had become "the most effective planned operation against a guerrilla target and its support organizations."[1] It was "a devastating measure that did more than any other single thing to defeat the Communists in Malaya."[2]

THE COMING OF TEMPLER

Meanwhile, in February 1952 Sir Gerald Templer arrived in the capacity of both High Commissioner and Director of Operations. Combining the chief civil and military posts in himself, he was "armed with the greatest powers enjoyed by a British soldier since Cromwell."[3] A former intelligence director, Templer understood the key role of good intelligence in counterinsurgency. Of course, the best source of intelligence was surrendered enemy personnel (SEPs). These began to show up in great numbers in response both to the visible fading of the prospects of a guerrilla victory and to impressive monetary rewards for information. Many SEPs led the British to their former encampments; their readiness to betray former comrades for cash quite amazed at least one student of this war.[4]

The British also used professional long-range jungle fighters to penetrate guerrilla areas. These units destroyed the guerrillas' food supplies, interrupted their messenger system, deprived them of sleep, and generally made life miserable. The British hardly ever used artillery. Their combat aircraft, mainly propeller-driven, normally engaged in close infantry support rather than area bombing. They had few helicopters, and these were used mostly for medical evacuations, which was good for morale. The destructive and counterproductive massive firepower that the Americans employed in Viet Nam was absent in Malaya.

As an integral part of his counterinsurgency, Templer, who may have coined the phrase about "winning hearts and minds," inaugurated a program designed to marginalize the insurgents politically as well as physically. All aliens born in Malaya (practically all of whom were Chinese) received citizenship. In the face of much skepticism, Templer saw to it that the Home Guard (local militia) enrolled and armed Chinese members (in the end, very few of their guns wound up in rebel hands). He also made it clear that independence would only come when the Emergency was over. Under his prodding, Malay and Chinese leaders formed an alliance in 1953; this sealed the fate of the rebellion, because it demonstrated that one could work for change without supporting the communists. Elections for a parliament were held successfully in July 1955.

By 1954, at the peak of the counterinsurgency effort, the authorities could muster approximately forty thousand regular troops, including British, Gurkha, Commonwealth, and Malayan elements. They deployed twenty-four thousand Federation police and thirty-seven thousand Special Constables. There were also 250,000 armed Home Guards.

All these converging programs—resettlement and food denial, uprooting the insurgent infrastructure, clear moves toward independence, high rewards for good information, penetration of the jungle, reliance on numbers rather than firepower, coordination of effort—eventually had a devastating effect on the guerrillas, and in September 1953 the authorities proclaimed the existence of the first "white" (guerrilla-free) area, in coastal Malacca. Out of fifty-one thousand square miles, fourteen thousand were "white" by the end of 1955, thirty thousand by June 1957. (The insurgency had only marginal support in Singapore, Kuala Lumpur, and other large towns.) When Templer left Malaya in 1954 the war was all but over; during the next two years there was very little combat, and the Emergency formally ended on July 31, 1960. During the dozen years of the Emergency, the guerrillas killed 512 British and Commonwealth soldiers, along with three thousand civilians. Roughly 6,700 guerrillas lost their lives, 1,300 were captured, and 2,700 surrendered.[5]

MALAYA AND VIET NAM

The British victory in Malaya contrasts dramatically with the French defeat in Indochina in the same period. But of course the circumstances of those conflicts differ as much as the outcomes. First of all, the Malayan communists received little or no outside assistance; apparently officers of the Chinese PLA arrived on the scene early in 1950, but they did not stay long. Also, because the Sultan of Malaya did not establish diplomatic relations with the USSR and China, there were no foreign embassies to act as brain centers for the insurgency. Secondly, the Malayan guerrillas had no sanctuary; the British navy isolated Malaya on three sides, and the Thais held the fourth; the latter permitted British aircraft and police to enter their territory. In the third place, the communists could not employ the nationalism issue effectively: the British were openly moving, hand in hand with politically prominent Malayans, toward independence. Fourthly, the issue of nationalism was ineffective also because of the ethnic divisions within the country; the communist appeal was limited to a minority of the Chinese, who were themselves a minority of the whole population—the Party failed completely in its halfhearted efforts to reach out to other groups. A fifth factor was the inability of the insurgents to develop an effective response to the resettlement program, which decisively separated them from their actual and potential supporters. Last in order, but not in importance, was geographical size: the relative smallness of Malaya hurt the rebels, making the isolation of the country and the supervision of its population relatively easy compared to French Viet Nam, which was two and a half times as big as Malaya.

NOTES

1. Anthony Short, *The Communist Insurrection in Malaya, 1948–1960* (London: Frederick Muller, 1975), 378.

2. Edgar O'Ballance, *Malaya: The Communist Insurgent War* (Hamden, CT: Archon, 1966), 108.

3. Geoffrey Fairbairn, *Revolutionary Guerrilla Warfare: The Countryside Version* (Harmondsworth, UK: Penguin, 1974), 151.

4. O'Ballance, *Malaya*, 174.

5. Ibid., 164, 177; and Gene Hanrahan, *The Communist Struggle in Malaya* (New York: Institute of Pacific Relations, 1954), 75.

13
The Huks

Once they had brought the Aguinaldo rebellion to an end, the American authorities in the Philippines began to make good on their promises to the Filipino peoples. They took visible and major steps toward self-rule and eventual independence. By 1907, the Philippines possessed the first popularly elected legislature in Southeast Asia; by 1916 all literate males had the vote. At the time of the Japanese invasion, Filipinos filled most positions in the civil service, including some of the highest.

Finally, on July 4, 1946, the Republic of the Philippines celebrated its Independence Day. Home to a population of twenty million, scene of the largest naval battle (Leyte Gulf) in the history of the world, the country had suffered severely during World War II. The economic mismanagement of the Japanese, their appalling atrocities, and the fierce fighting during the Liberation had devastated the Philippines physically and morally. The noted Philippine statesman Carlos P. Romulo expressed the belief that the Japanese had behaved so badly in his country because, whereas in Japanese eyes the Pacific War was a race war, the Filipinos by and large remained loyal to the Americans.

ORIGINS OF THE HUK MOVEMENT

During the Japanese occupation (1942–1944) several guerrilla organizations appeared. One of these was the People's Army Against Japan; its acronym in the Tagalog language, Hukbalahap, produced the nickname ''Huks.'' By late

1943 perhaps ten thousand of these Huks were engaged to one degree or another against the Japanese; they also sometimes attacked other guerrilla units organized by American forces. By the time of the Liberation, Huk units were well armed with weapons taken from the Japanese or shipped to them from the United States. Their stronghold was the island of Luzon, of forty thousand square miles, the size of Kentucky. The central districts of that island had for generations been the scene of violent agrarian unrest, with a deplorable record of peasant exploitation at the hands of Filipino government officials. Douglas MacArthur once observed that "if I worked in those sugar fields, I'd probably be a Huk myself."[1] Many Luzon landlords had cooperated with the Japanese occupation, and the Huks vehemently opposed the policy of the returning Americans of showing leniency toward such collaborators. By late 1946 there was open fighting between the Huks and the forces of the newly independent Republic.

Although operating almost exclusively in rural areas, the Huks did not wage a self-consciously Maoist-style war; the Chinese model had not yet become prominent. The leadership of the movement was largely urban, including several former university professors; perhaps most famous among the Huk leaders was Luis Taruc, a politician and former medical student.[2] A major activity of the Huks was the robbery of banks, payroll offices, and trains. The principal government force deployed against them was the Philippine Constabulary, with a paper strength of twenty-five thousand. This body was neither well-trained nor well-equipped; its usual tactics were encirclement and sweeps, which the guerrillas easily evaded. The Constabulary also systematically committed abuses against civilians, helping themselves to the possessions of the population they were supposed to be protecting. Luis Taruc cited these outrages as the main fuel that kept the rebellion going.

As the war went on, the leaders of the Huks more and more openly revealed their communist allegiance and plans; when the Maoists triumphed in China in 1949, the Philippine insurgents changed their name to the People's Liberation Army. In that same year the Huks (as they continued to be known) decided to support the reelection of President Elpidio Quirino, believing with good reason that the incompetence and corruption of his administration was their best guarantee of ultimate victory. Indeed the Quirino forces placed in the hands of the Huks an invaluable weapon: the presidential elections of 1949 were notably corrupt even for the Philippines, where ballot irregularities were a venerable art form. The fraudulent elections seemed to demonstrate that there was no peaceful and constitutional path to desperately needed change; hence that there was no alternative to armed insurrection. Thus the "dirty elections of 1949" brought recruits and sympathy to the Huk ranks. By mid-1950, when the North Korean army stormed into the South, the Huks had perhaps twenty-five thousand fighters and were able to carry out spectacular operations in the very outskirts of Manila.

Yet in fact the tide was just about to turn against them. Contrary to standard Leninist tactics, the Huks had failed to reach out and from a broad front with other disaffected and leftist groups. Peasants learned to fear the Huks because of the many common criminals in their ranks. Within the Huk organization punishment for infractions was severe, and they continually suffered important losses of support through such senseless acts of terror as the murder of the widow of President Manuel Quezon. In September 1950 a thoroughly alarmed President Quirino called in the Army to help the Constabulary, and, most importantly, appointed to the post of secretary of defense a congressman named Ramón Magsaysay.

MAGSAYSAY DEFEATS THE HUKS

From his own experience as a guerrilla against the Japanese, Magsaysay derived powerful insights into the nature of the Huk challenge. He moved vigorously to end abuses of civilians by the Constabulary and Army; in fact the Army began to provide medical assistance to villagers. He set up a telegraph system by which for a nominal fee any villager on Luzon could contact the secretary of defense's offices. Magsaysay also improved military tactics: he put an end to useless sweep operations and insisted on invasions of hitherto unmolested guerrilla areas, disrupting the insurgents' food supply and depriving them of rest. Soon the guerrillas found themselves forced back into the swamps, cut off from civilians, unable to obtain food, and subject to many illnesses.

To enforce his orders Magsaysay made numerous unexpected visits to the field in his small airplane, descending upon shiftless or venal local commanders like a true *diabolus ex machina*. He also brought the Constabulary under his personal control. He greatly improved the supply of intelligence, partly through offering huge rewards for the capture of guerrilla leaders. Magsaysay developed a special and effective twist to the reward system: he offered payment not for guerrillas in general but for this or that individual Huk leader, to answer charges not of insurrection but of specific criminal acts, such as particular instances of murder or rape. He greatly improved the amnesty program: realizing that many of the younger Huks had no place to go if they accepted amnesty, he put in place a resettlement program by which former Huks received twenty acres and a small loan.

Perhaps most importantly, Magsaysay undertook to ensure the propriety of the 1951 congressional elections. He deployed army units to guarantee a peaceful contest and an honest count, and the opposition Nacionalista party won in a landslide. This vivid demonstration of an alternative route to change did as much as anything to break the back of the Huk movement. (In 1953 Magsaysay ran against President Quirino and defeated him handily.)

The United States had an enormous emotional stake in the postwar Philippine Republic, and it wanted that country to be the showcase of democracy in Southeast Asia. President Truman sent American officers to help train the Philippine Army. President Quirino was anxious to have U.S. combat troops deployed against the Huks, but Washington was opposed to sending troops, being preoccupied with China, Greece, NATO, and the Marshall Plan. Then in mid-1950 came the Korean War, during which the Americans began to pick up as well an increasing share of the costs of the French campaign in Viet Nam. In any case, the American government believed that the roots of Huk successes were to be found in poor Philippine leadership and the need for land reform. Secretary of State Dean Acheson disliked President Quirino and thought that most of any assistance given his administration would be wasted. Above all, the Defense Department opposed sending combat forces; the Joint Chiefs were against employing American troops in a war whose primary causes it viewed as political. By the end of 1951 it had become clear that the Huks were not going to win.[3] For all these reasons American combat troops did not participate in the anti-Huk struggle.

Roughly ten thousand Huks died between 1946 and 1954; four thousand were captured, and sixteen thousand surrendered.[4] The Huk experience strongly suggests that communist-led guerrillas did poorly when they could not act as the spearhead of an outraged nationalism; communist efforts in the independent Philippines to rally support against ''American imperialism'' were a predictable flop. Already starved of foreign aid, the Huk movement began to collapse when Secretary Magsaysay produced clean elections—an alternative to revolution—in 1951. At the same time Magsaysay reduced mistreatment of civilians, instituted an effective amnesty program, and increased military pressure on the guerrillas without employing destructive weapons and tactics (in contrast, again, to the Americans in Viet Nam). In summary, the Philippine struggle provides a classic illustration of the vital link that should exist in any theory of counterinsurgency between good military tactics and good political strategy.

NOTES

1. William Manchester, *American Caesar* (Boston: Little, Brown, 1978), 420.

2. See his works *He Who Rides the Tiger* (New York: Praeger, 1967) and *Born of the People* (Westport, CT.: Greenwood, 1973 [orig. 1953]).

3. See *Foreign Relations of the United States, 1950*, vol. 6 (Washington, DC: Government Printing Office, 1976); and *Foreign Relations of the United States, 1951*, vol. 6 (Washington, DC: Government Printing Office, 1977).

4. Boyd T. Bashore, ''Dual Strategy for Limited War,'' in Franklin Mark Osanka, ed., *Modern Guerrilla Warfare* (New York: Free Press, 1962), 198.

14
The French in Indochina

At the end of World War II, France became the first European power to face a full-fledged Maoist revolutionary insurgency. The successful communist-led struggle against French rule over Viet Nam and the rest of Indochina had of course a regional genesis. But it was also one segment of a Eurasian-wide series of post–World War II communist uprisings that included Indonesia, Malaya, the Philippines, and Greece. The Cold War linked France's efforts to maintain its great-power status with American efforts to contain Sino-Soviet expansion; the French withdrawal from Viet Nam in 1954 would be succeeded by an American involvement there, at first tentative and later massive. A working knowledge of the main reasons for French failure in Viet Nam provides insight into both the political-military drama of the Cold War and the crisis that afflicted American society in the 1960s and after.

THE COMING OF THE FRENCH

Viet Nam has an area of 128,000 square miles, equivalent to that of Finland, or of Illinois and Missouri. The former South Viet Nam was the size of Washington State. The whole country is a thousand miles long, the distance from Rome to Copenhagen. The country consists of two great deltas, those of the Red and the Mekong rivers, joined together by a narrow strip of land tapering down from the mountains to only fifty miles at its waist. In 1945 the population of the country was approximately twenty-five million (sixty-five million in 1995).

By the middle of the seventeenth century, French Jesuit missionaries had built up a native Catholic community of 400,000 and had also invented the present written Vietnamese language. Viet Nam experienced a nativist reaction during the 1850s; many French civilians and Vietnamese Christian converts were killed. Powerful forces in France persuaded Napoleon III to intervene; in 1859 the French took Saigon and, beginning with Cochinchina, extended their control slowly northward.

The record of French colonialism in Viet Nam is of course an ambiguous one. The French brought peace, order, and modern medical facilities, and they developed the transportation system. On the other hand, the lives of most peasants were not improved, and some segments of the population showed a real deterioration in their circumstances. Certainly France made very little financial profit out of Viet Nam: in 1913 French external trade made up only 3 percent of GNP, and trade with *all* her colonies was only one-ninth of that 3 percent. The struggle to hold Viet Nam cost the French more money than they received from the Marshall Plan. Whatever the motives behind French tenacity in Viet Nam, they were not economic.

Most importantly for the future, the French built an educational system in Viet Nam that created a westernized elite steeped in French literature and political ideas. This elite, however, found that opportunities to play important roles in the affairs of their own society were blocked by hordes of Frenchmen who came to Viet Nam to fill up almost all the desirable administrative, educational, medical, and even clerical posts.

No Viet Nam–wide nationalist movement had seriously challenged French control before June 1940, when the Nazi juggernaut unexpectedly overwhelmed France. Two months later the Japanese military demanded and received from the French administration in Hanoi the right to occupy major cities and strategic points, so that they could stop the flow of Allied munitions to Chiang Kai-shek's forces. In March 1945 the Japanese cast aside even the appearances of French control and locked up all the Frenchmen they could catch. Understanding of this complete and public Japanese humiliation of the French in the sight of the Vietnamese is crucial for grasping how a communist-led Vietnamese revolution became possible in the postwar period. Before World War II the French had been able to maintain order among the twenty-five million Vietnamese with a military force of merely eleven thousand; to restore their control after the Japanese had exposed their weaknesses would require much, much more. The British and the Dutch soon came to the conclusion that the sun was setting on their Asian empires. Not the French: for many bitter years to come they would pursue their vision of *la mission civilisatrice* through the jungles of Viet Nam and across the sands of Algeria.

HO CHI MINH, THE COMMUNISTS, GIAP, AND THE PAVN

In May 1941, during the Japanese occupation, the Indochinese Communist Party proclaimed the formation of the League for the Independence of Viet Nam—Viet Minh for short. Following classic Leninist Front tactics, the Viet Minh was silent about standard communist doctrine on the collectivization of property and the dictatorship of the proletariat; it stressed instead the union of all classes of society against the Japanese. Under this nationalist guise the communists were able to penetrate areas of Vietnamese society hitherto closed to them. Such penetration was essential to their later success, because no communist party ever achieved and kept power through its own effort except under the banner of nationalism. The acknowledged leader of the Viet Minh front was the head of the Communist Party, Nguyen That Thanh, a man who was to achieve world notoriety under the alias Ho Chi Minh.

Ho Chi Minh had been born in 1890. Like every major communist revolutionary leader of this century he grew up in comfortable circumstances. In 1911, after having received a good education in French-model schools, he nevertheless failed to obtain a government job. He thereupon left his country and did not return for almost thirty years. In Paris in 1919, he participated in the founding of the French Communist Party; he visited the United States and Britain; in Moscow he took courses in Marxist theory and the techniques of political subversion; and he stayed for a while in China with Mao's army. His experience of the world was incomparably wider than that of any other Vietnamese revolutionary leader. But most of all, he was the acknowledged representative in Viet Nam of the mighty Soviet Union. The Soviets in those days were busy pursuing Lenin's "Two-Stage Theory of Revolution," which taught that the western democracies would fall to communism if only they could first be deprived of their colonial empires ("The road to Paris runs through Peking"). Anointed by Moscow, Ho had become the unchallenged leader of the fledgling Indochinese Communist Party by 1930.

Ho Chi Minh's principal collaborator was General Vo Nguyen Giap. Born in 1912, he graduated from the same school in Hué attended by Ho Chi Minh and Ngo Dinh Diem. Giap took a law degree at the University of Hanoi, married the daughter of a professor, and then taught history in a private preparatory school in the same city. Shortly after the Japanese invaded, Giap began organizing and training the tiny army of the Viet Minh. The Japanese were interested in controlling the cities, not the countryside; hence Giap's little army had the time and scope to develop leadership, identity, and tactics, and eventually grew into the formidable force known to the world as the People's Army of Viet Nam, or PAVN. Giap in later years boasted that the only military academy he had ever attended was "the bush."

THE FIRST TAKEOVER

After the announcement of the surrender of Japan in August 1945, confusion gripped Hanoi. The Japanese occupation army was interested in nothing except going home to Japan. Most of the French were still in prison. Emperor Bao Dai had some troops in the city, but ill-advised American OSS officers had given him the impression that the Viet Minh enjoyed the patronage of the United States government. In this chaotic situation, General Giap's small but well-organized army was able to impose itself on the capital; meanwhile elements of the Japanese occupation army handed over thirty thousand rifles to the Viet Minh. These events constitute the so-called August Revolution; and on September 2, 1945, Ho Chi Minh proclaimed the independence of Viet Nam from France. In those same days the Viet Minh were killing members of rival nationalist organizations and betraying others to the French police. They also fought bloody battles with the religious sects in the south, during which they assassinated the spiritual leader of the powerful Hoa Hao religion.

The Viet Minh had been able to occupy Hanoi because nobody on the spot could or would prevent them. The indifference of the Japanese and the absence of the French, rather than the strength of the Viet Minh, made the August Revolution possible. But the arrival of French forces from Europe and elsewhere was creating a new balance of power in Viet Nam.

Meanwhile, protracted negotiations in Paris between Ho Chi Minh and a newly-liberated but demoralized and divided France failed to produce any satisfactory result. The French recognized Ho's government and guaranteed it autonomy in the regions of Tonkin and Annam, with its own armed forces and treasury, but not full independence. Ho Chi Minh and his advisers could have accepted this autonomy and worked to extend it in time to full independence. Instead they insisted on total and immediate independence, and for this they were willing to unleash a series of terrible wars that would last thirty years and take the lives of millions of their countrymen—an awesome responsibility before history and the Vietnamese.

Giap now commanded fifty thousand troops, including many hundreds of Japanese deserters who provided invaluable help with training and arms production. Sporadic armed clashes flared between Viet Minh and French units. In November, in retaliation for Viet Minh action against French troops, the cruiser *Suffren* shelled the port of Haiphong, killing many innocent civilians. Sustained fighting was in progress by December 1946. The Viet Minh attempted to oust the French from Hanoi but failed; they then withdrew into the back country whence they had so recently emerged. The August seizure of Hanoi had been the Leninist phase of the Viet Minh revolution; the retreat into the jungles and mountains was the beginning of the Maoist phase.

A STALEMATED WAR

For the first three years the conflict consisted mainly of small actions, partly because the Viet Minh lacked sufficient modern weapons to assemble large formations. By 1949 the war had become a stalemate: the French and the troops of Emperor Bao Dai controlled the cities but lacked the numbers and training to flush the guerrillas out of their strongholds; on the other hand, the Viet Minh lacked the firepower to confront the French directly.

But late in 1949 Mao's triumphant communist armies established the Chinese People's Republic; the following year General Giap opened the way for the Viet Minh to receive supplies from China by capturing the key border posts of Cao Bang and Lang Son. The latter was a city of 100,000; the French abandoned it even before the enemy arrived, leaving behind a vast treasure of weapons and gasoline for the Viet Minh. Bernard Fall called the loss of Lang Son "France's greatest colonial defeat since Montcalm had died at Quebec." This was an absolutely vital victory for the Viet Minh, because without Chinese supplies they would never have had the firepower to defeat the French.

During 1951 newly appointed commander General Jean de Lattre set up a heavily fortified perimeter around Hanoi, hoping to establish a secure base area. Giap suffered severe reverses in conventional attacks on the de Lattre Line, defeats which Giap publicly blamed on the cowardice of his troops, but thousands of guerrillas still managed to infiltrate into the districts immediately adjacent to Hanoi.

FRENCH TACTICS

1953 was the height of the French effort. At that time General Giap was commanding around 300,000 fighters. According to the widely used formula that the defeat of guerrillas requires the government forces to have a force ratio of ten to one, in order to defeat Giap's forces the French needed three million soldiers in Viet Nam. In fact the French had deployed a mere fifty-four thousand troops from metropolitan France, which then had a population of forty-two million. Counting everybody—regular French soldiers, French colonial units, Foreign Legionnaires, Vietnamese in French uniform, Bao Dai's Vietnamese battalions, and the militias of the southern religious sects—pro-French forces totalled perhaps 550,000, giving them a ratio of less than two to one. In the 1950s more French officers were dying in Viet Nam than were graduating from the military academy at St. Cyr. (Among the officers killed, twenty-one were sons of marshals and generals of the French army, including the only son of General de Lattre.)

French numbers were grotesquely inadequate; their air power was exiguous—for example, they never had more than ten helicopters operational at one time; and they were deeply hostile to the idea of building up a real Vietnamese army under its own officers. Yet they insisted on trying to hold all sections of the country with units many of which were roadbound and had been armed and trained to fight in Europe. These conditions led to the system of outposts and convoys, which ate up manpower, equipment, and energy without establishing French control of the countryside. The system worked something like this: French outposts had to be supplied by road; the Viet Minh liked to ambush supply convoys; the French set up new outposts along the convoy routes to discourage ambushes; these outposts in turn had to be supplied by convoys; and so on. It was all very strange.

DIEN BIEN PHU AND PARTITION

The French high command in Hanoi always believed that with the superior discipline and firepower at its disposal, it could deal the Viet Minh crushing blows if the enemy would only abandon guerrilla tactics, and stand and fight. In building the fortress complex at Dien Bien Phu, on the Laotian border, the French intended to tempt the Viet Minh into accepting a conventional battle. Things developed differently from French expectations, disastrously so. During the spring of 1954, thirteen thousand French, Vietnamese, and colonial troops found themselves surrounded by 100,000 Viet Minh plus an unknown number of advisers from Mao's People's Liberation Army (Chinese assistance to the Viet Minh had greatly increased since the end of the fighting in Korea in mid-1953). The totally unexpected presence of Chinese artillery, compounded by the complete inability of the weak French air force in Viet Nam to drop sufficient supplies or reinforcements into the fortress, doomed the defenders from the very first day of the battle. After an epic eight-week defense, which the whole world paused to watch, what was left of the fortress and its garrison fell to the Viet Minh, exactly nine years after the surrender of Nazi Germany.

The French defeat at Dien Bien Phu was tactical, not strategic: that is, while the outcome of the battle was indeed a disaster, the French had lost only about 5 percent of their military assets in Viet Nam and could have carried on the war pretty much as before. But Dien Bien Phu galvanized growing disenchantment with the war inside France and helped bring to power a cabinet committed to a quick ending of the war.

The Viet Minh were much stronger in the northern provinces than they were farther south. Communist weakness in the southern provinces had several causes: Viet Minh military units there had been few during the Japanese occupation; savage fighting had broken out in the days after the Japanese surrender between Viet Minh on one hand and rival Trotskyite and nationalist groups on the other; Viet Minh terrorist incidents in the late 1940s had antagonized the large middle class; the Chinese border was relatively remote; and above all, large districts of the south were dominated by powerful anti-communist indigenous religious sects. Thus at their Geneva conference the great powers decided to partition Viet Nam into a communist north and a non-communist south (the latter based on Saigon and Cochinchina), with vague references to some sort of elections in the future to determine the final fate of the country. The United States did not sign the Geneva accords; neither did the Bao Dai government, which France, the United States, and other powers recognized as the legitimate government of Viet Nam.

THE UNITED STATES AND VIET NAM

In the late 1940s the United States was desperately eager to obtain the participation of the French in a new North Atlantic alliance to contain Soviet expansion. In June 1950 the Americans found themselves in a hot war in Korea, which soon included the Chinese. For both these reasons the Truman administration provided much financial support to the French effort in Viet Nam; by 1952 the United States was paying the lion's share of French war expenses there.

President Dwight Eisenhower believed that the idea that Dien Bien Phu could be saved by American air strikes alone was a delusion, and he was firmly opposed to sending American ground combat units into Viet Nam. Undergirding his position was the conviction that an anachronistic French imperialism had fueled the communist revolution, and that a truly independent Vietnamese state, assisted by the Americans, would be a much more effective obstacle to communist expansion.

REFLECTION

The soldiers who lost their lives fighting on the French side numbered twenty-one thousand from the regular French armed forces (including almost a hundred uniformed women); twenty-two thousand from Foreign Legion and African colonial units; and approximately eighty thousand Vietnamese soldiers serving in the French or allied Vietnamese forces, for a total of 123,000 dead. Of the Viet Minh, something close to 400,000 perished in the struggle.

There was nothing inevitable about the victory of the communist-led Viet Minh. Quite to the contrary, its victory would be hardly conceivable without the invasion of Viet Nam by Imperial Japan, an invasion that stripped the French of their aura of invincibility and permitted the Viet Minh to act as the leader of a broad nationalist coalition. It would be equally inconceivable without the triumph of the Maoists in neighboring China.

The French made their own major contribution to the Viet Minh victory by failing to develop a valid strategy. At the outbreak of serious fighting in late 1946, French political and military leaders had several options. First, they could have concluded that a major conflict with the Viet Minh was not worth the costs, and have withdrawn from Viet Nam. Second, they could have decided to send military forces into the country sufficient to at least hold both the deltas and harass the enemy in the hinterlands. Third, they could have attempted to defeat the guerrillas by building a sizable and well-equipped Vietnamese army out of the various and numerous non- or anti-communist elements. Fourth, they could have attacked their foes politically, by addressing some fundamental grievances of the Vietnamese peasantry, thereby isolating the middle-class leadership of the Viet Minh. As it turned out, the French chose none of these options, and in effect thrashed around for years fighting a war without a clear idea of how to win. When in 1949 the Chinese communist armies arrived on the northern border and the French were unable through either military or diplomatic means to prevent them from aiding the Viet Minh, the future outcome of the war was clear. The French still had one major card to play: rejecting all of the above courses of action, they could still have fought on and salvaged much by adapting their conduct to their inadequate means—that is, by withdrawing from the northern two-thirds of the country and retrenching their forces into the relatively secure bastions of Saigon and Cochinchina. But they declined to play that card as well. So the French counterinsurgency effort failed. Beneath the surface of this failure lay the continual French underestimation of their opponents, of which Dien Bien Phu was only the most spectacular example (and of which Haiti and Spain had been previous instructive instances).

During this grim struggle the politicians in Paris conducted themselves with stunning frivolity, setting up and then pulling down no less than sixteen prime ministers, and sending no less than eight different military commanders to Viet Nam.

Finally, even though the United States stepped in to fill the breach left by French withdrawal, there is little evidence that American leaders, civilian or military, imagined there was much of value for them to learn from the French experience.

15

Viet Nam: The American War

During the administrations of John Kennedy and Lyndon Johnson, the United States abandoned the strategy of indirect support for friendly governments facing insurgencies, a course that had worked so well in Greece and the Philippines. Instead, it undertook to confront a communist insurgency directly with a massive commitment of its own troops. (For events leading to the American commitment to South Viet Nam, see the chapter on French Indochina.)

NGO DINH DIEM

The French, the British, and the Americans recognized Emperor Bao Dai as ruler of independent Viet Nam. On June 18, 1954, in the midst of the collapse of the French effort in Indochina, he appointed as his prime minister Ngo Dinh Diem, a fifty-three-year-old graduate of the French School of Law in Hanoi. A lifelong nationalist and devout Roman Catholic, Diem had refused previous offers of the premiership by the Japanese, the French, and even Bao Dai; in 1946 Ho Chi Minh offered him the ministry of the interior in his new Viet Minh regime, which Diem also declined. By 1950 the communists had put a price on his head; since the French detested him and would not guarantee his safety, Diem left Viet Nam and went to Rome, France, and the United States.

When Diem became prime minister in the summer of 1954, he controlled hardly more than a few blocks in downtown Saigon. Over the next two years, however, he secured American help, brought Saigon, the army, and the powerful religious sects under control, settled almost a million northern refugees in new homes, and inaugurated the strategic hamlet program.

THE VIET CONG

After the French war ended and Viet Nam was partitioned, many Viet Minh (those who had fought the French under communist direction) stayed behind in the South. Their purpose was to destabilize the new southern state; their weapon was assassination. Between 1954 and 1958 they murdered 20 percent of South Viet Nam's village chiefs and schoolteachers.[1] The southern insurgency (henceforth referred to for convenience in these pages as the Viet Cong or VC), organized and directed by the Politburo in Hanoi, was a ladder of upward mobility for many. In contrast, to become an officer in the Army of South Viet Nam (ARVN) one needed a high school diploma, a rare commodity in a mainly peasant society. Nevertheless, the time soon arrived when the Viet Cong also employed abduction and threats against families as recruitment tactics.

The Eisenhower administration rendered substantial assistance to the Diem government. The Kennedy administration, however, found Diem to be a difficult ally who did not believe that visiting American "fact-finders" possessed superior insights into Viet Nam's culture and problems. Diem also endured constant, bitter attacks in the American press, because his strategic concepts did not coincide with those of young American journalists in Saigon. Powerful elements in Washington decided that Diem must go. The opportunity for his removal arrived in the summer of 1963 when anti-Diem Buddhist monks publicly burned themselves to death. Ambassador Henry Cabot Lodge, a foe of Diem, let ARVN generals know that the United States would look favorably on a military coup; accordingly, on November 2, 1963, President Diem was murdered, along with his brother. President Kennedy had often stated that the main purpose of the American presence in South Viet Nam was to reassure American allies all over the world about the reliability of American commitments. It is not clear how the murder of Diem advanced this purpose. Years later, CIA chief William Colby called the removal of Diem the first great American mistake in Viet Nam.

TET

By 1967 communist forces were taking enormous casualties, at a rate twice as high as the Japanese in World War II. General Giap said that between 1965 and 1968 alone, communist military losses totalled 600,000.[2] For comparison, between 1960 and 1967, thirteen thousand Americans died in Viet Nam, less than the number who died in the United States during the same years as the result of accidental falls; in 1975 alone, forty-six thousand Americans died in motor-vehicle accidents. Clearly, Hanoi had to do something. Thus plans developed for a great offensive that would break up the ARVN and provoke major uprisings in the cities—then the discouraged Americans would go home. The

Tet Offensive was thus an acknowledgement by Hanoi *that its guerrilla war in the South had failed.*

Even though American intelligence was aware that an offensive was brewing, it was still a shock when it came, in part because American forces simply could not believe that the communists would surface their guerrilla organization and thus expose it to destruction. Fighting was bloody and confusing for several days, but in the end the ARVN held together and the Viet Cong was stunned by the total lack of response to its pleas for a mass civilian uprising. Of eighty-four thousand Viet Cong involved in the offensive, thirty thousand were killed.[3] During the offensive the Viet Cong committed grisly atrocities, most notably in the historic city of Hué, where thousands of students, government officials, priests, and their relatives were found in mass graves, many clearly having been buried alive. Such events galvanized South Viet Nam: the government of President Nguyen Van Thieu distributed hundreds of thousands of arms to militia members. In years to come certain high-ranking Viet Cong would accuse Hanoi of having plotted Tet precisely to destroy their organization.

Yet while undeniably a military disaster for the communists, the Tet Offensive turned out to be a great propaganda victory, for it gravely undermined American determination to continue to resist the conquest of South Viet Nam. The shock of the Tet Offensive changed the policy of the United States from Americanization (see below) to "Vietnamization": Henceforth the United States simultaneously provided the South Vietnamese forces with better weapons and reduced the number of American troops in the country (which in President Johnson's last year had reached nearly 600,000). The first great test of the effects of Vietnamization was the 1972 Easter Offensive: after almost all U.S. ground combat troops had left the country, General Giap threw the entire North Vietnamese Army (NVA)—"the most efficient fighting machine in all Asia"[4]—against the South. The ARVN defeated the all-out offensive with the crucial support of U.S. air power, and once again, as in Tet, Hanoi's appeal to the population of South Viet Nam to rise up against its government went unheeded.

Thus the South Vietnamese had proven in the severe tests of 1968 and 1972 that with U.S. assistance they could stand against the best efforts of the North. Yet ever since Tet, the U.S. Congress had been turning increasingly hostile to the South Vietnamese. The main reasons for this growing rejection of their allies lie in the kinds of information that Americans received (more precisely, *did not* receive) about the conflict, and in the mistakes of the Johnson administration. The American news media completely ignored the South Vietnamese contribution to the common effort; night after night television reports dealt with American military actions as if the ARVN did not truly exist, despite the fact that throughout the war the ARVN took considerably more casualties than the American forces. One well-known American journalist, a candidate for the Pulitzer prize, published in a major newspaper statements provided to him by the Hanoi regime as if they were observed facts.[5] One of the major suppliers of war news to a major American newsweekly turned out to be a Hanoi agent.[6] President

Johnson did practically nothing to counter this deluge of negative and misleading reporting. However, if the news media overemphasized or misinterpreted American errors, they did not create them.

AMERICAN ERRORS

Clearly, the Americans made many mistakes in Viet Nam. Any list of the principal ones must surely include the following four: Americanization of the war, the bombing campaign in North Viet Nam, the so-called strategy of attrition, and the acceptance of permanent invasion of South Viet Nam via the Ho Chi Minh Trail.

Americanization

Most Americans, military and civilian, knew little of Vietnamese culture, of the Franco–Viet Minh conflict, or even of guerrilla conflict in general. Flooding the country with half a million young, not married, and (by local standards) fabulously rich Americans distorted the economy and debauched the culture. Yet it failed to provide the necessary numerical superiority, because North Viet Nam countered every increase in U.S. troop levels with an increase of its own. Besides, most Americans were not in Viet Nam to fight: for example, at the end of 1968, out of 536,000 servicemen in South Viet Nam, only eighty thousand were in combat infantry units. By sending this vast army across the Pacific, President Johnson prevented an immediate victory by the communists but also opened up deep fissures inside American society. Most of the money and energy that went into the transportation and supply of this vast American force would have been better spent training and equipping ARVN and the South Vietnamese militia.

Bombing North Viet Nam

Bombing was supposed to dissuade Hanoi from sending men and supplies into the South. Probably air interdiction would have failed anyway, but political considerations guaranteed both its failure and a high cost in American lives. For example, President Johnson ordered halts to the bombing no less than ten times, to "test Hanoi's good faith"; the communists instead used these respites to rebuild their forces. Even though great pains were taken in target selection—there was no "area bombing" like that used against Germany and Japan—Hanoi was able to paint itself in the eyes of much of the world, including many Americans, as a heroic David resisting a brutal and barbaric Goliath. The mismanaged bombing campaign cost American lives and damaged the international image of the United States but failed to stop the invasion of the South.

Attrition

Having taken up the task of fighting guerrillas, which was not their true responsibility or their best talent, the Americans then proceeded to fight the guerrillas in ineffective ways. Counterinsurgency is not about killing guerrillas; it is about depriving guerrillas of supplies, information, and recruits. This is accomplished by making sure that guerrillas cannot come among the civilians: in a word, true counterinsurgency means security in the countryside. The Americans rejected a policy of security on the grounds that it was too defensive; instead they determined to wear their enemies down by killing more of them in South Viet Nam than Hanoi could replace.

For attrition to work, the enemy must accept battle. But by definition guerrillas can control the tempo and magnitude of the fighting. The Viet Cong and NVA also practiced "hugging tactics," staying so close to American positions that U.S. air and artillery superiority could often not be employed. Very importantly, the strategy of attrition ignored the fact that Hanoi was quite capable of imposing horrific sacrifices upon its own people.

Since security—the clearing and holding of territory—was discounted, the war became a war without fronts, and the only way to measure progress was through the notorious body-counts, a method repugnant to many ordinary Americans and subject to grave inaccuracies. (As Clausewitz said, "Casualty reports on either side are never accurate, seldom truthful, and in most cases deliberately falsified.") Tactical military operations became the principal American activity, to the fatal disregard of civilian security. Sweep operations permitted occasions for abuse of civilians by American soldiers who understood neither the language, the culture, nor the perilous position in which many civilians found themselves. Out of such circumstances rose the tragedy of My Lai. The lavish use of aircraft and artillery to attack villages made many enemies for the Americans, as well as inflating the body count; very often the NVA or VC in a village would fire a few shots at American troops in the (usually fulfilled) hopes of calling down destructive retribution on its inhabitants. By some estimates the United States was eventually spending $400,000 for each communist soldier killed.[7] Meanwhile the guerrilla infrastructure in rural Viet Nam went mostly untouched, and the shocking destructiveness of the American style of war appeared on American television night after night.

Finally, having determined to kill the guerrillas rather than push them away, the Americans guaranteed that their own casualties in this dirty and dangerous enterprise would be much higher than necessary by instituting a one-year tour of duty: this meant that just when an American fighting man had learned something about the situation he was facing, he was sent home and replaced by a complete novice. It has been aptly observed that the Americans did not fight a ten-year war; they fought a one-year war ten times.

In the end, the Viet Cong was ground down; the NVA had to take over the war, and it too suffered stupendous casualties. So attrition did work, but not in time.

Permanent Invasion

Of all the American mistakes in the war, permitting the permanent invasion of South Viet Nam was the greatest. The Ho Chi Minh trail, eventually a multi-lane all-weather highway complete with oil pipeline, ran through "neutral" Laos and Cambodia to enter South Viet Nam at various points. By 1970 thousands of trucks came down the highway every month. The Trail amounted to a slow-motion Schlieffen Plan: if all the NVA who came down the Trail in small packets had entered South Viet Nam on the same day, it would have looked like the 1950 Korean invasion. The Trail enabled the communists to pick their target areas and concentrate on them, while the South Vietnamese and Americans had to be on the defensive everywhere. General William Westmoreland and others wanted to cut the Trail by building a defense line across Laos to the Thai border (a distance equal to that between Philadelphia and Washington, D.C.), but President Johnson and his key advisers forbade it. Attrition, like the bombing, was supposed to be a substitute for stopping the invasion of the South. Thus the Americans resorted to the most intensive bombing campaign in history, more intensive than that over Nazi Germany in 1944. Traffic on the Trail was slowed—but not stopped.

The destructive, escalating, and apparently endless war provoked increasingly large and violent antiwar and anti-administration demonstrations at home and abroad. The antiwar movement attracted many high-minded persons, and some of its original positions had a great deal of merit, but eventually it became dominated by exhibitionist and destructive personalities and degenerated into a pro-Hanoi claque. The elections of 1968 and 1972 were to show how limited the popular support for these later demonstrators really was.

STRATEGIC HAMLETS

One of the most successful and least expensive methods of counterinsurgency is the clear-and-hold strategy. The essence of clear-and-hold is that the government endeavors not to kill guerrillas but to deprive them of intelligence, supplies, and recruits. It accomplishes this aim by moving the guerrillas away from the civilian population, or vice versa, and keeping them there. Clear-and-hold is the opposite of guerrilla war. Guerrillas care nothing about holding territory; they move rapidly and by stealth in small numbers to inflict great damage. But in clearing-and-holding, the government occupies particular places openly, impressively, and permanently, using large numbers of troops to force guerrillas away and reassure the local population while inflicting as little damage as possible. Government forces advance methodically from cleared areas to contested ones, clearing and securing those in turn and moving on, eventually pushing the guerrillas back into the most inhospitable and least inhabited areas of the country, where they wither. In some key aspects, clear-and-hold resembles conventional war in slow motion. This was the heart of the successful British strategy in Malaya.

The Strategic Hamlet Program of the Diem government was a variation on this theme. Strategic hamlets were supposed to possess sufficient self-defense capabilities to hold off a guerrilla attack until outside help arrived. Like many things in South Viet Nam, the program was sound in conception but poor in execution. Strategic hamlets should have been erected slowly and steadily, from Saigon outward. But Diem moved too quickly; the program was announced in January 1962 and two years later there were officially twelve thousand strategic hamlets (in Malaya the British set up five hundred hamlets in three years). Instead of being on the fringes of cleared territory, many of the hamlets were deep inside contested country, situated haphazardly and unsupported by other strategic hamlets. Neither the ARVN nor the Americans wanted to spend resources on the program; hence many hamlets lacked even radios to call for help. The communists often staged an attack on a hamlet (always at night) in order to ambush the rescuing forces, who had to come by ground transport because they lacked sufficient helicopters. Nevertheless, captured documents indicated that the Viet Cong were very concerned about the strategic hamlet effort, because many hamlets did work, especially those inhabited by organized religious minorities such as Catholics or Cao Dai. The murder of Diem brought the program to a halt, and only the best organized hamlets were able to hang on.

THE SOUTH VIETNAMESE MILITARY EFFORT

Certainly, the ARVN had serious shortcomings. The Americans built the ARVN not to wage counterinsurgency but to resist a Korea-type invasion. The Americans gave it inferior weapons; for example, the ARVN did not receive the M-16 rifle in quantity until 1968, until then it was completely outclassed by communist forces using versions of the famed AK-47. The ARVN maintained French educational requirements for officers, thus severely limiting access to command slots for soldiers from peasant backgrounds. Training was very poor: most units were always in the field, so there was little time to train; officers were in short supply, and those who devoted themselves to training received scant recognition. Yet the ARVN did not break apart even under the furious pounding of the Tet and Easter offensives. This is a fact of fundamental importance, with which one might profitably contrast the utter collapse of the highly indoctrinated army of communist Hungary in 1956, the Cuban army in 1958, the PDPA army in Kabul in 1980 (see Chapter 17), or the Romanian army in 1989. In 1974 a noted British authority ranked the ARVN in fighting quality among free-world land forces second only to the Israeli army.[8] It was not the Viet Cong or the NVA that broke the ARVN but rather the self-inflicted calamity of an ill-planned and ill-executed retrenchment in combat conditions—the most difficult task for any army to carry out. The ARVN in fact did its best fighting when its back was to the wall, as in the defense of Xuan Loc in 1975.

Desertion rates in the ARVN were very high; so were they in the NVA and the Viet Cong. Desertion in the ARVN hardly ever had political implications; rather it was the response of peasant boys to the Saigon government's ill-advised policy of non-local service, a policy that resulted in "crippling the morale and effectiveness of the government's military forces."[9] Deserters from the ARVN often went home and joined the Territorial Forces (see below). Desertion hardly ever resulted in defection to the enemy, whereas in contrast 200,000 Viet Cong defected to the Saigon side.[10] Americans who like to express dismay over the ARVN desertion rates might recall that on the eve of the fateful battle of Gettysburg, when General George Meade arrived to take command of the Army of the Potomac, he expected to find 160,000 troops but in fact found only seventy-five thousand, because eighty-five thousand had deserted.

Every year from 1954 to 1975, the number of fatal casualties in the ARVN exceeded those in the American forces. About 200,000 ARVN personnel were killed. Some authors give a higher figure, and this number *does not include* the losses among the Territorial Forces. If in terms of total population American deaths had been proportionate to ARVN deaths, they would be not fifty-eight thousand—less than the number of highway fatalities in the United States in 1970 and 1971—but 2.6 million. In all of the wars of the United States, including the Civil War and World War II, total American military fatalities add up to less than one million.

After reorganization in 1964, the Territorial Forces (the militia) consisted of Regional Forces and Popular Forces (RF-PF, or Ruff-Puffs); Regional Forces were organized at the provincial level while Popular Forces were village self-defense units, with the former operating as rescue units for the latter. PFs received neither pay nor promotions nor training nor decent equipment. If a village were attacked, the PFs were supposed to hold out until the RFs arrived, but even if a village PF unit were lucky enough to have a radio over which to call for help, the RFs often lacked the mobility to effect a timely relief.

The Tet Offensive changed all this. During the crisis RFs and PFs often had to fight regular NVA units, and on the whole they did well. They then began to receive some good weapons and equipment. RF forces stood up especially well against the Easter Offensive. From 1968 to 1972, thirty-seven thousand ARVN lost their lives, compared to sixty-nine thousand RF-PFs. By 1973 the Territorial Forces numbered around 500,000; almost the whole of the vital Mekong Delta was under their control. The Territorial Forces received something like 3 percent of the war budget but accounted for 30 percent of Viet Cong and NVA combat deaths.[11]

"PEACE IS AT HAND"

On January 27, 1973, Washington and Hanoi signed peace agreements in Paris. Their principal effect was the removal of the small number of American fighting forces still in South Viet Nam and the cessation of air attacks on the North and on the Trail. In ominous contrast, the agreements tacitly allowed the North to retain 250,000 troops in the South. The Saigon government accepted these startlingly asymmetrical accords only after intense pressure from President Richard Nixon, who promised in writing that any serious violation of the agreement by the North would draw massive American retaliation. South Viet Nam was in much better shape by 1973 than in 1968: Saigon, with 2.5 million inhabitants, was almost completely free of terrorist acts; the government had carried out extensive land reform; Catholics, northern refugees, the urban middle class, the powerful religious sects, army officers and their families, all these were united in opposition to a forcible Hanoi takeover. And most important, the ARVN had shown in 1968 and 1972 that it could take whatever Hanoi could dish out—with American air support.

Given these circumstances, the desertion of the South Vietnamese by their American allies seems in retrospect inexplicable. In July 1973 Congress forbade any U.S. air combat over Viet Nam, thus repudiating President Nixon's pledges to Saigon. Congress also slashed aid to the South by two-thirds. The ARVN ran short of spare parts and gasoline; it had to cut radio communications and ground many fighter aircraft. Artillery batteries in the highlands were limited to four shells per day. By summer 1974 each ARVN infantryman was being issued eighty-five bullets per month. Bandages were removed from those who had died, and then washed and used again. Washington had spent perhaps $425 billion (in 1995 values) on the war; now Saigon would be allowed to go down for the want of less than $1 billion. At the same time, oil, weapons, and ammunition poured into Hanoi from the USSR. In December 1974 the NVA overran Phuoc Long province in a thunderous repudiation of the Paris Accords; a month later, in his State of the Union message, President Gerald Ford mentioned Viet Nam not even once. Hanoi had the green light.

The South Vietnamese were committed to holding every inch of their territory, while the North was able to assemble overwhelming force at a point of attack of its choosing. Thus in March 1975 the NVA seized strategic Ban Me Thuot, and Congress rejected President Ford's plea for emergency aid. President Thieu thereupon decided to carry out a strategic retrenchment: the ARVN would pull all of its forces out of the northern and central areas of the country to concentrate on the defense of Saigon and the populous Mekong Delta. Retrenchment was in fact a good idea, but Thieu embarked on it without sufficient preparation. Many roads and bridges turned out to be impassable to heavy traffic; hordes of civilians fearful of being left behind clogged the roads south, making an orderly army withdrawal impossible; throngs of refugees swept into Da Nang and Hué; soldiers left their units to search for their families and move them south. In this cauldron of chaos and despair, much of the ARVN melted away. On March 24 the NVA captured historic Hué; six days later Da Nang, where the first U.S. Marine battalions had landed exactly ten years before, fell amidst scenes of indescribable suffering.

But the ARVN still held the Mekong Delta and its sixteen provincial capitals.

Between Saigon and the Cambodian border many ARVN units were fighting fiercely; others were waging a furious defense of Xuan Loc, just north of the capital. Saigon was firmly under government control, and plans were afoot to turn the capital into another Stalingrad. Everyone expected that President Ford would send back the B-52s that would smash NVA power for a decade. Also, the rains were coming, the rains that would mire the NVA's Soviet tanks in impassable mud.

But on April 30, Acting President Duong Van Minh, assassin of Diem, ordered all southern forces to surrender. At that very hour the heavens opened and the rains poured down. It was twenty-five years almost to the day since President Truman first authorized U.S. assistance to the French war effort in Viet Nam.

WHY DID THE SOUTH FALL?

There are those who think the answer to this question is the corruption of the South Vietnamese government, the cowardice of the South Vietnamese Army, and the indifference of the South Vietnamese civil population. But in that case, why did Hanoi not just sit and wait for South Viet Nam to fall into its hands like a rotten peach? Why, if South Viet Nam was so decrepit, was it necessary for Hanoi to launch a massive World War II–style invasion in 1975?

An exhaustive list of the real causes of the fall of the South would not be a short one, but three in particular will receive attention here. First is what Napoleon called the moral factor. The South was fighting for a negative and ambiguous cause: whatever else it might entail, a northern victory meant the reunification of Viet Nam, while a southern success meant continued partition. Second, as Hanoi depended on the Soviets and the Chinese, Saigon depended on the Americans. It was no surprise that the Americans did not wish to maintain a great army on the Asian continent indefinitely. What was surprising was just how quickly the Americans tired of their responsibilities, and how utterly they abandoned their allies. Just when the war had become what the Americans had always said they wished it to be, a straightforward conventional conflict along the lines of Korea, the Congress began slashing assistance to the South. The effects of this abrupt and public rejection by their American allies both on the morale of the South Vietnamese and their physical capacity to wage war were of course disastrous. It is true that South Viet Nam could not have preserved its independence without long-term American assistance, but the same has been true of many U.S. allies, from Israel to West Germany to East Asia. American combat troops have been stationed in Europe since 1944, in Korea since 1950, and as of this writing (1996) they are still in both places. Nixon's sensational visit to Peking in 1972, however, sealed the doom of the South Vietnamese as far as the U.S. Congress was concerned.

However, a third factor in the fall of South Viet Nam was primary and decisive—over and above morale, over and above the drastic curtailment of American aid. It is in no way a denigration of the soldierly skills and the implacable determination of the North Vietnamese to observe that in the case of South Viet Nam, *geography was destiny*. If South Viet Nam had been a peninsula like South Korea or Malaya, or an archipelago like the Philippines, or if Laos had been a real state able to defend its borders, there would have been no Ho Chi Minh Trail, no piecemeal invasion from 1958 to 1971, no panzer-type invasions in 1972 and 1975. Geography made the Ho Chi Minh Trail possible. The Trail was Hanoi's decisive weapon; failure to close off the Trail was Washington's decisive mistake.[12]

APPENDIX: AN ALTERNATIVE STRATEGY

There is no easy way to beat a serious insurgency, but the Johnson formula was a case study of methods to avoid. A more promising strategy in South Viet Nam, one that took note of the experiences of the French in Viet Nam and the British in Malaya—as well as the Americans in Greece and the Philippines— would have been to minimize American casualties, neutralize the effects of the Ho Chi Minh Trail, deny the communists control over the bulk of the population, place the primary responsibility for hunting guerrillas on the South Vietnamese, and protect rather than endanger the civilian population by directing firepower *against the enemy*.

The simplest way to achieve most of these aims would have been to go into Laos and block the Trail on the ground, but that course was ruled out by the administration. An alternative would have been to create a sort of super-enclave out of Saigon and the Mekong Delta, by retrenching southward in a timely and orderly way. The Americans could have erected a front line bristling with heavy firepower and protected by the U.S. Air Force and Navy. The majority of the southern population would have been behind (south of) this American-ARVN line. The ARVN and the Territorials could have dealt with guerrilla units within the new borders. Highly trained ARVN units could have remained behind in the highlands to harass the enemy; American units could have held Hué and perhaps Da Nang as potential launching areas for flank invasions, on the model of Inchon (with the difference that the Americans would already be there). Refugees pouring into these enclaves could have been evacuated southward by ship. Creating a front line would have given full scope to American firepower, reduced the number of U.S. forces in the country, and held down American casualties (no more sweeps, no more booby traps). Bombing the North would have become unnecessary, the Ho Chi Minh Trail irrelevant. Desertion in the ARVN would have fallen drastically because potential deserters would already have been located close to home. The Hanoi Politburo would have had either to accept the independence of a South Viet Nam within defensible borders or launch frontal attacks against overwhelming U.S. firepower.[13] The South Vietnamese did in fact adopt a version of this strategy, but at the worst possible hour.

REFLECTION

The debacle of 1975 obscured perhaps the most important lesson of the American experience in Viet Nam: Maoist-style "people's revolutionary war" *had been defeated*. American firepower, the steadfastness of the ARVN and Territorials, land reform, and the Tet Offensive had broken the Viet Cong; to conquer the South, Hanoi had to commit its entire conventional army, one of the very best in Asia. Further, the defeat of Maoist strategy came despite the facts that the North was able to cover itself more or less in the garments of nationalism, that none of America's European allies supported the war, that the Americans imposed unprecedented limitations on the use of their air power, and that U.S.-Saigon forces were permanently outflanked via the Ho Chi Minh Trail.

At the height of its involvement, the armed forces that the United States committed to the Vietnamese conflict equaled about one-third of 1 percent of its population. Like the French before them, the Americans lost their objective in Viet Nam because of the increasing *political* difficulties of waging the war.

As for the triumphant Hanoi regime, after the departure of the Americans and the fall of Saigon came the exodus of refugees, of which the pathetic "boat people" were one example. But peace did not come to Viet Nam; instead there was more fighting, against Laotians, Cambodians, Thais, and Chinese. In fact, at the end of 1978 the mighty NVA, using American tactics and even American equipment, embarked on a massive, decade-long effort to defeat communist "Khmer Rouge" guerrillas in neighboring Cambodia—and failed.

NOTES

1. Bernard Fall, *The Two Vietnams: A Political and Military Analysis*, 2d rev. ed. (New York: Praeger, 1967), 281; Jeffrey Race, *War Comes to Long An* (Berkeley, CA: University of California, 1972), 83; and William J. Duiker, *The Communist Road to Power in Viet Nam* (Boulder, CO: Westview, 1981), 180.

2. *Washington Post*, April 6, 1969.

3. Maxwell Taylor, *Swords and Ploughshares* (New York: Norton, 1972), 383; and Phillip B. Davidson, *Viet Nam at War: The History, 1946–1975* (Novato, CA: Presidio, 1988), 475.

4. *The Economist*, April 15, 1972.

5. For this distressing episode see Guenter Lewy, *America in Viet Nam* (New York: Oxford University, 1978), 400–404.

6. Olivier Todd, *Cruel April: The Fall of Saigon* (New York: Norton, 1990), 253. And see the devastating criticism of the reporting on Tet in Peter Braestrup, *Big Story* (Boulder, CO: Westview, 1977).

7. *New York Times*, December 7, 1967.

8. Sir Robert Thompson, *Peace Is Not at Hand* (New York: David McKay, 1974), 169.

9. Jefferey Race, *War Comes to Long An*, 164n.

10. Thomas C. Thayer, *War without Fronts* (Boulder, CO: Westview, 1986), 202; and Douglas Pike, *PAVN: People's Army of Viet Nam* (Novato, CA: Presidio, 1986), 244.

11. Col. Hoang Ngoc Lung, *The General Offensives of 1968–1969* (Washington: US Army Center of Military History, 1981), 150; General Ngo Quang Truong, *Territorial Forces* (Washington: US Army Center of Military History, 1981), 77; William LeGro, *Viet Nam from Ceasefire to Capitulation* (Washington: U.S. Army Center of Military History, 1981), 330; James Lawton Colins, *The Development and Training of the South Vietnamese Army 1950–1972* (Washington: Department of the Army, 1975), 151; Thomas C. Thayer, "Territorial Forces," in W. Scott Thompson and Donaldson Frizzell, eds., *Lessons of Viet Nam* (New York: Crane, Russak, 1977), 256–61.

12. Naturally some of the most interesting writing about the various stages of this conflict is from the Communist side. See especially Truong Nhu Tang, *A Viet Cong Memoir* (New York: Harcourt, 1987); Vo Nhuyen Giap, *How We Won the War* (Philadelphia: Recon, 1976); Tran Van Tra, *Concluding the 30-Year War* (Rosslyn, VA: Foreign Broadcast Information Service, 1983); and Van Tien Dung, *Our Great Spring Victory* (New York: Monthly Review Press 1977).

13. For a development of these ideas, see Anthony James Joes, *Modern Guerrilla Insurgency* (New York: Praeger, 1992), 153–157.

16
The Khmer Rouge

Roughly 71,000 square miles in area, Cambodia is the size of North Dakota. In the mid-1970s its population was approximately seven million. Shortly thereafter the unfortunate little country became the scene of what is often described, not entirely accurately but quite suggestively, as "Viet Nam's Viet Nam."

The Khmer Rouge (or KR) originated mainly in elements that broke away amidst doctrinal and personal disputes from the official Cambodian communist organization. Many Khmer Rouge received military training from the North Vietnamese, or from East Germans after 1954.

During the American war in Viet Nam, the Hanoi regime, in flagrant violation of international agreements and its own public declarations, used the territory of neutral Cambodia as the locus for vital sections of that military highway quaintly and misleadingly named the Ho Chi Minh Trail. Cambodia's leader, Prince Norodom Sihanouk, pretended not to know about the permanent North Vietnamese occupation of parts of his country. Finally in 1970, with American encouragement, Cambodian General Lon Nol carried out a coup d'état and began to menace North Vietnamese supply routes in his country. A civil war ensued between Lon Nol's small Cambodian army, backed by the United States, and the Khmer Rouge, backed by the North Vietnamese Army. But in 1973 the United States Congress forbade further assistance to Lon Nol's government. The capital city of Phnom Penh inevitably fell to the communists, just two weeks before the fall of Saigon.

Once in power, the Khmer Rouge's leader Pol Pot (born Saloth Sar) proclaimed that it was now the Year Zero, and he proceeded to reveal the ghastly significance of that odd proclamation. The regime decreed that Phnom Penh, a city at that time of close to one million persons, must be emptied; it declared war on the educated classes, singling out members of the Buddhist clergy for particularly brutal slayings. Mass executions of condemned social categories, combined with maltreatment of prisoners and incredibly destructive economic policies, produced a true instance of auto-genocide: in a few years the Khmer Rouge succeeded in reducing the Cambodian population by something close to one-third. In American terms, this would be the equivalent of eighty million deaths.

THE VIETNAMESE INVADE

On December 25, 1978, powerful elements of the People's Army of Viet Nam invaded Cambodia and soon after captured Phnom Penh. Hanoi declared that its principal purpose was to stop destructive cross-border raids by the KR. Outside observers alluded to the long-standing desire of the Hanoi regime to bring all of former French Indochina under its control (an aspect of the famous Domino Theory of the 1950s and 1960s). The KR undertook guerrilla resistance to the Vietnamese invasion almost immediately. At the same time, Hanoi established a puppet regime called the People's Republic of Kampuchea (PRK); numerous figures in that establishment were former KR who joined the Vietnamese invaders in order to save themselves from Pol Pot's ever-widening blood purges. The PRK's record of atrocities was hardly less appalling than that of the KR proper. Eventually the Khmer Rouge leadership claimed that the massacres they perpetrated in the 1970s were really the work of Vietnamese agents.[1]

By 1982 there were perhaps 250,000 Vietnamese troops in Cambodia, and they had control of most of that country. But China and Thailand opposed Vietnamese hegemony over Cambodia: the Chinese viewed Hanoi as a major link in the Soviet Union's design to encircle it, and the Thais looked with alarm at the prospect of having Vietnamese military power right across their frontiers. To thwart the Vietnamese occupation of Cambodia, therefore, Thailand and China together helped to revivify the Khmer Rouge through arms shipments and the provision of sanctuary inside the Thai border; Pol Pot himself found refuge in Thailand in 1979. Then in February 1979 the Chinese army mounted a major invasion of Viet Nam's northern provinces. In this dramatic escalation the Soviet Union backed the Hanoi regime, as it had been doing for a quarter-century.

Thailand offered shelter from the Vietnamese army not only to the KR but also to other anti-Vietnamese guerrillas. Vietnamese efforts to solve or reduce this problem did not meet with success. In early 1985, for example, the Vietnamese launched a major offensive against Khmer Rouge bases along the Thai border, but the KR were still able to carry out raids to within ten kilometers of

Phnom Penh; and as late as June 1989 the Vietnamese army during one three-day period fired 2,700 artillery shells into a small KR base on Thai territory.[2]

All through the 1980s the KR used traditional guerrilla tactics against the Vietnamese occupation, disrupting road and railway traffic with mines and ambushes and attacking scores of small administrative centers. For its part the Vietnamese army employed tactics against the KR similar to those the Americans had employed against the Viet Cong and the North Vietnamese Army in the 1960s, with heavy emphasis on helicopters and artillery. Indeed the Vietnamese often harassed the KR with American-built jet aircraft of the former South Vietnamese air force. Meanwhile only international humanitarian assistance averted mass starvation in Cambodia.

In the summer of 1989 the foreign press was estimating the strength of the KR to be between thirty and forty thousand. Viet Nam announced the withdrawal of its forces from Cambodian territory in September 1989. Nevertheless, Prince Sihanouk declared that thousands of Vietnamese soldiers had remained behind disguised as Cambodian troops. Moreover, Viet Nam may have had to send several elite units back into the country in October to bolster the PRK, which was gravely weakened by the disintegration of the Soviet empire as well as by its identification with the unpopular Vietnamese. In 1991 the United Nations sponsored a peace agreement among the People's Republic of Kampuchea, the Khmer Rouge, and other insurgent groups. It then sent twenty-two thousand peacekeeping troops to the country, one of the largest operations in UN history. In May 1993 UN-supervised elections took place (at a cost of $2 billion), but the Khmer Rouge boycotted them and peace still did not return to devastated Cambodia.

In early 1994 the Khmer Rouge controlled perhaps as much as a fifth of the country's territory, centered on Battambang province, and a fighting force of fifteen thousand, armed with sophisticated weapons. Subsequently, thousands of KR fighters took advantage of a government amnesty program. Nevertheless murderous attacks on Vietnamese civilians in Cambodia, as well as PRK officials and Western tourists, were common. Meanwhile, widespread and increasing accusations of corruption undermined the legitimacy of the government in Phnom Penh.

Although China, under United Nations pressure, has apparently cut off aid to the KR, the same is not true at this writing for Thailand, whose army continues in active support of the guerrillas. Thailand remains hostile to the occupation of all French Indochina by the mighty Vietnamese army and receives support for this position from its partners in the Association of Southeast Asian Nations (ASEAN). Some observers believe that the KR, by selling lumber and gem concessions in territory it controls, has accumulated many millions of dollars in Thai banks, enough to fuel insurgency for years to come.[3] In April 1994 the Cambodian government accused Bangkok of helping Pol Pot escape capture by crossing the border.[4]

A PRELIMINARY SUMMING-UP

The profound historical aversion of Cambodians for the Vietnamese explains much of the failure of Hanoi and its puppet PRK government to defeat the Khmer Rouge, but not all. As so often happens, external forces have played a powerful role in this guerrilla conflict. Thai-Vietnamese rivalry has deep historical roots, and the two peoples fought each other over control of Cambodia in the nineteenth century; in fact, only the establishment of a French protectorate over Cambodia saved it from complete disappearance. China, moreover, felt deep anxiety about the Moscow-Hanoi axis, especially in the 1980s when the Soviets, already closely aligned with China's unfriendly neighbor India, sent large military forces into Afghanistan, yet another state along the Chinese frontier. The violent hostility between Viet Nam and the Khmer Rouge and between Viet Nam and China all brought to the surface in the grim Cambodian tragedy, shattered whatever might have remained of the myth of Asian communist solidarity.

Finally, the People's Army of Viet Nam, the former North Vietnamese Army or NVA, was a fighting force that had bloodied the French, the Americans, and the Chinese, an army many of whose principal leaders had themselves once been impressive guerrilla tacticians. The failure of this army to suppress the Khmer Rouge guerrillas invites, or perhaps requires, a thorough reexamination of the French and American experiences in Viet Nam from 1946 to 1972.

NOTES

1. See, for example, *Far Eastern Economic Review*, May 9, 1985.
2. *Far Eastern Economic Review*, June 29, 1989.
3. See *New York Times*, December 19, 1993, 1.
4. See *New York Times*, April 7, 1994, A12.

17
The Soviets in Afghanistan

In December 1979 the Soviet Union carried out a swift and massive invasion of its neighbor Afghanistan. This event provoked the "largest single national uprising in the twentieth century," it involved the Soviets in their longest military conflict, and it provided a textbook study of how a major power can fail to win a war against guerrillas. Most of all, it contributed to the most profound reshaping of the world balance of power in this century.[1]

PRE-INVASION AFGHANISTAN

Afghanistan lies at the intersection of the Middle East and East Asia, astride the historic trade routes between Persia and India. With an area of a quarter-million square miles, it is equal in size to the combined territories of France, Belgium, the Netherlands, and Switzerland, or those of Illinois, Indiana, Ohio, Michigan, and Wisconsin. Covered for the most part by forbidding mountains, the country has no railways at all, and few all-weather roads. An artificial buffer state separating czarist and British imperialisms, the country found itself suddenly exposed to pressures from the north when the British left India in 1947. The pre-invasion population was about sixteen million, of whom most were hardy peasants living simple lives centered around family, village, and religion. Divided into many ethnic, religious, and racial groups, of which the six million Pushtuns were the most numerous, Afghanistan was a decentralized country with little national consciousness. But there was a powerfully unifying cultural force: Sunni Islam, professed by 90 percent of the inhabitants.

THE PDPA AND THE SOVIET INVASION

In April 1978 a bloody military coup in Kabul took the lives of President Mohammed Daoud and his family. Although the weight of evidence indicates that the coup was not Moscow-inspired, the tiny Afghan communist party (or PDPA, the People's Democratic Party of Afghanistan) soon emerged in control of the government.

The PDPA had been founded only in 1965, principally by Babrak Karmal, who was probably a KGB agent. By its own admission the new regime in a short time executed thousands of political prisoners; it also killed Islamic religious teachers and attacked peasant family structure and customs (the party even forbade dancing at weddings). Predictably, this attempt by an exiguous minority in Kabul to produce overnight a Central Asian Stalinism provoked widespread violent reaction. On the eve of the Soviet invasion, fully twenty-three of Afghanistan's twenty-eight provinces were under rebel control.

The principal motive of the Soviet invasion seems to have been the desire to prevent the ignominious destruction of the PDPA regime, which had been advertising itself as communist-directed and pro-Moscow. In preparation for the incursion, Soviet advisers to the Afghan army sabotaged most of its tanks and other heavy weapons. Then, on December 24, 1979, Soviet airborne troops descended on Kabul. One of their first actions was to kill the incompetent and bloodthirsty PDPA President Hafizullah Amin.

Apparently the Soviets expected to encounter little effective resistance to their takeover either from inside or outside the country. Least of all did they count on anything more than verbal reaction from the United States: the Americans were still traumatized by Viet Nam and Watergate and distracted by the approaching presidential contest, as the Carter administration reeled from the effects of domestic and foreign policy reverses.

RESISTANCE: STRATEGY AND TACTICS

The disparity in size, population, wealth, and military power between the Soviet Union and Afghanistan was tragicomic: the world's largest country and mightiest land power opposed a backward and isolated buffer state that possessed not even a railroad. Also, the KGB was able to make use of Soviet Central Asians to infiltrate guerrilla areas and train children as assassins.

The guerrilla resistance, however, was not without important assets. It was so amorphous, so local or regional, that it could not be destroyed with one or a few powerful blows. In addition, the guerrillas almost from the start enjoyed the priceless blessing of a sanctuary in Pakistan, where they could find refuge, obtain arms, and launch infiltrations. But most of all, the guerrillas possessed that supreme weapon, high morale: fighting in a holy cause, calling themselves *mujahideen* ("warriors of God"), they were convinced that they would one day emerge victorious over their enemies.

By 1985 estimates of the number of guerrillas were running anywhere between eighty and 150 thousand. Arrayed against them were thirty thousand Afghan army troops (down from 100,000 since the Soviet invasion), fifty thousand local militia more or less purchased by Kabul, and 115,000 Soviet soldiers, providing the invader with at best a ratio of five to two over the guerrillas—totally inadequate.

The insurgents' basic tactics were ambushing convoys and mining roads. In a country with Afghanistan's topography, such actions were extremely effective: from time to time the guerrillas were able so to isolate major cities that they had to be supplied with much difficulty by aircraft. Sniper fire was a specialty of a rifle-loving population; despite lupine Soviet security efforts, assassinations of government and army figures and collaborators were common events in the very streets of the capital city. When the Soviets launched their periodic sweeps, the guerrillas, even entire villages, faded into the high hills, taking every item of food with them; when the Soviet tide receded, the guerrillas and villagers returned. The essence of the resistance strategy was not of course to try to defeat the Soviets but to make their continued occupation of the country too costly. Stalemate was the objective of the mujahideen, and they had clearly achieved it before the sixth year of the war.

THE KABUL REGIME AND ITS ARMY

Once the Soviet occupation got under way, the only accomplishment that the PDPA regime could point to was the total ruination of the country's system of higher education. By 1982, for example, almost the entire prewar faculty of Kabul University was dead, in prison, or in hiding, with Russians or unqualified PDPA members called in to take their places.

As they had gutted the country's universities, so the PDPA destroyed its army. Among the many unpleasant surprises that greeted the Soviets was the disintegration of Afghanistan's pre-invasion army and the total inability of their Kabul clients to build a new one. Most Afghan officers who had not been killed, fired, retired, or exiled by the PDPA joined the resistance. To replace these, men received appointment as officers after only three months' training. Desertion, defection, and distribution of weapons to the guerrillas were the norm; on one memorable occasion an entire Afghan army brigade surrendered without firing a shot. Morale suffered further serious depredations because murderous infighting between rival PDPA factions interfered with appointments and promotions.

In response to all this, Soviet advisers adopted the practice of disarming Kabul troops when they were not actually in the presence of the enemy. Afghan army posts were surrounded with minefields, not to keep the guerrillas out but to keep the soldiers in. All ranks in the army, and especially officers, received pay much higher than comparable posts in the civil government. Kabul offered accelerated promotions, high school diplomas, and university credits in return for completing military service; it lowered the draft age to sixteen in 1984, and then to fourteen. All this was to little avail: the Kabul army never exceeded three-tenths of 1 percent of the population. Thus, dismayed and resentful Soviet Army troops had to shoulder almost the entire burden of serious fighting against the resistance.

SOVIET STRATEGY

The Soviet Army lacked an effective doctrine of counterinsurgency, it had no experience of serious combat since the 1940s, and the quantity of troops assigned to Afghanistan was grotesquely inadequate to their mission. Predictably, therefore, the Soviet invasion forces carried out ineffective sweeps by essentially roadbound units. It was this combination of insufficiencies—of doctrine, of experience, of numbers, of tactics—that lay at the root of the Soviet decision to resort to a policy of systematic destruction of the countryside and its inhabitants. The campaign against crops, animals, and people eventually made it impossible in many areas for civilians to supply food to the guerrillas. The Soviets were especially determined to empty the provinces along the borders with the USSR and with Pakistan, a program described as "migratory genocide."[2] In their campaign to denude whole provinces, the Soviet armed forces employed poison gasses and dropped small explosive devices shaped like toys and designed to kill or maim children.[3]

By 1988 this deliberately genocidal campaign had reduced fully four million Afghans to refugee status, by far the largest number of such unfortunates on the face of the planet. Estimates of the number of civilian deaths as a direct consequence of Soviet policy range beyond 1.3 million, equivalent to the deaths of twenty million Americans.

THE COURSE OF THE CONFLICT

In the first year following the invasion, the Soviet forces pursued a very conservative line of action, staging only a few, mainly roadbound, operations and thus giving the mujahideen time to organize and consolidate. Thereafter they launched several large sweep operations, mainly in the Panjshir Valley near Kabul. Elite special forces (known by the Russian acronym "Spetsnaz") learned how to carry out damaging attacks on mujahideen areas. Soviet domination of the air, especially through the helicopter gunship, was their most effective weapon. The acquisition by the guerrillas of surface-to-air missiles in 1983 profoundly changed the face of the war by forcing Soviet pilots to fly at higher-than-optimal altitudes. Soviet air power suffered further drastic diminution in 1986 when the mujahideen began receiving Stinger hand-held anti-air missiles in large numbers; these weapons made it very dangerous for Soviet helicopters to fly protection for ground convoys and seriously reduced the mobility of Spetsnaz troops.

With Soviet air supremacy to a great degree neutralized, the guerrillas were able to reduce or even halt for extended periods land communications between major cities. Eventually they so thoroughly penetrated the Kabul government and army that surprise operations by units of significant size became close to impossible. Meanwhile life had become very dangerous for PDPA members and the large Soviet community in Kabul, with assassinations, explosions, and rocket attacks occurring with increasing frequency and effect.

When one considers how vast was the destruction and suffering that engulfed the Afghan people for so many years, the reaction of the outside world to this spectacle seems incredibly restrained. Pakistan of course began giving material aid to the resistance almost immediately. Conferences of foreign ministers of Islamic countries issued sharp protests. Chinese weapons began arriving, French medical missions entered the country (at great personal risk), and the United Nations voted year after year that "foreign troops" should leave Afghanistan. But the slaughter raged on. For its part, the government of India, which had denied the right of the United Nations even to criticize the Soviet invasion, openly favored the Kabul puppets as late as 1988.

THE AMERICANS AND THE WAR

It is as close to certain as such things can ever be that the Politburo in Moscow expected little reaction from Washington beyond verbal protest. In fact, the American government responded with great agitation. In a notable hyperbole that undoubtedly appalled the Soviets, President Jimmy Carter called the invasion of Afghanistan the "greatest threat to peace since the Second World War." The United States declared a boycott of the Moscow Olympics (in which action it was joined by many countries, including Communist China), placed an embargo on wheat shipments to the USSR, offered vastly increased aid to Pakistan, rushed the Secretary of Defense to Beijing, and proclaimed that any further Soviet advance toward the Persian Gulf area would constitute a direct threat to vital American interests. Carter's successor, Ronald Reagan, in a bold challenge to the "Brezhev Doctrine," declared that it would henceforth be the policy of the United States to assist "subjugated peoples" who were seeking to throw off the communist yoke.[4] American help to the mujahideen, little enough at first, amounted to $470 million in 1986 and $700 million in 1988.

THE SOVIETS DEPART

By 1987, after seven years of war, it was clear that the insurgents could not take or hold any major city of Afghanistan. It was equally clear that the Soviets controlled nothing much beyond those cities, two key airports, and the north-south highway from the USSR to Kabul. Most importantly, the Russians had lost their air supremacy.

In return for this tenuous hold on a rebellious neighbor, Moscow had alarmed the West and offended the Islamic world and many nonaligned states. It suffered fifty thousand casualties, of which fifteen thousand were fatal. Over one thousand aircraft, six hundred tanks, and several thousand other vehicles were destroyed. The conflict helped President Reagan pry big defense budgets out of Congress and was bringing Washington and Beijing closer together. Perhaps most crucial of all, the USSR's fifty million Muslim subjects, most of whose territories had been conquered relatively recently, were witnessing the mighty Red Army frustrated by Islamic peasants, the Red Star eclipsed by the Crescent, Lenin tamed by Mohammed—what a spectacle.

The Soviets had plunged themselves into a forbidding terrain inhabited by hardy and recalcitrant peoples. They had disastrously overestimated their ability to prevent outside help reaching the rebels; arms and supplies poured in from Pakistan, the United States, Saudi Arabia, China and Iran—especially the decisive Stinger missile. Moscow's marionettes in Kabul proved incompetent to gather up any but the slimmest threads of popular support, despite the ethnic, religious, and linguistic divisions in the country and the opportunities these should have provided for venerable tactics of divide-and-rule. The number of Red Army troops committed to the war was hopelessly insufficient: this was the root of the terror campaign against the civilian population, a campaign that was uniting almost the whole world against Moscow. To achieve the traditional ten-to-one ratio of troops to guerrillas, the Soviets would have had to put at least 900,000 soldiers into Afghanistan, eight times the size of their actual commitment, and even then there would be no assurance of a speedy solution.

Why should Gorbachev continue to commit himself to this costly imbroglio inherited from Leonid Brezhnev? Why, indeed? And so in April 1988 Pakistan and the PDPA signed their Geneva Accords, with the United States and the Soviet Union as guarantors; the Russians began their UN-monitored withdrawal the following month.

"RUSSIA'S VIET NAM"

It became fashionable in the 1980s to refer to the Afghanistan war as "Russia's Viet Nam." The obvious similarities, however, between these two conflicts cannot obscure some crucial differences. First, Afghanistan was right over the border from the Soviet Union, whereas Washington was closer to the South Pole than to South Viet Nam. Second, the Soviet political system was ideally suited to the conduct of a destructive war aimed at civilians: there were no intrusive media, no congressional investigations, no troublesome Amnesty International interlopers. Third, however brave and tenacious the mujahideen, they simply were not comparable as a fighting force to the excellently trained and equipped North Vietnamese Army; comparatively speaking, the Soviets had it easy. Last (for this list), in contrast to the Americans, the Soviets did not abandon their allies in Kabul, although they owed them incomparably less than the Americans owed their allies in South Viet Nam; instead, after it pulled its troops out, Moscow continued to pour vast quantities of supplies into the country up until the very eve of the surrender of Kabul.

THE MEANING OF THE WAR

The insurgency in Afghanistan offers one of the very few instances in human history in which guerrillas successfully contested their conventional opponents even though, in contrast to Carolina or Spain or China or Viet Nam, they themselves were not operating in conjunction with conventional military forces. But it is above all the political consequences of this struggle that make it so worthy of note. For the first time since the end of World War II, the vaunted Soviet military machine had been brought to a halt. The common folk of Afghanistan, marginalized or ignored by the world's politicians and intellectuals for centuries, bombed and gassed and chased from their ruined villages by the world's mightiest army, this remote and martyred people inflicted *the first clear-cut military reverse* on what had hitherto been so often called the historical inevitability of Marxism-Leninism. The successful resistance of the Afghan people contributed mightily to the gathering forces of disintegration within the Soviet empire. In one of history's most profound and sensational ironies, Trotsky's famous aphorism about the road to Paris lying through the towns of Central Asia received a spectacular twist: the cries of battle in the Afghan mountains had their echo in the shouts of freedom at the Berlin Wall.

NOTES

1. David Isby, "Soviet Strategy and Tactics in Low-Intensity Conflict," in Richard H. Shultz, Jr., et al., eds., *Guerrilla Warfare and Counterinsurgency: U.S.-Soviet Policy in the Third World* (Lexington, MA: Lexington Books, 1989), 330.

2. Louis Dupree, quoted in Joseph J. Collins, *Soviet Invasion of Afghanistan* (Lexington, MA: Lexington Books, 1985).

3. See *Christian Science Monitor*, October 26, 1988, 11; *New York Times*, December 10, 1985, 30; Edward Girardet, *Afghanistan: The Soviet War* (New York: St. Martin's Press, 1985), 213, 219–20; Claude Malhuret, "Report from Afghanistan," *Foreign Affairs* 62 (Winter 1984); 430; Anthony Arnold, *Afghanistan: The Soviet Invasion in Perspective* (Stanford, CA: Hoover Institution, 1985, revised); Henry Bradsher, *Afghanistan and the Soviet Union* (Durham, NC: Duke University, 1985), 211; and J. Bruce Amstutz, *Afghanistan* (Washington, DC: National Defense University, 1986).

4. At the time of the invasion of Czechoslovakia in 1968, Leonid Brezhnev proclaimed that once communists had come to power in any country, the Soviet Union would not permit that country to leave the "socialist camp."

18
The New People's Army

The latest chapter in the long story of revolutionary insurgency in the Philippines concerns the New People's Army (NPA). Its roots are located in the historic and persisting dichotomy between a westernized elite and the peasant masses, a tendency toward governmental corruption notable even for Southeast Asia, and a tradition of rural rebellion going deep into the Spanish colonial past. Like the Huk uprising of the post–World War II period, the NPA guerrillas are the military arm of a communist revolutionary organization—the "Communist Party of the Philippines–Marxist Leninist" (CPP-ML), a self-proclaimed Maoist group. (This group should be distinguished from the older Philippine Communist Party, the PKP, from which the CPP-ML split off during 1967–1968.) Some former Huks (see chapter 13) were prominent in the leadership of the NPA, which sought to generate support by decrying the presence of major U.S. military installations on Philippine territory.

The NPA embarked upon a guerrilla campaign in 1968. By 1972 it had carried out a sufficient number of operations against military and civilian targets to attract international attention and was receiving arms shipments by sea from China. President Ferdinand Marcos, first elected as a reform candidate in 1965, claimed that the NPA had succeeded in infiltrating student and Catholic Church groups and labor unions. He imposed martial law on September 23, 1972. Martial law seems to have both helped and harmed the NPA: by closing off legal and political avenues to change it undoubtedly made recruits and sympathizers for the insurgents, but it also allowed the government forces to carry out a more centralized and vigorous campaign against the guerrillas. Efficient military intelligence work resulted by 1976 in the arrest of almost all the top leaders of the movement. Internal splits and noisy purges further weakened the insurgency. Martial law remained in effect until suspended by President Marcos in January 1981.

Upheavals in domestic politics impacted heavily on the fortunes of the NPA. In 1983 Senator Benigno Aquino, an implacable critic of Marcos, was assassinated as he returned to Manila from the United States. Popular demonstrations against presumed presidential involvement with the assassination resulted in serious clashes between Aquino supporters and the police. Opposition parties made considerable gains in the 1984 congressional elections; more ominously, the turmoil set off by the assassination led to increased NPA activity. In the presidential election of February 1986, Marcos claimed victory over Corazon Aquino, widow of the slain senator, amid widespread charges of massive electoral fraud. Huge demonstrations supported the Aquino cause. Significant sectors of the army officer corps under Lieutenant General Fidel Ramos joined with Secretary of Defense Juan Ponce Enrile to defy Marcos and support Mrs. Aquino. The Catholic Church also threw its powerful influence behind her. President Reagan advised Marcos to step down, which he did on February 25, 1986. The whole picture for the NPA had suddenly and dramatically changed for the worse: it now confronted the popular President Corazon Aquino, backed by the resources of the Church and the army.[1] In addition, within Philippine society energetic anticommunist vigilantism had become widespread, while in the wider world there were portents of profound upheavals within international communism.

Nevertheless the NPA still represented a potent challenge. General Ramos stated that over 1,100 soldiers and militia had died at the hands of the insurgents during 1985. In July 1986 press estimates of NPA strength reached thirty thousand fighters in control of 20 percent of the nation's rural territory. The NPA was especially strong on the islands of Samar and Luzon, but it was present in most provinces of the country.

In February 1987 President Aquino offered an amnesty to NPA members. During the same year vigilante groups, formed to identify and attack NPA supporters, grew strong with army support. But in August the Secretary of Local Government, an outspoken advocate of vigilantism, was shot near his Manila home; in October three U.S. servicemen were killed in an NPA attack near Clark Air Force Base, the first American military casualties in the country since 1974. As 1988 began President Aquino asked the army to do whatever was necessary to defeat the NPA threat by the end of her administration. Subsequently the NPA announced that it would increase its attacks on U.S. installations, and in April 1989 an NPA assassination squad (groups of this nature are called "sparrow units") killed Lieutenant Colonel James Rowe. At the same time, elements in the Philippine army, dissatisfied with the progress of the war against the NPA, staged several unsuccessful coups against President Aquino that included a bombing of the presidential palace on December 1, 1989.

In May 1992 General Fidel Ramos, supported by Mrs. Aquino, won the presidential election. During the first half of that year the NPA killed three hundred soldiers and police, including a colonel in the army intelligence service; this number was considerably smaller than the year before. The NPA appeared to be running out of steam. In 1992 their fighters were estimated to number 13,500, down from twenty-five thousand four years before. Also, the issue of the U.S. bases ceased to be a major source of nationalist agitation in Philippine politics with the American withdrawal from Subic Bay at the end of 1992.

In these circumstances, in August 1992 President Ramos freed NPA leader Romulo Kitanan, who had been arrested the year before. (Kitanan had been first seized in a raid in 1988 but had escaped.) A month later Ramos legalized the Communist Party, inviting it to exchange armed struggle for political competition; he also released several dozen NPA leaders.

By the middle of the 1990s it was clear that the NPA guerrillas were not going to overturn the government, but it was not so clear that the government would be able, through its own efforts, to bring the insurgency to a completely satisfactory conclusion in the near future.

NOTE

1. The armed forces had grown from twenty-five thousand in the army and fifteen thousand in the paramilitary Constabulary in 1965 to seventy thousand for the army and forty thousand for the Constabulary by 1985. See Institute for International Security Studies, London, *The Military Balance*, for the years indicated.

Section V: Latin America

From the late 1950s into the 1970s, Latin America seemed the ideal setting for guerrilla revolution. In many countries the profound social problems implanted by the Spanish conquest had been neglected or aggravated during the succeeding century and a half of independence. As the Cold War entered its second decade, the general situation was perfectly suited, so it seemed to many, to a rising tide of Soviet and Cuban adventurism. But, with the deeply ambiguous exception of the Sandinistas, who came to power in part with the help of the Carter administration, the widely heralded march of Cuban-style guerrilla revolution fizzled. In Bolivia, Colombia, Venezuela, Guatemala, and El Salvador, guerrilla revolutionaries failed; in most other countries they did not even mount a serious challenge.

At least three major factors produced this historic debacle. The first was the utter inadequacy of the so-called Cuban model of revolution. In the first place, as will be shown below, this model was profoundly misinterpreted even by those who developed it; second, Castro's noisy proclamations of his adherence to the Soviet camp and his intent to spread his revolution to all Latin America alerted the United States and galvanized the military and middle classes in the region. Third, Latin American guerrilla groups not only failed to form broad alliances with moderate and middle class elements, as Castro had done, but could not even form alliances among themselves. Fourth, in part as a result of pressure from the United States, governments threatened by guerrilla revolution began to conduct relatively open and honest elections.

A second main factor in the guerrilla failure was a notable decline of

Soviet interest in Latin America during the 1980s, followed by the ending of the Cold War and then the collapse of the Soviet empire. Hence leftist guerrillas—and not only in Latin America—found themselves bereft both of crucial outside assistance and of the psychological comfort of feeling themselves part of a great worldwide movement whose triumph was inevitable. This element above all helps to explain the arrival of peace in El Salvador.

The third factor was the inability of revolutionary groups to gather together sufficient long-term popular support. This failure is strongly suggested (although not conclusively proven) by the relatively small vote for guerrilla-backed candidates in El Salvador in 1989 and 1994, the surprising and overwhelming defeat of the Nicaraguan Sandinistas in 1990, and the dismal showing of the presidential candidate backed by former guerrillas in Colombia in 1994.

19
Continental and Caribbean Struggles

CUBA

Many have identified the seizure of power by Fidel Castro and his followers as the first communist revolution in the Western Hemisphere. This description is completely erroneous: Castro indeed imposed a communist regime on the Cubans, but he had not led a communist revolution. Nevertheless, the Castro phenomenon did produce a transformation of politics in the hemisphere, including important and longlasting changes in the way Washington viewed the Cold War.

Cuba before Castro

Castro and his followers confronted the dictatorship of Sergeant Fulgencio Batista, a regime that can accurately be characterized as a mafia in khaki. The confrontation succeeded because of profound peculiarities of Cuban society and history. By the 1950s, although there were serious pockets of poverty on the island, by all international statistical measures Cuba was one of the most prosperous countries in Latin America. Yet Cuban society was shallow and sick. Although Cuba before Batista had been superficially democratic, its main political parties were mere channels for funnelling government patronage to opportunists. More importantly, those social organizations that everywhere else constituted the foundation of traditional Latin American society—the Church, the army, and the landed aristocracy—were either absent, or present in a most attenuated form. The Catholic Church, with few priests, many of them foreign missionaries, had only the most nominal presence in extensive areas of the countryside. In contrast to other Latin states, Cuba had remained a Spanish possession until the early twentieth century; the Cuban army, whose existence post-dated independence, had no glorious tradition of struggle against Spanish imperialism. No great landowning class, rooted in the land and maintaining stability, existed; instead of aristocrats there were only plutocrats, many of them Americans or Spaniards, who viewed rural Cuba not as a venue in which to pursue and preserve a way of life but rather as a sugar field from which to extract profits.

Over this artificial and brittle society presided the decidedly uncharismatic figure of Batista. He had been the dominant political actor in Cuba for a decade after 1933, indeed a sort of tribune for the disinherited. When it became clear that he would lose the 1952 presidential election, he placed himself in power through an army coup. Batista's repressive and exploitative methods soon alienated large elements of Cuban society across all classes and regions. In July 1953, a twenty-seven-year old law school graduate and landowner's son named Fidel Castro led a band of mainly student followers in an attack on an army base. Security forces crushed the attack within a few hours, and Castro was captured and sent to prison. Pardoned by the government in 1955, Castro and some of his friends shortly afterward went to Mexico, where they studied the rudiments of guerrilla tactics under a veteran of the Spanish Civil War. On December 2, 1956, Castro and about eighty armed followers landed in Cuba. Most of these soon found themselves in the hands of the security forces, but the remainder were able to find refuge in the Sierra Maestra, in the extreme southeastern section of the island. Adopting the techniques of guerrilla war, they attacked small patrols, withdrawing immediately to prepared ambush sites. The Cuban army responded by consolidating its smaller outposts, in this way undermining its own morale and abandoning the countryside to the guerrillas. Castro proclaimed his goal to be restoration of constitutional government and free elections, and he soon attracted wide attention and support within and without Cuba.

The Collapse of Batista

Batista had an army of fifteen thousand, a force that should have been quite adequate to deal with Castro's puny challenge. But the Cuban army, like Cuban society, was not what it seemed on the surface. It was less a fighting force than a uniformed extortion ring. Within the officer corps promotion depended almost exclusively on political favoritism. The high command was "a demoralized gaggle of corrupt, cruel and lazy officers without combat experience."[1] None of its elements had had proper counterguerrilla training. Army campaigns against the rebels in the Sierra Maestra were desultory and unsuccessful, partly because Castro had come into possession of army codes and was thus able to call down strikes by Batista's air force on Batista's own soldiers. Unable to come to grips with the guerrillas, the Cuban army predictably took out its frustrations on the helpless civilian population, under the very eyes of the North American press. In May 1958 a thunderbolt struck the Batista regime: the Eisenhower administration proclaimed an embargo on arms shipments to Cuba. This meant in effect that Batista would be unable to obtain American weapons to reequip his forces. Here was a signal to all Cubans, including the army, that Washington wanted, or at least expected, the rebels to win. Then on December 10, 1958, the State Department announced it was withdrawing its recognition from Batista's government. Three weeks later, on New Year's Eve, the dictator fled the country and elements of Castro's small forces began to enter Havana.

In subsequent years, many, including members of Castro's inner circle, sought to replicate "the Cuban model" of guerrilla revolution in other Latin American countries, most notably Venezuela and Bolivia. These efforts failed, for several reasons. One of them, to be sure, was that Cuba had no land borders; but the main reasons for the failures and even fiascos in trying to export Castro's revolution stemmed from a misapprehension of what had actually happened in Cuba. There were two main sets of circumstances that defeated efforts to transfer the Cuban model to South America, one political and the other military.

In the Sierra, Castro had presented himself as a democratic political reformer interested in restoring integrity and dignity, and most of all clean elections, to Cuban politics. There was no talk of a Leninist regime, class war, expropriation of property, or undying animosity to the United States, only of cleaning out the embarrassingly dirty Batista regime. In stark contrast, during the 1960s and even later, Castro's would-be imitators on the southern continent campaigned as open Leninists or Maoists, proclaiming their intent to carry out social revolution, help bury the United States, etc. These proclamations aroused the deeply rooted and broadly influential Latin American establishments, which had not existed in Cuba. They also aroused the United States, which during the Cuban struggle had put pressure on Batista to give up, to begin a program of counterguerrilla training for the national armies. Also, the spectacle of hundreds of thousands of middle-class Cubans fleeing to the United States during the years when Castro was solidifying his dictatorship provided an object lesson to would-be reformers and democrats (not to mention the upper classes and their allies) all over the southern continent.

On the military side, the Castroite guerrillas had faced a Cuban army whose weaknesses were unique in Latin America. The Cuban command structure was hazy and riddled by political divisions. During the struggle Castro frequently urged Army officers to desert Batista and come over to his side, and many did so. Aware that the Castro forces usually released prisoners after disarming them, army units often surrendered, after the exchange of a few shots, to guerrilla bands only a fraction of their number. During the two-year conflict Batista's forces suffered fewer than three hundred fatalities, or less than three per week.[2] By the time Batista fled his capital, many units of the army *had not fired so much as a single shot* in combat. The primary and decisive military facts of the Castro victory, ignored by his would-be imitators (and by many of his enemies), were these: first, the Batista regime did not experience a defeat but a collapse; second, no Latin America guerrilla force of the future would ever encounter a national army so utterly unprepared to defend itself; and third, very importantly, the numerous and publicized executions of former Batista army officers by the new Castro regime made a most profound and lasting impression on armed forces all over South America.

Castro has remained in sole power for four decades, more and more dependent on handouts from the Soviet Bloc, handouts that abruptly ceased when the Bloc imploded. His regime, the first communist dictatorship in the new world, became one of the very last communist dictatorships anywhere at all.

GUEVARA IN BOLIVIA

What happened to Ernesto Guevara in Bolivia constitutes a brief but valuable compendium of advice to guerrillas on exactly how not to follow their chosen path.

Ernesto (''Che'') Guevara was born in 1928, in Argentina, son of an architect. He graduated in medicine in 1953 but spent little time practicing his profession. He went to Guatemala and worked for the Arbenz regime until it was over-thrown in 1954. Then he moved to Mexico, where he met the Castro brothers. Soon he was leading guerrillas in the deceptively easy contest with Batista. In fact it was he who led the guerrilla forces into Havana on January 1, 1959; Fidel arrived a little later. Guevara became head of the Cuban national bank, and then minister of industry. His tenure in each of those posts was a disaster; he therefore left Cuba, went off to the Congo to seek the true revolution, and returned quite disillusioned.

Soon, however, he became enamored of a truly vast idea. The continent of South America seemed excellent for guerrilla warfare: full of mountains and jungles, bad roads, impoverished peasants, and the very worst aspects of arrested capitalism. Right in the middle of this continent so pregnant with revolution sat Bolivia. Given its central location, a Castroite regime in Bolivia could turn all of South America into an anti-U.S. inferno—or, at the very least, relieve the American pressure on Cuba. So off went Guevara to Bolivia, which he entered in November 1966 by way of the La Paz airport. Eventually about two dozen men and women joined him, mostly Cubans and Argentines, supposing them-selves to be the nucleus of a great guerrilla army that would engulf the Yankee imperialists in a war ten times as big as Viet Nam.

From an orthodox Marxist-Leninist point of view, Guevara was guilty of a central and irredeemable heresy, namely ''focoism.'' That set of ideas derived in part from a disastrously wrong interpretation of Castro's guerrilla war in Cuba. In focoist thinking, the ''objective conditions'' for revolution need not be clearly present: the guerrillas themselves can create, or perhaps uncover, these conditions through acts of violence against the oppressor state. Such revolutionary romanticism would have appalled the Bolivian Communist Party, but no matter, Guevara landed in the country and began his activities without having so much as informed the local Party that he was coming.

True enough, Bolivia was a poor country, four times the size of Colorado, with a strategic location and a primitive transportation system, all of which should have made it prime guerrilla territory. But all the *political* factors were wrong. Guevara went to Bolivia to preach the revolution, but Bolivia had *already had* a revolution, a real one, which had resulted in extensive land redistribution; whatever else the peasants of Andean Bolivia may have been thinking, they did not think of themselves as landless. The president of the republic, René Barrientos, was a popular leader of Indian heritage. Moreover, he had come to power through a national election that in the Bolivian context could pass as a democratic one. Had not Guevara himself warned, in his justly famous little handbook on guerrilla warfare, that no revolution can succeed against a regime that was democratic, or even against one that tries to appear so?[3] After all, to make revolution one has to mobilize every available resource, but in a democratic or pseudo-democratic system many even of the dissatisfied will not support violent revolution because, and as long as, there appears to be a bloodless road to change.

So, according to Guevara's own teaching, he and his band were in the wrong country. But there was more. The Bolivian army was composed largely of peasant conscripts, drawn from the very villagers among whom Guevara wandered seeking to ignite the revolutionary fire. For their part, Guevara's followers, almost all of them non-Bolivians, almost all of them obviously petit-bourgeois, could not speak Guarani, the language of the Indians of the province in which Guevara had located. It is no wonder that the local Indians, suspicious with good reason of strangers under any circumstances, not only declined to become recruits for Guevara's South American guerrilla army but supplied intelligence to the Bolivian authorities and withheld it from the Guevaristas.

Even all this was not the end of the troubles afflicting Guevara's band. Clausewitz rightly advises guerrillas to operate in areas of rough terrain, where the impedimenta of the enemy conventional army will slow it down. It can happen, however, that the terrain can be *too* rough, so that it works worse hardships on the guerrillas than on the army, and this is what occurred in Bolivia. Besides, the guerrillas are supposed to be familiar with the terrain in which they operate, more so than the troops sent to chase them; this of course was not so with Guevara's band, so many of whom were strangers to Bolivia. In their remote corner of the Andes, Guevara's followers, mostly city folk, found themselves exhausted by the difficult passages from one place to another, without medical supplies, without even enough food. In contrast, the Bolivian army, though it moved ponderously, did so in relative comfort. Guevara himself, who was an asthmatic, should never have been in the Andean mountains in the first place.

The stage was obviously set for a rapid and bloody denouement. President

Barrientos accepted a sixteen-man team of American Special Forces to train Bolivian counterguerrilla units. In October 1967, less than a year after Guevara had entered the country, some of these soldiers captured and executed him, and put his body on public display.

In Cuba, the collapse of the Batista regime had resulted from a combination of factors—a corrupt and incompetent army led by bored and despised politicians; widespread support in the urban areas, including large strata of the bourgeoisie and the Church, for the guerrillas in the mountains; and the open distaste of the American government for the incumbent regime. In Bolivia, there was nothing like that, nothing at all, quite the contrary. Consequently the Guevara expedition to Bolivia was, in fact and perhaps also in intention, a suicide mission.

THE SANDINISTAS

For one hundred years after it achieved independence in the 1820s, Nicaragua was the scene of endemic civil conflict between its Conservative and Liberal parties. Both parties maintained their own armies, an unusual situation in Latin America. In 1912 President Adolfo Diaz, facing another outbreak of civil war, requested U.S. assistance to maintain peace. Nicaragua was of strategic importance to Washington both because of its proximity to the Panama Canal and because German and Japanese firms were interested in constructing a Nicaraguan canal. U.S. sailors and Marines landed in the country, where by and large they remained until the 1930s, although the number of U.S. troops actually in Nicaragua sometimes fell as low as a hundred men. By the 1920s both Conservatives and Liberals had come to support the American presence. Eventually the State Department presented the Nicaraguans with a plan "to transform Nicaragua's armed forces into a nonpolitical force dedicated to defending constitutional order and guaranteeing free elections."[4] In May 1927 a new Guardia Nacional began training under the supervision of the U.S. Marines.

The Marine trainers soon discovered that they had not only to train raw recruits but to combat disease. Campaigns were undertaken against rampant venereal infections as well as malaria and smallpox. Regular pay, uniforms, good food, and medical treatment made recruitment of young men into the Guardia easy, although the Marines soon had to drop the literacy requirement for membership. The Marine-led Guardia supervised the 1928 presidential elections, in which the opposition Liberal candidate José Maria Moncada won a clear victory. Even the ruling Conservatives acknowledged that they had lost fairly. For the first time in the history of Nicaragua, the ruling party had lost an election and permitted the inauguration of the victors. Nevertheless, the Marine presence in Nicaragua called forth much criticism, especially in the U.S. Senate.[5] All parties agreed that the Marines would go home right after the 1932 elections, in which the Liberals again won a clear mandate. When the Marines left, the leadership of the two Nicaraguan parties agreed to destroy completely the nonpartisan nature of the Guardia by dividing the officerships equally between them. (The American model for the Guardia had been not *bipartisanship* but *nonpartisanship*.)

The Coming of the Somozas

Anastasio Somoza Garcia, a leading Liberal, received presidential appointment as commander in chief of the Guardia. The long-standing animosity between the two parties soon broke out into the open once again. In 1936, Somoza ran for and won the presidency, thus combining within himself the presidential office and the direct command of the Guardia. This was the true beginning of the Somoza dynasty.

One of the major objectives of the Marine-built Guardia Nacional was to restore order in the northern countryside, which had become the scene of the activities of Augusto Sandino. Born in 1895, after a stormy youth Sandino had joined the Liberal rebellion against President Emiliano Chamorro. He rejected the bipartisan agreement for U.S. supervision of the 1928 elections and led his band of followers into attacks on Guardia outposts during and after 1927. In 1931 he seized the headquarters of a lumber company and massacred its American and British employees. In February 1933 Sandino came to Managua and signed with the Liberal president a peace accord that allowed him to maintain a force of armed men at the expense of the national government. Again in Managua a year later for further discussions, Sandino was forcibly taken at night by bitterly anti-Sandino officers to the airport and shot dead. The act was denounced by the American ambassador, but Sandino's followers allowed themselves to be disarmed, and that was apparently the end of the Sandino episode.

In a very common reversal of the Marxist model, the Somozas used political power to acquire economic dominance. The Somozas reaped much wealth from family or partnership business enterprises, real estate, lotteries, and graft (but not from taxation, which was low). Somozan Nicaragua looked a lot like Batista's Cuba. The long history of hostility between Conservatives and Liberals had weakened the upper class; the small middle class to a remarkable degree worked directly for the Somozas, either in the government or in business; the political parties were invertebrate and corruption-ridden (Somoza several times reached accommodation with the opposition Conservatives by giving them a share of the take); the army was not the shield of the republic but the tool of the dictator. Anastasio Somoza was assassinated in 1956, but the dynasty remained. His son Luis succeeded him in the presidency; Luis's brother Anastasio, Jr. ("Tachito") held the presidency from 1967 to 1972 and again from 1974 until the overthrow.

The FSLN

In 1962 a group of communists and other leftists, with the assistance of Fidel Castro, founded the FSLN, the Sandinista National Liberation Front. (Augusto

Sandino had been no communist, nor did he align himself with communists.) The Front's purpose was to ignite guerrilla revolution against the Somozas, but their efforts during the 1960s sank amidst the apathy of the peasantry and the vigilance of the Guardia. In the 1970s, however, things began to go very wrong for the Somozas. The second generation of the dynasty abandoned the relative restraint of the past and began to make egregious mistakes that created allies for the FSLN. After the terrible Managua earthquake of December 1972, emergency aid flowed into Nicaragua from all over the world and especially from the United States; Guardia officers and Somoza henchmen looted the stricken capital and stole much of the foreign assistance. The elites of the nation were repelled by the spectacle of this cesspool of graft amid an inferno of misery. Then in a spectacular raid in December 1974 guerrillas captured several prominent cabinet figures, seriously undermining the regime's self-confidence and image of impregnability. Committing a classic, textbook error, Somoza allowed the Guardia, in its frenzied search for Sandinista guerrillas, to terrorize helpless countryfolk, making it easier for the Front to increase its ranks. In January 1977 the Nicaraguan bishops publicly condemned the regime's violence, and soon thereafter President Carter announced that the United States would not renew its security treaty with Nicaragua. Six months later, President Somoza suffered a heart attack, an event that grimly suggested to many of his followers that the days of the regime might indeed be numbered. In January 1978 the murder of Pedro Chamorro, internationally respected publisher, critic of the regime, and possessor of the most impeccable elite credentials, really alarmed the upper classes and turned them further toward an alliance with the Front. There seemed no other way to oppose the Somoza dictatorship than through revolution. The Church, the universities, and business groups all made common cause with the FSLN, which itself had eschewed radical programs, promised free elections, and won the accolade of the *New York Times*. The regime continued to crumble: in March 1978 Sandinistas assassinated the second in command of the Guardia; the following August, disguised guerrillas were actually able to seize the presidential palace and hold it for nearly forty-eight hours.

By that time the Guardia Nacional numbered about twelve thousand, one of the smallest armies in all Latin America. Hostile to the population and isolated from it by special privileges, much of the Guardia's energy was taken up with collecting and distributing graft. Then the Managua earthquake scandals and the killing of Pedro Chamorro alienated every sector of Nicaraguan civil society; thereafter neither the Guardia nor the regime it protected could reach out for allies against the Sandinistas, who had been obtaining valuable assistance from Castro's Cuba. Nevertheless, unlike Batista's army, the Guardia had received counterinsurgency training. Besides, its members greatly feared that after a Sandinista victory they would suffer the same bloody fate that Castro had meted out to Batista's military. Thus right up until the end the Guardia fought much better than Batista's forces ever had. Under these circumstances the war might have gone on for years. But President Carter's special envoy in San Jose induced the FSLN to sign an agreement foreswearing blood vengeance against the Guardia if the latter laid down its arms. In these circumstances the fighting came to an end, and the Sandinistas established their control of the country.

The Contras

Relations between the new regime and the Carter administration began to deteriorate almost immediately, and the Reagan administration adopted a stance of open hostility to the Sandinistas. A heterogeneous group, including long-time opponents of Somoza, disillusioned supporters of the FSLN, and former *Somocistas* came together to form an anti-Sandinista guerrilla group that soon became universally known as the *Contras* (from the Spanish for counterrevolutionary). They set up training camps in Honduras and received instruction from the Argentine armed forces. At about the same time, the former Sandinista commander Eden Pastora launched another anti-Sandinista guerrilla effort, independent of the Contras, in Costa Rica. In December 1981 President Reagan told members of congressional intelligence committees that United States assistance to the Contras would help slow down the shipment of arms from Nicaragua to the guerrillas in El Salvador. American support for the Contras was extremely controversial in Washington, and eventually involved the administration in an embarrassing scandal, the so-called Iran-Contra Affair. In mid-1984 Congress forbade assistance to the Contras, then permitted ''humanitarian aid'' in late 1985, and finally lifted the ban on aid entirely in October 1986. The Contras meanwhile received help from Saudi Arabia, Brunei, and elsewhere. Supporters of the Contras have insisted that the guerrillas deserve much of the credit for the 1990 decision of the Daniel Ortega regime to hold national elections under international observation. In any event, those elections resulted in a defeat for the Sandinistas as resounding as it was unexpected.

EL SALVADOR

El Salvador, the only Central American republic without an Atlantic coastline, is the size of Massachusetts. Its population at the time of the outbreak of the recently concluded guerrilla war was 3.5 million. The very stereotype of a Central American society, El Salvador has been almost from the beginning a commodity-export economy, with grave maldistribution of land and wealth, and a dreary history of oligarchical control and military dictatorship. The army consisted of an officer elite presiding over peasant conscripts; the common soldiers did not receive decent training or care, and the unprofessional officer corps had no real mechanism for rewarding competence or weeding out incompetence. In close alliance with the oligarchy, this army compiled a notable record of human rights abuses, including massacres of peasants.

The FMLN

The combination of social backwardness, government unresponsiveness, and liberation theology led to demands for serious change among the growing middle class, including some army officers. In December 1980, in Havana, several revolutionary groups organized the Faribundo Marti National Liberation Front (FMLN), named in honor of a Salvadoran communist contemporary of the Nicaraguan Augusto Sandino.

The FMLN, displaying good leadership and bold tactics, and benefitting from army ineptitude, very rapidly mounted a serious challenge approximating a conventional war. In reply, elements of the oligarchy, army, and police sanctioned the organization of "death squads," whose activities encompassed the murder of anyone dangerous to the regime—including Oscar Romero, Archbishop of San Salvador, in 1980. In its efforts to get at guerrillas the army killed many civilians who found themselves in the way. In spite of these circumstances, in the spring of 1980 the Carter administration decided that the United States must help the Salvadoran government overcome the challenge from an insurgency that was clearly communist-controlled. In retrospect this decision was the most important event of the entire conflict.

Nevertheless, the inadequacies of the Salvadoran government and army seemed to indicate their imminent collapse. The guerrillas were able to mobilize ten to twelve thousand fighters, a formidable array indeed and one far greater than either the Castro or Sandinista insurgencies had commanded. Yet in January 1981 the much-heralded "final offensive" of the insurgents failed completely—before any appreciable U.S. aid had arrived. (The popular uprising predicted by FMLN in conjunction with the 1981 insurrection was a resounding flop; this was the first major indication that support for the insurgents was not as widespread as many outside El Salvador claimed it to be.)

President Reagan was determined to prevent the victory of the FMLN, which would be interpreted as a triumph for the Sandinistas and Castro, and behind them the Soviet Union. A small number of U.S. military advisers arrived in the country, and in January 1982 Salvadoran officers began training in counterinsurgency techniques at Fort Bragg, North Carolina. Out of these efforts eventually arose a better-equipped and more competent army.

From 1982 to 1985 bitter fighting raged across the little country. The small size of El Salvador should have worked to the disadvantage of the guerrillas, but the border with Honduras had never been well-defined; both governments had no-entry zones for their troops, and these areas ("*bolsones*") provided the insurgents with excellent sanctuaries. The rebels received priceless assistance, including military training, from neighboring Nicaragua, and from the USSR, Cuba, Bulgaria, East Germany, and Viet Nam.[6] Additionally, the Salvadoran army suffered from peculiar weaknesses. Among these were the "*tanda*" system, whereby an entire class of officers received promotion at the same time, negating any concept of merit; structural corruption, whereby officers profited from government payments for non-existent soldiers and sold goods at inflated prices to their troops; and a lack of enthusiasm on the part of many officers to see the war end, because U.S. aid would then also end.

By 1985 it was clear that El Salvador would not fall, but the insurgents continued to fight tenaciously. The war had become stalemated; with perhaps seven thousand fighters still active, the FMLN abandoned its semi-conventional tactics and reverted to the classic pattern of protracted guerrilla war.

Meanwhile, the Americans were making their presence felt. In December 1983 Vice President George Bush visited the capital, San Salvador, to deliver the tart message that if government forces did not visibly decrease abuses of human rights then American assistance would cease. A month later the so-called Kissinger Commission reported its findings that the United States had important strategic and ideological interests in Central America. The Commission urged the strengthening of the Salvadoran military and the building of democratic practices to deprive the rebels of a legitimate cause.[7] Both these events improved the climate for congressional support of the El Salvador government. Between 1979 and 1987 the United States provided $2 billion in economic and $700 million in military assistance. During the same period Salvadoran security forces increased from ten to fifty-six thousand.[8] In 1980, the ratio of security forces to insurgents was 1.5 to one; by 1987 it was close to eight to one. Certainly one must be cautious about such figures, because they can mask important qualitative questions; but clearly if the ratio is changing over time in favor of the guerrillas, the government is losing the war. The opposite was the case in El Salvador.

As the military situation stabilized in favor of the government, democracy was slowly establishing itself in the society. In May 1984 Jose Napoleon Duarte was elected president. A Notre Dame graduate, civic activist, and critic of the status quo, he was one of the founders of the Christian Democrats, a party that for years had been the principal opponent of the Salvadoran establishment. (Most observers believe that Duarte had won the presidential elections of 1972 but had been counted out.) This 1984 election was the first time in the history of El Salvador that an opposition candidate had peacefully attained the presidency.

By 1989, after more years of inconclusive fighting, major figures in the FMLN, such as Ruben Zamora, had renounced guerrilla warfare and opted for political action. In the March presidential elections, Alfredo Cristiani, candidate of the ultra-conservative ARENA party, won an easy victory witnessed by the international press. The inauguration of Cristiani represented the first civilian-to-civilian transfer of power in the country's history. Soon the FMLN entered into negotiations with its former archenemies of the ARENA. Following the failure of these talks, the FMLN launched another major offensive, its largest ever, in November 1989; it was unsuccessful. At the same time elements in the army executed six Jesuit priests, setting off an uproar in the U.S. Congress.

A principal characteristic of Salvadoran society during the eighties had been the disappearance of moderate opinion and the strengthening of the extremes. But the end of the Cold War put new pressures on both sides: the FMLN was increasingly unable to count on support from communist countries, while the army realized that the Americans now felt themselves in a position actually to be able to cut off aid. Accordingly, in January 1992 the government and the FMLN signed peace accords in Mexico City, in the presence of UN Secretary-General Boutros Boutros-Ghali and U.S. Secretary of State James Baker. The FMLN undertook to disarm under UN supervision and become a normal political party; some of its members were to be permitted to enroll in a new national police force. The UN pledged to send up to a thousand military and civilian supervisors into the country. The treaty marked the end of a twelve-year insurgency which had taken an estimated seventy-five thousand lives. In the April 1994 presidential election ARENA candidate Armando Calderon won an overwhelming victory over Ruben Zamora, candidate of a Marxist coalition based on the former insurgents.

El Salvador: Neither Viet Nam Nor Cuba

Contrary to fashionable predictions, El Salvador had not turned into "another Viet Nam." Indeed the differences between the wars in El Salvador and Viet Nam were (or should have been) much more impressive than the similarities. One contrast lay in the dimensions of the struggle: El Salvador has one-eighth the area and one-fifth the population of South Viet Nam alone. Another is its location: if Washington is nearer the South Pole than Saigon, San Salvador is nearer to Houston and San Diego than is either of those cities to New York.

Besides these fundamental factors of demography and geography, any list of factors powerfully affecting the outcome would include the following elements. First, the Salvadoran army had the near-unanimous support of the upper and upper-middle classes. This unity was rooted in the defeat of the peasant-based communist uprising of 1932, which had solidified "the strongest anticommunist sentiment in Latin America."[9]

Second, the repeated failure of predicted popular uprisings to materialize, and the less than impressive showings of leftist candidates in national elections, indicated that the authoritarian Marxism of the FMLN was unattractive to broad strata of Salvadorans. The Front never had much organized support in urban areas to begin with[10]; by the late 1980s terroristic activities on the part of some elements of the Front, such as the laying of mines near populated areas, were clearly alienating large elements of the war-weary population. On the other hand, conservative forces were able to mobilize or purchase considerable support among workers and peasants; thus in the 1991 congressional elections the ARENA party obtained 44 percent of the vote. Third, the struggle against the FMLN had the clear support of three U.S. presidents, and this eventually produced improvements both in the army's military capabilities and in its treatment of civilians.

Fourth, the return of free elections in 1984, as in the Philippines in 1951, deprived the insurgents of the most powerful argument in favor of violent revolution. Clearly the El Salvador of 1989, in which a freely elected opposition civilian candidate was inaugurated as president for the second time in a row, was not the El Salvador of 1979, and during the administration of President Duarte international support had increased for the government and decreased for the guerrillas.

Fifth, it is no denigration of the Salvadoran guerrillas to state that they depended both psychologically and materially on outside support. But the Soviets were rapidly losing interest in the contest even before the end of the Cold War; there was no China in Central America; and the electoral defeat of the Sandinista regime in neighboring Nicaragua in March 1990 gave the coup de grace to whatever hopes of military victory the guerrillas may still have entertained.

In summary, El Salvador's government, seeking to legitimize itself by moving toward democratic elections, retained the support of most of the country's middle classes and also of the United States: this contrasted *fundamentally and decisively* with the Cuban and Nicaraguan experiences. Rather than another Viet Nam, El Salvador was in some key ways another Greece: the Americans mainly provided the allied government with economic and military assistance, while both insisting that the ally clean up its more egregious flaws and sending small numbers of military advisers to tone up the armed forces. Moreover, the insurgents in both Greece and El Salvador had clearly failed even before they lost their sanctuaries (Yugoslavia in the one case and Nicaragua in the other).

Like the campaign against Aguinaldo, the war in El Salvador deserves a great deal closer and more dispassionate scrutiny than it is likely to receive.

COLOMBIA

With an area of 439,000 square miles, Colombia is roughly the size of Arizona, New Mexico, Colorado, and Utah combined. From the late 1940s through the 1980s the country was the scene of some of the cruelest and most extensive violence ever witnessed in South America. In 1948 the assassination of the populist politician Jorge Gaitán unleashed a rural civil war, called by the Colombians *la violencia*. In its outward aspects a struggle between adherents of the Conservative and Liberal parties, the war eventually degenerated into an orgy of atavistic atrocities. Estimates of the death toll, men, women, and children, from this dreadful conflict range around 200,000 (out of a population in those days of fifteen million). Increasingly desperate appeals to put an end to la violencia resulted in the dictatorship of General Gustavo Rojas Pinilla (1953–1957). His failure to control the bloodletting then produced the National Front (1958–1974), a pact whereby the Conservative and Liberal parties agreed to alternate the presidency between them every four years and to share seats in the congress equally.

In the midst of this national emergency, the Castro regime proclaimed the exportability of revolution from Cuba to the mainland. Guerrilla organizations proliferated. Colombian Fidelistas returning to Santander from Cuba in 1965 launched the guerrilla Army of National Liberation (ELN). In response, the following year the pro-Moscow Colombian Communist Party created the Revolutionary Armed Forces of Colombia (FARC). Then the Maoists set up their People's Liberation Army (EPL) in 1967. When former dictator General Rojas Pinilla claimed (probably correctly) that he had been defrauded of his victory in the 1970 presidential elections, some of his more tempestuous followers eventually launched yet another guerrilla movement, the M-19. Each of these groups produced split-offs, so that Colombian guerrilla forces have been very fragmented, competitive, and even hostile to one another. These guerrilla units represented not the uprisings of oppressed peasants so much as efforts by out-of-power middle-class intellectuals to obtain peasant support for revolutions to place themselves in power.

Engagements between Colombian security forces and the various guerrilla bands dragged on for years. In the mid-1980s several thousand guerrillas were still active, but they were highly sectarian; thus they were unable to form alliances with broad moderate or even leftist elements in civil society, of the sort that had been so successful in Cuba and Nicaragua. Indeed the diverse guerrilla "armies" could not even form tactical alliances with each other. Their principal sources of support were kidnaping, extortion from foreign companies, and drug trafficking; such activities were bringing in perhaps $200 million every year. To combat this cash inflow, the government eventually started to freeze the assets of kidnap victims' families and to threaten cancellation of contracts of foreign companies that paid protection money to guerrillas. In the late 1980s various guerrilla groups, especially ELN, cost the government the equivalent of a half-billion U.S. dollars from attacks on oil pipelines; in the process enormous damage was done to the natural environment.

The government began peace talks with EPL and FARC in October 1989. In March 1990, the M-19 guerrilla group, after sixteen years of fighting, agreed to accept amnesty and surrender its weapons. M-19 then ran candidates in the May 1990 national elections; their presidential ticket drew only 13 percent of the total vote. The EPL accepted the same deal in February 1991.

Nevertheless, there were still thousands of unreconciled guerrillas in the country. In November 1990 FARC and ELN launched major attacks, preceded by the murder of the bishop of Arauca. In December the army began its largest offensive in three decades, against guerrilla strongholds in the eastern Andes. After the collapse of peace talks in 1992 the government began to forbid contacts between the media and guerrillas, and launched an effort to criminalize individual guerrillas. Clashes continued through the early 1990s: for example, in August 1993 an ambush on the outskirts of Bogota took the lives of thirteen policemen, and the following month land mines killed fourteen army personnel in Antioquia province. The government rejected peace overtures from elements of the ELN in the spring of of 1993. Instead it conducted against the remaining guerrilla groups a three-pronged attack, which included (1) professional counterinsurgency units rather than draftees to hunt guerrillas; (2) huge rewards for information leading to their apprehension; and (3) not only amnesty but resettlement loans to guerrillas who turned themselves in. The *New York Times* reported on July 1, 1994, that in the preceding three-month period 1,200 guerrillas had indeed surrendered.

To the outside observer it seems fairly clear at this point that there will be no peace in Colombia in the foreseeable future, if peace means the complete absence of guerrilla activity. Colombia is and will remain for some time a violence-ridden country, but "violence is not a revolution."[11] Strategically, the guerrillas have been beaten; in fact, several factors came together to defeat them almost before they began. In the first place, the Colombian army has long been vehemently united against the guerrillas and has proven itself willing and able to wage vigorous counterinsurgency campaigns, about which it already knew quite a lot from its experiences during la violencia and in the Korean War. In short, the Colombian army is a real army: if Castro had had to face an army like that, backed by the United States, instead of Batista's gaggle of uniformed extortionists, the whole contemporary history of Latin America would have been very different.[12] Beyond that, the United States rendered timely and extensive assistance to the Colombian government. In addition, Colombia is one of the few countries in Latin America where the influence of Roman Catholicism is pervasive rather than nominal, and the Colombian Church has for years thrown its influence behind the constitutional regime. Finally, the Colombia of the 1990s is not the Colombia of the 1960s. Vigorously contested elections have taken place through decade after decade of guerrilla violence, the Soviet Union has collapsed, and the Castro regime is decomposing. As this unhappy century nears its end, the principal threat to the Colombian constitutional order comes not from guerrilla chiefs but from narcotics lords.

VENEZUELA

Venezuela has an area of 352,000 square miles, the size of Montana, Wyoming, and Colorado. With the overthrow of the dictator Pérez Jiménez in 1958 and the democratic election to the presidency of Romulo Betancourt, Venezuela entered an era in which it would emerge as one of Latin America's most successful democratic polities. Every five years one freely elected civilian president handed power over to another freely elected civilian, the latter being almost invariably the leader of the opposition party. At almost exactly the same time (the early 1960s), Latin America was about to experience the euphoria, or hysteria, that arose from the apparent prospect of the export of Fidel Castro's revolution. Several guerrilla groups came out of the incubator of the Venezuelan Communist Party, most notably the FALN (Armed Forces of National Liberation), to which some junior army officers adhered. Small actions by Castroinspired and Cuban-assisted guerrillas began to occur in 1961. In dramatic contrast to the Cuban experience, however, the Venezuelan guerrillas were openly Leninist in their aspirations. In addition, the ruling Democratic Action party of President Betancourt (elected 1958) was sincerely reformist and enjoyed deep sympathy in the countryside, where the guerrillas would have to get their main support if they were to achieve any success. A main tactic of the guerrillas, moreover, was to kill policemen; this proved very unpopular, because police were usually recruited from the poorer classes.

In 1963, the revolutionary elements suffered a profound defeat with the election of Raul Leoni as president. He promised legality to the Communist Party if it would only renounce violence and participate openly in the electoral struggle. In fact, after 1964 the Venezuelan Communist Party publicly disavowed guerrilla tactics.

In these unpromising circumstances, Fidel Castro landed some of his own guerrillas on the Venezuelan coast in mid-1966. Hardly anything came of this venture except to puncture further the myth of the exportable revolution; by 1969 there were no serious guerrilla operations anywhere in the country.

Everything in Venezuela was stacked against the guerrillas. The Venezuelan Army remained cohesively hostile to the insurgents and generally supportive of the civilian presidency. The United States provided counterinsurgency training. Oil money paid for social programs, including the land reforms of President Betancourt and his successor. Free and democratic elections provided an alternative to violence for opponents of the regime, closing off the possibility of the broad alliance between guerrillas and civilian moderates that had developed in pre-revolutionary Cuba and Nicaragua. Pursuing its own foreign agenda, in 1969 the USSR instructed Castro to stop helping the Venezuelan guerrillas. Finally, in addition to all these advantages, the democratic government knew how to employ amnesty effectively to encourage splits between and within the guerrilla groupings.

GUATEMALA

Guatemala's forty-two thousand square miles make it equal in size to Tennessee. In 1954, the U.S. Central Intelligence Agency orchestrated the revolutionary overthrow of the increasingly left-leaning President Jacobo Arbenz. This controversial action set the stage for Central America's longest insurgency; decades of violence and civil war would destroy the lives of scores of thousands of Guatemalans, send thousands more to seek refuge in Mexico and the United States, and deeply agitate several American administrations.

Faithful to the pattern of Latin American insurgency, Guatemala had several rival guerrilla bands. The best known was the Rebel Armed Forces (FAR), started in 1962 by young military officers in company with communist elements from the Guatemalan Labor Party. During 1966–1967, FAR suffered a severe beating in the countryside from intensive army operations aided by American

Green Berets; nevertheless members of this group killed the American and West German ambassadors in 1968 and 1970 respectively.

In the early 1970s the Guerrilla Army of the Poor (EPG) attempted to revive guerrilla insurgency after the failure of FAR. EPG carried out numerous assassinations during 1975; ransom money bought many good weapons from Mexican suppliers, and a certain amount of help from Cuba, the USSR, Viet Nam, and Nicaragua; and a serious earthquake in 1976 distracted the Guatemalan government from counterinsurgency operations. In the next decade EPG and several smaller groups came together in Managua, Nicaragua, to form the Guatemalan National Revolutionary Unity (URNG), in imitation of the Salvadoran FMLN, whose proclamations they closely copied. This umbrella organization, however, failed to unite the Guatemalan guerrillas militarily or ideologically. At the same time, the new president, General Efrain Rios Montt, launched a combination of ferocious military campaigns against guerrilla strongholds, with generous policies toward cooperative villages. The Guatemalan army extended its presence in the countryside through distribution of food and land, the creation of local village self-defense forces, and the break-up of pro-guerrilla peasant communities in guerrilla-infested areas.

The counterinsurgent activities of the Guatemalan army included the abduction or killing of known or suspected guerrilla sympathizers, which aroused much criticism in the United States. The American government suspended military assistance to Guatemala in December 1990. The following year President Jorge Serrano refused to accept a renewal of aid, because it came with too many conditions. (President Serrano was the first elected civilian in Guatemalan history to receive presidential power from an elected civilian predecessor.) After a constitutional crisis, the Guatemalan congress named the well-known human rights advocate Ramiro de Leon Campio to the presidency in June 1993.

Strenuous army operations in the 1980s, along with a return to electoral democracy, seemed to put an end to any serious chances for the guerrillas to come to power in the foreseeable future. In the first months of 1991 talks took place in Mexico City between the Guatemalan army and the URNG; they were inconclusive, as were further discussions in 1993. Meanwhile, on September 5, 1993, the *New York Times* reported the discovery of a huge cache of Guatemalan guerrilla arms and supplies inside Nicaragua.

PERU: EL SENDERO LUMINOSO

Peru has an area of 496,000 square miles, the size of Arizona, California, New Mexico, and Oregon combined. The eastern part of the country is sparsely populated jungle; the great Andean chain dominates the central provinces. When Sendero violence began in 1980, the population was about seventeen million, of which five million lived in the Lima area. Half the population is Indian; the other half is mostly mestizo, with some European, African, and Asian elements. Although it has one of the best air forces in Latin America, Peru is neither a modern society nor a modern state. The large Indian population, heirs of the great empire of the Incas, has never been part of Peruvian society; more than a quarter of the population speaks only Indian languages, mainly Quechua.

Since independence from Spain, Peru's history has been tumultuous, with countless military coups and civil conflicts. In 1968 a military junta seized power and pledged itself to carry out radical reforms, especially the breakup of the great landed estates in favor of the peasantry. By 1980 the bright promises of the reformist dictatorship had resulted in deep disappointment, and the military handed power back to the civilian it had overthrown in 1968, President Fernando Belaúnde Terry. Belaúnde's administration ended in failure in 1985, and his elected successor, the charismatic Alan García, left office in 1990 amidst near-universal criticism.

Guzman: The Fourth Sword

Abimael Guzman, the founder of Sendero Luminoso ("The Shining Path"), taught his followers to call him the "Fourth Sword of the Revolution," after Marx, Lenin, and Mao. He got the name for his movement from the Peruvian communist José Carlos Mariátegui, who wrote that "Marxism will provide the shining path to victory." Born in the southern province of Arequipa in 1934, Guzman obtained university degrees in philosophy and law. As an instructor in philosophy at San Cristobal University in Ayacucho province, Guzman headed the local Communist Party organization; he thereafter became involved in the breakaway Maoist Red Flag faction and founded Sendero in 1970. Students and other professors at the university made up the original core of his followers, upwardly mobile young adults who aspired to be the rulers of a new Peru. Guzman also spent several years in China in the 1960s and 1970s, observing the Cultural Revolution.

Ayacucho province, where in 1824 the climactic battle of the South American wars of independence took place, has a population of about half a million. In Quechua, Ayacucho means "corner of the dead"; most of the area is unsuited for agriculture, and thus its Indian cultivators are very poor. The peasant perception that the agrarian reform of the 1970s had failed, plus the remoteness of the area, provided Sendero's original nucleus of academics with opportunity to recruit and expand. The poverty and isolation of Ayacucho have placed an indelible mark on Sendero's ideology and tactics: Sendero is a movement of "the geographical, social, economic and political periphery."[13]

Sendero's central belief is suggestive of Cambodia's Khmer Rouge: all of Peruvian society is thoroughly corrupt and therefore needs to be destroyed and rebuilt from scratch; indeed every aspect of western civilization, including democracy, is rotten. But Guzman also repudiated the former Soviet Union and continues to condemn post-Mao China and Castro's Cuba as betrayers of true communism; thus Sendero neither requests nor apparently receives help from other Marxist movements. The Senderistas expect that their utopia will emerge from a racial socialism based on Guzman's interpretation of the indigenous Indian culture and its glorious Inca past. Yet despite its rhetorical *indigenismo*, Sendero has always drawn its leaders from the semi-Europeanized provincial petit-bourgeoisie.

The first acknowledged act of public violence by Sendero was the destruction of ballot boxes during the May 1980 elections. After that, the guerrillas began to attack local police posts and destroy modern farm equipment. Assassination became a staple of their campaign, targeting especially government officials and judges, village elders, school teachers, priests, social workers, agricultural extension personnel, leaders of left-wing and reformist organizations, and foreigners. The guerrillas established "liberated zones" based on compulsory subsistence-level farming. Establishing a "Reign of Terror and Virtue," Guzman closed all bars and houses of prostitution and insisted that his followers practice personal cleanliness. (Sendero prisoners to this day keep their cells spotless.) Mainly because of its self-imposed isolation from the rest of the Marxist-Leninist world, Sendero has obtained few weapons from outside Peru. In a mining country, however, the guerrillas could obtain plenty of dynamite; they captured or stole rifles from policemen and soldiers; and through their alliance with the drug traffickers of the Huallaga Valley they received mortars and heavy machine guns.

With its Lima-centric view of the world, the Peruvian establishment at first chose to ignore reports of increasing Sendero violence in remote Ayacucho. The guerrillas became the responsibility of the police, who were underpaid, poorly trained, and divided into rival branches. Peru has considerable armed forces, but these are conventionally armed and trained. More importantly, as late as 1988 most of the army units continued to be deployed along the borders with Ecuador and Chile, with which neighbors Peru has experienced considerable tension for many years.[14] When Lima finally began to commit sizeable army units to the anti-Sendero campaign, they proved ineffective. The low pay of the soldiers opened the way to deals with drug lords; the army lacked the necessary mobility for fighting in the mountains and in jungle areas, and their road-bound columns frequently suffered bloody ambushes. Predictably, the army resorted to punishment of the local peasantry, and even here and there to mass murder, but the guerrillas simply moved to other locales. Meanwhile the government's notorious human rights violations caused Washington to cut off aid. All this time Peru was experiencing prolonged and serious financial and economic problems under the democratically elected presidencies of Belaúnde and García.

Prospects

The final defeat of the Sendero Luminoso may take a very long time. The combination of ancient racial and social cleavages with a mountainous topography and governmental failure seem to make Peru an ideal setting for guerrilla war. At the end of 1992, estimates placed the number of Sendero activists at around fifteen thousand. It is nonetheless very difficult to see how the insurgents can ever come to power, or even present a serious challenge to the Peruvian state. Four factors stand out most clearly in opposition to the prospect of a guerrilla victory, or even a stalemate, in this struggle.

First, recall Guevara's teaching that a revolutionary movement cannot defeat a state that has plausible pretensions to being a democracy.[15] Sendero is fighting against just such a government. The freely elected Belaúnde handed power over to the freely elected García in 1985, who in turn was succeeded by the freely elected Alberto Fujimori. Even though Fujimori took emergency powers in April 1992, he promised a speedy return to constitutional normality, and his actions received overwhelming approval in a plebiscite. Nor does Sendero monopolize criticism of the government: left-wing parties openly campaign for votes and have themselves been victims of the fanatical sectarian violence of the Senderistas. In a word, the Shining Path is not the only road to change. (In April 1995, President Fujimori won reelection to the presidency, defeating former UN Secretary General Javier Pérez de Cuéllar in a landslide.)

Second, even before the collapse of the Soviet empire, Sendero had deliberately isolated itself from the outside world. Consequently, aside from payments from international drug lords, it receives no outside assistance, the sine qua non of very nearly every successful guerrilla insurgency. Third, in a scenario reminiscent of the disastrous tactics of the Greek communist insurgents of the 1940s, Sendero terrorism has deeply antagonized many of the peasant communities in whose territory it operates. In the early 1990s, local village militias counted perhaps fifty thousand members, poorly armed but bitterly hostile to Sendero.

Fourth and finally, the government has become much more effective against the guerrillas. The number of troops in guerrilla-disturbed areas, especially well-trained marines supported by helicopters, has increased. Simultaneously the Peruvian intelligence services have greatly improved; in the early 1990s they were able to arrest several high-ranking Senderistas. Then in September 1992 came their greatest coup: the capture of the Fourth Sword himself. Guzman had gone to Lima to obtain treatment for a skin disease and apparently was turned over to the police by one of his former mistresses. This sensational event, as well as the sentencing of Guzman to life imprisonment, punctured the air of mystery and inevitability around Sendero and opened up an internal struggle among the sub-leaders still at large.

By the middle of 1994 the Sendero war had caused approximately twenty-seven thousand deaths and done billions of dollars in damage. In the year following Guzman's capture there were 1,600 violent deaths, but this figure was only one-half that of the previous year, and several thousand Senderistas have deserted the cause. Under a Law of Repentance, whereby guerrillas who help in the apprehension of former comrades receive reduced sentences and resettlement, many more have been taken captive.

NOTES

1. Hugh Thomas, *The Cuban Revolution* (New York: Harper and Row, 1977), 215.

2. Thomas, *The Cuban Revolution*, 258.

3. "Where a government has come to power through some form of popular vote, fraudulent or not, and maintains at least an appearance of constitutional legality, the guerrilla outbreak cannot be promoted, since the possibilities of peaceful struggle have not yet been exhausted." Ernesto Guevara, *Guerrilla Warfare* (New York: Vintage, 1969), 2.

4. Richard Millet, *Guardians of the Dynasty* (Maryknoll, NY: Orbis, 1977), 70.

5. For most of the time, the Marine "occupation force" in Nicaragua consisted of approximately a hundred men, considerably smaller than the ten thousand Cuban troops who would be present in the country during the 1980s.

6. James LeMoyne, "El Salvador's Forgotten War," *Foreign Affairs* 68 (Summer 1989); 105–26.

7. Henry Kissinger et al., *Report of the Bipartisan Commission on Central America* (Washington, DC: Government Printing Office, 1984).

8. All figures in this paragraph are adapted from A. J. Becevich et al., *American Military Policy in Small Wars: The Case of El Salvador* (Washington, DC: Pergamon-Brassey's, 1988).

9. Timothy P. Wickham-Crowley, *Guerrillas and Revolutionaries in Latin America: A Comparative Study of Insurgents and Regimes since 1956* (Princeton, NJ: Princeton University, 1992), 287.

10. LeMoyne, "El Salvador's Forgotten War."

11. Wickham-Crowley, *Guerrillas and Revolutionaries*, 296.

12. Ibid., 58.

13. David Scott Palmer, ed., *The Shining Path of Peru* (New York: St. Martin's, 1992), 244.

14. In fact, in January 1995, after the Sendero threat had subsided, serious border conflict broke out between Peru and Ecuador.

15. Guevara, *Guerrilla Warfare*, 2.

Section VI: Post-Colonial Conflicts

From North Africa to Southeast Asia, the ebb tide of European imperialism after 1945 provided space for the outbreak of bloody conflicts both old and new. In some places, such as Algeria, conflict raged between elements of the indigenous population against a colonial power supported by other indigenous elements. In some newly independent areas, like Angola, the artificial boundaries of the imperialist age, boundaries vociferously declared immutable by the successor governments, provided the ethnic and religious fuel for civil conflagration. On the Horn of Africa, one of the longest wars in the history of the contemporary world—fully thirty years—resulted in the birth of the new state of Eritrea and the collapse of the pseudo-Marxist dictatorship in Addis Ababa. Close by, in the Sudan, a protracted struggle was being waged literally against the reimposition of racial slavery; while far away in the heart of Asia, the remote and pacific people of Tibet waged a tenacious but losing struggle for the survival of their language and religion.

20
From Algeria to Zimbabwe

ALGERIA

"The Algerian War was to be the last, probably, and certainly the greatest and most dramatic of colonial wars."[1] A struggle of Muslim nationalists for independence from France, it also generated a rebellion of much of the French army against its own government, a rebellion that brought an end to the Fourth Republic. The conflict concluded with the complete defeat of the Muslim guerrillas, the handing over of Algeria to these same defeated rebels, the political decimation of the victorious French officer corps, and the bloody massacre of France's loyal Muslim allies in Algeria. The Algerian war is a textbook case of how military success can become political disaster.

Genesis

Serious French involvement in Algeria dates from the 1830s. Although a huge country—larger than France, Germany, Britain, Norway, Denmark, Sweden, and Finland combined—at the beginning of the rebellion the population was less than ten million. Of these, one million were *colons*, descendants of immigrants mainly from France, Italy, and Spain. The *colons* tended to treat Muslims as an inferior race, and their presence in Algeria greatly complicated and embittered the Algerian question.

The second exacerbating complication was the French army's emotional attachment to Algeria. The army was profoundly aware that the liberation of France from the Nazis had begun in the African empire. It also felt estranged from metropolitan French society and looked upon Algeria as its own congenial preserve. But most of all, the Algerian insurgency began just a few months after the French effort in Viet Nam ended. Many French officers felt that the politicians in Paris had given the army an impossible task there, that the politicians had forced the army to suffer not only the humiliation of defeat but the shame of abandoning the countless Vietnamese who had placed their trust in the French. The army was determined not to betray and be betrayed again. Algeria must remain French, even if against the will of God or man.

Viet Nam had not been the only recent humiliation of the French army: the Algerian war broke out only a decade and a half after the French collapse in the face of the *blitzkrieg* of 1940. Colonial peoples all over the world, and not least in Algeria, saw then the military weakness of the French and drew far-reaching conclusions from it; in that same world war, thousands of Algerian Muslims received military training. During World War II, French leaders had promised reforms to the colonies, but little of substance occurred once the war was over. Thus the Muslim nationalist Front de Liberation National (FLN) and its military arm, the Armée de Liberation National (ALN), was able to attract the support of men like Ferhat Abbas. A middle-class intellectual educated in France and a deep admirer of French culture, Abbas had long advocated a true integration of the Algerian Muslims into French society. Concluding reluctantly that few in France truly shared this aim, Abbas eventually became political head of the FLN.

Defeat of the Guerrillas

The Muslim revolt began in October 1954, when five hundred insurgents attacked fifty French military posts and police stations across eastern Algeria. The FLN received substantial advice and support from the Gamal Abdel Nasser regime in Egypt. By April 1956 the French army had committed 450,000 men to the Algerian conflict. They used *quadrillage* tactics, a variant of the system employed in the Vendée in the 1790s: the army holds the major towns in strength, places small garrisons in the lesser communities, constantly expands the number of places held, and meanwhile mounts frequent patrols to scour the interstices between garrisoned towns, depriving the guerrillas of a secure base and keeping them off balance, on the move.

The guerrillas possessed sanctuaries in Morocco to the west and Tunisia to the east. These might have played a decisive role in the war, but through prodigious efforts the French negated them: the army constructed barriers that reduced passage across the borders to a trickle. The most famous of these barriers was the Morice Line, extending hundreds of miles along the Tunisian frontier. It consisted of electrified wire, with mine fields on both sides and watchtowers at intervals. Any break in the wire would call down fire from French artillery as well as fighter planes and helicopters. The French deployed eighty thousand men along the Line.

Cutting off most outside aid, the army also deprived the guerrillas of internal support by regrouping peasants. Eventually two million Muslims moved or were moved out of guerrilla areas, many into new villages and towns where the army provided them with medical care and schooling, even employment, and undertook to convert hostile or indifferent peasants into loyal French subjects. The army also increased the number of its Muslim auxiliary troops, called *harkis*, to 180,000. And during 1957 paratroopers broke up the terrorist organization in the Muslim quarter of Algiers, the fabled Casbah.

The results of all this activity—sending in great numbers of troops to close the sanctuaries, hunt the guerrillas, regroup the peasantry, and smother the urban terrorists—were soon quite obvious: at the end of 1957, there were twenty-five thousand insurgents outside Algeria but only fifteen thousand guerrillas left inside the country. During 1958, guerrillas were surrendering at the rate of three hundred a month. The army had clearly broken the back of the insurgency.

Before that victory had become clear, however, the French army found itself cast into the Suez fiasco. In July 1956 President Nasser of Egypt, who was, not incidentally, a source of arms for the FLN, seized the Suez Canal. The French government, in collusion with Britain and Israel, determined to break the Nasser regime by a tripartite military assault. To this end the French reequipped the Israeli army, which invaded Egypt on October 29, 1956; within a week the Israelis had been joined by major French and British military formations. But in the midst of a successful campaign, on the brink of driving Nasser from power, the politicians decided to call off the war, a decision that sent a chill down the collective spine of the French army in Algeria.

The Army Revolts

At the same time, public opinion in metropolitan France was perceptibly shifting against the continuation of the Algerian conflict. The Suez affair was one element in this change. Incidents of French soldiers torturing Muslim terrorists to obtain information about future outrages, the unpopularity of the draft, the agitation of the still-powerful French Communist Party, the unattractive face presented by the *colons*, the spread of Muslim-on-Muslim terrorism to Paris itself, were all eating away at popular support for the war. Then in January 1958 occurred the Sakiet Incident. The Tunisian village of Sakiet had been used by the FLN/ALN as a base for infiltration into Algeria. When French aircraft bombed the village, a storm of criticism swept over the United Nations and the U.S. Congress, revealing how isolated France was becoming internationally as a result of the Algerian conflict.

In May 1958 the French parliament installed a new cabinet committed to negotiations with the FLN. In Algiers the *colons* rioted and seized control of key buildings. To many army leaders, it seemed clear that the politicians who had required them to crush the Algerian rebels were now ready to betray the army, its victory, and most of all its promises of fidelity and security to pro-French Muslims, just as four years previously the politicians had forced the army to betray its promises to pro-French Vietnamese. Refusing to bow to this scenario, units of the army in Algeria landed on and took control of the island of Corsica, without resistance. Faced with this unprecedented crisis, the Paris politicians summoned Charles de Gaulle from his attentive retirement, as the only man in France who could restore army discipline and prevent civil war. De Gaulle would be the last premier of the Fourth Republic.

As the outstanding French hero of World War II, de Gaulle elicited much sympathy within the army. But de Gaulle was a neo-Carolingian, not a neo-Roman: that is, like the technocrats of the metropolis, he disdained Algeria and the whole African empire; he believed that France's destiny lay not in possession of "Eurafrica" but in domination of the emerging European Community. Besides, de Gaulle realized that as long as the Algerian conflict went on, the French army there would be less than completely under his control; he knew that the army in Algeria that had brought him to power could turn against him.

In November 1960 de Gaulle (now president of the Fifth Republic) announced a referendum on the future of Algeria. The plan triggered a second revolt by the French forces in Algeria, in April 1961. Wearing his army uniform, de Gaulle broadcast a plea to the French army in Algeria to remain loyal, a plea heeded by most of its officers; opinion in metropolitan France rallied to him, and many army draftees in Algeria refused to follow mutinous officers. The revolt collapsed.

An ugly postscript to the Algerian conflict was the formation of the OAS, the Secret Army Organization, a group of former French officers who in their bitterness and despair tried to assassinate de Gaulle and launched terrorist acts against Muslim civilians and even against the army itself. By 1967 the sad, misshapen thing had come to its end.

Algerian Independence Day was July 4, 1962; before that date over one and a half million people had left the country, among them many Muslims. The French army had suffered eighteen thousand deaths, including Muslim troops. European civilian casualties numbered ten thousand. The insurgents had killed sixteen thousand Muslim civilians, and another fifty thousand were "missing." The insurgents themselves had lost 141,000 men at the hands of the French and another twelve thousand in internecine fighting. After independence, the new Algerian government began killing the Harkis, Muslims who had fought for the French; estimates of their deaths run from thirty thousand to 150,000.

ERITREA

The insurgency for the independence of Eritrea is instructive for several reasons. It lasted for an unusually long time, from 1961 to 1993; it represents "the most comprehensive defeat of a regular army in the Third World since the 1954 French loss of Dien Bien Phu in Viet Nam'';[2] and it is an example of a major failure for Soviet and Cuban intervention in Africa, although few heralded or perhaps even realized it at the time.

Eritrea has an area of forty-eight thousand square miles, the size of the state of Mississippi. Its population of about 2,700,000 consists mostly of poor, pastoral nomads. For centuries the country was loosely governed by Ethiopia. Eritrea became an Italian possession in 1890 and remained so until World War II, when it was occupied by the British. In 1952, under United Nations auspices, Eritrea entered into a federal union with Ethiopia. At first, the Christian minority in Eritrea welcomed the Ethiopian connection, but by 1962 Emperor Haile Selassie had abolished Eritrean autonomy, and Ethiopian interference in Eritrea had united Christians and Muslims there in opposition to Addis Ababa.

The Eritrean Liberation Front (ELF) was born in Cairo in 1958 and undertook guerrilla insurgency in September 1961. The backbone of the guerrilla forces were Eritrean deserters from the Sudan army and former members of the Eritrean police. The ELF found a sanctuary in Sudan, where it established training camps and supply dumps, and received recognition and aid from several other Islamic countries, especially Syria and Iraq. Soon the Soviets and Cubans were helping with arms and training; some ELF cadres also received training in Iraq, in China, and from the PLO in Lebanon. The Ethiopian army, on the other hand, obtained assistance and training from the United States and Israel.

Fighting dragged on inconclusively for a decade. In 1971 the Ethiopian army constructed a chain of fortified villages along the Sudanese frontier. By that time Ethiopian casualties were running at fifty per month, and the ELF possessed many weapons captured from the Ethiopian army. In 1974, an army coup in Addis Ababa displaced the venerable Emperor Haile Selassie, who was eventually murdered. Out of these events emerged the disastrous Ethiopian communist dictatorship of Colonel Mengistu Haile Mariam. But the immediate effects of the coup were to cripple the Ethiopian regular army with factionalism and purges. The Eritreans might have won a swift victory during the confusion, but internal splits—the Eritrean People's Liberation Front (EPLF) had seceded from ELF in the early 1970s—and even fighting among rival Eritrean guerrilla groups prevented any unified action.[3] Nevertheless, by 1977 the insurgents were engaging in semi-conventional warfare in their stronghold in the mountainous northern third of Eritrea and waging classical guerrilla war in the rest of the country. By then the rebels may have numbered around twenty-two thousand.

Despite the bloody revolution in Addis Ababa in 1974, which introduced many calamitous programs, the policy of Ethiopia toward Eritrea did not change. What did change was the position of the USSR and Cuba, who deserted the Eritreans and now backed the Addis Ababa regime. Soviet aid, including tanks and MIG aircraft, poured into Ethiopia. It was this equipment that enabled the Ethiopians to defeat the Somalis in the war of 1977–1978 in Ogaden and around Djibouti. In May 1978 Soviet General Vassily Petrov commanded a renewed

Ethiopian offensive against the EPLF.[4] All this was to no avail: the war raged on, and between 1982 and 1986 Ethiopian casualties may have run as high as eighty-five thousand.[5]

At the beginning of the 1990s, the EPLF may have commanded as many as forty-five thousand members; this was a very large fighting force for Africa, and many of the insurgents carried good Soviet weapons, taken from the Ethiopian army. The guerrilla war was escalating to conventional proportions: in February 1990 the insurgents captured the Red Sea port of Massawa. Eight months later talks between the Ethiopian regime and the EPLF opened in Washington. The denouement of the conflict was rapidly approaching. The thoroughly incompetent Mengistu faced a strategic combination of the EPLF and growing numbers of his domestic opponents, especially the Tigre People's Liberation Front (TPLF), founded after the 1974 coup. The TPLF scored impressive victories over the exhausted Ethiopian troops in December 1989 and January 1990, and the following year the Soviets drastically curtailed their aid to Addis Ababa. All this seems to have produced a general collapse of morale in the army, which reached its nadir by May 1991. With rebel forces approaching the capital itself, Mengistu resigned and fled to Zimbabwe on May 22. Three days later EPLF forces entered Asmara, capital of Eritrea, and four days after that, Tigréan forces were in Addis Ababa itself. That same day the EPLF announced a provisional government in Eritrea, and requested the United Nations to supervise a referendum on independence. On May 24, 1993, the independent republic of Eritrea came into existence, for which fifty thousand Eritrean lives had been given.

RHODESIA/ZIMBABWE

Zimbabwe has an area of 150,000 square miles, equal to that of Alabama, Mississippi, and Louisiana combined. In the 1960s, Zimbabwe was the British colony of Southern Rhodesia; while all sub-Saharan Africa seemed to be hurtling toward independence, the distribution of the best lands in the colony was wildly disproportionate in favor of the 100,000 whites and against the interests of the five million blacks. In an attempt to block eventual black enfranchisement, the white minority unilaterally proclaimed the independence of Rhodesia in 1965. This move resulted in the imposition of sanctions, first by Britain and then by the UN, and the outbreak of guerrilla war.

Two principal groups waged the insurgency in Rhodesia: ZAPU, the Zimbabwe African People's Union, and ZANU, the Zimbabwe African National Union. ZAPU was founded in 1961 by the father-figure of Zimbabwe nationalism, Joshua Nkomo. ZAPU received training and arms from the USSR and its Cuban comrades, as well as from China and North Korea. In July 1963, dissident ZAPU members organized ZANU and obtained weapons from and training in China, and also from Tanzania, Ghana, and (after 1975) Mozambique.

ZAPU guerrillas invaded Rhodesia from Zambia (the former Northern Rhodesia) during 1967; their attempts to establish themselves in border areas were defeated by Rhodesian security forces but were renewed in 1972. ZAPU engaged in relatively little combat, because Nkomo was husbanding his resources for the civil war he believed must follow the inevitable fall of the white minority regime; Nkomo also engaged in extensive negotiations with the white government of Prime Minister Ian Smith in Salisbury. The two insurgent organizations were further divided from each other by tribal animosities and personal rivalries. Zambia expelled ZANU from its territory in 1975 because of assassinations of rival leaders; nevertheless, by 1975 ZANU directed several thousand guerrillas. The guerrilla tactics of both ZANU and ZAPU consisted largely of attacks on farm houses, the ambush of lone vehicles, and the destruction of railways. Both groups also vigorously engaged in intimidation of African peasants to obtain recruits and supplies.

To separate peasants from guerrillas, the Smith government began creating "protected villages" in 1974; by mid-1976 between 175,000 and 200,000 peasants lived in such villages. It also established a special constabulary to patrol white areas at night. Security forces numbered twelve thousand in the army, eight thousand police, and thirty-five thousand reserves, including several thousand blacks. The government announced that between December 1972 and December 1976, 225 white and black security personnel were killed, along with 2,260 guerrillas, sixty-five white civilians, and 1,027 black civilians.

For more than a decade after its declaration of independence, Rhodesia had been able to exist and indeed prosper in spite of UN sanctions, because of the friendly support of neighboring South Africa and Portuguese Mozambique. But in 1975 Mozambique became independent; its territory now became a sanctuary for Rhodesian guerrillas. This was a crucial turning point. The South Africans decided that their own interests required a settlement in Rhodesia rather than continued war; accordingly, South Africa withdrew all its police units from Rhodesia and urged Smith to reach some accommodation with the insurgents.

Despite serious divisions between and within ZANU and ZAPU, and despite the continuing willingness of thousands of Africans to serve with government antiguerrilla forces, Rhodesia's white population was simply too small and too internationally isolated to defeat or even to hold off the increasingly well-armed, well-trained, and optimistic guerrillas. Thus talks between Smith and Nkomo opened in Salisbury in October 1975. A year later a multilateral conference on the future of Rhodesia took place in Geneva. Smith and several black leaders agreed that majority rule would come to Rhodesia by December 31, 1978. But as the political settlement went forward, insurgency and counterinsurgency intensified. Rhodesian forces hit guerrilla camps in Mozambique to forestall invasion in October 1976; in late 1977 and early 1978 they entered into both Mozambique and Zambia, and into Angola as well. Meanwhile, in November 1976, in Dar-es-Salaam, the presidents of several African "front line" states summoned the communist bloc to increase arms shipments to the guerrillas.

After elections with universal suffrage in April 1979, Methodist Bishop Abel Muzorewa took office as prime minister in a new state then called Zimbabwe-

Rhodesia. A ceasefire agreement was signed in London in December 1979, between Muzarewa's government and dissident guerrilla groups, and two months later new elections took place. ZANU defeated ZAPU 63 percent to 24 percent; ZANU leader Robert Mugabe became prime minister, and the Reverend Caanan Banana, another Methodist, took office as president in April 1980.

PORTUGUESE AFRICA

In the early 1960s Portugal possessed one of Europe's oldest and largest African empires, dating from the days of the fifteenth-century, seaward-looking monarchs. Angola, Mozambique, and Portuguese Guinea together totalled 790,000 square miles, twenty-three times the size of Portugal, and had a population of twelve million.

The independence parties in these colonies were led by well-educated city dwellers, far removed from the simple peasants whose destinies they wished to control. They suffered as well from serious internecine hostilities based on tribal rivalries. Although Portugal was small, poor, and far away, nevertheless by 1974 the Portuguese eventually were maintaining 142,000 troops in Africa (half of whom were native African, recruited from tribes hostile to the tribes supporting the local or regional guerrillas).

Guerrilla activity, especially in Angola and Mozambique, consisted of small attacks at short range from across the border. At any given time only a very small proportion of the guerrillas were inside the target colony. Until 1968 the Portuguese response to the guerrillas was generally passive; after that year they became more aggressive, gathering together civilians in protected villages and trying to seal off frontier transportation routes by means of air interdiction and raids by elite commando and marine units (many of whom were African).

By 1974 Portuguese security forces had lost eleven thousand men, European and African, with thirty thousand wounded, but nowhere except possibly Guinea-Bissau could it be said that the guerrillas were winning. The coup d'état in Lisbon on April 25, 1974, completely changed the situation: the new Portuguese military government, eager to rid itself of the colonial wars as quickly as possible, handed over power in the colonies to anybody who had a plausible claim to it. Under those circumstances the ex-colonies, now independent states, plunged into civil war.

Angola

The principal independence parties in this colony were: the FNLA (National Front for the Liberation of Angola), led by Holden Roberto, a member of the Bakongo royal house; the MPLA (Popular Movement for the Liberation of Angola), a 1956 merger of the tiny Angolan Communist Party and several other small groups; and UNITA (National Union for the Total Independence of Angola), which split from FNLA in 1966. UNITA, strong among the Ovimbundu people of the south, had as its leader Jonas Savimbi, an alumnus of the universities of Lisbon and Lausanne. Ideology, personal ambition, and most of all tribalism deeply divided the various groups.

In 1961 an MPLA invasion of Angola from the newly independent Congo Republic ended in the massacre of several hundred whites and seven thousand Africans. Angola, with a 1961 population of five million, had a Portuguese security force of less than ten thousand, many of whom were native African. After the initial explosion, guerrilla activities were very low-level, consisting mainly of the laying of mines, which accounted for 40 percent of the Portuguese casualties. By 1974 the MPLA had been largely forced out of the colony, but the new military regime in Lisbon recognized it as the official government of independent Angola.

The MPLA then proceeded, with Cuban and Soviet help, to win a bitter civil war against UNITA. (Cuban troops also helped the MPLA wipe out the FNLA.) Badly mauled, Savimbi's UNITA embarked on a new guerrilla war in 1977. Savimbi turned for help to South Africa, as well as to China, the United States, and Zaire. By the mid-1980s, South African troops were fighting openly for UNITA, Cuban troops for the MPLA (estimates of Cuban strength in Angola run from forty to sixty thousand). With the collapse of the Soviet empire and the admitted failure of the MPLA's economic policies, a peace agreement took effect in May 1991, calling for a ceasefire, exchange of prisoners, demobilization, a new national army, and free elections.

In the September 1992 presidential elections, MPLA candidate José Eduardo dos Santos was proclaimed the winner over Savimbi, who then charged fraud and resumed the guerrilla struggle. In a few months the country was experiencing full-scale civil war, for which, on March 12, 1993, the United Nations Security Council declared UNITA "solely responsible." In November 1994, Angolan army units, bolstered by advice and training from South African mercenaries, entered Savimbi's capital of Huambo, even as a peace agreement between the warring parties was about to be signed in Lusaka, Zambia.

Mozambique

In 1962, three small revolutionary groups founded Frelimo—the Mozambique Liberation Front. Frelimo had its support mainly among the Makonde tribe, less than 3 percent of the population, and Makonde support automatically earned Frelimo the hostility of the numerous Macua tribe.

In 1964 Frelimo launched major attacks against the Portuguese colonial administration from Tanzania, its principal sanctuary. Its guerrillas also received training in Egypt and Algeria. By 1971 Frelimo had perhaps eight thousand fighters. Having killed off rival nationalist groups, it inherited the government when the Portuguese pulled out, proclaiming itself to be a vanguard Leninist party in a one-party people's republic. Frelimo power meant the dictatorship of the small urban minority over the peasant majority, and the version of communism it introduced resulted in economic disaster. Frelimo also vigorously persecuted all forms of religion.

Under such circumstances, civil war predictably followed independence. The main anti-Frelimo force was Renamo, the Mozambican National Resistance. It was founded in 1976, under the auspices of Rhodesian Intelligence, gathering together former African members of Portuguese counterinsurgency units who had fled to Rhodesia after 1974. It also included disenchanted Frelimo members. In 1980, after African majority rule came to Rhodesia (now Zimbabwe), South Africa took over the care and training of Renamo. Renamo used forced recruitment, and its combat tactics in areas not controlled by it were brutal, not distinguishing between military and civilian targets. Mozambique, a very poor and deeply disunited country, was hard-pressed to deal with a serious guerrilla movement; by 1990 Renamo had perhaps twenty thousand members and was active in most provinces.

After two years of negotiations organized by the Italian government and Catholic Church officials, peace accords were signed in Rome in October 1992 between the Mozambique government and Renamo. Weapons would be surrendered under the supervision of the UN, which undertook to send 7,500 peacekeeping troops.

The long and brutal post-independence conflict had caused perhaps as many as a million deaths and created two million refugees.

Guinea-Bissau

With an area of fourteen thousand square miles, Guinea-Bissau (called thus to distinguish it from neighboring French Guinea) was the smallest of Portugal's African possessions, smaller than the combination of Massachusetts, Connecticut, and Rhode Island. But the little colony produced perhaps the most notable leader of any revolutionary movement in Portuguese Africa, Amilcar Cabral (1924–1973), a graduate of Lisbon University. In 1956 Cabral founded the PAIGC (African Party for the Independence of Guinea and Cape Verde) and in 1963 turned to overt armed struggle. Guinea-Bissau was the one territory where the rebels were actually able to achieve a stalemate with the Portuguese forces, even though the local Muslim tribes, a quarter of the population, remained loyal to Portugal. By 1972 Cabral led seven thousand guerrillas; the yearly blood cost of the conflict was three hundred Portuguese casualties and about a thousand guerrilla deaths. Cabral had Cuban advisers and Soviet weapons, including ground-to-air missiles, and a sanctuary in neighboring Guinea. In 1973 dissidents murdered Cabral in Conakry. The movement might have fallen apart after that, but the Lisbon coup occurred the next year. Post-independence and post-Cabral Guinea-Bissau descended to the status of a police state, riven by violent ethnic and personal rivalries.

The Moros

During the 1970s the Philippine Republic found itself facing not one but two distinct armed insurgencies, one revolutionary and the other secessionist. The latter was made up of Muslim Filipinos, called Moros since the days of the Spanish. Islam had entered the Philippines in the fifteenth century, from Indonesia. The census of 1970 reported that out of a total of thirty-eight million Filipinos, a little over two million were Muslim, most of whom were concentrated in the southern provinces of Sulu, Lanao del Norte, Lanao del Sur, and Cotabato. For centuries the Philippine Muslims have been poor, uneducated, and largely ignored by the central government of the day.

The Moros have a venerable tradition of armed conflict with the governing authorities of the archipelago, first with the Spanish, then the Americans, and lately the Christian Filipinos. A principal cause (or circumstance) of the latest uprising was the steady stream into southern provinces of Christian Filipino immigrants from other parts of the country. The exact date of the outbreak of the insurgency is hard to identify, but the clash of private armed groups of Muslims and Christians began to attract attention from the Manila government in 1971. During 1972 and 1973 Moro leaders formed the Moro National Liberation Front (MNLF).

In 1976, the Philippine government, the MNLF, Libya, and the Organization of the Islamic Conference (OIC) signed the Tripoli Accord,[6] which provided that a plebiscite on the question of local autonomy would take place in thirteen provinces on the island of Mindanao, where most Philippine Muslims live. The autonomy plebiscite of April 1977, a free election under foreign observation, resulted in a resounding defeat for the Moros—predictably, because the population was mostly non-Muslim. The Moro movement never quite recovered from this setback, but fighting continued, at great cost to civilians. For example, a grenade attack on the cathedral in Davao City on Easter Sunday 1981 killed thirteen and wounded two hundred. By then there were thirty-five thousand Philippine army troops in the disturbed provinces of the south. Government sources and the media have provided differing estimates for casualties in the Moro insurgency, but in 1988 there was general agreement that by then the figure had reached at the very minimum fifty thousand.[7]

On January 19, 1987, President Corazon Aquino met with Moro leaders in Cotabato City; additional high-level talks took place in Jeddah, Saudi Arabia. Following these conferences major Moro leaders announced that they would accept the government's offer of provincial autonomy rather than continue an apparently hopeless and destructive struggle for full independence. But some Moro groups found the degree of autonomy insufficient, and guerrilla conflict continued. As the 1980s drew to a close the MNLF may have controlled as many as fifteen thousand well-armed fighters, and its leaders sought full membership in the OIC.

The Moros are a small minority of the Philippines population, and do not constitute a majority even on the island of Mindanao, which the outside world supposes to be their stronghold. Yet even in these perilous circumstances serious internal splits and disagreements abound among them. Differences among ethnic and dialect groups are compounded by hostility within the MNLF between Marxist elements and traditional Muslim elites. Important leaders of the MNLF have long lived outside the country, usually in the Middle East. The MNLF itself split in 1975, with Libya backing the incumbent leadership and Egypt supporting a new group calling itself the Moro Islamic Liberation Front (MILF). The national government has known how to take advantage of these internal troubles, offering amnesties and coopting local Muslim elites into jobs within autonomous governing bodies. The Philippine army has from time to time given added point to these political ploys by carrying out large and destructive assaults on Moro strongholds. Consequently, over the years numerous Moro guerrilla chiefs and their followers have made separate peaces with the Manila government.

Nonetheless, the principal Moro problem is not numerical inferiority or internal divisions: it is rather that the rebellion contains within itself a fundamental strategic weakness that is permanent and fatal. No Philippine government, no matter its institutional origins or political coloration, can possibly countenance partition of the country. Therefore the MNLF cannot rely on a war of exhaustion for achieving its aims (which strategy always has double effects anyway): the government will not, because it cannot, grow tired of a war to preserve the territorial integrity of the nation. To win independence, therefore, the MNLF would have to carry the war directly into the heavily populated areas of Luzon. But the MNLF cannot—by its very nature—effectively wage guerrilla war outside of predominantly Muslim areas.[8] The Moro insurgency by definition seeks support among a well-defined constituency that is permanently a small minority of the total population and is also concentrated in localities that are not contiguous to one another, all in a limited geographical area remote from the seat of national power. At the same time, potentially sympathetic Arab countries are far away, and besides, the Manila government has often supported the Arab bloc on international questions, thus undercutting the prospect of the MNLF obtaining serious aid from Middle Eastern states.

Thus the only real hopes of victory for the MNLF, however slim, seem to lie in making an alliance with the NPA or receiving substantial outside assistance. But devout Muslims have been unable to make effective common cause with the Maoist-dominated NPA. The most likely scenario for the late 1990s thus seems to be that the rebellion will sputter on, to no lasting effect or dramatic conclusion. Bloody guerrilla attacks on the authorities, kidnapings of foreigners (which has greatly reduced international sympathy for the Moros), and massacres of Catholic church workers continued—as on December 25, 1992, when Moro insurgents killed eighteen Catholic church workers.

East Timor

East Timor has an area of 7,300 square miles, smaller than the state of New Jersey. A Portuguese possession from the sixteenth century to the 1970s, East Timor is predominantly Roman Catholic, one of the oldest communities of that faith in Asia. But today it is a marginal part of the world's largest Muslim state; thus its inhabitants find themselves in a position the reverse of the Moros in the Philippines. Much of its population of about 680,000 exhibits the maladies associated with generations of malnutrition and illiteracy.

The Indonesian independence movement defined the area of Indonesia to be exactly coextensive with the former Netherlands East Indies. Thus, in effect, the Dutch created Indonesia, much as the Spanish created the Philippines and the British, Nigeria. The immediate relevance of this observation lies in the fact that the Indonesian independence movement of Sukarno, and the early Indonesian republic, identifying themselves as the heirs to the Dutch empire, did not lay claim to East Timor, because it was not Dutch but Portuguese.

Following the 1974 military coup in Lisbon, the Portuguese were obviously heading for decolonization in Timor as well as in Africa. Accordingly, the Revolutionary Front for the Independence of East Timor ("Fretilin"), under the leadership for the most part of self-identified Marxists, proclaimed the independence of East Timor on November 28, 1975. In response to this declaration, thousands of Indonesian soldiers "volunteered" to enter East Timor on December 7, 1975. This date should be seen in relation not only to the Lisbon coup and the Fretilin declaration but also the fall of Saigon to the communists (April 30, 1975). Among the several motives influencing the decisions of the government in Jakarta was fear of possible communist influence in or control of an independent East Timor. Whatever the validity of these apprehensions, the regimes in Hanoi and Peking did eventually send military supplies to the Fretilin guerrillas.

Some observers have charged that the invading Indonesian forces singled out Chinese inhabitants for murder and looting, with hundreds of Chinese killed in the very first days, and also that the Catholic seminary and several churches were pillaged and burned. Two weeks after the invasion the United Nations Security Council called for the withdrawal of Indonesian troops from East Timor, still a Portuguese territory under international law. Nevertheless in 1976 Indonesia proclaimed East Timor to be its twenty-seventh province and maintained an occupation force there of close to twenty thousand.

The number of deaths resulting from the invasion and subsequent counterinsurgency is greatly in dispute. At a press conference in April 1977, Indonesian Foreign Minister Adam Malik reportedly asked: "So what if fifty thousand people [in East Timor] have been killed? This is a war."[9] In 1985, Amnesty International published a report stating that since 1976 over a hundred thousand East Timorese had been killed.

By the 1980s East Timor presented the classic picture of guerrilla struggle: the Indonesian army controlled the towns and the roads between them, with the guerrillas concentrated in marginal and remote areas. The Indonesians employed the all-too-familiar tactics of counterinsurgency: the burning of houses and crops, the liberal use of artillery, napalm, and defoliants, the forced evacuation of civilians to resettlement sites. To flush guerrillas out of their hiding places, they also made use of "fence of legs" operations, reminiscent of British "drives" during the Boer conflict. In the fence of legs, the army forced Timorese civilians to link hands, forming a human chain (or "fence") stretching for many miles. Two of these human chains, parallel to each other and miles apart, then moved toward each other with Indonesian soldiers behind each chain.

Some observers estimated that in the mid-1980s Indonesia was maintaining twenty-five thousand troops in East Timor, at a cost of a million dollars a day, to fight against three thousand guerrillas.[10] The Indonesian government publicly stated that Fretilin had no more than two to three hundred fighters, but in December 1988 guerrillas staged several attacks near Dili, the capital, during which scores of Indonesian soldiers reportedly lost their lives.

A central element of Fretilin guerrilla strategy has been to attract international attention and sympathy to its cause, especially in Portugal, Australia, the Vatican, and the United Nations. These efforts have encountered some major setbacks: for example in August 1985 the Labour government of Australia recognized Indonesian sovereignty over East Timor. Pope John Paul II, in his October 1989 visit to the island, called on Indonesia to observe fundamental human rights but said nothing about independence. Nevertheless, neither the Vatican nor Portugal recognizes the Indonesian incorporation of East Timor; Portugal has continually insisted that the United Nations supervise a free election on East Timor's future. In September 1988 the European Parliament called upon Indonesia to withdraw its forces. In 1988 and again in 1989 scores of members of both houses of the U.S. Congress formally requested the American Secretary of State to raise questions with the Indonesian government about human rights abuses in East Timor.

One student of the conflict has suggested that elements of the Indonesian army are not eager to see the fighting end, because it provides its officers with combat experience, as well as with opportunities for graft.[11] Nevertheless, in March 1990 the Indonesians launched a major new offensive against Fretilin with perhaps as many as forty-six thousand troops, including six thousand East Timor conscripts.

On November 20, 1992, Indonesian troops captured Xanana Gusmao, leader of the Fretilin insurgents; six months later he received a sentence of life imprisonment. The Portuguese government vigorously protested what it viewed as the severity of this sentence; Amnesty International declared that no Indonesian court has clear jurisdiction over Gusmao because the United Nations has not recognized Indonesia's occupation of East Timor. Hundreds of Fretilin guerrillas reportedly surrendered in the wake of the arrest. In the same month Indonesian troops opened fire on a crowd of thousands of East Timorese who had gathered in a cemetery in Dili; according to some reports hundreds of unarmed civilians were killed in the incident.

Tibet

Like Afghanistan, Tibet is a Central Asian state invaded by a massive totalitarian neighbor. The effort of the Tibetan people to reclaim their independence and preserve their culture produced one of the longest and most strenuous guerrilla wars in the history of Asia, as well as a major armed clash between China and India.

Tibet is larger in area than Spain, France, and Portugal combined, or Texas, Oklahoma, and New Mexico. Four of Asia's mightiest rivers—the Yangtse, Mekong, Indus, and Brahmaputra—have their sources within its borders. The Plateau of Tibet, twelve thousand feet high, is surrounded by forbidding mountains, notably the Himalayas to the south and west. The population in 1950 was perhaps three million; the capital, Lhasa, had about twenty-five thousand inhabitants. Religion, in the form of Lamaist Buddhism, was the very essence of Tibetan society. At least one male from every family became a monk; before the Chinese invasion there were 300,000 monks of various grades—one-quarter of the entire male population. Since the fourteenth century, the leader of Tibetan society, both temporal and spiritual, had been the Dalai Lama (a term used outside, not inside, Tibet). Upon the death of a Dalai Lama, his reincarnated successor was traditionally discovered among the country's poorest classes.

Tibet was once the center of a great empire extending from Afghanistan to Burma, and from Siberia to India. The Tibetan tongue is still spoken in parts of Kashmir, Burma, Nepal, and Sinkiang. Tibetan influence in Mongolia and Manchuria has been profound, and the leader of the Mongolian church, the Grand Lama of Urga, was traditionally selected from Tibet. The country never experienced foreign colonization, until today. Even Ghengiz Khan did not subdue the fierce Khambas of eastern Tibet. On the contrary, Tibet formed the strategic heart of Asia, out of which horsemen had come several times to invade China to the east.

For two thousand years the Chinese have considered the Tibetans a race distinct from them. Spoken Tibetan is not like Chinese, and its script derives from India, not China.[12] "By the mid-nineteenth century if not earlier, Manchu Chinese influence was miniscule . . . [;] the Tibet-Dogra war of 1841, the Tibet-Nepal War of 1857, the Nyarong War of 1862–1865 and the British invasion of Tibet in 1903–1904 were fought and settled without Chinese assistance."[13] The collapse of the Manchu dynasty in 1911 enabled the Dalai Lama to expel all remaining Chinese officials and troops. Nevertheless, the Nationalist regime of Chiang Kai-shek continued, like the Manchu empire before it, to claim sovereignty over Tibet, a claim the Tibetans explicitly repudiated. As the victory of the communists in China approached, isolated Tibet did not even have a radio station.

The Invasion. The Maoist victory in 1949 signalled a new era not only for China: for the first time in a century China had a government both willing and able to impose control over remote areas like Tibet. Peking informed the Tibetan government that it must acknowledge Tibet as part of China, with Chinese control over Tibetan defenses as well as diplomatic and trade relations with foreign states. In the face of Tibetan reluctance to accede to these demands, on October 5, 1950, ninety thousand Communist Chinese soldiers invaded Tibet from the east and north. The regular Tibetan army counted only nine thousand men, poorly equipped and trained. Within two weeks the Chinese invaders had captured the major part of this army, then sent them to their homes. Chinese troops had received instruction not to mistreat Tibetan civilians, and they proclaimed that they would not injure Tibet's religion or the monastic system.

Throughout the twentieth century Tibetans had relied on support from the India-based British against Chinese encroachment. But by 1950 the British were gone from India, and they in any case believed that no Tibetan resistance could have any chance of success. Tibet appealed for help to the UN, but only El Salvador and Ireland were openly sympathetic. India did not oppose Chinese occupation of Tibet: among other things, the British-trained Indian army had been badly upset by partition and had been fighting both the Pakistanis in Kashmir and several internal communist-inspired uprisings.[14] Above all, when the Chinese moved into Tibet, world attention was focused on the war in Korea.

The Dalai Lama fled from the Chinese invaders to the Indian border in December 1950. After receiving Chinese promises of respect for Tibetan culture, however, he urged his people to submit. The Chinese at first showed restraint, while they brought in more troops and built access roads and fortifications. Once these projects were well under way they felt strong enough to crush the Tibetans. Then the Chinese began imposing "reforms," which included settling large numbers of Chinese immigrants. In the mid-1950s, they looted, closed, or destroyed scores of monasteries, gave Tibetan lands to Chinese squatters, and imposed higher taxes on the Tibetan people. Tibetan schoolchildren now received instruction only in Chinese. Tibetan culture suffered vicious ridicule: the Chinese tied lamas to horses and dragged them through the towns; many were beaten to death. By late 1953 there were around 300,000 Chinese troops in Tibet, bringing with them venereal diseases hitherto unknown in that isolated country. During his 1956–1957 visit to India, the Dalai Lama asked for asylum, but Prime Minister Jawaharlal Nehru persuaded him to return home.

Armed clashes between Chinese and Tibetans had been occurring since 1952, but a major guerrilla-style rebellion broke out in the eastern regions of the country by the turn of 1955–1956. Fresh from their "victory" in Korea, the Chinese leaders tried to deal with this revolt by brute force, which in turn produced more recruits for the guerrillas. In July 1956 Vice-Premier Marshal

Chen Yi went to eastern Tibet to see what the trouble was; guerrillas attacked his escort, killing or capturing three hundred men.

The various guerrilla groups formed the National Volunteer Defense Army (NVDA), with headquarters in Loka province. The Chinese air force attacked the rebels with napalm and gas as well as explosive bombs. The guerrillas, mostly Khamba tribesmen, had never before been bombed, or even seen bombing aircraft. But they were "the last cavaliers of the fierce warrior tribes of Central Asia,"[15] with a long history of armed resistance to Chinese incursions.

The Dalai Lama declined to bless the revolt. His innate pacifism, the absence of any outside help for the Tibetans, and the overwhelming power of the Chinese led him to conclude that Tibet could not survive if it resisted. In contrast, guerrilla leaders believed they could inflict heavy losses on the Chinese, who would not wish the outside world to witness so large a rebellion and hence might make concessions. The Chinese declared the uprising the work of a decadent religious aristocracy; aside from the obvious question of how such a group could sustain a widespread and vigorous guerrilla war, Nehru himself pointed out that the growing numbers of Tibetan refugees in India were mainly from the humble classes.

Outclassed in numbers, training, and equipment, ignored by the great world, the Tibetans seemed doomed to quick defeat. Nonetheless, the guerrillas were not without advantages. Tibet is four times the size of Italy, most of it covered by the world's most daunting mountains, with the few roads often impassable in winter. (In good weather the NVDA closed the Kanting-Khamdo-Lhasa road with landslides, isolating the Chinese garrison at Lhasa.) Familiar since childhood with guns, animated by religious conviction, organized into kinship units, the Tibetans of Kham and Ando provinces summoned up as well "their fearless fighting qualities, their knowledge of mountain warfare, and their implacable hatred of the Chinese."[16] They were used to a spartan life and had no real supply problems, living on mare's milk and hiding from Chinese aircraft in caves. For allies, they had their excellent horses and fierce mastiffs. The guerrillas found a sanctuary in the Tibetan-speaking border districts of Nepal (which the Chinese sometimes violated). In Katmandu the NVDA had contact with the CIA and Chiang Kai-shek's regime, from which some of them received training in communication and parachuting. By 1957 perhaps eighty thousand guerrillas were in the field; in the previous year Khamba bands had wiped out Chinese garrisons in Khamdo, Litang, and elsewhere.

The standard formula for counterinsurgency required the Chinese to have 800,000 troops in Tibet. But in fact they seem only to have between two and three hundred thousand, "occupied in an all-out war of extermination in East Tibet."[17] Finding the air of Tibet too thin, Chinese soldiers were exhausted after short marches. Tibet did not produce enough food to sustain massive armies, nor did the Chinese like the staple barley and dried meat of the Tibetan diet. With truck convoys taking sixteen days to get from Sinkiang to Lhasa, it was costing the communist regime fifty times as much to feed a Chinese soldier in

Tibet as in Peking. During 1956–1958 alone, forty thousand Chinese died in eastern Tibet. The Khambas rarely took prisoners and often killed their own wounded to prevent them from falling into Chinese hands.

In July 1958 Peking withdrew its invitation to Nehru to visit Tibet, fearing large anti-Chinese demonstrations in Lhasa. On March 18, 1959, Chinese troops tried to kill the Dalai Lama by shelling the Norbulinka Palace, believing him to be inside. The population of Lhasa, swollen with refugees from the east, rose in revolt. The Dalai Lama fled under NVDA protection to their stronghold in Loka province, on the border of Bhutan, and from there decided to go on to India. This escape from Tibet, across some of the most rugged terrain on earth, with 200,000 Chinese troops in the country (between thirty and fifty thousand in Lhasa alone) was a remarkable feat. The Dalai Lama has lived in exile ever since.

China and India. The Dalai Lama's friendly reception in India placed an immediate strain on that country's relations with China. By 1961–1962 the Chinese held the towns, and the NVDA controlled the mountains and the remote valleys; the only reliable link between Lhasa and Peking was by air. The Chinese fought the guerrillas with aircraft, great numbers of troops, and new roads: they built a strategic road from Sinkiang into northern Tibet across Indian territory. These events would soon embroil China in a wider conflict.

Prime Minister Nehru had long pursued good relations with Communist China, even at the cost of lying about what was happening in Tibet and suppressing Lhasa's efforts to communicate with the outside world. He failed to see the strategic implications for India of China's massive occupation of Tibet. Nevertheless, long-standing suspicions between newly independent India and newly Communist China, and also Chou En-lai's deep personal distaste for Nehru, helped make a clash between the two Asian giants inevitable. In 1962, after the Chinese built their new invasion road across territory claimed by India and established military posts in it, Nehru ordered the Indian army to kick them out. The results were a resounding humiliation for the Indian army and for Nehru himself. India turned to the Soviets and the Americans for help and allowed outside assistance for the Tibetans to cross the Indian border.[18]

Meanwhile, the International Commission of Jurists issued a press statement condemning Chinese massacres of Tibetan civilians, forced labor, forced marriages, and the destruction of monasteries, manuscripts, and art works: "It would seem difficult to recall a case in which ruthless suppression of man's essential dignity has been more systematically and efficiently carried out."[19]

Nevertheless, by 1970, the overwhelming power of the Chinese had brought major fighting to an end. The Tibetan economy and ecology had been devastated by the "modernizing reforms" of the Communist occupation, including forced collectivization, compulsory cultivation of wheat, the destruction of the external culture, and an influx of Chinese settlers. "The old Tibet was gone."[20]

Sudan

Since the 1950s Sudan has experienced major guerrilla conflicts. These continue today in a context of a worldwide Islamic upsurge. Muslim northern Sudan, closely identifying itself with the Arab world, is pitted against a black, animist, or Christian southern Sudan. Southerners usually refer to northerners as "Arabs" (approximately half of Sudan's twenty-five million people are Arabic-speaking, and perhaps two-thirds Muslim). A break-up of Sudan along religious and ethnic lines would reverberate mightily throughout sub-Saharan Africa.

With one million square miles, Sudan is the biggest country on the continent, five times the size of Spain, ten times that of Wyoming. Thirteen hundred miles from north to south, Sudan links the Middle East with the heart of Africa. Most of the fighting has taken place in the three southernmost provinces, totalling about 250,000 square miles, the size of Texas or Afghanistan.

Islam did not come to Sudan until a thousand years after that faith had conquered Egypt; Sudan is in more than one way marginal to the Islamic world. Arabs traditionally looked upon black Sudanese as inferiors; for generations, Arab slavers carried on disastrous raids in southern Sudan. In the late nineteenth century, the British contemplated erecting southern Sudan as a sort of Christian barrier against Muslim penetration of central Africa.

The regime of the Mahdi (1881–1898) tried to force Islam on the blacks, and it legalized slavery. Opposition to Anglo-Egyptian efforts to suppress the slave trade had been a major cause of Mahdism.[21] After the final defeat of the Mahdist state, Sudan became an Anglo-Egyptian condominium, although its southern boundaries with Uganda and Ethiopia were not settled until 1913. The predatory, slave-catching Mahdist state, which is some ways resembled that of Khomeini in Iran, has important residues in present-day Sudan: the great-grandson of the Mahdi served as prime minister during 1967–1969 and 1986–1989, and the Mahdist movement possesses a private militia.

The First Sudan War, 1955–1972. As independence approached, an overwhelmingly northern constitutional commission rejected federalism, wishing to make Islam the religion and Arabic the language of the state. In contrast, southerners wanted protection for English and Christianity in their own region. Many southerners, their consciousness long aroused by northern efforts to enslave, Arabize, and Islamicize them, believed that a benevolent British rule was about to be replaced by a malevolent Arab one. Thus rebellion broke out even before independence, which came in 1956. A military regime soon took power in Khartoum and "adopted a policy of unabashed Islamization and Arabization in the South. Protest was met with violent assertions of government authority."[22] The government closed southern missionary schools, abolished the Sunday holiday, and expelled hundreds of Catholic and Protestant missionaries.

Early guerrillas called themselves the Land Freedom Army and also Anya-

Nya ("snake venom"); later, most of these groups gathered together in the Southern Sudan Liberation Movement (SSLM). They built small base camps deep in the forests or in border regions. In the first days of the rebellion, Anya-Nya mistreated civilians, having no doctrine of organizing the civil population to support the guerrillas. Rival guerrilla groups and self-proclaimed "southern governments" sprang up, mainly based on the tribal divisions that have permitted the conquest and exploitation of the southerners for centuries. The period 1955–1963 was mainly one of survival for the guerrillas, due in part to the weaknesses of the Khartoum army, operating in a large area with poor communications (Anya-Nya mined the few roads and bridges, so the northern army became dependent on inadequate air transport). By the end of 1964 Anya-Nya counted perhaps five thousand fighters, only a tenth of whom possessed firearms.[23] After 1965, the guerrillas were able to get some good weapons from outside Sudan or from defeated rebels from Zaire. By the end of 1968 the guerrillas numbered perhaps ten thousand; equipment, discipline, organization, and coordination remained poor.

In May 1969, Colonel Gafaar Numeiry, commander of the Khartoum garrison, came to power in a coup d'état. Declaring that a military solution to the rebellion in the south was impossible, he promised regional autonomy and better treatment of civilians by the army. At the same time Numeiry built up his armed forces (to thirty-six thousand), receiving Soviet instructors and arms, and the fighting went on.

Before 1949, there were no secondary schools in the south. The consequent absence of a large educated southern class meant a lack of good political leadership and of effective spokesmen to arouse interest abroad. Thus, when the guerrillas appealed to the UN and to the Organization of African Unity to investigate government atrocities, they received no response. (The United States during the 1960s was of course increasingly enmeshed in Viet Nam.) But the guerrilla movement benefitted from the eventual emergence of Joseph Lagu. Born in Equatoria Province in 1931, of the Madi tribe, son of an Anglican mission teacher, Lagu received an army commission in 1960. Three years later he joined Anya-Nya and was made a colonel. By 1971, thanks in part to his ability to procure arms from Israel, Lagu had imposed his leadership over almost all of the southern fighting groups, which may have enrolled twenty-five thousand men.

But the principal factor in favor of the guerrillas was the weakness of the government army. This force had little or no counterinsurgency training; on the contrary, Soviet instructors inculcated the doctrine of the Big War. Its numbers were always too small (never more than forty thousand) to control a huge territory with primitive communications. Northern soldiers look upon assignment to duty in the south as punishment. Despite Soviet help, air power remained very weak. Most black Sudanese were hostile to the central government, an attitude reinforced as government military operations burned missions, schools, clinics, even whole villages.

Foreign governments interested themselves in the long struggle. Khartoum received help at various times not only from the USSR but from Iran, China, and Libya (a Libyan pilot flying a government MIG-23 was taken alive by guerrillas in December 1988). The Israelis helped the guerrillas in both conflicts and trained some of them in Uganda.[24] Ethiopia also aided the guerrillas, because Khartoum was assisting Eritrean rebels. During the second war the nucleus of the guerrilla forces received training, arms, and sanctuary in Ethiopia.

In March 1972, a ceasefire came into effect, mainly through the efforts of the World Council of Churches and Emperor Haile Selassie. According to the Addis Ababa Agreement, the Khartoum government promised amnesty, self-government for the black provinces, equality of all religions, recognition of English as a major language in the south, and incorporation of thousands of guerrillas with their present rank into the national army. Joseph Lagu received command of all Sudanese armed forces in the southern provinces.

The Conflict Renewed, 1983. The Addis Ababa agreement was not an end to the conflict but only a truce. Small groups of bandits and anti-Khartoum guerrillas had been operating in the south in the early 1980s. The government made no distinction between these bands and loyal southern army units. Indeed, distrusting all southern regular forces, it began to try to disarm these and move them into the north. In May 1983 at Bor, the 103d Battalion under Lieutenant Colonel John Garang mutinied and went across the border into Ethiopia. This unit and other groups, usually former Anya-Nya men, composed the nucleus of the Southern People's Liberation Army (SPLA) and the Southern People's Liberation Movement (SPLM), proclaimed in Ethiopia in July 1983. Khartoum then imposed the Islamic penal code on the whole country. The war would almost certainly have recommenced eventually, but "it was Numeiry's unilateral abrogation of the Addis Ababa agreement . . . that led to the resumption of hostilities in 1983 by the leadership of the [SPLM]."[25] The government responded with a conventional military offensive. It captured a dozen towns held by rebels, but this merely forced their defenders back into the impenetrable forests. Khartoum ignored any possibility of attacking the insurgents politically.

Government units suffered many casualties, which was especially important since now most of the fighting was being done by troops from the north; Khartoum was not accustomed to so many northern casualties. The government therefore resorted to the formation of local militias, which had first been used in the mid-1960s to fight the Anya-Nya. Khartoum needed these militias because its army was too small and conscription would have been unacceptable in the north. Some militia groups were very distracting to SPLA units.

The early tactics of the SPLA were to attack small police and army outposts while consolidating its hold in south-central Sudan and working out supply lines from Ethiopia. Civilian sympathy came to SPLA in response to the bad behavior of government troops. SPLA leaders proved immune to bribes, and their military successes humiliated the regime (Numeiry was ousted in a coup in 1985). By 1989 SPLA had moved to conventional war, holding three-fourths of the territory of the south including the three provincial capitals, plus much of the Ethiopian border. (In contrast, the old Anya-Nya had never held an important town.)

By 1991 the rebels were besieging the main government garrison at Juba, which had to be supplied, very expensively, by air. But in that same year a split, partly tribal-based, developed inside the SPLM, when those desiring an independent south broke away from the leadership of John Garang, who advocated not secession but only southern rights.[26] At the same time the fall of the Mengistu dictatorship in Ethiopia ended the SPLA sanctuary there, a major blow. In these circumstances Khartoum planned a final offensive, fueled by Chinese arms and Iranian gold. Proclaiming jihad against the southern rebels, the government drove 400,000 southern refugees out of Khartoum into the desert.[27] The offensive began in March 1992, the rebels retreating in the face of overwhelming government power; it ended in July with the capture of the key town of Torit, although fierce guerrilla fighting continued.

In February 1993, John Paul II, in Khartoum, in the presence of the dictator General Omar Al-Bashir, deplored forced Islamization. The judiciary, the civil service, and the teaching profession had been purged of non-Muslims; according to the human rights group Africa Watch slavery had reappeared in Sudan, and U.S. Secretary of State Warren Christopher declared Sudan to be one of the states sponsoring international terrorism.

The black Africans of southern Sudan had many historical and contemporary grievances against the Khartoum government. Their rebellion, over a vast area of very difficult terrain, received assistance from foreign sources. The inadequate material resources of the Khartoum government meant it would have been hard pressed to cope with such a development in the best of circumstances, but the outrages against civilians committed by its troops in the southern areas undermined its ability to play on traditional tribal rivalries and guaranteed that the war would be protracted and bitter. The war helped produce one of the worst famines in African history. By the mid-1990s the conflict had cost at least one million lives and generated another million and a half refugees.

NOTES

1. Paul-Marie de la Gorce, *The French Army: A Military-Political History* (New York: George Braziller, 1963), 447.

2. Roy Pateman, "The Eritrean War," *Armed Forces and Society* 17 (Fall 1990): 94.

3. ELF, the parent Eritrean nationalist group, found itself pushed by 1981 into the Sudan, where it disintegrated amid internal squabbling.

4. Pateman, "Eritrean War," 89.

5. Ibid., 91–92.

6. In 1992 the OIC included forty-seven Asian and African states plus the Palestine Liberation Organization.

7. *Far East Economic Review*, February 18, 1988, 30.

8. Even an ability to do so would by no means guarantee victory, as the Huks discovered in the 1940s.

9. John G. Taylor, *Indonesia's Forgotten War: The Hidden History of East Timor* (London: Zed, 1991), 83.

10. *Far Eastern Economic Review*, April 10, 1986.

11. Taylor, *Indonesia's Forgotten War*, 185.

12. H. E. Richardson, *A Short History of Tibet* (New York: E. P. Dutton, 1962), chap. 1.

13. Melvin C. Goldstein, *A History of Modern Tibet 1913–1951* (Berkeley: University of California, 1989), 44.

14. B. N. Mullik, *My Years with Nehru: The Chinese Betrayal* (Bombay: Allied Publishers, 1971), 79–80.

15. Michel Peissel, *The Secret War in Tibet* (Boston: Little, Brown, 1973), 4.

16. George Patterson, *Requiem for Tibet* (London: Aurum, 1990), 150.

17. George Patterson, *Tibet in Revolt* (London: Faber and Faber, 1960), 152.

18. See Neville Maxwell, *India's China War* (New York: Anchor, 1972); and Sir Michael Carver, *War since 1945* (New York: G. P. Putnam's Sons, 1981), chap. 11.

19. International Commission of Jurists, *The Question of Tibet and the Rule of Law* (Geneva: 1959), 59.

20. Patterson, *Requiem*, 149.

21. P. M. Holt, *The Mahdist State in Sudan* (Oxford, UK: Oxford University, 1958), 24, 34, 117; and Gerard Prunier, "Le Sud-Sudain depuis l'indépendance (1956–1989)," in Marc Laverge, ed., *Soudan Contemporain* (Paris: Karthala, 1989), 383.

22. M. W. Daly, "Broken Bridges and Empty Basket: The Political and Economic Consequences of the Sudanese Civil War," in M. W. Daly and A. A. Sikainga, eds., *Civil War in the Sudan* (New York: British Academic Press, 1993), 14.

23. Edgar O'Ballance, *The Secret War in the Sudan* (Hamden, CT: Archon, 1977), 79.

24. Ibid., chap. 10.

25. Francis Mading Deng, "War of Visions for the Middle East," *Middle East Journal*, vol. 44 (August 1990), 596. Catherine Miller has written: "Au Sud, la politique d'arabisation et d'islamisation forcée accompagnant la domination politique et économique du Nord provoqua la guerre civile et l'éclatement de la société sudiste" ("In the South, the policy of forced Arabization and Islamicization accompanying the political and economic domination of the North provoked civil war and the explosion of southern society."); Laverge, *Soudan Contemporain*, 106.

26. See M. Khalid, ed., *John Garang Speaks* (London: KPI, 1987).

27. *New York Times*, February 22, 1992, and June 3, 1992.

Section VII: Toward a Summing-Up

At this point, having completed an analytical survey of forty guerrilla conflicts on five continents, it is time to ask what general principles or conclusions suggest themselves. Chapter 21 offers a comparison of the "styles" of counterinsurgency of four major powers. Chapter 22 then outlines a general approach to effective counterinsurgency. Such an approach needs to combine (1) military tactics appropriate to the geography of the region with (2) a realistic appreciation of the political factors that generate and sustain a particular guerrilla insurgency.

21
Styles of Counterinsurgency Compared

Many of the guerrilla conflicts analyzed in this volume, including some of the most spectacular, have involved the French, British, Americans, and the Russians/Soviets. The following is a brief comparative overview of the general approach, or "style," of counterguerrilla warfare each of those societies have displayed.

THE BRITISH

The British developed their counterinsurgency techniques mainly during the six or seven decades preceding the outbreak of World War II. Those techniques reflect three characteristics of the British Empire: first, its vast extent included peoples of many different races and religions, elements of which—from time to time, for diverse reasons, and in myriad circumstances—rose in armed rebellion against British control; second, the imperial power did not maintain a large standing military force; and third, Britain was in those decades transforming itself into a democratic polity.

The necessity to confront faraway rebellions with quite limited numbers of British troops suggested a policy of relying as little as possible on conventional military force. It was also clearly desirable to recruit soldiers from among the local populations, a practice that usually provided useful intelligence about the nature of the particular rebellion. In addition, British authorities were often ready to consider that a given rebellion might derive at least in part from a legitimate grievance that they should mitigate to the degree possible.[1]

As a consequence of these influences, the British style of counterinsurgency came to consist of a varying mix of the following principles. First, employ the minimum possible amount of conventional military force, and in a highly selective manner (as contrasted to a French tendency to resort rather quickly to general punishment and intimidation, and to the American overemphasis in Viet Nam on indiscriminate, tremendously destructive firepower). Second, emphasize the role in counterinsurgency of police and administrative measures. Third, foster the closest cooperation among the military, police, and civil government, especially for gathering and sharing intelligence. Fourth, identify and remove or decrease, where possible, political or socioeconomic irritants. Fifth, provide effective security for civilians, regrouping exposed settlements into more easily defensible areas. Sixth, harass guerrilla base areas with small, highly trained units. Last, place special emphasis on denying the guerrillas a reliable supply of food (a technique that received special emphasis in the Malayan campaign).[2]

These principles reached their highest point of development after the Second World War, so that the Malayan conflict has become a textbook example of British counterinsurgency style. One ought nevertheless to keep in mind certain peculiarities of that struggle which limit the wholesale applicability of its lessons to other conflicts. Among the most outstanding of those peculiarities was British awareness that retention of Malaya was neither strategically nor psychologically vital to the survival of the British state: the authorities could move forward rather quickly toward granting independence. Another was the ease with which the British, because of Malaya's geography, were able to isolate the insurgents from outside assistance.

THE FRENCH

In the Revolutionary and Napoleonic periods, France confronted two major guerrilla crises, one in its own Atlantic provinces, the other in Spain. The French provoked both uprisings by outraging the religious sensibilities of generally law-abiding peasants and prolonged them by the unbridled violence of their troops against civilians.

The Revolutionary government at first failed to take the Vendean rebellion with sufficient seriousness; later, it unleashed a campaign of extermination akin to that of the Soviets in Afghanistan. Even though foreign assistance failed to reach the Vendée, and even though the Paris regime eventually employed overwhelming numbers of troops, the insurgents were still able to extract serious concessions from the government in return for laying down their arms, and they took vengeance on the regime at the time of Waterloo.

In contrast to the Vendée, the French were unable to isolate the Spanish rebels from foreign aid; quite the contrary, the country became a testing ground for the future Duke of Wellington and a bleeding gash in the body of the Imperial army. In addition, the French neither sent in enough troops to achieve even superficial pacification, nor properly coordinated the operations of the forces they had, nor deployed those forces in correct counterinsurgency tactics. Despite these key differences, there were several glaring similarities between the French campaigns in Spain and the Vendée, including a marked tendency to underestimate the enemy's capabilities and the wanton and ultimately very expensive mistreatment of the civil population.

In the nineteenth century, French colonial warfare produced three major figures in the field of counterinsurgency. They were Robert-Thomas Bugeaud (1784–1849), Joseph Gallieni (1849–1916), and Louis Lyautey (1854–1934). Bugeaud, a veteran of Napoleonic Spain, received appointment as governor-general and commander in chief in Algeria in 1840. Finding the French forces there demoralized and doing poorly against Muslim rebels, Bugeaud restored his army's offensive spirit, but he also followed a policy of punishing civilians for activities of the guerrillas. His men raped at will, burned fields, destroyed orchards, and took the lives of hundreds of unarmed civilians, an "orgy of brutality and excess" that undermined the discipline of the troops and offended public opinion in France.[3]

Joseph Gallieni is associated with the famous analogy of the "oil stain," whereby French control of a restive colony would spread slowly outward from strong bases. In practice, this meant that military occupation would be followed by civil administration, aiming at the establishment of peace, justice, and prosperity, and thus attracting native support. Gallieni worked out his ideas with much success in Senegal, Tonkin, and Madagascar. He then went on to climax his already distinguished career by serving as military governor of Paris and becoming the key figure in the crucial French victory on the Marne in 1914.

Louis Lyautey, conqueror and administrator of Morocco, published very enlightened articles on colonial conquest and administration. He declared that the French empire in Africa must respect local customs and especially the Muslim religion, while at the same time liberating the native peoples from inter-ethnic violence and from oppression and extortion by traditional rulers. Lyautey was, in short, the evangel of *la mission civilisatrice*. In time, however, Lyautey showed that, rhetoric aside, he was little different from other French commanders, responding to rebellion with brutality: "If [his soldiers] could not punish the guilty, they would punish whom they could."[4]

It is, of course, the French effort in Viet Nam that ranks as one of the classic examples of an inappropriate and therefore unsuccessful approach to counterinsurgency. True enough, the French confronted a massive problem of a type that afflicted neither the Americans in the first Philippine war nor the British in Malaya: the presence over the border of Communist China, willing and able to extend significant help to the Viet Minh guerrillas. But the Chinese presence did not begin to affect the war until 1949, when the fighting had been going on for almost three years. In any case, the problem of Chinese supplies was magnified into needlessly damaging proportions precisely because of French policies: they neither committed their own troops in numbers sufficient to control the frontier nor raised and equipped a Vietnamese force that could do the job for them. In addition to these fundamental failures, two other venerable French counterinsurgency tactics, notable in the Vendée and in Spain, made their contribution to the Viet Minh victory. These were punishing the civilians, as in the scandalous bombardment of defenseless Haiphong, and underestimating the enemy, which produced the defeat at Dien Bien Phu.

Hard on the heels of the debacle in Indochina came the conflict in Algeria. There, in contrast to Viet Nam, the French deployed an abundance of manpower, interdicted almost all outside aid to the rebels, and undertook a sustained program of winning popular support among the Arab majority, which achieved some significant success. As a result, the French defeated the guerrillas on every front, the eventual political outcome notwithstanding. In these respects at least, the French campaign in Algeria provides a model, like the British effort in Malaya, for the successful suppression of guerrilla insurgency.

THE AMERICANS

Americans showed that they could play the role of guerrillas effectively during their own Revolutionary War and War of Secession. Their record as counterinsurgents is more ambiguous. The principal insurgencies in foreign parts against which Americans have contended include the post-1898 Philippine rising under Aguinaldo, the Greek Civil War and the Huk rebellion after World War II, and the Viet Nam conflict.

The campaign against Aguinaldo ultimately met complete success. The Americans easily cut the guerrillas off from outside aid. They paid close attention to separating the guerrillas from the civilian population. Relying mainly on small-unit infantry tactics, they employed little heavy weaponry. And they fought the guerrillas with the weapons of political and social reform, effecting impressive improvements in basic sanitation, health care, and education, making credible promises of self-government and eventual independence. The defeat of the Aguinaldo insurgency is the American version of the British victory in Malaya.

In both the Greek and Huk conflicts after World War II, American efforts were largely indirect, but nevertheless (or perhaps "and therefore") crowned with success. The Americans sent no combat units, only advisers. They vigorously pressed for military and social reforms and supported effective leaders (especially Magsaysay). They provided timely economic assistance that enabled the allied governments to wage counterinsurgency without disrupting their national economies. Of at least equal importance, from the beginning of the Philippine conflict, and toward the end of the Greek war, the allies of the Americans were able to isolate the insurgents from outside aid.

In Viet Nam, the United States turned away from the successful Greek and Philippine models, Americanizing the struggle against Hanoi and the Viet Cong to an extreme degree. By the time the Kennedy and Johnson administrations committed the United States to massive intervention in South Viet Nam, the Americans' concepts of conflict had become almost totally dominated by their experiences in World War II: the successful pursuit of total victory through the unprecedentedly massive employment of power. Both strategically and psychologically, this American approach to war was not only inappropriate but diametrically opposite to sound counterinsurgency doctrine. Thus, with the notable and neglected exception of the Marines in the northernmost provinces of South Viet Nam, the Americans insisted on fighting a conventional war, relying on massively destructive firepower ("spend shells, not men") that afflicted friend as well as foe, and defining victory in terms of attrition of the enemy rather than security of the civilians.[5] They failed to isolate the theatre of combat, so that great quantities of enemy troops and supplies were constantly rolling into South Viet Nam; this last was a failure, of course, not of the military commanders on the scene but of the politicians and pundits in Washington. This combination of unnecessarily aggressive tactics with unnecessarily passive strategy has few if any precedents in the history of warfare. Yet even while laboring under these grim, self-inflicted adversities, the Americans broke the back of the guerrilla insurgency in South Viet Nam. That is why the final conquest of that country required a full-scale conventional invasion by Hanoi's army, at the time one of the largest and best-equipped forces on the planet.

THE RUSSIANS/SOVIETS

Undoubtedly Afghanistan is the Russian/Soviet experience in counterinsurgency most widely known in the West. But the Russians have a long history of such conflicts, going back far before the Bolshevik Revolution. In the nineteenth century, for example, the czarist empire was busy suppressing guerrilla uprisings in its newly conquered territories in the Caucasus and Central Asia. In these lands, the basic Russian formula for defeating guerrillas included: isolating the area of conflict from outside interference; establishing firm control of the cities or major towns first and extending control out from these; constructing successive lines of forts by which the enemy was pushed into an ever more constricted area; slashing the taproots of guerrilla resistance through the destruction of settlements, livestock, crops, and orchards; and deploying numbers of troops in the affected areas sufficient to carry out these tasks simultaneously and effectively.

The successor Soviet regime also gained extensive experience in combatting insurgencies, most notably in Daghestan, Western Siberia, the Caucasus, Central Asia, the Ukraine (post-1918 and post-1944) and Lithuania. Many of these insurgencies flowed from popular hostility to the Kremlin's policies of agricultural collectivization and religious persecution. In the first decade or so after the October Revolution, Soviet counterinsurgency emphasized the assassination of the insurgent leadership, the concept of collective guilt (which permitted the massacres of local civilians and the taking of heads of families as hostages, to discourage further resistance), and large-scale permanent deportation. The suppression of insurgency in the Ukraine after 1918 resulted in the deaths of 200,000 peasants and the deportation of 100,000 families.

Writing in the 1920s, Mikhail Tukhachevsky (1893–1937), often called the father of Soviet counterinsurgency, stressed the need for antiguerrilla forces to show respect for local cultures, recruit former guerrillas, establish a unified political-military command, and proclaim opportune amnesties. Ideology nevertheless required him to emphasize that all serious anti-Bolshevik uprisings must have their origins in the machinations of foreign agents and ''kulaks'' (rich peasants), and he endorsed the tried-and-true methods of collective guilt and deportation. (Tukhachevsky died in Stalin's purges.)

After World War II the Kremlin faced guerrilla insurgencies in Lithuania and the Ukraine. In neither case did the guerrillas have a sanctuary. On the contrary, closed off from and forgotten by the outside world, both were inundated not only by Red Army troops but by swarms of the dread political police, successors to Lenin's Cheka. As many as 350,000 Lithuanians may have suffered deportation between 1944 and 1952.[6]

A summary of the Soviet style of counterinsurgency up to 1979 would therefore include closing off the rebellious area, deploying an abundance of troops and secret police, and unleashing mass terror against civilians. In Afghanistan, the Soviets certainly turned their awesome power upon the civilian population, but they chose to deploy troops whose numbers were utterly insufficient to deal with such a determined and popular national uprising. Consequently, they were unable to seal off Afghanistan from the outside world—a fatal failure, because once the Afghans were able to obtain sophisticated weapons, the Soviets had neither the requisite numerical nor technical superiority to defeat or even contain the insurgents.

NOTES

1. John Pimlott, ''The British Experience,'' in Ian F. W. Beckett, ed., *The Roots of Counter-Insurgency: Armies and Guerrilla Warfare 1900–1945* (London: Blanford, 1988).

2. See the good discussion of these points in Thomas R. Mockaitis, *British Counterinsurgency 1919–1960* (New York: St. Martin's, 1990).

3. Douglas Porch, ''Bugeaud, Gallieni, Lyautey: The Development of French Colonial Warfare,'' in Peter Paret, ed., *Makers of Modern Strategy: From Machiavelli to the Nuclear Age* (Princeton, NJ: Princeton University, 1986), 381.

4. Porch, ''Bugeaud, Gallieni, Lyautey,'' 393.

5. Andrew F. Krepinevich, *The Army and Viet Nam* (Baltimore: Johns Hopkins, 1986).

6. Ian F. W. Beckett, ''The Soviet Experience,'' in Beckett, ed., *Roots of Counter-Insurgency.*

22
Reflections: Combatting Guerrillas

A skillfully led guerrilla campaign is a mortal challenge for any government. Consider the frustrations and even debacles that so many powerful countries encountered when they entered the marshes of counterinsurgency. The British in the Carolinas, the Bonapartists in Spain, the Japanese in China, the Germans in Yugoslavia, the French and then the Americans in Viet Nam, the Soviets in Afghanistan, the Vietnamese in Cambodia—governments of every political complexion and economic system have found counterinsurgency an exceedingly difficult undertaking.

On the other hand, there are sufficient examples of successful counterinsurgency to demonstrate that guerrilla warfare is not magical. The supposedly invincible Maoist model especially needs a skeptical reexamination in light of its resounding failures in Malaya, the Philippines, Peru, El Salvador, and elsewhere. Nor ought we continue to ignore the fact that in the dawn of the twentieth century, in the faraway Philippines, under unpromising circumstances, American forces were notably successful at combatting guerrillas.

One way to develop a model of successful counterinsurgency is to examine and compare instances in which guerrilla warfare failed. There is no foolproof formula to be applied by counterinsurgents, or by guerrillas either; each case requires careful and dispassionate analysis of its peculiar causes and circumstances. But unsurprisingly, certain elements, certain patterns, do appear time and again. Antoine Henri Jomini, a Swiss officer who served with the Napoleonic armies in Spain, reflected on the bitter French experiences there and concluded that victory over the substantial guerrilla movement eluded the French because of their insufficient numbers, inappropriate tactics, and destructive conduct toward civilians.[1] His views about fighting guerrillas with both effective military tactics and a sound political program eventually found resonance in the counterinsurgency doctrine of the U.S. Marines.[2] The following discussion of the elements of a successful counterinsurgency is to a large degree an elaboration of Jomini's views.

To defeat guerrillas, a government needs to present to the population a *peaceful alternative to revolution*. One should never overlook the key insight of Guevara—he himself did so, to his destruction—that one cannot wage insurgency successfully against a government that is democratic or at least wears the trappings of democracy. That is because recruitment to the cause of the guerrillas will be difficult as long as there is a widespread belief that warfare is not the only road to change.[3]

Sufficient numbers are essential. This may seem to be a heroically banal observation, yet in fact the road of guerrilla war is littered with the wreckage of counterinsurgencies that tried to win on the cheap. Many students of the subject have concluded that in order to beat the guerrillas, a government needs a preponderance over them of as much as ten to one. But from the British army in America in 1780 to the Soviet army in Afghanistan in 1980, the actual ratio has often fallen far below this figure; indeed, sometimes it is the guerrillas who have a numerical preponderance, at least in certain areas. The guerrillas may strike where and when they choose, and thus the government or occupying army has to garrison all the important population centers, police the roads between them, protect the railways and bridges and airports, maintain relief forces to rush to any point under attack, and still have a supply of troops actually to go around hunting for guerrillas. All this requires a great commitment of personnel, probably for a protracted period: governments that cannot or will not make such a commitment *should not undertake to wage counterinsurgency*.

Clearly, however, numbers alone are not enough: *rectitude* is required. Government forces must conduct themselves correctly among the civilian population. Severity toward civilians who live in secure areas but continue to assist guerrillas is permissible, indeed advisable. But systematic maltreatment of the civil population per se, especially in uncontrolled areas, not only makes recruits for the guerrillas but dries up essential intelligence sources, and even undermines the discipline and morale of the soldiers themselves. The Vendée, Napoleonic Spain, Magsaysay's Philippines, Batista's Cuba, Afghanistan, and El Salvador all illustrate the centrality of this concept. A government can limit costly abuses of civilians by effective indoctrination of junior officers. An additional method is to deploy troops as much as possible in their native areas. The counterinsurgent command needs to be especially alert to potential problems of this sort when deploying indigenous troops who are members of an ethnic or religious minority.

Correct conduct toward civilians also requires the *avoidance of inappropriate technologies*. Governments train and equip conventional armies to fight other conventional armies, not guerrillas; military promotions, decorations, and reputations derive from the handling of ever larger regular formations, not from beating guerrillas, and certainly not from devoting years of study to the techniques of counterinsurgency. Hence regular armies have employed tactics of encirclement or "sweeps," which guerrillas can evade. Guerrillas are often immune to the power of heavy weapons: tanks, for instance, are not suited to rapid pursuit of small groups in mountains, jungles, and marshes; artillery will be ineffective if the guerrillas "hug" (stay very close to) government installations or troop units. In any case, guerrillas can always simply decline to fight in unfavorable circumstances. At the same time, lavish use of destructive modern firepower can alienate the civil population and make recruits for the insurgents. No Americans would wish to see their homes or neighborhoods liberated from enemy control in the manner that was employed by U.S. forces in Viet Nam, or in Korea. Effective counterinsurgency *does not mean the killing of guerrillas*, it means *the security of the civil population*.

From the Swamp Fox to the mujahideen, nothing is clearer than that the government must endeavor to *interdict outside assistance* to the guerrillas. It must also *close off any guerrilla sanctuary*, or at least restrict access to it. Attaining the latter goal requires a combination of diplomatic pressure on the country providing or permitting sanctuary, and employment of sufficient troops in the border areas. The French effectively shut down the Tunisian sanctuary of the Algerian guerrillas with their Morice Line. Conversely, Laos was the key to the fall of South Viet Nam, and the bitter Soviet experience in Afghanistan is only the latest example of the consequences of the failure of counterinsurgent forces to control borders.

A good intelligence system is as essential to the counterinsurgency as it is to the guerrillas. Rectitude toward the civilian population and recruitment of troops, militia, and police from the local population are fundamental to a good intelligence program. Guerrillas who have been captured or who have accepted amnesty can be a gold mine of valuable information: hence the guerrillas need to understand that falling into the hands of government forces will not be equivalent to or worse than death. Coordination of the efforts of various intelligence-gathering groups is essential. Also, counterinsurgents need always to be sensitive to the fact that civilians may be unsympathetic to the guerrillas and yet fearful of reprisals if they cooperate with the authorities. Hence soldiers and police must set up procedures whereby civilians can furnish information against the guerrillas in safety. One such method is for the authorities to provide each family in a given neighborhood with sheets of paper and an envelope, and then carry into each house a box into which all such papers must be deposited. Above all, counterinsurgent forces must never—but *never*—withdraw from a district after they have invited or allowed their civilian sympathizers to reveal themselves.

One of the great lessons of the Malaya conflict is the value of *unity of direction*. In imitation of the wartime Churchill cabinet, the control of the entire British effort in Malaya—military, police, intelligence, and administration—

rested in the hands of one person, assisted by a very small group of advisers. The Americans in Viet Nam did not follow this example, to their cost: for highly debatable political reasons, the American and South Vietnamese efforts were kept separate, but the Americans failed to coordinate effectively even those activities directly under their control.

"The guerrilla fighter must be separated from the people. The guerrilla must be fought with his own tactics. These are the essence of anti-guerrilla strategy."[4] As Clausewitz observed, everything in war is simple, but even the simplest thing is very difficult. One can pursue the *separation of the guerrillas from the civil population* in several ways. One is relocation, concentrating the previously dispersed population into areas that are relatively easy to protect. Such relocation of population can be a very effective tool, provided it is done well. If it is done hastily, forcibly, on the cheap, without regard for the feelings and basic needs of the civilians, relocation can become a disaster and a rich source of recruits for the guerrillas. Relocation worked out very well in Malaya, and fairly well in the Philippines (1901–1902), but it was generally unsuccessful in French Algeria and in South Viet Nam.

Another strategy for separating guerrillas and civilians is the clear-and-hold method. In relocation, one moves the civilians; in clear-and-hold, one moves the guerrillas. In the ideal clear-and-hold scenario, the government forces solidify their control of their own base areas (usually the urban centers) and move outward, very slowly and methodically, into guerrilla-dominated sections of the countryside. They occupy a new district or village in great strength, making it clear that they can provide security for civilians and that they will under no circumstances abandon that place to the guerrillas. The patient application of basic police methods begins to uproot the all-important guerrilla infrastructure— the underground organization that supplies the insurgents with intelligence, food, and recruits. A volunteer militia is formed that, once the regular army has moved on, can resist guerrilla reentrance until government forces come to the rescue. For such a militia to be viable, the civilians need to believe that the government is preferable to the guerrillas, or—just as useful—that it is going to win. The most effective local militias will often be found in areas inhabited by religious or ethnic minorities who do not identify with the group or groups predominant among the guerrillas. Once a systematic attack on the guerrilla infrastructure is well under way and a militia has been put in place, the troops can move out into the next area to be cleared.

Finally, small, well-trained *hunter groups* can enter the more remote territories of the guerrillas. Their main aim is not to kill guerrillas but to harass them and, above all, to find and destroy their supply dumps and food-raising areas. Such efforts, when combined with effective policies of supervising the civil population and interrupting outside aid, will create a true crisis of supply for the guerrillas.

In summary, successful counterinsurgency requires superior numbers of troops practicing appropriate tactics to isolate the guerrillas and conciliate the civilians. The main objective is not to kill guerrillas but to increase security. Even with such a program, the elimination of a well-led guerrilla movement might take years. Such a long-term engagement, with its unwelcome financial burdens, inevitable military setbacks, and undeniable moral ambiguities, in a faraway place and under the eyes of sensationalist media, may be exceedingly stressful to any democratic polity, and especially to the United States.

NOTES

1. Antoine Henri Jomini, *The Art of War*, trans. G. Mendell and W. Craighill (Westport, CT: Greenwood, 1971 [orig. 1862]), 26–31 and passim.

2. "The occupying force must be strong enough to hold all the strategical points of the country, protect its communications, and at the same time furnish an operating force sufficient to overcome the opposition wherever it appears. . . . While curbing the passions of the people, courtesy, friendliness, justice, and firmness should be exhibited." U.S. Marine Corps, *Small Wars Manual* (Washington, DC: Government Printing Office, 1940), section 1–9d.

3. Ernesto Guevara, *Guerrilla Warfare* (New York: Vintage, 1961).

4. General Abdul H. Nasution, *Fundamentals of Guerrilla Warfare* (New York: Praeger, 1965 [orig. 1953]), 64.

PART II
Biographical Profiles

The following section offers brief sketches of persons whose activities, either as guerrilla chieftains, military commanders, government officials, party leaders, theorists, or instructors (or in any combination of these roles), exerted notable influence or illustrate important points in the conflicts discussed in preceding chapters.

ABBAS, FERHAT (1899–1985). Algerian independence leader. He received a French education, including a degree from the University of Algiers, and served two separate enlistments in the French army. Abbas was originally an advocate of the permanent union of France and Algeria and the assimilation of Algerian Muslims into French society. He grew increasingly disillusioned, however, with the lack of response on the part of the French authorities to petitions and requests for greater equality for Algerian Muslims. In 1956 he went to Cairo and joined the Algerian FLN (National Liberation Front). Soon thereafter he was chosen first president of the revolutionary Provisional Government of the Algerian Republic. The struggle for independence produced deep fissures within the ranks of Algerian Muslims and even in the FLN; after the peace settlement with France, the FLN expelled Abbas from its ranks (1963) and placed him under house arrest (1964). Abbas wrote several books, including *La Nuit coloniale* (1962).

ABRAHMS, CREIGHTON WILLIAMS, JR. (1914–1974). American military commander. Abrahms graduated from West Point in 1936 and was a tank commander in World War II, playing a major role in the relief of Bastogne during the Battle of the Bulge (1944). In 1967 President Johnson appointed him to be deputy commander in Viet Nam under William Westmoreland, with special responsibility for upgrading the equipment and training of the South Vietnamese army (ARVN). Abrahms succeeded Westmoreland as American commander in Viet Nam, holding that post from 1968 to 1972; during that time the war in Viet Nam became much more a conventional than a guerrilla conflict. Abrahms finished his career as Army Chief of Staff (1972–1974), dying in office.

AGUINALDO, EMILIO (1869–1964). Philippine guerrilla leader. Of Chinese and Tagalog descent, Aguinaldo was the leader of the Katipunan, the secret Philippine independence society, in Cavite. Having participated in the insurrection against Spanish rule in 1896, he was in exile in Hong Kong when the Spanish-American war broke out; Commodore Dewey brought him back to the Philippines. Proclaiming himself Provisional President of the Philippine Republic in June 1898, he soon led his forces into clashes with American military units around Manila and later embarked upon guerrilla resistance. Captured in March 1901, he took an oath of allegiance to the United States and accepted a pension from the U.S. government. In 1935 he ran unsuccessfully for president of the Philippine Commonwealth against Manuel Quezon. Used as a figurehead by the Japanese occupation authorities, he was imprisoned briefly in 1945. He published *A Second Look at America* (1957).

AMIN, HAFIZULLAH (1929–1979). Afghan communist leader. The son of a government employee, Amin graduated from Kabul university; he also took a master's degree in education at Teachers College, Columbia University, but failed to obtain a Ph.D. there. He became foreign minister and the real power in the PDPA regime after the coup of 1978 and then deposed President Taraki to take supreme power. It appears that embarrassment over the bloodthirstiness and incompetence of the Amin regime was one of the principal motives for the Soviet invasion of Afghanistan in 1979. Amin died in a shoot-out with Soviet paratroopers in the presidential palace.

AQUINO, CORAZON (b. 1933). President of the Philippines. A graduate of St. Vincent College in New York City, she married the politically prominent Benigno Aquino in 1955. After her husband's assassination, she became the presidential candidate of a broad coalition for the 1986 election. The Manila government declared President Marcos the victor, but Aquino supporters claimed fraud and took to the streets. Opposed by key units of the Philippine armed forces and the Reagan White House, Marcos left the country and Mrs. Aquino assumed the presidency. Her administration (1986–1992) had to confront the continuing rebellion of the communist-led New People's Army, outbreaks of Moro violence on Mindanao (which she sought to end through negotiation), and several coup attempts by elements of the armed forces. She successfully supported the candidacy of her secretary of defense, Fidel Ramos, in the presidential election of 1992.

BAO DAI [NGUYEN VINH THUY] (b. 1913). Vietnamese monarch. A son of Emperor Khai Dinh, he was educated in France and acceded to the throne in 1926. His plans for the modernization of Vietnamese society were rebuffed by the French. After the seizure of Hanoi by the Viet Minh in 1945, Bao Dai fled to Hong Kong. Seeking a political counter-figure to Ho Chi Minh, the French government in 1949 recognized Bao Dai as leader of an independent state of Viet Nam. He appointed Ngo Dinh Diem as prime minister in 1954. After the October 1955 referendum that ended the monarchy and established a republic, Bao Dai went into exile in France.

BATISTA Y ZALDIVAR, FULGENCIO (1901–1973). Cuban president and dictator. The son of poor farmers, of mixed blood, Batista joined the army in 1921. In the turmoil of the revolution of 1933 and through his influence in the army, Batista wielded power behind the scenes. Elected president of the republic in 1940, Batista was a friend to organized labor and greatly expanded education and public works. Widespread dissatisfaction in Cuba with corrupt politicians allowed Batista to return to power in 1952 in a military coup. After an initial period of popularity, Batista's second regime became notable for corruption and repression. When it became clear to him that his army was totally unprepared to cope with Castro's insurgency, Batista fled the country, going first to the Dominican Republic, then Portugal, and finally to Spain, where he died. His interesting analysis of the Castro insurgency, *Cuba Betrayed*, emphasizes how little actual fighting took place during that struggle and how easily key commanders of his army succumbed to bribery by Castro.

BAYO, ALBERTO (1892–1967). The man who trained Fidel Castro in the rudiments of guerrilla warfare, Bayo was born in the Cuban province of Camagüey. The son of a Spanish army officer, he received much of his early schooling in New Orleans. He enlisted in the Spanish army at age fourteen and later graduated from the Infantry Academy in Madrid. During the 1920s he flew combat aircraft missions against Arab guerrillas in Spanish Morocco; he subsequently served in the Spanish Foreign Legion, where he continued his education in counterguerrilla fighting. In the Spanish Civil War he was an officer in the Republican (loyalist) air force. After the war he returned to Cuba and then went to Mexico, where he participated in unsuccessful conspiracies to remove the Somoza and Trujillo dictatorships. In 1955 he encountered Fidel Castro and his companions and taught them the basics of guerrilla warfare. After Castro came to power, Bayo returned once more to Cuba; he died there, holding the rank of "commandante" in Castro's army. See his *150 Questions for a Guerrilla*.

BONIFACIO, ANDRES (1863–1897). Philippine nationalist leader. Born in Manila, he was the principal founder (1892) of the secret nationalist society called the Katipunan. He instigated the 1896 revolt against Spanish rule at the head of 100,000 Katipunan members. During that struggle Bonifacio became involved in a bitter dispute over authority in the nationalist movement with Emilio Aguinaldo, who had him executed by firing squad in April 1897.

BORGE MARTINEZ, TOMAS (b. 1930). Nicaraguan Sandinista leader. The son of a pharmacist, Borge studied law and became active in communist youth organizations. He was one of the principal founders, with Carlos Fonseca, of the Sandinista National Liberation Front (FSLN) in 1961. After the fall of Somoza Borge became minister of the interior.

BOR-KOMOROWSKI. *See* Komorowski, Tadeusz.

BOTHA, LOUIS (1862–1919). Boer leader. With little previous military experience, he skilfully led the epic siege of British forces in Ladysmith. In 1900 he received command of the army of the Transvaal and led it with distinction in guerrilla action. After the war he advocated cooperation with the British, serving as prime minister of the Transvaal (1907–1910) and then as first prime minister of the Union of South Africa (1910–1919). Botha led the British Imperial forces that conquered German Southwest Africa (later known as Namibia) in World War I.

BRIGGS, HAROLD (1894–1952). British military leader. A lieutenant general of the Indian Army, Briggs also saw service in Burma from 1946 to 1948. After he took command in Malaya in April 1950, he developed a scheme of operations that came to be known as the Briggs Plan. The principal elements of the Plan were: (1) to concentrate on providing security from guerrilla contacts for the civilian population (including, among other things, resettlement of squatters living near the guerrilla-infested jungle); (2) to ensure close coordination of military, police, and administrative functions; and (3) to expel guerrillas permanently from one district after another, proceeding from south to north. When Briggs's appointment expired in December 1951, he was deeply discouraged at what he perceived as a general lack of cooperation, and morale among British and pro-British forces in the peninsula was low. Nevertheless, Briggs had launched the strategy that under his successor would lead to victory.

CABRAL, AMILCAR (1921?–1973). West African independence leader. Born in Portuguese Guinea, Cabral was educated as an agronomist in Lisbon. In 1956 he founded a party to work for independence, proclaiming guerrilla war in 1963. With the help of Soviet weapons and Cuban advisers, he achieved a stalemate against Portuguese counterinsurgency forces. Cabral was assassinated in Conakry. He wrote *Guinea in Revolution*.

CADOUDAL, GEORGES (1771–1804). Breton guerrilla leader. An able commander of Chouan forces, Cadoudal escaped to England in 1801. There, with British financial support, he ran a camp near Southampton for anti-Bonapartist activists and agents. Returning to France, he involved himself in a conspiracy to assassinate Napoleon and was guillotined. The discovery of the Cadoudal plot helped Napoleon transform the Consulate into the Empire.

CALLWELL, CHARLES EDWARD (1859–1928). British military figure. Born in London, he attended the Royal Military Academy. Involved with both artillery and intelligence, he saw action in the Afghan war (1880) and in South Africa (1899–1902). Callwell resigned from the army in 1909 but was recalled to the War Office in 1914. He was made a major general and attained knighthood. He wrote several books on military affairs, most notably the counterinsurgency classic *Small Wars*. In that work he notes that counterguerrilla forces, in order to win, must constantly assume the offensive, but that this required aggressiveness is easily thwarted by the greater mobility of irregular forces. Hence he warns that well-led guerrillas can present a nearly insuperable challenge to even the most powerful states.

CARRIER, JEAN-BAPTISTE (1756–1794). French Revolutionary official. Elected to the national Convention in 1792, he was sent to supervise events in the Vendée after most of the organized fighting had come to an end. There he helped organize a campaign of genocide against the peasantry. His plans included burning down churches, poisoning wells, and spreading infections. He overrode even the rather casual legal proceedings of the revolutionary tribunals and had persons killed on mere suspicion or accusation. To save ammunition and dispose more rapidly of corpses, he invented the *noyades* (drownings), whereby hundred of living persons were tied up together naked and placed in boats, which were then sunk in the Loire River. Carrier also experimented with poison gases, but without much success. Some estimates place the number of his victims in the area of ten thousand. In one of the endless factional struggles in Paris he helped bring down his patron Robespierre and was then himself sent to the guillotine.

CASTRO (RUZ), FIDEL (b. 1926). Communist dictator of Cuba. The son of a landowner and his cook, Castro was educated in Catholic schools and studied law at the University of Havana. In 1953 he and companions unsuccessfully attacked the Moncada army barracks in Santiago. Released from prison in 1955, he went to Mexico where he and a few followers studied guerrilla tactics under Alberto Bayo. The next year they made an armed landing in Oriente Province. Many of the participants were killed or captured, but the remainder retreated into the Sierra Maestra. From this base Castro would during the next two years harass the Batista regime until its fall. Castro appointed himself prime minister in 1959.

Castro succeeded in taking power by force in Cuba because: (1) much of the terrain of Cuba was excellent for sheltering guerrilla operations; (2) the armed forces of the regime were corrupt, badly led, and poorly armed; (3) he promised the Cubans not communism but Western-style democracy; and (4) the Eisenhower administration imposed an arms embargo, which profoundly disheartened the supporters of President Batista (q.v.). The so-called Cuban Revolution was much less a guerrilla victory than the collapse of a regime. Failure to grasp this elemental fact gave rise to the belief that it would be relatively easy to export Castroism to other Latin American states, but all attempts to do this ended in failure.

CASTRO, RAUL (b. 1930). Cuban communist official. While a student at the University of Havana, he joined the communist youth organization. He participated in his brother Fidel's attack on the Moncada barracks, guerrilla training in Mexico, and the landing in Cuba in 1956. After Fidel came to power, Raul became a member of the Politburo of the Cuban Communist Party and Minister of the Armed Forces. He was perhaps the single most influential person in bringing his brother to embrace Marxism-Leninism.

CATHELINEAU, JACQUES (d. 1793). Vendean guerrilla leader. Born in Anjou, Cathelineau became a linen merchant. During the revolt in the Vendée he displayed a natural talent for guerrilla war but died as the result of wounds received at the siege of Nantes.

CAYETANO CARPIO, SALVADOR (1920–1983). Salvadoran communist guerrilla leader. As a youth he was a student for the priesthood. Later he attended the Party School in Moscow and became head of the Salvadoran Communist Party, which he afterward rejected. He was the principal founder of the guerrilla umbrella organization called the Farabundo Marti Popular Liberation Front (1980). After being implicated in the murder of a female guerrilla leader, Cayetano committed suicide in Managua.

CHALLE, MAURICE (b. 1905). French military leader. Born in the Vaucluse, he graduated from St. Cyr in 1927 and went into the air corps. A general in Algeria, he participated in the military-civilian uprising of May 1958 that brought de Gaulle back to power and the Fourth Republic to an end. The Challe Plan for counterinsurgency in 1958–1959 improved on the existing French system, emphasizing strongpoints, patrols, ambushes, and rapid deployment of strike forces once the enemy's location had been spotted. By 1960 the Algerian guerrillas were very close to complete defeat. When, despite the army's success, de Gaulle made it unmistakably clear that he was moving inexorably toward Algerian independence, Challe led another coup in 1961. This one failed, owing mainly to the disunity within the army in Algeria and the fact that de Gaulle was so much more formidable than the politicians of the defunct Fourth Republic had been. General Challe received a prison sentence of fifteen years but was pardoned by de Gaulle.

CHARETTE DE LA CONTRIE, FRANÇOIS-ATHANASE (1763–1796). Vendean guerrilla leader. Trained as a naval officer, Charette became a major figure in the Vendean revolt. He accepted a pardon in February 1795. When the Quiberon landing occurred, Charette again took up the sword of rebellion but was captured and shot.

CHEN PING [ALSO FREQUENTLY CHIN PENG] (b. 1921?). Malayan communist guerrilla leader. Born in Perak, Malaya, Chen became deputy leader of the Malayan Communist Party under Lai Tek. After Lai Tek absconded with the Party funds, Chen became leader in 1948 and proclaimed the Communist Republic of Malaya. After the clear failure of the protracted insurgency, Chen sought safety along the Thai-Malayan border some time around 1955; he and a few followers remained in semi-activity in the area for many years.

CHIANG KAI-SHEK (1887–1975). Chinese military and political leader. Born in Chekiang province, Chiang graduated from a Japanese military academy in 1909 and within a few years had become Sun Yat-sen's military assistant in Canton and commandant of Sun's military academy at Whampoa. In 1926 Chiang led the Northern Expedition from Canton to unify fragmented China. As Chiang's army moved north, many provincial warlords adhered to its standard; by 1928 he had established a national government at Nanking. During the so-called Nanking Decade China made visible progress toward economic development and elementary human rights, especially for women. Simultaneously, Chiang vigorously attacked the communists in several extermination campaigns, the last of which drove them to their desperate Long March. The Chinese Communist Party was saved from destruction, however, by the Japanese invasion of 1937.

During World War II Chiang came to personify to the world the indomitable spirit of embattled China. But inside the country, the Japanese had badly mauled Chiang's armed forces, thereby undermining the prestige and legitimacy of the regime. The unexpectedly abrupt ending of World War II found the Nationalists unprepared to deal with China's profound problems of postwar adjustment. In addition, large-scale warfare between Chiang's Nationalists and Mao's communists soon broke out again. Chiang attempted an immediate takeover of Manchuria, which was far from his base; the effort ended in military disaster. Moreover, as the head of an extremely diverse party and army for twenty years, Chiang had learned to emphasize loyalty over ability in his subordinates. The consequences of this practice during the Civil War with the communists were disastrous: Chiang's generals, often incompetent or worse, used static defense tactics against Mao's fast-moving armies. Mao and his lieutenants knew how to take advantage of all these Nationalist mistakes and weaknesses, so that by 1950 Chiang's regime controlled only the island of Taiwan. Chiang remained president of this remnant republic, which eventually developed into one of the most prosperous states in Asia, until his death.

CHRISTOPHE, HENRI (1767–1820). Haitian revolutionary leader. A freed slave, he served Toussaint L'Ouverture and later commanded under Dessalines, of whose murder he was an instigator. In control of northern Haiti, he waged a long and inconclusive struggle with Haitian mulatto forces and built the impressive citadel at La Ferrière. Faced with revolt, he committed suicide.

CHU TEH (ZHU DE) (1886–1976). Chinese communist military leader. The major architect, after Mao, of the revolution, he was born in Szechwan, graduated from Yunnan Military Academy (1911), and served in the forces of Sun Yat-sen. Going to Europe in 1922, he studied political science at Göttingen University, met Chou En-lai, and secretly joined the Chinese Communist Party. He was one of the few early communists with military training and experience in troop command. In 1926 he attended the University of the Toilers of the East in Moscow. Becoming associated with Mao Tse-tung in 1928, they together constructed the Fourth Red Army. Chu Teh helped build up the famous Kiangsi Soviet and led the Red Army on the Long March (1934–1935). During the second Sino-Japanese War, Chu became commander in chief of all communist armed forces. He perfected the strategy of (1) concentrating on control of the countryside, thereby (2) avoiding long and costly sieges of great cities, and (3) being able to destroy the static, city-anchored forces of the enemy piecemeal. In 1954 he relinquished command of the Red Army and became Deputy Chairman of the Chinese People's Republic.

CHURCHILL, WINSTON (1874–1965). British prime minister. In December 1943, at the height of World War II, Churchill decided, on the basis of information from sources whose political motives were to say the least questionable, to jettison General Mihailovic, the representative of the legitimate Yugoslav government, and throw British support behind the guerrillas led by Tito, in those days a fervent Stalinist and a former loyal supporter of the Hitler-Stalin pact.

CLAUSEWITZ, KARL VON (1780–1831). Prussian military theorist. Of Polish descent, Clausewitz entered the Prussian army at the age of twelve and later attended the Berlin Military Academy under the great Scharnhorst, whose student, protegé, and assistant in later years he became. He saw service with the Prussian army during the French Revolutionary and Napoleonic Wars. Unwilling to accept the Franco-Prussian peace, he served in the Russian army from 1812 to 1814 but returned to Prussia and was present at Waterloo. He served from 1818 to 1830 as superintendent of the Berlin Kriegsakademie, where he had previously delivered a series of lectures on guerrilla war.

His great achievement was to distill the realities of Napoleonic warfare into lessons for the education of the Prussian army. He accomplished this mainly through his great posthumously published work, *On War*, which Bernard Brodie called "not simply the greatest book but the only truly great book on war." It contained little about guerrilla war beyond the section titled "A People In Arms" in Book Six, where two of his main concepts—that "the defensive is the stronger form of war" and that military operations must be congruent with political objectives—find cogent expression. Clausewitz completely ignored the fact of seapower, which of course played so important a role in the Spanish guerrilla struggle against Napoleon, as well as in later insurgencies in Arabia, Malaya, the Philippines, and elsewhere. Certainly he would have amplified and polished his theories over time, but unfortunately he succumbed to the great cholera epidemic that swept over Eastern and Central Europe in 1831.

CLINTON, SIR HENRY (1738?–1795). British military leader. Born in Newfoundland, son of a colonial governor of New York, he served for a while in the New York militia and distinguished himself in the French and Indian War. He succeeded Howe as commander of all British forces in America in 1778. He commanded the successful Charleston invasion of 1780 and then, leaving Cornwallis behind to hold the Carolinas, returned to New York. He later became governor of Gibraltar (1794–1795). His controversial account of the campaigns in America has been published under the title *The American Rebellion*.

CORNWALLIS, CHARLES (1738–1805). British military and political figure. A graduate of Eton, Cornwallis joined the army and saw service in the Seven Years' War. In parliament he opposed those measures that were clearly stirring up discontent in the American colonies. Sent to America in 1776, Cornwallis hoped for reconciliation. He became second-in-command of British forces in the colonies under General Clinton. In 1778 he embarked on his ill-fated Carolina campaign, which called forth the efforts of such great guerrilla chiefs as Francis Marion, the Swamp Fox, and which culminated in the surrender of his army at Yorktown. The British establishment did not hold Cornwallis culpable for this disaster; afterwards he was made governor general of India and viceroy of Ireland.

CRISTIANI BURKHARD, ALFREDO (b. 1947). President of El Salvador. Graduating from Georgetown University in 1968, Cristiani pursued the life of a Salvadoran coffee magnate. He was held hostage by guerrillas in 1980. Chosen head of the ARENA party in 1985, he attained election to the National Assembly in 1988. As the candidate of ARENA in the presidential contest of 1989, during which many foreign observers were present, he defeated his Christian Democrat opponent in the runoff by attracting 54 percent of the vote. His inauguration was the first time in the history of El Salvador that an opposition candidate had taken office after a free election, and also the first time that a civilian had been followed in the presidential office by another civilian. He pursued a course of negotiations with the main guerrilla groups in the country, and in 1992, in the presence of the Secretary-General of the United Nations, signed peace accords with the FSLN.

D'AUBUISSON ARRIETA, ROBERTO (1944–1992). Salvadoran political figure. From a modest family background, D'Aubuisson joined the army as a youth, eventually reaching the rank of major. Dismissed from the army in 1979, he was frequently accused of masterminding the notorious "death squads" that assassinated suspected pro-communists and also of being implicated in the assassination of Archbishop Oscar Romero in 1980. He founded the ARENA

(National Republican Alliance) party in 1981, served as president of the Constituent Assembly from 1982 to 1984, and ran unsuccessfully for president against Napoleon Duarte in 1984. The *Washington Post* called him "the most charismatic politician" in El Salvador.

DEBRAY, REGIS (b. 1940). French theorist of guerrilla war. From an upper-class Parisian background, he briefly taught philosophy. He first visited Cuba in 1961 and became an ardent admirer of Fidel Castro. He was made professor of philosophy at the University of Havana in 1966. Perhaps the best-known of his several books is *Revolution in the Revolution* (1967). In that volume Debray set forth the "foco theory" of guerrilla war, that in Latin America conditions were so volatile that a few armed men, even foreigners, could begin a struggle that would ignite a whole country. In accordance with this unusual view, Debray went to join Guevara in Bolivia, where he was arrested and jailed until 1970. Several persons have since suggested that information Debray gave out at a press conference may have helped the Bolivian army find and kill Guevara. Upon release from prison he went to Chile and eventually back to France. In 1974 he declared the doctrine of the foco fallacious because it had disassociated the military from the political aspects of revolutionary struggle. In 1981 French President Mitterand appointed Debray to the post of special assistant.

DE GAULLE, CHARLES (1890–1970). French general, first president of the Fifth Republic. De Gaulle owed his return to power in 1958 to the army's determination to keep Algeria French. Believing, however, like Charlemagne, that the anvil of France's destiny lay between the Rhine and the Elbe, he rejected as a distraction and a delusion the army's Eurafrican vision of a French Algeria. Thus he eventually granted independence to that country, at the cost of an unsuccessful army rising against his government (ironically, in 1940 de Gaulle himself had mutinously rejected the authority of the Third Republic), the careers of hundreds of French officers, and the lives of tens of thousands of *harkis*, Algerian Moslems who had served the French.

DE LA REY, JACOBUS (1847–1914). Boer military leader. The grandson of an immigrant from Holland, he fought the Bantu and served as a member of the Transvaal parliament. Although he had originally opposed a war with Great Britain, upon the outbreak of the South African conflict he revealed himself to be a talented guerrilla leader. He eventually became commander of all guerrilla operations in western Transvaal. After the war he was a member of first Senate of the Union of South Africa (1910–1914). In the early days of the First World War, he became involved in a plot for a Boer uprising against the British, but before these plans came to fruition he himself was killed in a shootout with police.

DE LATTRE DE TASSIGNY, JEAN (1889–1952). French military leader. Born in the Vendée, he was educated at the Jesuit school at Poitiers and the military academy at St.-Cyr. Arrested by the Vichy regime in 1942, he escaped to London with the help of the RAF in 1943. He took a major part in the liberation of France, leading the capture of Toulon and Marseilles, and was a signer of the German surrender. In December 1950 he received appointment as both high commissioner and commander-in-chief of French Indochina. De Lattre restored French morale there after the shattering defeats along the China border, cancelling plans for an evacuation of French civilians and bringing his own wife to live with him in Hanoi. He constructed the de Lattre line, 1,200 small, mutually supportive strongpoints around the Red River delta (near Hanoi), against which Giap launched futile and disastrous offensives in winter-spring 1951. De Lattre tried to build up the loyal Vietnamese armed forces to defend the Line so that his own French troops could pursue Giap. But a Vietnamese army, well enough trained and armed to confront Giap, could one day have confronted the French as well, so de Lattre's plans in this regard met much resistance. Consequently neither he nor his successors ever had enough manpower for an effective campaign against the Viet Minh. De Lattre's only child, a lieutenant, died fighting in Tonkin. Afflicted with cancer, he left Viet Nam in November 1951 and returned to France. He was posthumously created a Marshal of France.

DESSALINES, JEAN-JACQUES (1758–1806). Haitian military and political leader. Born in West Africa, he worked as a slave for a black master. Joining the slave revolt of 1791, he established himself as a military leader of consequence, earning the nickname the "Tiger." At first supporting Napoleon, Dessalines revolted against him in 1803 and launched an extermination of Haitian whites, in which thousands were killed. He also persecuted Haitian mulattoes. Proclaiming an independent Republic of Haiti in 1804, he later assumed the title of Emperor Jacques I. He died in an ambush plotted by Christophe and other Haitian guerrilla leaders.

DE WET, CHRISTIAN RUDOLF (1854–1922). Boer guerrilla leader. A dashing commander, de Wet once captured an enemy wagon train with 140,000 rations. Opposed to South Africa's entrance into World War I, he participated in the 1914 rebellion, which Smuts effectively stamped out. De Wet went to prison but later received a pardon. He wrote *The Three Years' War* (1902).

DIEM. *See* Ngo Dinh Diem.

DIEZ, JUAN MARTIN (1775–1825). Spanish guerrilla leader. He achieved fame fighting against the French invaders of Castile and acquired the nom de guerre El Empecinado, "the stubborn one." Diez had been a cavalryman in Spain's war against the French Republic (1793–1795). After the defeat of

Spain's regular armies in 1808–1809 he turned to guerrilla warfare. He captured numerous couriers, convoys, and detachments of enemy troops. Contrary to the usual Spanish practice, he treated his prisoners well, and in return the French usually did not harm his men when they captured any. By 1810 Diez commanded a thousand men. The Cadiz regency named him a brigadier general, and he won the outspoken admiration of his principal opponent, General Joseph Leopold Hugo. By 1814 his followers had increased to five thousand. After the defeat of Napoleon Diez served the Liberal revolution of 1820; King Ferdinand hanged him in 1825.

DJILAS, MILOVAN (b. 1911). Yugoslav guerrilla leader and government official. Born in Montenegro, Djilas obtained a law degree from the University of Belgrade in 1933. He became associated with Tito in 1937 and achieved membership in the Yugoslav Communist Party Central Committee in 1938 and the Politburo in 1940. He played a major role in the guerrilla fighting against the Nazi occupation and the Chetniks, becoming a close adviser to Tito. His publicly expressed disillusionment with communism led to his expulsion from the party in 1954; two years later he went to prison for publicly supporting the Hungarian uprising. His major books include *The New Class, Conversations with Stalin,* and *Wartime.* Referring to the shedding of the blood of many fellow Yugoslavians during and after the war by Tito's Partisans, Djilas wrote (in *Wartime*): "With my present outlook, I would not have been able to do what I had done then."

DUARTE FUENTES, JOSÉ NAPOLEON (1925–1991). President of El Salvador. He earned a degree in civil engineering from Notre Dame University. Duarte was a founder of the Christian Democratic Party of El Salvador in 1960 and served as mayor of San Salvador three times beginning in 1964. It is close to a certainty that in 1972 he won the presidential election, but he was counted out, thrown into prison, beaten, and exiled to Venezuela until 1979. In the crisis of the communist-led guerrilla insurgency, however, he was called back, and from 1980 to 1982 he governed the country as head of a reformist junta. He finally achieved election as president of the republic in 1984. During his term he held the line against the guerrillas, carrying out political and social reforms and maintaining close ties to the United States. By the end of his presidency in 1989 it was clear that the insurgents would not win.

DUPONT DE L'ETANG, PIERRE ANTOINE (1765–1840). Napoleonic military commander. A veteran of Valmy, Marengo, Ulm, and Friedland, Dupont surrendered his army to Spanish regular and guerrilla forces at Bailén in 1808, a shattering blow to French military prestige. For this Napoleon broke him and kept him under arrest until 1814. Under Louis XVIII, Dupont served as minister of war.

ESPOZ Y MINA, FRANCISCO (1781–1836). Spanish guerrilla leader. Gabriel Lovett has called him "the true genius of the guerrilla war in the peninsula." Born near Pamplona, he was a literate, landowning peasant. Within two years of the French invasion he had made himself leader of the guerrillas of Navarre; his 3,500 men tied down thirty thousand Imperial troops, thus contributing certainly to Wellington's key victory at Torres Vedras. Ferocious atrocities on both sides characterized the guerrilla struggle, especially the reprisal execution of prisoners. In the mountains Espoz y Mina established arms factories, munitions dumps, and hospitals, and he supported his troops by collecting "customs duties" from French and Spanish merchant convoys passing through his territory. Like other Spanish guerrilla chiefs he became a master of rapid movement based on excellent intelligence, and consequently for much of the war communications between Madrid and Paris were non-existent. By 1813 his units had developed into a conventionally armed force of 13,500, with which he captured Zaragoza. After 1814 he was prominent in Liberal politics and revolts.

EWING, THOMAS (1829–1896). American political and military figure. Born in Ohio, he was the son of President Zachary Taylor's secretary of the interior. He graduated from Cincinnati Law School and eventually became first Chief Justice of the Kansas Supreme Court. At the outbreak of the Civil War he organized and led the 11th Kansas Volunteers. He became brigadier general in 1863, in charge of Kansas and western Missouri. It was Ewing who issued the notorious General Orders No. 11, forcibly removing civilians from guerrilla-troubled counties of western Missouri; the homes of many of these people were afterwards burned by Kansas troops. This was the most drastic measure the Union government took against civilians in a Union state during the war (Sherman's March taking place in seceded states), and it was soon suspended because of the resulting outcry. Ewing successfully resisted the 1864 invasion of Missouri by Sterling Price. He served in the U.S. House of Representatives from 1877 to 1881.

FAISAL AL HUSEIN AMIR (ALSO FEISAL) (1885–1933). Arab national leader and monarch. Born in Mecca, he was the son of the ruler of the Hejaz. Faisal became the principal figure in the Arab revolt against Turkish rule, and the ally and protector of T. E. Lawrence. For years after the 1916 rising, Arabs in many different quarters viewed him as the natural leader of a restored pan-Arab state. The British established him as King of Iraq in 1921, which he remained until his death.

FANON, FRANZ (1925–1961). Third-world revolutionary figure. Born in Martinique, he served in the French army during World War II, then studied medicine and psychiatry at the University of Lyon. In 1953 he went to Algeria, and joined the FLN the following year. His best-known work is *The Wretched of the Earth* (1961), in which he advocated personal and lethal violence as a cleansing and liberating force whereby Africans would lose their inferiority complex vis-à-vis the colonialists. Fanon died in Washington, DC.

FONSECA AMADOR, CARLOS (1936–1976). Nicaraguan communist guerrilla leader. A student activist, his training was in the Nicaraguan communist youth organizations. He spent 1957 in the Soviet Union and in 1957 wrote *A Nicaraguan in Moscow*, which painted the USSR as a model for Latin America's future. He spent some time in Cuba in 1959. Fonseca was one of the two principal founders of the Sandinista National Liberation Front (FSLN) in Honduras in 1961 (the other being Tomas Borge).

FRENCH, JOHN (1852–1925). British military leader. He joined the army in 1874 and became a successful cavalry leader in the South African war. After being made field marshal and Chief of the Imperial General Staff in 1913, he suffered severe reverses in many bloody campaigns on the Western Front in World War I. He received the title First Earl of Ypres and held the post of Lord Lieutenant of Ireland in the troubled years 1918–1921. He wrote *1914*.

FUNSTON, FREDERICK (1865–1917). American military leader. Born in Ohio and raised in Kansas, he attended Kansas State University for a while. After widely varying employment as a young man, he served with Cuban guerrillas against the Spanish in the 1890s. At the outbreak of the Spanish-American War he received command of a Kansas volunteer regiment. In the Philippines, he won the Congressional Medal of Honor. By a clever ruse Funston captured the guerrilla leader Aguinaldo in March 1901. This act, called by Secretary of War Root ''the most important single military event of the year in the Philippines,'' brought the conflict to a close. Funston was made a brigadier general at age thirty-six. In 1914 he participated in the landing at Vera Cruz and was appointed military governor of that city. See his *Memories of Two Wars: Cuban and Philippine Experiences* (1911).

GALLIENI, JOSEPH SIMON (1849–1916). French military leader. A graduate of the military academy at Saint-Cyr, Gallieni participated in the pacification of the French Sudan as well as in the Franco-Prussian War. During his service first in Indochina (1892–1896) and then as Governor General of Madagascar (1896–1905) he developed and perfected his *tache d'huile* (oil stain) strategy of counterinsurgency, consisting of moving methodically from strength to strength while dividing and weakening the enemy by making clear to them the benefits of French rule: peace, social services, and prosperity. Called out of retirement in 1914 to defend Paris, he became Minister of War the next year. He was (posthumously) created a Marshal of France in 1921.

GIAP. *See* Vo Nguyen Giap.

GODOY, MANUEL DE (1767–1851). Spanish political figure. The favorite of King Charles IV and reputedly the lover of his wife Maria Luisa, Godoy was appointed prime minister at the age of twenty-five. He brought Spain into alliance with France and was thus partly responsible for the disaster that befell the Spanish navy at Trafalgar. In 1807 he allowed a French army to enter Spain on its way to Portugal; in return for this favor, Godoy received the promise that after Napoleon had reorganized the Iberian peninsula he himself would get a little kingdom of his own in southern Portugal. After the anti-Napoleonic uprising broke out in Spain, Godoy went into exile and died in Paris. His memoirs have been translated into English.

GREENE, NATHANAEL (1742–1786). American general in the Revolutionary War. Born in Rhode Island, he was expelled from the Quaker community because he attended a military parade. He was active in the iron business and served in the legislature several times between 1770 and 1775. At the outbreak of the Revolution he became a commander of militia. He was placed in command of American troops in Boston after the British evacuated that city. He participated in Washington's spectacular coup at Trenton in 1776 and shared the terrible winter at Valley Forge. As Quartermaster-General of the Continental Army, he was "Washington's right arm." Washington placed him in command of the remains of the southern forces after Gates's disaster at Camden in 1780. Greene fought Cornwallis at Guilford Court House, where the British achieved a tactical victory but a strategic defeat. Throughout the Carolina campaign, the cooperation between Greene's little army and the partisan bands led by Marion and Sumter would reverse the British conquest of the southern colonies and lead to Yorktown. Before Cornwallis began his journey toward Virginia, he established a line of forts to hold South Carolina in submission. But Greene plunged into the colony and captured these garrisons or drove them into the British base at Charleston, which the British finally evacuated. During the darkest period of the War of Independence, Greene's ability to hold his little army together through defeat after defeat while the enemy wore himself into exhaustion, along with his grasp of the possibilities of sustained guerrilla operations, mark him as second only to George Washington himself as the outstanding commander of the American Revolution.

GUEVARA, ERNESTO ("CHE") (1928–1967). Latin American guerrilla leader. He was born in Rosario, Argentina, and received a medical degree in 1953. He was in Guatemala in the last months of the Arbenz regime and met Fidel Castro in Mexico in 1955. A member of the little band that landed in Cuba in 1956, he was influential in guiding Castro to embrace a version of Marxism-Leninism. In the new regime Guevara held office as minister of industry and as head of the Cuban state bank; he failed spectacularly in both positions. Mutually disillusioned with Castro, Guevara went to the Congo, where he engaged in guerrilla activity. Returning to Cuba, he decided to lead a revolution in Bolivia, primarily for its geographical position: sharing a border with many other South American countries, a Castroite Bolivia would become a continental center of revolution. Intending to ignite "many Viet Nams," Guevara went to Bolivia in November 1966 with about two dozen men and women, mainly Cubans and Argentines, who were to be the nucleus of a great guerrilla army (he himself entered the country in disguise via the La Paz airport). But the would-be revolutionaries failed completely to win the support of the local Indian population, and the physical conditions of highland Bolivia proved much too harsh for these petit-bourgeois foreigners; indeed they could not even obtain the blessing of the Bolivian Communist Party. Less than a year after the beginning of the revolutionary attempt, most of Guevara's followers had been captured, and he was killed in October 1967. In spite of, or perhaps because of, this egregious and fatal fiasco, during the 1970s Guevara became an icon for self-styled revolutionaries throughout the world.

GUSMAO, JOSÉ ALEXANDRE XANANA (b. 1947). East Timorese guerrilla leader. In May 1993 Indonesian troops captured him in a suburb of Dili. Hundreds of Fretilin rebels reportedly surrendered after this event. Gusmao received a sentence of life imprisonment. President Soares of Portugal, among other world leaders, called for his release; President Suharto of Indonesia reduced his sentence to twenty years.

GUZMAN REYNOSO, ABIMAEL (b. 1934). Peruvian Maoist guerrilla leader. Born in Mollendo, his natural father sent him to a good high school and then the University of San Augustín in Arequipa. Guzman then became a philosophy instructor at the University of San Cristóbal de Huamanga in Ayacucho. He visited China several times between 1965 and 1976. In 1970 he founded the Sendero Luminoso, the Shining Path (a phrase from the Peruvian Marxist writer Mariategui). For the next several years he built up and indoctrinated his new organization, resigning his academic post in 1976. Sendero unleashed its "People's War" in 1980. It claimed many lives over the next dozen years but was unable to expand its base beyond some Indian communities in remote regions. Arrested in Lima in September 1992, Guzman received a sentence of life imprisonment.

HALLECK, HENRY WAGER (1815–1872). American military figure. Born in Oneida county, New York, he graduated from Union College and then from West Point (1839). He saw action in the Mexican War and resigned from the army in 1854 to enter law practice and business in California, in which endeavors he enjoyed notable success. At the outbreak of the Civil War he received a commission as major general in the regular army and succeeded Frémont as commander of the Department of the Missouri. In that troubled area he proclaimed that guerrillas were not soldiers but bandits who could be killed upon capture, a policy that was not rigidly enforced. He publicly supported the notorious General Orders No. 11 of General Ewing but in fact cancelled its further application. For most of the war he served in Washington as Lincoln's general in chief, i.e., his personal military adviser. He wrote *The Elements of Military Art and Science* and *International Law, or Rules Regulating the Intercourse of States in Peace and War,* and translated Jomini's life of Napoleon.

HEKHMATYAR, GULBUDDIN (b. 1949?) Afghan guerrilla leader. He is reported to have been for several years a member of the PDPA before switching to radical Islamic politics. During the struggle against Soviet occupation he became leader of Hezb-i-Islami (the Party of Islam). His enemies accuse him of responsibility for the deaths of several leaders of rival guerrilla bands and other political opponents, and of secret collusion with the Kabul puppet government and with the Soviet KGB. Violently anti-Western as well as anticommunist, he advocates a profoundly revivalist and theocratic Islam. He became prime minister of post-communist Afghanistan in June 1993.

HO CHI MINH (1890–1969). Vietnamese communist leader. Born in Nghe An province, his original name was Nguyen That Thanh; his pseudonym, adopted around 1940, means "he who enlightens." He attended an elite high school in Hué founded by the father of Ngo Dinh Diem. Rejected for a position in the French colonial administration, Ho left Viet Nam in 1911 as a crewmember on a steamship; he did not return to his country for thirty years. He visited the United States, Britain, Thailand, and China (spending some time with Mao's Eighth Route Army), helped found the French Communist Party at Tours in 1920, studied Leninist techniques at Moscow's University of the Toilers of the East, and learned to speak passable English, Russian, and Mandarin (as well as French, of course). He remained unmarried all his life. During his many adventures abroad Ho fell into the hands of unfriendly security services several times, always managing somehow to escape; critics have attributed many of these miraculous deliverances to Ho's willingness to give information about other nationalist leaders.

After the fall of France and the Japanese occupation of Viet Nam, Ho and his lieutenants formed a resistance national front, called the Viet Minh for short. This organization emphasized not Leninist class war but the collaboration of all classes against the Japanese marauders. Thus Ho established a claim to being "a nationalist first, a Communist second." In the chaotic interregnum between the surrender of the Japanese and the return of the French, Ho and his little Viet Minh army entered Hanoi and proclaimed national independence; he would hold the title of president of the Democratic Republic of Viet Nam from 1945 until his death. Negotiations with the French followed, but by December 1946 serious fighting had broken out. With the collapse of French willpower after Dien Bien Phu, Ho took over control of Viet Nam north of the seventeenth parallel. The remainder of his life was subsumed in the epic struggle to conquer the South Vietnamese and defeat their American supporters.

HOCHE, LOUIS-LAZARE (1768–1797). French revolutionary commander. In 1794 he received the unenviable commission to suppress the flaming rebellion in the Vendée and Brittany. Provided with overwhelming numbers of troops, he was able to isolate the Vendée from the rest of the country with a line of mutually supporting fortified posts, and to subject the province to incessant patrols. He disarmed the population by the expedient of seizing hostages and cattle, which he would release in exchange for weapons. But Hoche also sought to remove the underlying causes of the rebellion: he introduced religious toleration and granted amnesties and exemptions from conscription. He repulsed the British-supported royalist landing at Quiberon in the summer of 1795 and a year later signed a peace agreement with the last of the important Breton guerrilla chiefs. The Directory conferred on him the title of ''Pacificator of the Vendée.'' In 1796 he commanded the ill-fated expedition to Ireland and died the next year of pneumonia, at the age of twenty-nine.

JAMES, JESSE WOODSON (1847–1882). Confederate guerrilla and bandit. Born in Clay County, Missouri, at the age of fifteen he joined Quantrill's band. After the Civil War he and his brother Frank (1844–1915) led their gang in robbery and murder across the middle west. In Iowa in 1873, the James Gang invented a new form of crime, the train robbery. Jesse was killed for the price on his head by a member of his gang, in St. Joseph, Missouri.

JAMESON, SIR LEANDER STARR (1853–1917). British political figure in South Africa. A native of Edinburgh, he went to Kimberley, South Africa, to practice medicine, where he became closely associated with Cecil Rhodes. In December 1895 he led an incursion into the Transvaal Republic during which he was captured. The Boers handed him over to British authorities, who imprisoned him. This notorious ''Jameson Raid'' helped precipitate the Boer War. Jameson served as prime minister of Cape Colony from 1904 to 1908 and was made baronet in 1911.

JOMINI, ANTOINE-HENRI (1779–1869). Soldier and military theorist. Born in Switzerland, Jomini joined the French army. While on service in Spain, he observed firsthand how difficult it is to wage or even conceptualize a successful counterinsurgency. He later accompanied Napoleon's disastrous expedition to Russia, served as chief of staff to Marshal Ney, and after 1812 was military adviser to czars Alexander I and Nicholas I. He died in Paris, knowing that he had achieved the reputation as the premier military theorist of his age. He left behind many books on military history and theory; the most famous of these is *The Art of War* (*Précis de l'arte de la guerre*), published in 1838, a book that had a tremendous influence among officers of the United States Army, especially during the Civil War. In that work, and in others, he warned of the enormous difficulties of opposing guerrillas, a warning which, after the passage of a century and a half, is valid today. In his view, to attempt to wage counterinsurgency on the cheap invites disaster; the government must deploy troops in numbers sufficient both to garrison all key points and provide hunter groups for incessant operations against guerrillas. At the same time, he stressed the political aspects of counterinsurgency, advising those who would defeat guerrillas above all to practice justice and moderation toward the civilian society.

KARMAL, BABRAK (b. 1929). Soviet puppet leader of Afghanistan. Son of an Afghan army general and member of the wealthy Kabul elite, he was a founder of the Afghan Communist Party (PDPA) and an active collaborator in the 1979 Soviet invasion of Afghanistan. The Soviets installed him in power in 1980; he proved to be a pliable tool of Soviet administration. As the anti-Soviet and anti-Kabul revolution grew in intensity, the Soviets removed Babrak from power in 1986. He reportedly returned to Afghanistan from exile in the USSR in 1991.

KITCHENER, HORATIO (1850–1916). British military leader. Born in County Kerry, he graduated from the Royal Military Academy at Woolwich. He was commander of the Egyptian Army by 1892 and crushed the Mahdists in the Sudan in 1898. He was made commander-in-chief of British forces in South Africa during the Boer War (November 1900). He adopted stern measures to bring the Boer guerrillas to heel, including farm burning, the first so-called concentration camps for civilians, and an elaborate and reasonably effective system of blockhouses. In later years he served as commander-in-chief in India and was created field marshal. In 1914 he was made Secretary of State for War; while on a wartime mission to Russia, his ship struck a German mine, and he drowned.

KLÉBER, JEAN BAPTISTE (1753–1800). French revolutionary general. Born in Strasbourg, he attended military school in Munich and served for several years in the Bavarian army. He was sent to fight the Vendean insurgents in 1793 but was transferred out because his methods were not considered brutal enough. Later he commanded Napoleon's army in Egypt and was assassinated in Cairo by a Turkish fanatic.

KOMER, ROBERT W. (b. 1922). American public official and counterinsurgency expert. A native of Chicago, Komer graduated magna cum laude from Harvard in 1942, served in the army during World War II, and then worked for CIA and also the National Security Council. Beginning in 1966 he was special assistant to President Johnson for pacification in Viet Nam; in 1967 he was given full charge of pacification efforts, with the personal rank of ambassador. Komer brought renewed life to the CORDS program (Civil Operations and Revolutionary Development Support), labored to upgrade the training of the sadly neglected Regional and Popular Forces, and developed the controversial Phoenix program to coordinate the various intelligence agencies in Viet Nam. President

Johnson appointed him ambassador to Turkey in 1968, and he was undersecretary of defense in the Carter administration. See his *Bureaucracy Does Its Thing: Institutional Constraints on US/GVN Performance in Viet Nam.*

KOMOROWSKI, TADEUSZ (BOR-KOMOROWSKI) (1895–1966). Polish resistance leader during World War II, known by his underground name of General Bor. Born in Lwow, he joined the armed forces and was a colonel when the Nazis overran Poland in 1939. He received overall command of the Polish Home Army in 1943 and was made a general. During the early years of the German occupation the Home Army engaged mainly in acts of sabotage while it prepared for the national uprising. That doomed struggle took place between August and October 1944, under Komorowski's leadership. See his revealing work *The Secret Army.*

KRUGER, STEPHANUS PAULUS (1825–1904). Leader of the Boers. A veteran of the Great Trek of 1836, he was a soldier, farmer, and politician and held office as president of the Transvaal Republic from 1883. Known as "Uncle Paul," he was an implacable foe of the imperial vision of Cecil Rhodes (q.v.). His policy of denying the vote to "outlanders" in the Transvaal served as an excuse for the Jameson Raid. In 1900, at the height of the Boer War, he journeyed to Europe in a Dutch cruiser to seek help for his people. Kruger died in Switzerland.

LA ROCHEJAQUELEIN, HENRI DU VERGIER, COMTE DE (1772–1794). Vendean commander. He was born in Poitou. Killed in action against republican forces at the age of twenty-one, he is most remembered for his exclamation: "If I advance, follow me; if I retreat, kill me; if I die, avenge me."

LAI TEK (sometimes LOI TAK) (b. 1900?). Malayan communist political leader. The facts of this man's early life and later career are scanty and disputed. He was probably born in Viet Nam and may have been of Vietnamese and Chinese parentage. A Comintern agent and also probably a French police informer in Saigon, he joined the Malayan Communist Party around 1934 and was its secretary general by 1939. He preceded Chen Ping (q.v.) as head of the Malayan communists. It is widely believed that his rapid rise in the party was the result of his being in the pay of the British, who obligingly arrested his potential rivals. During World War II, the Japanese occupation forces at least twice made seemingly miraculous discoveries and arrests of the top leaders of the Malayan Communist Party—all except Lai Tek. He fled the country in 1947, taking the Party funds with him. He may have been killed in Thailand by a communist hit team some years later.

LANE, JIM (1814–1866). Kansas political and military leader. Lane was born in Indiana, from which state his father had been elected to the U.S. House of

Representatives during the presidency of Andrew Jackson. A lawyer with no previous military experience, Lane commanded an Indiana regiment in the Mexican War and acquitted himself well at Buena Vista. He became lieutenant governor and later a member of the U.S. House. In 1855 he moved to Kansas Territory where he became active among the free-state forces and participated in vicious fighting against pro-slavery elements. Upon the admission of Kansas to the Union, he went to the U.S. Senate (1861). Soon thereafter he received appointment as a brigadier general of volunteers and fought against the secessionist forces of former Governor Sterling Price in western Missouri. As a supporter of President Andrew Johnson's Reconstruction policy, Lane lost popularity in Kansas and died a suicide. Critics of Lane have placed upon him a large share of the blame for the horrors of the guerrilla conflict in Missouri and the postwar criminality rampant in that unhappy state.

LANSDALE, EDWARD G. (1908–1987). American guerrilla war specialist, called ''America's near-legendary Clausewitz of counterinsurgency.'' Lansdale was born in Detroit and graduated from UCLA. During World War II he served with the OSS and became a major general in the U.S. Army Air Force. He was an especially close adviser to Ramón Magsaysay in the Philippines, and from 1954 to 1956 he assisted Ngo Dinh Diem in Saigon. He returned to South Viet Nam in 1961 and again in 1965, with Ambassador Henry Cabot Lodge. He was the model for characters in several novels in several languages. He wrote *In the Midst of Wars* (1977).

LAWRENCE, T(HOMAS) E(DWARD) (1888–1935). Most famous British guerrilla. Born in Wales, he grew up in the town of Oxford and attended Jesus College. Before the war he went exploring and mapmaking in the Middle East, and in 1914 he was made an intelligence officer because of his knowledge of Arabic. He eventually became British liaison and political adviser to Faisal (q.v.), the organizer of the Arab revolt against the Turkish empire. Lawrence correctly understood the Arab uprising as a ''sideshow of a sideshow,'' but due to the romanticization of his exploits (which Lawrence certainly aided), his has long been one of the best-known names in guerrilla war. His tactics perfectly fulfilled the classic task of the guerrilla: by rapid assembly and dispersal of his forces he tied down thousands of Turkish soldiers who could have been of good use elsewhere. In December 1917 he accompanied British forces as they entered Jerusalem and was made a lieutenant colonel. For a while after the war he worked, with little success, to advance the cause of Arab independence. In 1922 he joined the RAF as a private under an assumed name but was soon discovered; the same occurred in the tank corps. He was again in the RAF from 1925 until his death in a motoring accident. In 1927 he legally changed his name to T. E. Shaw. See his widely read classic, *Seven Pillars of Wisdom* (1926 and 1935).

LECLERC, CHARLES (1772–1802). French military figure. He married Pauline Bonaparte in 1797. In January 1802 Napoleon sent him at the head of twelve thousand troops to subdue the Haitians, where on Napoleon's orders he treacherously arrested Toussaint. Driven from Haiti by the insurgent forces, he died of fever on Tortuga. His defeat temporarily ended French imperial ambitions in America and led to the Louisiana Purchase.

LETTOW-VORBECK, PAUL VON (1870–1964). A German soldier, one of the outstanding guerrilla leaders of World War I. Born in the Rhineland, he joined the army and saw action in the Boxer Rebellion and against the Hottentots in German Southwest Africa. By 1914 he was the commander of the German East Africa (Tanganyika) forces. Cut off by the British, Belgians, and Portuguese, he waged a campaign to keep British forces in Africa from being sent to reinforce the French front. His field of operations extended over 650,000 square miles. In 1916 the pro-British General Smuts invaded Tanganyika with a large force of Boers; late in 1917 Lettow-Vorbeck began a three-thousand-mile "Long March" south from the Kilimanjaro area to Mozambique and then back into Tanganyika. His few thousand men, white and African, tied up twenty to thirty times their number of British, Belgian, and Portuguese forces. Lettow-Vorbeck was a member of the Reichstag from 1929 to 1930.

LIDDELL HART, B. H. (1895–1970). British military writer. Born in Paris, he left his studies at Cambridge in 1914 to become an army officer. After the Great War, reacting against the appalling casualty lists and poor tactics of that conflict, he stressed the importance of the indirect approach to the enemy, as well as mobility and surprise. His writings on tank warfare influenced the views of the creators of the blitzkrieg more than those of his own compatriots. He was military correspondent for the *Daily Telegraph* from 1925 to 1935 and military adviser to the *Times* from 1935 to 1939. He wrote numerous books. In his *Strategy* he emphasized the long-term negative effects on a society that even a successful guerrilla uprising can produce and was dismissive of the contributions to victory of resistance movements in Western Europe.

LIN PIAO (LIN BIAO) (1907–1971). Chinese communist leader. Born in Hupeh province, he was educated under Chiang Kai-shek at the Whampoa Military Academy. He participated in the KMT Northern Expedition (1926–1927) but broke with Chiang when the latter turned against the Communist Party. He became one of Chu Teh's leading lieutenants. In 1947 and 1948 he was commander of communist forces during the decisive battles in Manchuria. He became minister of defense in 1959. In 1965 Lin published a manifesto which set forth the thesis that, just as the communist triumph in China had developed out of communist control of rural areas surrounding the cities, so the rural areas of the world (Asia, Latin America, Africa) would surround and then defeat the capitalist "cities," namely the Americans and their Western European allies.

For some unfathomable reason this bizarre idea attained world notoriety and alarmed the administration in Washington. By 1966 Lin achieved the position of Mao's heir apparent, but within a few years the two had become estranged and Lin died under very mysterious circumstances.

LYAUTEY, LOUIS HUBERT (1854–1934). French colonial soldier. Lyautey learned counterinsurgency theory and tactics under Gallieni (q.v.) in Tonkin and Madagascar. He also had experience in Algeria. His career in pacification reached its zenith from 1912 to 1925, when he was governor general of Morocco. There he undermined armed rebellion by seeking support among traditional forces and emphasizing the benefits of peaceful life under benevolent French administration. He was especially successful during the difficult days of World War I when the French massively shifted their attention and resources from the African empire to the Western Front. Lyautey was created a Marshal of France in 1921.

MACARTHUR, ARTHUR (1845–1912). American military leader. Born in Springfield, Massachusetts, MacArthur saw action in the Civil War and many years later in Cuba and the Philippines. He had a reputation for bravery under fire and mastery of assault tactics, which he had learned under Sherman. He was made military governor of Manila in 1898. He defeated the initial attacks of Aguinaldo on Manila and soon cleared most of southern Luzon. MacArthur recommended amnesty for his opponents, but Aguinaldo retreated into the Bataan peninsula. MacArthur became military governor of the Philippines in 1900, and he befriended the captured Aguinaldo and his young assistant, Manuel Quezon. Conflicts between MacArthur and William Howard Taft led Secretary of War Elihu Root to relieve MacArthur as governor in 1901. He was promoted lieutenant general in 1906 and retired in 1909.

MAGSAYSAY, RAMÓN (1905–1957). President of the Philippines. After attending the University of the Philippines, he managed a bus company. He joined a guerrilla unit after the Japanese invaded his country. After the war he served in the Philippine House of Representatives (1946–1950). In 1951, with the Huk guerrillas growing ever bolder, President Quirino appointed Magsaysay to be secretary of defense. In that post Magsaysay improved the conduct of troops toward the civilian population, sent small hunter squads into places that had hitherto been safe for the guerrillas, offered huge rewards for information leading to the capture of specific guerrilla leaders, and paid unexpected visits by private plane to field units to make sure his directives were being followed. Later he began a policy of inducing guerrillas to surrender by offering them resettlement on land of their own. Perhaps most importantly, Magsaysay marginalized the guerrillas by using troops to reestablish the honesty of elections. He defeated President Quirino by a landslide in 1953. President Magsaysay died in a plane crash while campaigning for reelection in 1957.

MAO TSE-TUNG (1893–1976). Chinese communist leader. Born in Hunan Province of a middle-class family, Mao participated in the seminal May Fourth Movement (1919) at Peking University. He became a founder of the Chinese Communist Party in 1921. From the late 1920s to the early 1930s he organized guerrilla units to fight the Nationalist regime of Chiang Kai-shek. He emerged as dominant leader of the communist party during the calamitous flight from Chiang's armies known as the Long March. After the victory over the Nationalists, Mao was chief of state of the People's Republic from 1949 until 1959: in the latter year he found it expedient to resign in the wake of the unparalleled disasters of the Great Leap Forward (in which perhaps thirty million lives were needlessly lost). Nevertheless, a few years later Mao felt able to unleash the destructive turmoil known as the Great Proletarian Cultural Revolution. Immediately after Mao's death his life-long collaborators and lieutenants began to jettison or reverse his policies.

Most of Mao's important writings on the subject of guerrilla warfare date from the period 1936–1940, after the Long March. Among his most important and familiar concepts are that guerrillas must (1) seek to wage a protracted conflict, (2) be supported by conventional units, (3) develop base areas, (4) practice ceaseless political indoctrination, and (5) cultivate good relations with the peasantry. These are all good ideas, but hardly original. Nevertheless, it is still fashionable even in some knowledgeable circles to write of Mao as a veritable Genius of War, the man who invented the strategy whereby ill-armed guerrillas defeated the mighty hosts first of the Japanese imperialists and then of the Chinese Nationalists. But this interpretation is difficult to square with certain facts. First, Japanese occupation forces in China were very thinly spread relative to area and population, and they directed most of their efforts against Chiang's army, which they very badly damaged, to the long-term benefit of Mao. Second, starting from 1942 at the latest, Mao's communist forces devoted most of their efforts to fighting not the Japanese but the Nationalists. Finally, it was the Americans, not the Chinese, and most certainly not Mao's guerrillas, who defeated the Japanese. Although these elementary circumstances are easily ascertainable, many of Mao's would-be imitators chose to ignore them, to their supreme cost.

MARCOS, FERDINAND (1917–1989). President of the Philippines 1965–1986. Educated in law at the University of the Philippines, he served with Philippine and U.S. forces during World War II. After membership in the House of Representatives (1949–1959) and the Senate (1959–1965) he was elected president, as a young reformer. Marcos confronted both the new People's Army and the Moro rebels; in response to the continuing internal crisis he proclaimed martial law in 1972. In 1986, after a hotly contested electoral struggle with Corazon Aquino that brought the country to the edge of paralysis, Marcos left the Philippines for Hawaii, only to face lawsuits and criminal charges in his own country and the United States.

MARION, FRANCIS (1732–1795). American guerrilla leader, called the "Swamp Fox." Born in South Carolina, he was a planter and in 1775 a member of the Provincial Congress; at that time he accepted a commission in a provincial regiment. Because of a leg injury he was not in Charleston at the time of the American debacle there (1780). Thus, after the further American disaster at the battle of Camden, it fell to Marion to organize his guerrilla band, which became the only important American armed force still active in South Carolina. His tactical genius and especially his emphasis on mobility enabled his men to disrupt British communications between Charleston and Camden, a state of affairs that seriously distracted Cornwallis. His activities were of tremendous assistance to the little American regular army of General Nathanael Greene. Marion was careful of the lives of his men, scrupulously honest, and above all successful; Christopher Ward wrote that "he was in all respects unexcelled as a partisan leader." After the war he served in the South Carolina state senate, in which body he advocated reconciliation with that state's numerous loyalists.

MARKOS VAFIADES (b. 1906). Greek guerrilla leader. Born in Asia Minor, Markos worked in tobacco fields and went to Greece in 1923. Active in the Greek civil war from its beginning, he became commander of the Democratic Army (the communist insurgents) in 1947. Markos was a talented leader of guerrillas, taking full advantage of the sanctuaries open to him in Yugoslavia, Albania, and Bulgaria. He eventually clashed unsuccessfully with Communist Party boss Zachariades over the question of continuing with classic guerrilla tactics, which Markos advocated, or turning to conventional tactics, as Zachariades demanded. After the end of the civil war he may have gone to Poland; he was officially expelled from the Greek Communist Party in 1961.

MARSHALL, GEORGE C. (1880–1959). American soldier and statesman. He was born in Uniontown, Pennsylvania, and graduated from the Virginia Military Institute. During World War II he was Army Chief of Staff and President Roosevelt's principal strategic adviser. He later served as secretary of state (1947–1949) and secretary of defense (1950–1951). In 1953 he received, as author of the Marshall Plan, the Nobel Peace Prize. As Truman's ambassador to China (1945–1947) he attempted unsuccessfully to end the fighting between the Nationalists of Chiang Kai-shek and the communists of Mao Tse-tung.

MARTÍ, AGUSTIN FARABUNDO (1900–1932). Salvadoran revolutionary. Son of a landowning farmer, he had to flee to Guatemala when he was a university student (1920), returning to El Salvador in 1925. He served in Sandino's armed band in Nicaragua from 1927 to 1929, but, having by now become a communist, Martí found Sandino's goals too narrow. As a participant in the failed 1932 communist-organized revolution in El Salvador, he ended up before a firing squad.

MASSOUD, AHMED SHAH (b. 1954?). Afghan guerrilla leader. He became one of the best known of the resistance commanders in Soviet-occupied Afghanistan. From his exploits against Soviet forces in the Panjsher Valley, he acquired the title of the "Lion of the Panjsher." Later he shifted most of his operations to the northern provinces. He emerged as the chief rival to Hekmatyar. Appointed minister of defense in the post-PDPA government in May 1992, he nevertheless resigned the next year at the insistence of Hekmatyar. See articles on him in the *Christian Science Monitor*, April 22, 1992, and the *Washington Post*, April 23, 26 and 29, 1992, and January 23, 1994.

MASSU, JACQUES (b. 1908). French military leader. A graduate of St.-Cyr, he entered the paratroops. He rallied to de Gaulle's resistance in 1940; the end of World War II found him in French Indochina, and he also served in French West Africa (1951–1954) and Tunisia before assignment to Algeria. He participated in the ill-fated Suez expedition. He has received most of the credit for stamping out the terrorist activities emanating from the Casbah. While he was preeminent in the 1958 Algerian uprising against the Fourth Republic, he did not join the 1961 rebellion against de Gaulle. Consequently he became military governor of Metz and then commander of French forces in West Germany. He wrote *The Truth about Suez* and *The Real Battle of Algiers*.

MENGISTU, HAILE MARIAM (b. 1937). Ethiopian general and dictator. A member of the Amhara ethnic group, he was an army major at the time of the overthrow of Emperor Haile Selassie in 1974. Mengistu soon made himself dictator, a position he held until 1991, in large part by killing off his opponents and potential rivals inside the ruling clique. A client of the USSR, he ruined Ethiopia's agricultural economy through forced collectivization, fought a war with Somalia, and provoked armed resistance from the country's ethnic and religious minorities. When Soviet support began to dry up he was unable to contain the numerous rebellions in the country and in 1991 fled to Zimbabwe.

MIHAILOVICH, DRAZA (1893–1946). Yugoslav military figure and guerrilla leader. He was born at Ivanjica in Serbia. A General Staff officer at the time of Germany's conquest of Yugoslavia, he took to the mountains and summoned all who could to join him; his followers became known as Chetniks. The Yugoslav government-in-exile appointed him minister of the armed forces and legitimate head all resistance forces in Yugoslavia; he was acknowledged by the Churchill cabinet. Because Mihailovich believed that Germany was doomed to lose the war, because he foresaw that at war's end Tito's Partisans would attempt to seize power, and because he was deterred by the Nazi reprisal policy (fifty Yugoslavs executed for every German soldier killed), Mihailovich sought to preserve his forces, and the lives of his countrymen, for a better day. This policy, as interpreted by Churchill's informants, convinced the latter to abandon Mihailovich and throw support to Tito, a move that was controversial then and remains so today. At war's end the Tito forces hunted down Mihailovich, whom, after a show trial, they executed and buried in a secret grave. President Truman posthumously awarded him the Legion of Merit in 1948.

MILNER, ALFRED (1854–1925). British political leader in South Africa. He was born in Bonn and had a great success as a student at Oxford. He served as undersecretary of finance in Egypt (1890–1892). Appointed High Commissioner for South Africa and Governor General of the Cape Colony in 1897 shortly after the Jameson Raid, he exacerbated tensions with the Boers and helped bring on war. From 1901 to 1905 he governed both the Transvaal and the Orange River Colony. He held other important posts in Britain during and after World War I, including Colonial Secretary (1919–1921).

MOSBY, JOHN SINGLETON (1833–1916). Confederate guerrilla leader. Born in Virginia, he attended the University of Virginia and was practicing law in that state when it seceded. He served in the cavalry of Jeb Stuart until January 1863, when he began guerrilla operations in northern Virginia at the head of the group that came to be called Mosby's Partisan Rangers. Although Mosby was wounded and had several narrow escapes, he was never taken prisoner, nor were his Rangers defeated. Operating among a friendly population, he practiced to perfection the classic guerrilla tactics of boldness and mobility. Shortly after Appomatox Mosby disbanded his followers and was later freed on parole by General Grant. Partly from admiration for Grant, partly from a desire to help heal the wounds of war, Mosby joined the Republican Party. In later years he served as United States consul in Hong Kong and in the Justice Department, and published his *War Reminiscences.*

MUGABE, ROBERT (b. 1924?). Nationalist leader of Zimbabwe. Educated in Roman Catholic mission schools, he became a schoolteacher. He joined Nkomo's ZAPU, but differences with the latter led Mugabwe to form ZANU (the Zimbabwe African National Union). He was held in detention by the Rhodesian government from 1964 to 1974, during which time he obtained a law degree by correspondence. He lived in Mozambique from 1974 to 1979, helping to direct the guerrilla insurgency in his own country. In 1980 he became the first prime minister of independent Zimbabwe, and the first president in 1987. By 1989 he had dismantled the parliamentary governing structure, creating a one-party socialist state.

NAJIBULLAH, DR. (b. 1947). Afghan communist leader. Born in Paktia province in 1946 into a middle-class family, he entered Kabul University to study medicine and took ten years to get his degree. He joined the Communist Party (PDPA) in 1965 and became a member of its central committee in 1977. After the PDPA took power, he headed the secret police (KhAD) from 1980 to 1985, under the direction of the Soviet KGB, by whom he was thoroughly trained. In

1986 he became leader of the PDPA and de facto boss of those parts of Afghanistan still under communist control, following the Soviet ouster of Babrak Karmal. In April 1992, after more than thirteen years of foreign occupation and civil war, he declared the PDPA regime at an end.

NAPOLEON (BONAPARTE) (1769–1821). Emperor of the French. His invasion and occupation of Spain provoked a ferocious and tenacious national resistance, and gave the world the term "guerrilla." French defeats in Spain undermined the aura of invincibility that had hitherto surrounded the Napoleonic system and set the stage for united European resistance. The Spanish reversals followed the defeat of French forces by guerrillas in Haiti. It is indeed fortunate for Napoleon's reputation in our own day that it does not depend on French counterinsurgency efforts in Haiti and Spain.

NASUTION, ABDUL HARIS (b. 1918). Indonesian guerrilla leader and military commander. A native of the Batack country, he taught school for a while and then from 1940 to 1942 attended the cadet officers' academy in Bandung, in what was then the Netherlands East Indies. During the Japanese occupation he served in a collaborationist military unit. In the conflict between the Indonesian nationalist parties and the Dutch following World War II, Nasution directed guerrilla operations. In 1959 he became minister of defense and in 1962 chief of staff of the armed forces; in these and other posts he often had to confront guerrilla insurgencies in various parts of the country. Thus, like Ramón Magsaysay, he had first-hand experience of both leading guerrillas and suppressing them. When communist and other forces sought to assassinate the leaders of the Indonesian army in 1965, Nasution was one of the few who escaped; he was instrumental in rallying the army and the country to a successful resistance, which resulted in the destruction of the Indonesian Communist Party, once one of the largest in the world, and the displacement of President Sukarno. See his *Fundamentals of Guerrilla Warfare* (1953).

NAVARRE, HENRI (1898–1983). French soldier. Commander in Viet Nam from May 1953 to June 1954, he was responsible for the erection of the doomed fortress at Dien Bien Phu. Navarre had served in World War I and later fought against guerrillas in Syria and Morocco. He worked in army intelligence, was active in the underground in World War II, and held commands in Algeria and Germany before going to Viet Nam.

NGO DINH DIEM (1901–1963). Vietnamese political leader. He was born in Quang Binh province, the birthplace also of General Giap. His ancestors embraced Catholicism in the seventeenth century. Of a mandarin family, he graduated first in his class from the French-run School of Law and Public Administration in Hanoi. He served as governor of Binh Thuan province and briefly as Bao Dai's minister of the interior (1933), but the French distrusted him as a nationalist and blocked his plans for reforms, causing his resignation. Toward the end of World War II both the Japanese occupiers and Bao Dai offered him the premiership, and he also received an offer from Ho Chi Minh to be minister of the interior in a Viet Minh government. Diem refused all these appointments, because he felt his freedom of action would be too constricted. With a communist price on his head, and disliked by the French, Diem left Viet Nam in 1950, journeying to Rome, France, Belgium, and the United States. Finally, in June 1954, he accepted another offer of the premiership from Bao Dai.

The government of which Diem became the head controlled hardly more than a few square blocks in downtown Saigon. But Diem won the admiration and support of powerful Americans like Senators Mike Mansfield, John Kennedy, and Hubert Humphrey. Within a few years he had brought the rebellious army leadership under control, broken the hold of organized crime in Saigon, tamed the armed religious sects, attacked malaria, extended education, settled a million northern refugees, and secured his election as first president of the Republic of Viet Nam. Diem's prickly independence and lack of public relations skills, however, as well as suspicions that he was moving toward a compromise peace with North Viet Nam, got him into trouble with elements of the Kennedy administration; also opposition from certain Buddhist factions weakened his position at home and in Washington. In 1963 a coup by a group of South Vietnamese generals, in which high-ranking Americans in Saigon and Washington were complicit, resulted in his assassination; CIA Director William Colby later characterized the removal of Diem as America's first big mistake in Viet Nam.

NGUYEN VAN THIEU (b. 1923). A native of Ninh Thuan province, Thieu was the son of a small landowner and fisherman. In 1945 he joined the Viet Minh but later became a supporter of the French. He was a member of the first graduating class of the Vietnamese Military Academy at Dalat (1949); after 1954 he was superintendent at the academy for four years. In 1958 he embraced Catholicism, the religion of his wife. He was involved in the coup against President Diem in 1963 and was elected president of the republic in 1967 and in 1971. He bitterly opposed the Paris accords negotiated by Henry Kissinger. In the spring of 1975, as the U.S. Congress continued to slash assistance to South Viet Nam, Thieu decided to consolidate South Viet Nam's armed forces, bringing those units in the northern and central parts of the nation into the Saigon area. In itself, such a retrenchment was a good idea, in fact long overdue, but the process was carried out on the basis of such inadequate planning and communication that it produced a rout and then the disintegration of much of the South's army. The retrenchment began on March 16; two weeks after that Da Nang fell, and one month later North Vietnamese regulars entered Saigon. Up to almost the last hour of this ordeal, President Thieu retained his faith that the Americans would use air strikes to save the country for which so many thousands of their young people had died. After the fall of Saigon, Thieu went to Taiwan, and then to England.

NKOMO, JOSHUA (b. 1917). Guerrilla and political leader in Rhodesia/Zimbabwe. The son of a teacher and lay-preacher, he became a leader in the railwaymen's union. He sojourned in England in 1959 and 1960, and in 1961 founded ZAPU. Rhodesian authorities held him in detention for ten years, beginning in 1964. His followers played a relatively minor role in the fighting against the Rhodesian government, apparently because Nkomo wanted to preserve his strength for what he viewed as the inevitable post-independence ethnic civil war. In the 1980 elections he and his party suffered a resounding defeat at the hands of Robert Mugabe's ZANU. In 1987 Nkomo was chosen one of Zimbabwe's two vice presidents.

ORTEGA SAAVEDRA, DANIEL (b. 1944). Nicaraguan political figure. Born in La Libertad, he studied for a few months at the Jesuit-run Universidad Centro-Americana in Managua. He joined the fledgling FSLN in 1963 and spent the years from 1967 to 1974 in prison for bank robbery. Released in a hostage exchange, he went to Cuba to receive training in guerrilla warfare. After the fall of the Somoza regime he became a member of the ruling junta. (His brother Humberto, born in 1946, also held high posts, including minister of defense, and commanded the Nicaraguan army until 1995.) He was elected sole president of Nicaragua in 1984, without serious opposition. In the 1990 presidential elections, despite Sandinista control of the security forces, the patronage power, and the media, he suffered a decisive (56 to 41 percent) defeat at the hands of Violeta Chamorro, in a high turnout. After much hesitation and internal dispute, the Sandinistas decided to accept the results of the election, and Ortega relinquished his office.

PAPAGOS, ALEXANDER (1883–1955). Greek military leader and statesmen. Born in Athens, he received an officer's commission in 1906. He fought in the Balkan Wars and also in the Greek invasion of Turkey (1919–1922). He became minister of war in 1935. He commanded Greek forces against the Italian invasion of 1940 and was held as a hostage in Germany until 1945. In January 1949, towards the end of the Greek civil war, he became commander-in-chief of the national forces. In that position he infused his troops with new discipline and energy. He cleared Greece from south to north, eliminating the communist infrastructure and forcing the guerrillas up against and then over the northern frontiers. Created field marshal in 1949, he served effectively as prime minister from 1952 to 1955.

PASTORA GÓMEZ, EDEN (b. 1937). Nicaraguan guerrilla leader. Born into a family of middle-class landowners, he was educated at the Jesuit preparatory school in Managua. Later he studied medicine at the University of Guadalajara

(Mexico) but did not complete the course. He joined the guerrillas fighting the Somoza regime in 1959 but accepted amnesty a few years later. In 1970, while in Mexico, he joined the FSLN. Uniting with the Ortega brothers in 1978, he served as deputy minister of the interior and then deputy minister of defense. Pastora spent time with guerrillas in Guatemala. In 1982, while in Costa Rica, he denounced the betrayal of the Sandinista revolution by the Ortegas and others, with their "mansions and Mercedes-Benz's." Throughout the rest of the decade he led a guerrilla struggle against the regime.

PHAM VAN DONG (b. 1906). Vietnamese communist leader. Born into an Annamese mandarin family. He attended the same lycée as Vo Nguyen Giap and Ngo Dinh Diem. He was a co-founder of the Vietnamese Communist Party (in China) and was held in French prisons from 1930 to 1938. He became official head (prime minister) of the Viet Minh revolutionary government in 1950, a post he held for three and a half decades, through the Geneva Conference of 1954, the death of Ho Chi Minh, and the conquest of South Viet Nam. In the face of his country's worsening economic situation, he finally resigned in 1986.

PICKENS, ANDREW (1739–1817). American Revolutionary guerrilla leader. Born in Pennsylvania, he was at the outbreak of the Revolution a farmer and justice of the peace in South Carolina. He served as an officer of militia, returning to his home on parole after the fall of Charleston (1780). When British forces nevertheless raided his plantation, he returned in anger to the struggle as a guerrilla commander, and he played a major role at the Battle of the Cowpens (January 1781). After the war Pickens served in the South Carolina state legislature and the U.S. House of Representatives.

POL POT (b. 1925–1928). Cambodian revolutionary. Born in Kompong Thom province, Pol Pot (a nom de guerre) served under Ho Chi Minh during World War II. He joined the Communist Party in 1946. He went to Paris and studied electronics, but apparently failed his examinations several times. He taught school in Phnom Penh from 1954 to 1963, becoming prominent in the communist-led Khmer Rouge. He led the overthrow of the Lon Nol government in 1975 and launched the campaign of societal reorganization that within four years would take the lives of more than a quarter of his countrymen, make Cambodia a desolate scene of starvation and disease, and invite a Vietnamese invasion and occupation. He officially stepped down as leader of the Khmer Rouge in 1985, but many believe that he continued to dominate that organization.

PRICE, STERLING (1809–1867). American political and military leader. Born in Virginia, he moved to Missouri, where he practiced law and became involved in politics. He served in the U.S. House of Representatives, from which he resigned to participate in the Mexican War. He was governor of Missouri from 1853 to 1857. Opposed to secession in 1861, he nevertheless joined the Confederate army. In September 1864, in the last important Confederate effort in the West, he led an invasion force of twelve thousand from his base in northern Arkansas into southern Missouri. He called for a guerrilla uprising across the state; the response was quite disappointing, only about five thousand Missourians heeding the call, and those not for long. Price was driven out of Missouri by Union forces under General Ewing.

PUISAYE, JOSEPH DE (1755–1827). French nobleman and Chouan leader. The son of a marquis of modest means, he first studied for the priesthood and then trained as a cavalryman. During the Breton rising he led the unsuccessful effort to take Rennes (May 1794). He worked constantly but without great success for greater cooperation among the various Chouan guerrilla bands. Puisaye went to England in 1794 to seek aid. He was the commander of the disastrous landing at Quiberon in 1795. Unlike most of the other western guerrilla leaders, he did not make peace in 1796. He retired to Canada in 1797 and to England in 1802, where he died.

QUANTRILL, WILLIAM CLARKE (1837–1865). Confederate guerrilla leader. Born in Ohio, he went to Kansas in 1857, where he became involved in violent enterprises in that disorderly Territory. At the outbreak of the Civil War he joined the forces of Missouri's former governor Sterling Price but soon deserted. He eventually formed his own irregular band, operating on the bloody Kansas-Missouri border. He is most remembered for the raid on Lawrence, Kansas (August 21, 1863), in the course of which he and his followers killed more than 150 unarmed men and boys. The raid shocked the entire nation, and Confederate General Henry McCulloch described Quantrill and his men as "the wildest savages." In January 1865 Quantrill raided Danville, Kentucky; a few months later in that same state he was taken prisoner after suffering serious wounds.

QUIRINO, ELPIDIO (1890–1956). President of the Philippines. A graduate of the law school of the University of the Philippines, he served in the Philippine House of Representatives and Senate (1919–1931). Elected the first vice president of the independent Philippines under Manuel Roxas, Quirino succeeded to the presidency upon the latter's death in 1948. The corruption of his administration, and especially the blatant fraud of his reelection in 1949, re-energized the communist-dominated Huk guerrillas. Faced with possible disaster, Quirino appointed Ramón Magsaysay, the architect of the Huk defeat, to be secretary of defense in 1950. Magsaysay overwhelmingly defeated Quirino for the presidency in 1953.

RAMOS, FIDEL (b. 1928). President of the Philippines. A graduate of West Point (1950) and a Protestant in an overwhelmingly Catholic country, Ramos received appointment as chief of the Philippine Constabulary by President Marcos. Turning against Marcos in the wake of the upheavals following the controversial 1986 presidential election, Ramos supported Mrs. Corazon Aquino. As chief of staff of the armed forces under President Aquino, Ramos sustained her through half a dozen attempted coups. He became secretary of defense in 1988. In the 1992 presidential election, Ramos ran with the endorsement of President Aquino. Receiving 24 percent of the vote, he was elected over six other candidates.

REAGAN, RONALD (b. 1911). President of the United States 1981–1989. Toward the end of his first term he proclaimed the Reagan Doctrine, under which anticommunist insurgent movements would receive assistance from the United States. This was a challenge to the Brezhnev Doctrine, according to which the Soviet Union would never allow any communist government to be removed from power. Under the Reagan Doctrine, U.S. assistance reached guerrilla forces in Afghanistan, Angola, Ethiopia, and Nicaragua.

RHODES, CECIL (1853–1902). British financier and empire-builder. He went to Natal in 1870, was elected to the Cape Colony parliament in 1881, organized the De Beers diamond conglomerate in 1888, and held the office of prime minister of the Cape Colony from 1890 to 1896. From his personal funds he helped finance pioneers in what came to be called Rhodesia. He resigned as prime minister in the wake of the Jameson fiasco. Most of his fortune went to establish the famous Rhodes scholarships to Oxford.

ROMULO, CARLOS P. (1899–1985). Philippine statesman. A publisher, Romulo won a Pulitzer Prize in 1941 for coverage of the war in the Philippines. Aide-de-camp to Douglas MacArthur on Corregidor, Romulo accompanied the latter to Australia. He served as president of the United Nations General Assembly from 1949 to 1950. He accepted appointment as Philippine secretary of foreign affairs in 1950 and as ambassador to the United States in 1952. A candidate for president in 1953 against Quirino, Romulo withdrew in favor of Ramón Magsaysay, who subsequently won a great victory. Romulo went on to become president of the United Nations Security Council in 1957, president of the University of the Philippines, 1962–1968, and secretary of foreign affairs, 1968–1984. He published several works, including the autobiographical *I Walked with Heroes* (1961).

ROXAS Y ACUNA, MANUEL (1892–1948). President of the Philippine Republic. A graduate of the law school of the University of the Philippines, Roxas served as speaker of the Philippine House of Representatives. Although he collaborated with the Japanese occupation, his actions were defended after the war by General Douglas MacArthur. Roxas was elected first president of the Republic of the Philippines in 1946. His administration's ill-advised tactics against the Huk guerrillas were producing a crisis when he died in 1948, to be succeeded as president by Elpidio Quirino.

SALAN, RAOUL (1899–1984). French military figure. Born in Roquecourbe to become the "most decorated soldier in the French army," in 1950 he became second in command in French Indochina to de Lattre. He served as commander-in-chief and high commissioner there from 1951 to 1953. In 1956 he became commander in Algeria and was active in the events of May 1958. Retiring from the army in 1960 as a protest against de Gaulle's policies in Algeria, he went to Spain and helped organize the Secret Army Organization (OAS), a group that engaged in terrorism in Algeria (even against the French army) and sought to murder President de Gaulle. Arrested in Algeria, Salan received a sentence of life imprisonment in 1962 but was granted amnesty by de Gaulle in 1968.

SANDINO, CÉSAR AUGUSTO (1893–1934). Nicaraguan guerrilla leader. The son of a landowner and an Indian woman, he worked as a farmer and a mining engineer. As a young man he had to flee to Mexico because of his involvement in a brawl. During the mid-1920s he joined the Liberal Party revolt against the Conservative administration in Managua and raised an armed band. He engaged in actions against the small U.S. Marine detachment in Nicaragua from 1927 to 1933. In 1931, in a raid on a lumber company headquarters, he killed several British and American civilians. Sandino entered into negotiations with the Managua government in 1934; while on one of his visits to the capital he was murdered by members of the Guardia Nacional. His fame rests not on his achievements, which were minor, but on the use of his name many years later by Central American communists, with whose objectives he was not in sympathy while he lived.

SAVIMBI, JONAS (b. 1934). Angolan guerrilla leader and politician. Educated by Protestant missionaries, he embraced their religion. He attended an elite Portuguese preparatory school in Angola, studied medicine at the University of Lisbon, and graduated with a degree in political science from the University of Lausanne. He apparently went to China in 1965 for training in guerrilla warfare. The next year he founded UNITA (Union for the Total Independence of Angola). From then on he would be engaged in warfare first against the Portuguese and then against the Leninist MPLA regime of independent Angola. Over the course of these many years he received assistance at different times from South Africa, China, France, and the United States, as well as several conservative African and Arab states.

SCIPIO AFRICANUS MINOR (also SCIPIO AEMILIANUS) (185–129 BC). Roman soldier and politician. It was he who finally destroyed the city of Carthage (146 BC). Sent to Spain, where the Romans had suffered many reverses in what was essentially a series of guerrilla insurgencies, Scipio eventually trapped the Celtiberian rebels in their capital of Numantia, which fell in 133. This victory put Roman control of Spain on an unchallengeable footing.

SHERMAN, WILLIAM TECUMSEH (1820–1891). American military leader. Born in Ohio, he served in the Union armies during the Civil War, achieving a lasting place in the history books because of events and policies associated with his Atlanta Campaign and March to the Sea (May–December 1864), and the invasion of South Carolina (February 1865). His campaigns exemplified the "raiding strategy" analyzed by Archer Jones in *The Art of War in the Western World*: his "policy of exhaustion" showed the dwindling ranks of supporters of the Confederacy that the defenses of their heartland were brittle indeed. Thus, although he in fact commanded a great conventional army, Sherman exerted an effect on the Confederacy akin to that of a massive guerrilla campaign.

SISON, JOSÉ MARIA (n.d.). Filipino guerrilla leader. A founder of the communist guerrilla New People's Army, he was captured in November 1977, north of Manila.

SMITH, IAN (b. 1919). Rhodesian political figure. He saw service as a fighter pilot in World War II. In 1961 he helped found the Rhodesian Front, a political party in favor of immediate independence for a white-controlled Rhodesia. He held office as prime minister from 1964, proclaiming unilateral independence in November 1965 and directing resistance against African guerrillas. In 1975 Smith began participating in talks with African insurgent leaders, which culminated in majority rule for the renamed state of Zimbabwe in 1979.

SMUTS, JAN CHRISTIAN (1870–1950). South African military and political figure. He was born a British subject in the Cape Colony and made a brilliant record at Christ's College, Cambridge. After he returned to Pretoria with a law degree, President Kruger appointed him state attorney. During the South African (or Boer) War he distinguished himself as a guerrilla leader; in 1902, when the fight was clearly lost, he nevertheless led a band of warriors to within a hundred miles of Capetown. During World War I Smuts smashed a Boer uprising and led South African forces into German East Africa. He then returned to England and helped lay the foundations of the Royal Air Force and was a signer of the Treaty of Versailles. After the war he was an advocate of the League of Nations and served as South African prime minister from 1919 to 1924. Again at the head of the government (1939–1948), Smuts led South Africa to declare war on Germany in 1939. During and after World War II he was active in organizing the United Nations. All the while, however, Smuts's vision of South Africa as a responsible member of a worldwide British Commonwealth was costing him support among his fellow Afrikaaners; Daniel Malan and the Nationalists finally drove Smuts from office in the election of 1948.

SOMOZA FAMILY. Dynasty of president-dictators of Nicaragua. The founder of the dynasty, Anastasio Somoza (1896–1956), became president through his command of the National Guard; that organization, plus the Liberal Party, became the twin pillars of the regime. Anastasio held the presidency from 1937 to 1947 and again from 1950 to 1956, when he was assassinated. He pursued worthwhile reforms, especially an effort to lessen the country's dependence on banana exports. His son Luis Somoza Debayle (1922–1967) succeeded him in the presidency from 1957 to 1963; he sought to relax the more repressive aspects of the family's rule, and during his administration real progress was made in housing and education. During their reign the Somozas had become the richest family in Nicaragua and probably in Central America. They spread much of this wealth among their friends and potential enemies; many elements in the country benefited financially from the dynasty. This was a secret of the long Somoza rule, along with careful control over commissions in the Guardia. But under Luis's brother, Anastasio Somoza Debayle (1925–1980), who held the presidency from 1967 to 1972 and from 1974 to 1979, things began to come unglued. Hitherto the Somoza family had exercised relative restraint, in comparison with many Third World regimes. Anastasio Jr. (''Tachito''), however, was so corrupt financially and so inept politically that during the 1970s he succeeded in forcing the Nicaraguan middle class to make common cause with the Sandinista FSLN, which had hitherto been a fringe organization. Just before the Sandinistas took over Managua, Anastasio fled to Paraguay; he died by assassination in Asunción.

SOPHOULIS, THEMISTOCLES (1860–1949). Greek political leader. Educated as an archaeologist, he participated in revolutionary activities against the Turkish regime on his native Samos. He served as prime minister in 1924 and again during the Greek Civil War (1945–1946 and 1947–1949).

SPINOLA, ANTONIO SEBASTAO (b. 1910). Portuguese military commander. His father was a close adviser of Prime Minister Antonio Salazar. Spinola graduated from the national military academy in 1933 and soon after was commanding Portuguese volunteers in the Spanish Civil War. He was an observer with German troops during the siege of Leningrad. In 1968 he became governor and military commander of Portuguese Guinea. In that territory he carried out many reforms; by 1973, half the forces in Portuguese uniform were native Guineans, and he had brought the rebellion to a stalemate. After returning to Portugal, he published *Portugal and the Future* (1974), calling for a negotiated settlement in Africa and economic reforms at home. The book caused an uproar in official circles. After the army coup that toppled the successors of Salazar, Spinola served as president of the republic for several months but resigned in the face of violent leftist criticism.

STOFFLET, NICOLAS (1752–1796). Vendean guerrilla leader. A professional soldier, he joined the Vendean uprising and played an important role in the victory at Saumur (June 1793). He was made a major general in the royal army. He signed a truce with Hoche in May 1795 but rose up again at the time of the Quiberon landing. A talented guerrilla chief, he was nevertheless hunted down, going before a firing squad in February 1796.

SUMTER, THOMAS (1734–1832). American guerrilla leader in the Revolutionary War. Born in Virginia, he visited England as a young man but by 1765 had become a planter in South Carolina. Simultaneously an Episcopalian and a Baptist, he served in the first and second South Carolina Provincial Congresses. At the outbreak of the Revolution he received a colonel's commission in the Continental Army but retired to his plantation in 1778. After the fall of Charleston British troops pillaged and burned his home, and Sumter was back in the fight. Leading bands of well-mounted men that sometimes numbered several hundred, he fought many fierce battles with British regular units. His men were always short of arms and ammunition and almost never had so much as a single piece of artillery. But he supplied General Greene with invaluable intelligence, frightened the regional loyalists into quietude with his lightning movements, and wore out the British with constant alarms and fruitless chases. Well might Cornwallis complain to Clinton about ''the indefatigable Sumter.''

Sumter was not without blemish: he was careless of casualties, expropriated private property as he felt the need, and had other notable faults. But he was merciful to prisoners (unlike several leaders in Carolina on both sides), and when the fighting was over he worked for reconciliation between patriots and loyalists.

After the war, he declined election to the Continental Congress. He did, however, serve several terms in the South Carolina House of Representatives, was a member of the first United States House of Representatives (1789), and sat in the U.S. Senate from 1801 to 1810. President Madison appointed him ambassador to Brazil, and a fort named after him in Charleston harbor achieved much notoriety in a later war. He was the last of the Revolutionary commanders to die, surviving Yorktown by half a century.

SUN TZU (fl. 4th century BC). Chinese strategist and writer. He is the author of the famous classic *The Art of War*. In the thought of Sun Tzu, competently conducted warfare is based on deception and the indirect approach; good intelligence is of primary value; rapid concentration of forces at the point of the enemy's weakness is the secret of success; and the intelligent commander fights only when victory is certain, at the lowest possible cost to himself and to the enemy. Sun Tzu exerted pervasive and obvious influence on the military thought of Mao Tse-tung, as well as on other modern Chinese and Japanese military thinkers.

TARAKI, NUR MOHAMMED (1917–1979). Afghan communist figure. As a young man he learned English in Bombay and may have joined the Indian Communist Party. He worked in the U.S. aid mission and the U.S. embassy in

Kabul. Active within the PDPA, Taraki became president of Afghanistan after the 1978 coup. Following a visit to the Kremlin, Taraki returned to Kabul and, apparently on Soviet advice, attempted to arrest or kill party boss Hafizullah Amin, who instead threw him into prison and a few months later announced Taraki's death.

TARLETON, BANASTRE (1754–1833). British soldier and politician. Educated at Oxford, he arrived in America in 1775 with Cornwallis. As a commander primarily of loyalist forces he was to become a major figure in the Carolina campaign; "He wrote his name," says Christopher Ward, "in letters of blood all across the history of the war in the South." The phrase "Tarleton's quarter" signified the killing of surrendered enemies. He commanded the loyalist and British forces that were annihilated at Cowpens. From 1790 to 1812 he served in Parliament. He wrote *A History of the Campaigns of 1780 and 1781 in the Southern Provinces of North America* (1787).

TARUC, LUIS (b. 1913). Philippine revolutionary and leader of the Huks. Born in Pampanga province near Manila, the son of poor peasants, Taruc attended the University of Manila for two years (1932–1934) but had to withdraw for lack of funds. He took command of the Hukbalahap units on Japanese-occupied Luzon in 1942. Elected to the House of Representatives in 1947 as a radical, he was rejected by the House because of alleged election irregularities. In 1948 he became co-founder of a new Huk movement, the People's Liberation Army. In 1954, taking advantage of Magsaysay's amnesty program, Taruc turned himself in, an event that was taken as the irrefutable sign that the rebellion had been defeated. After a trial he received a sentence of twelve years; eventually President Ferdinand Marcos granted him a full pardon, and he turned to activity among peasant organizations. He wrote *Born of the People*, a pugnacious communist tract, and the more autobiographical and conciliatory *He Who Rides the Tiger.*

TEMPLER, SIR GERALD (1898–1979). British military figure. A graduate of Sandhurst, he achieved the rank of lieutenant-colonel in World War I and was an armored division commander in World War II. When in 1952 he received appointment as both High Commissioner and Director of Operations for Malaya, he was "armed with the greatest powers enjoyed by a British soldier since Cromwell" (Geoffrey Fairbairn, *Revolutionary Guerrilla War*, p. 151). Although the communists had clearly lost their chance for victory by 1952, British morale in Malaya was low. Templer soon changed that, carrying out the resettlement program laid down by his predecessor General Briggs. By the end of 1954 close to 600,000 squatters had been moved away from the edges of the guerrilla-infested jungles; many of these received title to a piece of land for the first time in their lives. By this resettlement, and by vigorous efforts to control the movement of foodstuffs, Templer created a very serious food problem for the guerrillas. A former intelligence officer, Templer believed that the counter-insurgency needed greatly improved collection and collation of timely intelligence; he therefore placed emphasis on the taking of prisoners. While specially trained hunter squads made the jungles unsafe for the guerrillas, retraining of the police forces increased the security of the civil population. Like Magsaysay, Templer made unexpected visits to various local headquarters, a practice that had a tonic effect on the whole anti-guerrilla effort. As the capstone of his campaign to "win the hearts and minds" of the population, Templer took major steps toward an independent Malaya based on cooperation between law-abiding elements of the Malay and Chinese populations. When Templer left Malaya in 1954 to become Chief of the Imperial General Staff (1955–1958), the conflict was all but finished. He was created field marshal in 1956.

THIEU. *See* Nguyen Van Thieu.

TITO, JOSIP (BROZ) (1892–1980). Yugoslavian communist guerrilla and politician, president of Yugoslavia. Born in Croatia, he was the seventh of fifteen children of a Croatian father and a Slovenian mother. Captured by the Russians in World War I, he became a communist activist, fought in the ranks of the Red Army in the Russian Civil War, and was trained by the Comintern in Moscow from 1935 to 1937. Although the Nazis overran Yugoslavia in April 1941, Tito, loyal to the Hitler-Stalin Pact, did not organize resistance to them until after the German invasion of Russia. Tito's followers, calling themselves the Partisans, deliberately provoked reprisals by the Germans upon the civilian population, a strategy rejected by the rival guerrilla leader Mihailovich. Assisted by British supplies and the approach of Soviet troops during 1944, Tito emerged as the dictator of Yugoslavia and the loyal disciple of Stalin. He nevertheless broke with the Soviets in 1948 and pursued a "national road to communism" until his death.

TORRES, CAMILO (1929–1966). Colombian guerrilla. A son of one of the country's privileged families, he was ordained in the Catholic priesthood and studied at the Louvain. He later taught sociology at the National University in Bogotá. Growing increasingly radical in his views and associates, Torres officially left the priesthood in 1965. He then joined the ELN (the Castroite Army of National Liberation) and after a guerrilla career of two months was killed in a fight with Colombian soldiers. Like Guevara, although on a much lesser scale, he became a cult figure for several years.

TOUSSAINT, FRANÇOIS-DOMINIQUE (TOUSSAINT-L'OUVERTURE after 1796) (c. 1743–1803). Haitian independence leader. With no formal education, he became a plantation steward, receiving emancipation in 1777. He joined the slave revolt in 1791 and soon built a guerrilla army in opposition to other black leaders whose abilities and motives he held in contempt. Allying himself at first with Spanish and English forces against the French, Toussaint changed sides in 1794, virtually expelled the Spanish, and made himself dictator under nominal French sovereignty. A devout Catholic and a vegetarian, he preached reconciliation among blacks, whites, and mulattoes in Haiti. He also instituted compulsory labor on plantations. Overrunning Santo Domingo in 1801, he freed the slaves there and protected peaceful non-blacks. With the French invasion of 1802, Toussaint found himself deserted by whites, mulattoes, and even his lieutenants and allies Christophe and Dessalines. Arrested through treachery, he was imprisoned in France, where he died.

TRINQUIER, ROGER (b. 1908). French officer, a parachutist. He did service in China, Indochina, and Algeria. His most well-known work, *La guerre moderne*, a theory of counterinsurgency, has been seen by many as a blueprint for military totalitarianism.

TRUMAN, HARRY S (1884–1972). President of the United States, 1945–1953. Reacting to the opening of the Cold War, and specifically to the civil war then raging in Greece, he proclaimed before a joint session of Congress in March 1947 a profound innovation in American foreign policy that came to be called the Truman Doctrine. The essence of that doctrine was, in the president's words, "that it must be the policy of the United States to support free peoples who are resisting attempted subjugation by armed minorities or by outside pressures." This doctrine, along with the Marshall Plan and the North Atlantic Treaty, constituted the foundations of the policy of containment, which was to guide the leaders of the United States for the next four decades.

TRUONG CHINH (b. c. 1910). Vietnamese communist leader. Born Dang Xuan Khu, he changed name to "Long March" in honor of Mao and his People's Liberation Army. A founder of the Vietnamese Communist Party 1930, he was its secretary-general from 1941 to 1956. The bloodshed and disruptions attendant upon the land reforms in North Viet Nam in 1955 forced his resignation. Along with Pham Van Dong and Le Duan, he ran North Viet Nam after the death of Ho Chi Minh. He was made first secretary of the Vietnamese Politburo in 1986 but was forced to relinquish the post a few months later. Among his writings is a small treatise on guerrilla war, *A Primer for Revolt.*

TUKHACHEVSKY, MIKHAIL (1893–1937). Soviet military figure. Born in Slednevo, Russia, descended from a noble family, Italian on his mother's side, he became an officer in the czarist army in 1914. He joined the Bolsheviks in 1918. He saw action in the civil war that followed the Bolshevik seizure of power in 1917 and played an important role in the Russo-Polish war of 1920. He also helped to suppress the famous Kronstadt rebellion in 1921. He held a command in the fighting against anti-Soviet guerrillas in central Asia (the so-called *Basmatchis*). During the purges of the armed forces the Stalinists, after a secret trial, executed him for treason.

VANN, JOHN PAUL (1924–1972). American military officer and counterinsurgency expert. Born in Norfolk, Virginia, he enlisted in the army as a youth and did service in the Korean War. He was educated at Rutgers and Syracuse universities and the Command and General Staff College at Fort Leavenworth (1958). He became a lieutenant colonel in 1961. During 1962 and 1963 he was senior adviser to an ARVN division in the Mekong Delta. Retiring from the army in 1963, he returned to Viet Nam in 1965 as a province pacification officer under the Agency for International Development. In 1966 he became chief of civilian pacification programs for the eleven provinces surrounding Saigon and in 1971 was made senior adviser for the II Corps area of South Viet Nam. By then he was, in the words of his biographer, "the most important American in the country after the ambassador and the commanding general in Saigon." A vigorous advocate of American participation in the Vietnamese War, he was also an implacable and persistent critic of the strategy employed under President Johnson and General Westmoreland. He died in a helicopter crash in Kontum province. See Neil Sheehan's best-selling *A Bright Shining Lie: John Paul Vann and America in Viet Nam* (1988).

VILLALOBOS, JOAQUIN (b. 1951). Salvadoran guerrilla leader. Villalobos was active in radical politics after his days as a university student. In the late 1970s he became leader of the ERP (People's Revolutionary Army), the largest guerrilla group in El Salvador.

VIRIATHUS (d. 139 BC). Guerrilla commander in Roman Spain. A leader of the Celtiberian peoples, he inflicted notable defeats on Roman forces sent to pacify the country, often by employing classic guerrilla methods of rapid concentration and rapid dispersal. The Romans finally succeeded in bringing about his assassination through the treachery of his followers.

VO NGUYEN GIAP (b. 1912). Vietnamese communist military leader. Born in Quang Binh province, he attended the same elite high school in Hué as Ho Chi Minh, Pham Van Dong, and Ngo Dinh Diem (qq.v.). He obtained a bachelor of laws degree from the University of Hanoi and then taught history in a private school in that city. In 1937, under the influence of Truong Chinh (q.v.), he joined the Communist Party. Giap's wife and sister were active in subversive activities during World War II; the French guillotined the latter and the former died in prison. By 1941 Giap had established his first small military unit; in later days he would boast that the only military academy he ever attended was the bush. In the chaotic days after the Japanese surrender, Giap led his little army into Hanoi for the so-called August Revolution; he became minister of the interior and consolidated his control over the communist armed forces, the People's Army of Viet Nam (PAVN). At this time Giap displayed the love of fine clothes and gracious living that would characterize him even during the worst days of the fighting with the Americans. Another characteristic was his disregard for casualties among those he commanded. He publicly blamed the failure of his attacks on de Lattre (q.v.) on the cowardice of his troops.

A close student of Mao, Giap insisted that the troops be thoroughly indoctrinated and always display proper behavior toward civilians. In 1954 he achieved world fame through his victory at Dien Bien Phu, a victory to which Chinese assistance, inadequate French numbers, and the tendency of the French to underestimate their adversaries all contributed. Evidence suggests that Giap was opposed to the launching of the great Tet Offensive of 1968, which turned out to be the military disaster Giap is understood to have predicted. Four years later he directed the Easter Offensive, the largest military operation in the world since the Chinese intervention in the Korea War.

Throughout his career, Giap simultaneously held high posts in the army and in the party, a perfect illustration of a key communist concept and practice. But factional enemies deprived Giap of his position as minister of defense in 1980 and his seat on the Politburo in 1982.

WELLINGTON, DUKE OF (ARTHUR WELLESLEY) (1769–1852). British soldier and statesman. Born in Dublin in the same year as Napoleon, Wellesley attended Eton (it is close to a certainty that he *never* said "The battle of Waterloo was won on the playing fields of Eton"). He entered the army in 1787 and saw service in India from 1796 to 1805. He landed in Portugal with a small army in 1808. Owing not only to his excellence as a commander but also in good part to the efforts of tens of thousands of Spanish guerrillas, who inflicted huge casualties on the French and disrupted their communications, after five years of combat in Spain he was ready to invade southern France. The victor of Waterloo represented Great Britain at the Congress of Verona in 1822 and served as prime minister from 1828 to 1830.

WESTERMANN, FRANÇOIS-JOSEPH (1751–1794). French revolutionary commander. Born in Alsace, Westermann was commander of Republican troops in the Vendée from May to December 1793. Because of the unprecedented atrocities committed with his approbation ("I have crushed the children under horses' hooves, I have massacred the women," he wrote to his superiors in Paris), he earned the title "the Butcher of the Vendée." As a result of the constant factional fighting within the ranks of the French revolutionaries, he went to the guillotine.

WESTMORELAND, WILLIAM CHILDS (b. 1914). American military figure. A native of Saxon, South Carolina, Westmoreland graduated from West Point in 1936. He saw service in North Africa, Normandy, and the Bulge. In 1949 he became an instructor at the Command and General Staff College at Fort Leavenworth, Kansas, and later taught at the Army War College. He fought in Korea and was superintendent of West Point from 1960 to 1963. From 1964 to 1968 he commanded U.S. forces in Viet Nam. He became Army Chief of

Staff in 1968 and retired in 1972. He sought the Republican nomination for the governorship of South Carolina in 1974.

General Westmoreland has been the object of severe criticism, inside and outside the army, over his search-and-destroy strategy in Viet Nam, the one-year tour of duty, the grisly "body-count" controversies, and other fundamental matters. Various defenders have pointed out that the army that Westmoreland took over was prepared neither materially nor psychologically for counterinsurgency; that President Johnson's insistence on keeping the American forces on the strategic defensive, and specifically the prohibition against closing the Ho Chi Minh highway through Laos, severely circumscribed Westmoreland's options; and that by the end of 1968 the Viet Cong guerrillas had in fact ceased to play a major role in the conflict. See his *A Soldier Reports* (1976).

YOUNGER, COLE (THOMAS COLEMAN) (1844–1916). Confederate guerrilla and desperado. Born in Missouri, son of a Union-supporting father, Cole nevertheless joined Confederate guerrilla bands under Quantrill and others. He was later appointed a captain in the regular Confederate forces. He did not settle down after the war (during which his father was murdered by Unionist irregulars) but joined the James brothers and their band of brigands. He participated in the disastrous attempt to rob the bank at Northridge, Minnesota, in 1876, where he was wounded and captured. He received a pardon in 1903 and returned to Missouri and there lived out his remaining years in tranquility.

ZABIULLAH KHAN (d. 1984). Afghan guerrilla leader. One of the lesser-known resistance commanders but one of the most effective, Zabiullah's assassination by agents of the Kabul secret police (KhAD) was a great loss to the insurgent forces.

ZACHARIADES, NIKOS (b. 1902). Greek communist leader. Born in Asia Minor, he received training in revolutionary activity in the Soviet Union from 1922 to 1925; he again lived in the USSR from 1928 to 1931, when the Comintern appointed him to head the Greek Communist Party. Caught by the Germans, Zachariades was confined in Dachau from 1942 to 1945. During the Greek civil war, he was the principal author of the disastrous policies pursued by the communist side, including alienation of the peasantry and the premature abandonment of guerrilla tactics in favor of conventional warfare. After causing many of its prominent leaders to be expelled from the Greek Communist Party, he was himself expelled in 1956. He may have ended up working in a factory outside Moscow.

ZAMORA, RUBEN (b. 1942?). Salvadoran political leader. He discontinued studies for the priesthood in 1961 to work in peasant reform movements. He later joined Napoleon Duarte's Christian Democratic party and taught briefly at the Catholic University in San Salvador. Returning to El Salvador in 1987 after eight years of exile, he soon achieved the status of most prominent member of what was called the "democratic left." Although the political group he led was affiliated with the revolutionary FMLN, Zamora engaged in bitter public criticism of terrorist acts perpetrated by that organization in the late 1980s. His voluntary return to his country to engage in electoral politics was widely viewed as a major step toward national reconciliation, or at least peaceful competition. Elected to the National Assembly in 1991, Zamora ran for president of the republic in 1994. He was defeated by a two-to-one margin and accepted the result in a nationwide television address.

PART III
Bibliographical Essays

This bibliographical section provides the reader a selection of English-language works on guerrilla warfare that is wide-ranging, representative, and intensive. (For publication data on articles and books mentioned in the essays, see the alphabetical listing accompanying each.)

STUDIES OF WAR

Even a select list of works on the general subject of war and its relation to insurgency and guerrilla combat would be exceedingly long. Hence the titles that follow in this paragraph (some of which contain excellent bibliographies) are only a sampling from among the best-known or suggestive works. One could perhaps make no better beginning on the general subject than to consult Karl von Clausewitz, *On War*, and especially Book 6, chapter 26, "The People in Arms." Antoine-Henri Jomini, *The Art of War*, has insights into counterinsurgency, acquired the hard way through service in Napoleonic Spain, that are still of great value today. Archer Jones, *The Art of War in the Western World*, is filled with useful discussions of various aspects of guerrilla warfare, although he does not like to use that term. John Keegan's *A History of Warfare* is a broad historico-anthropological treatment. Peter Paret, ed., *Makers of Modern Strategy: Machiavelli to the Modern Age*, is an inexhaustible treasurehouse, especially chapter 27, "Revolutionary War." Sun Tzu, *The Art of War*, is deceptively brief and simple; the profound influence of this work on the thinking of Mao Tse-tung is apparent throughout the latter's writings. Two works by Martin van Creveld, *Command in War* and *Technology and War: From 2000 BC to the Present*, discuss the problems and techniques of commanders from the Stone Age to the computer era. Russell Weigley, *The American Way of War*, provides much matter for reflection, especially the chapter dealing with the Carolina campaign in the American Revolution.

For broad reference works that catalog guerrilla and insurgent groups of every description, see Henry W. Degenhardt, ed., *Revolutionary and Dissident Movements: An International Guide*; Peter Janke, *Guerrilla and Terrorist Organizations: A World Directory and Bibliography*; and U.S. Department of Defense, *Casebook on Insurgency and Revolutionary Warfare: 23 Summary Accounts*.

Two useful comparative historical treatments are Robert B. Asprey, *War in the Shadows: The Guerrilla in History*, and Walter Laqueur, *Guerrilla: A*

Historical and Critical Study. Most of Asprey's book is about the Viet Nam wars; the second edition (1994) contains a foreword that is marred by some remarkably intemperate statements. Laqueur, for his part, wrote that the age of guerrilla war was passing; in addition, the work has some puzzling omissions, and much of the extensive bibliography consists of non-English works. In spite of these difficulties it is still a must-read for students of the subject.

On Roman counterinsurgency experience and techniques, see F. E. Adcock, *The Roman Art of War under the Republic*, and two solid studies of the long Iberian resistance: E. S. Bouchier, *Spain under the Roman Empire*, and C.H.V. Sutherland, *The Romans in Spain*. One should also consult Appian, *Roman History*, vol. i, and *The Cambridge Ancient History*, vol. viii. Caesar, *Commentaries on the Gallic Wars*, also has interesting passages on what today would be called counterinsurgency.

Among older works that are still useful for studies of particular periods or questions are Otto Heilbrunn, *Partisan Warfare*, a small classic; P. Kecskemeti, *Insurgency as a Strategic Problem*, stressing the very limited ability of a foreign power, such as the United States, to carry out or force reforms in an allied country; Abdul H. Nasution, *Fundamentals of Guerrilla Warfare*, written in 1953 by a soldier with the uncommon experience of having commanded both Indonesian guerrillas against the Dutch and later Indonesian conventional forces against secessionist guerrilla movements; Richard J. Barnett, *Intervention and Revolution: The United States in the Third World*, is a skeptical view of American power and motives; C. W. Thayer, *Guerrilla*, can still be read with profit; so can B. Singh and Ko-Wang Mei, *Theory and Practice of Modern Guerrilla Warfare*. J. Bowyer Bell, *The Myth of the Guerrilla*, is a solid and well-received work skeptical of the "invincible guerrilla." See also Nathan Leites and Charles Wolf, *Rebellion and Authority: An Analytical Essay on Insurgent Conflicts*; Richard H. Sanger, *Insurgent Era*; Andrew M. Scott, *Insurgency*; I. L. Idriess, *Guerrilla Tactics*, and Percy Cross Standing, *Guerrilla Leaders of the World*, which presents sympathetic portraits of nineteenth-century partisan chiefs. Otto Heilbronn, *Warfare in the Enemy's Rear*, is mainly concerned with what today would be called special forces operations, but it has a useful bibliography. Brian Crozier, *The Rebels*, is a broad study in a journalistic vein. Harry Eckstein, ed., *Internal War*, offers the contributions of thirteen social scientists of diverse interests; and Franklin Mark Osanka, ed., *Modern Guerrilla Warfare: Fighting Communist Guerrilla Movements 1941–1961*, presents thirty-seven essays of varying quality and a good bibliography for the time; T. N. Greene, ed., *The Guerrilla—and How to Fight Him*, is a valuable collection of essays from a more tactical viewpoint. See also Victor Krulak, ed., *Guerrilla Warfare*; Virgil Ney's early study, "Guerrilla Warfare: Annotated Bibliography"; Leo Heiman, "Guerrilla War: An Analysis"; J. K. Zawodny, "Guerrillas and Sabotage: Organization, Operations, Motivation, Escalation"; Franklin Lindsay, "Unconventional Warfare"; and Klaus Knorr, "Unconventional Warfare: Strategy and Tactics in Internal Political Strife."

Among other more contemporary and broadly comparative works are Ian F. W. Beckett, ed., *The Roots of Counterinsurgency: Armies and Guerrilla Warfare 1900–1945*, which examines British, French, German, and Russian/Soviet experiences, and Anthony James Joes, *Modern Guerrilla Insurgency*, which analyzes six insurgencies in Greece, the Philippines, Indochina, and Afghanistan. Additional useful treatments are Arthur Campbell, *Guerrillas: A History and Analysis from Napoleon's Time to the 1960s*; Ronald Haycock, ed., *Regular Armies and Insurgency*, produced from a symposium at the Royal Military College of Canada, treating five cases from the Mexican Revolution to Viet Nam; Bard O'Neill, *Insurgency and Terrorism: Inside Modern Revolutionary Warfare*; and Bard O'Neill et al., eds., *Insurgency in the Modern World*. N. K. O'Sullivan, ed., *Revolutionary Theory and Political Reality*, has chapters on Latin America and sub-Saharan Africa; and no one should overlook the small but invaluable study by Lewis Gann, *Guerrillas in History*, which emphasizes the importance of outside help for successful guerrillas. G. Chaliand, ed., *Guerrilla Strategies: Revolutionary Warfare and Counterinsurgency*, exhibits a universal sympathy for all guerrillas, whatever their cause, but the essays are well-selected and informative. D.E.H. Russell, *Rebellion, Revolution and Armed Force.*, is quite worthwhile, and so is John Ellis, *A Short History of Guerrilla Warfare*. One should also consult Ted Robert Gurr's *Why Men Rebel*, which discusses the social and psychological roots of rebellion. Max G. Manwaring, ed., *Uncomfortable Wars: Toward a New Paradigm of Low Intensity Conflict*, is a brief volume with contributions from the military, the foreign service, and academia, seeking to present a formula for successful counterinsurgency. Edward G. Corr and Stephen Sloan have edited a useful collection entitled *Low Intensity Conflict: Old Threats in a New World*. Other collections of essays include Lewis B. Ware, ed., *Low-Intensity Conflict in the Third World*; Michael T. Klare and Peter Kornbluh, *Low Intensity Warfare: Counterinsurgency, Proinsurgency, and Antiterrorism in the Eighties*; and Loren B. Thompson, ed., *Low-Intensity Conflict: The Pattern of Warfare in the Modern World*; Stephen Blank et al., *Responding to Low-Intensity Conflict Challenges*; D. M. Condit, ed., *Challenge and Response in Internal Conflict*; and Walter Laqueur, *The Guerrilla Reader: A Historical Anthology*. See also J. Bowyer Bell, "Revolutionary Insurgency," in "Revolutionary War: Western Response," a special issue of the *Journal of International Affairs*; "Subnational Conflict," a special issue of *World Affairs*; Richard H. Shultz, "The Low-Intensity Conflict Environment of the 1990s," and "Coercive Force and Military Strategy: Deterrence Logic and the Cost-Benefit Model of Counterinsurgency Warfare"; and last but by no means least, Harry G. Summers, "Principles of War and Low-Intensity Conflict."

A good grasp of Maoist revolutionary war theory is essential to any student of guerrilla war and counterinsurgency. Very accessible are Mao Tse-tung, *Basic Tactics* and *On the Protracted War*, but consult also his *Selected Military Writings*, as well as the later manifesto by Lin Biao, *Long Live the Victory of People's War*. Samuel B. Griffith, *Mao Tse-tung on Guerrilla Warfare*, is brief and valuable. "Revolutionary Warfare" by John Shy and Thomas Collier is illuminating. For a broader portrait, see J. Chen, *Mao and the Chinese Revolution*.

The complex problems of counterinsurgency are addressed in Douglas Blaufarb, *The Counterinsurgency Era: United States Doctrine and Performance 1950 to the Present*, by a former member of CIA and RAND researcher who criticizes a lack of clarity in U.S. goals in the 1960s. John McKuen, *The Art of Counterinsurgency Warfare*, seeks a counter-strategy to Maoist people's war. Ian F. W. Beckett and John Pimlott edited *Armed Forces and Modern Counterinsurgency*, which contains several very helpful essays, especially on Portuguese Africa and Rhodesia. Additional useful works are W. J. Pomeroy, *Guerrilla and Counterguerrilla Warfare*, R. L. Garthoff, *How Russia Makes War*, and Harriet Scott and William Scott, *The Soviet Art of War*; Thomas A Grant, *Little Wars, Big Problems: The United States and Counterinsurgency in the Postwar World*, a doctoral dissertation; Charles Wolf, *Insurgency and Counterinsurgency*; and Michael Carver, *War since 1945* (Lord Carver served as Chief of the British General Staff). John S. Pustay, *Counterinsurgency Warfare*, is also useful. D. Michael Shafer, *Deadly Paradigms: The Failure of U.S. Counterinsurgency Policy*, is scathingly critical of the American performance in Viet Nam. One should also consult two illuminating essays by Elliot Cohen, "Constraints on America's Conduct of Small Wars," and "Dynamics of Military Intervention." See as well two articles by Michael J. Englehardt, "America Can Win, Sometimes: U.S. Success and Failure in Small Wars," and "Democracies, Dictatorships and Counterinsurgency: Does Regime Type Really Matter?" Consult also William C. Staudenmaier and Allen Sabrossky, "A Strategy of Counterrevolutionary War"; Charles Maechling, "Insurgency and Counterinsurgency: The Role of Strategic Theory"; Gustav Gilbert, "Counterinsurgency"; Andrew Mack, "Why Big Nations Lose Small Wars: The Politics of Asymmetric Conflict", and Peter J. Woolley's provocative "Geography and the Limits of U.S. Military Intervention."

Focusing specifically on the British approach to counterinsurgency, C. E. Callwell's *Small Wars: Their Principles and Practice*, although written at the turn of the century, is still full of useful tactical obervations, and so is Byron Farwell's more historical *Queen Victoria's Little Wars*. Charles Gwynn's *Imperial Policing* presents several cases from the 1920s and 1930s. Bringing the account several decades further are Thomas R. Mockaitis, *British Counterinsurgency, 1919–1960*, and Julian Paget, *Counterinsurgency Campaigning*, on Cyprus, Malaya, and Kenya.

For comparative treatments of the neglected relationship between a state's armed forces and internal conflict, see Katherine Chorley, *Armies and the Art of Revolution*, Anthony James Joes, *From the Barrel of a Gun: Armies and Revolutions*, and John Ellis, *Armies in Revolution*.

Informative studies of peasantry and insurgency include Chalmers Johnson's really excellent *Peasant Nationalism and Communist Power*; Timothy P. Wickham-Crowley, *Guerrillas and Revolution in Latin America: A Comparative Study of Insurgents and Regimes since 1956*; Eric Wolf's aging but still interesting *Peasant Wars of of the Twentieth Century*; John Wilson Lewis, ed., *Peasant Rebellion and Communist Revolution in Asia*; John Walton, *Reluctant Rebels*, a comparison of Colombia, the Philippines, and Kenya; Guy Pauker, *Sources of Insurgency in Developing Countries*; Theda Skocpol "What Makes Peasants Revolutionary?''; Raj Desai and Harry Eckstein, "Insurgency and Peasant Rebellion''; and Ralph Thaxton, "On Peasant Revolution and National Resistance.''

Books, and especially articles, that treat U.S. armed forces and insurgency from a technical or professional point of view are of course voluminous. For broad discussions of the U.S. military approach to guerrilla warfare, one sound place to start would be the U.S. Marine Corps, *Small Wars Manual* (1940), which stresses good relations between troops and civilians. In 1960 the U.S. Army Special Warfare Center published *Readings in Guerrilla Warfare*, which is still of interest, and in the 1980s the services' Joint Low Intensity Conflict Project published an *Analytical Review of Low Intensity Conflict*, an effort to establish some conceptual order among a multitude of disparate topics.

Works that address certain detailed considerations of guerrilla struggle are: Alberto Bayo *150 Questions for a Guerrilla*, by a veteran of the Spanish Civil War who taught guerrilla techniques to the Castro brothers; Ernesto Betancourt, *Revolutionary Strategy: A Handbook for Practitioners*, despite its title a very academic treatment; and Alexander Orlov's old but intriguing *Handbook of Intelligence and Guerrilla Warfare*. Useful specialized studies of particular subjects are Ssu-Yu Teng, *The Nien Army and Their Guerrilla Warfare 1851–1868*; and Patrick O'Sullivan and Jesse Miller, *The Geography of Warfare*.

Additional useful general bibliographies include: Robin Higham, ed., *A Guide to the Sources of United States Military History* and *A Guide to the Sources of British Military History*; and see Benjamin R. Beede, *Intervention and Counterinsurgency: An Annotated Bibliography of the Small Wars of the United States 1898–1984*.

Adcock, F. E. *The Roman Art of War under the Republic*. Cambridge, MA: Harvard, 1940.

Appian. *Roman History*. Trans. Horace White. New York: Macmillan, 1899. vol. 1.

Asprey, Robert B. *War in the Shadows: The Guerrilla in History*. Garden City, NY: Doubleday, 1975 [Revised 1994]. 2 vols.

Barnet, Richard J. *Intervention and Revolution: The United States in the Third World*. New York: World Publishing, 1968.

Bayo, Alberto. *150 Questions for a Guerrilla*. Boulder, CO: Pantheon, 1963.

Beckett, Ian F. W., ed. *The Roots of Counterinsurgency: Armies and Guerrilla Warfare 1900–1945*. London: Blanford, 1988.

Beckett, Ian F. W., and John Pimlott. *Armed Forces and Modern Counterinsurgency*. New York: St. Martin's, 1985.

Beede, Benjamin R. *Intervention and Counterinsurgency: An Annotated Bibliography of the Small Wars of the United States, 1898–1984.* New York: Garland, 1985.

Bell, J. Bowyer. *The Myth of the Guerrilla: Revolutionary Theory and Malpractice.* New York: Knopf, 1971.

———. "Revolutionary Insurgency." *Conflict,* vol. 9, no. 3 (1989).

Betancourt, Ernesto F. *Revolutionary Strategy: A Handbook for Practitioners.* New Brunswick, NJ: Transaction, 1991.

Blank, Stephen, et al. *Responding to Low Intensity Conflict Challenges.* Maxwell Air Force Base, AL: Air University Press, 1990.

Blaufard, Douglas. *The Counterinsurgency Era: United States Doctrine and Performance 1950 to the Present.* New York: Free Press, 1977.

Bouchier, E. S. *Spain under the Roman Empire.* Oxford, UK: Blackwell, 1914.

Caesar, *Commentaries on the Gallic War.* Various editions.

Callwell, C. E. *Small Wars: Their Principles and Practice.* Wakefield, UK: EP Publishing, 1976 [orig. 1906].

Cambridge Ancient History, The. vol. 8. 1989, pp. 118–42 (on the Romans in Spain).

Campbell, Arthur. *Guerrillas: A History and Analysis from Napoleon's Time to the 1960s.* New York: John Day, 1968.

Carver, Michael. *War since 1945.* New York: Putnam, 1981.

Chaliand, G., ed. *Guerrilla Strategies: Revolutionary Warfare and Counterinsurgency.* Berkeley, CA: University of California, 1982.

Chen, J. *Mao and the Chinese Revolution.* London: Oxford University, 1965.

Chorley, Katherine. *Armies and the Art of Revolution.* London: Faber and Faber, 1943.

Clausewitz, Karl von. *On War.* Ed. and trans. Michael Howard and Peter Paret. Princeton, NJ: Princeton University, 1976.

Cohen, Eliot A. "Constraints on America's Conduct of Small Wars." *International Security,* Fall 1984.

———. "Dynamics of Military Intervention." Ariel E. Levite, Bruce W. Jentleson, and Larry Berman, eds., *Foreign Military Intervention: The Dynamics of Protracted Conflict.* New York: Columbia University, 1992.

Condit, D. M., et al., eds. *Challenge and Response in Internal Conflict.* Washington, DC.: American University, 1967–1968.

Corr, Edwin G., and Stephen Sloan, eds., *Low-Intensity Conflict: Old Threats in a New World.* Boulder, CO: Westview, 1992.

Cross, James Eliot. *Conflict in the Shadows: The Nature and Politics of Guerrilla War.* Garden City, NY: Doubleday, 1963.

Crozier, Brian. *The Rebel: A Study of Post-War Insurrections.* Boston: Beacon, 1960.

Degenhardt, Henry W., ed. *Revolutionary and Dissident Movements: An International Guide.* London: Longman, 1988.

Desai, Raj, and Harry Eckstein. "Insurgency: The Transformation of Peasant Rebellion." *World Politics,* vol. 42 (July 1990).

Eckstein, Harry, ed. *Internal War.* Glencoe, IL: Free Press, 1964.

Ellis, John. *Armies in Revolution.* New York: Oxford University, 1974.

———. *A Short History of Guerrilla Warfare.* London: Ian Allen, 1975.

Englehardt, Michael J. "America Can Win, Sometimes: U.S. Success and Failure in Small Wars." *Conflict Quarterly,* vol. 9 (Winter 1989).

———. "Democracies, Dictatorships and Counterinsurgency: Does Regime Type Really Matter?" *Conflict Quarterly,* vol. 12 (Summer 1992).

Farwell, Byron, *Queen Victoria's Little Wars*. London: Harper and Row, 1972.

Gann, Lewis H. *Guerrillas in History*. Stanford, CA: Hoover Institution, 1971.

Garthoff, R. L. *How Russia Makes War*. London: Allen and Unwin, 1954.

Gilbert, Gustav. "Counterinsurgency." *Military Review*, April 1965.

Grant, Thomas A. *Little Wars, Big Problems: The United States and Counterinsurgency in the Postwar World*. Doctoral dissertation. University of California, Irvine, 1990.

Greene, T. N., ed. *The Guerrilla—And How to Fight Him*. New York: Praeger, 1962.

Griffith, Samuel B. *Mao Tse-tung on Guerrilla Warfare*. New York: Praeger, 1961.

Gurr, Ted Robert. *Why Men Rebel*. Princeton, NJ: Princeton University, 1970.

Gwynn, Charles. *Imperial Policing*. New York: St. Martin's, 1934.

Haycock, Ronald, ed. *Regular Armies and Insurgency*. London: Croom Helm, 1979.

Heilbrunn, Otto. *Partisan Warfare*. New York: Praeger, 1962.

———. *Warfare in the Enemy's Rear*. New York: Praeger, 1963.

Heiman, Leo. "Guerrilla War: An Analysis." *Military Review*, vol. 43 (July 1963).

Higham, Robin, ed. *A Guide to the Sources of British Military History*. London: Routledge and K. Paul, 1972.

———. *A Guide to the Sources of United States Military History*. Hamden, CT: Archon, 1975.

Idriess, I. L. *Guerrilla Tactics*. Sydney: Angus and Robertson, 1942.

Janke, Peter. *Guerrilla and Terrorist Organizations: A World Directory and Bibliography*. New York: Macmillan, 1983.

Joes, Anthony James. *From the Barrel of a Gun: Armies and Revolutions*. Washington, DC: Pergamon-Brassey's, 1986.

———. *Modern Guerrilla Insurgency*. Westport, CT: Praeger, 1992.

Johnson, Chalmers. *Peasant Nationalism and Communist Power*. Stanford, CA: Stanford University, 1961.

Jomini, Antoine-Henri *The Art of War*. Trans. G. H. Mendell and W. P. Craighill. Westport, CT: Greenwood, not dated [orig. 1862].

Jones, Archer. *The Art of War in the Western World*. New York: Oxford University, 1987.

Kecskemeti, Paul. *Insurgency as a Strategic Problem*. Santa Monica, CA: RAND, 1967.

Keegan, John. *A History of Warfare*. New York: Knopf, 1993.

Klare, Michael T., and Peter Kornbluh, eds. *Low Intensity Warfare: Counterinsurgency, Proinsurgency and Antiterrorism in the Eighties*. New York: Pantheon, 1988.

Knorr, Klaus. "Unconventional Warfare: Strategy and Tactics in Internal Political Strife." *Annals of the American Academy of Political and Social Science*, vol. 341 (May 1962).

Krulak, Victor N. ed. *Guerrilla Warfare*. Annapolis, MD: U.S. Naval Institute, 1964.

Laqueur, Walter. *Guerrilla: A Historical and Critical Study*. Boston: Little, Brown, 1976.

———. *The Guerrilla Reader: A Historical Anthology*. New York: New American Library, 1977.

Leites, Nathan, and Charles Wolf, Jr. *Rebellion and Authority: An Analytical Essay on Insurgent Conflicts*. Chicago: Markham, 1970.

Lewis, John Wilson, ed. *Peasant Rebellion and Communist Revolution in Asia*. Stanford, CA: Stanford University, 1974.

Lin Biao. *Long Live the Victory of People's War*. Peking, 1965.

Lindsay, Franklin. "Unconventional Warfare." *Foreign Affairs*, vol. 40 (January 1962).

Mack, Andrew. "Why Big Nations Lose Small Wars: The Politics of Asymmetric Conflict." *World Politics*, vol. 27 (January 1975).

Maechling, Charles. "Insurgency and Counterinsurgency: The Role of Strategic Theory." *Parameters*, vol. 14 (Autumn 1984).

Manwaring, Max G., ed. *Uncomfortable Wars: Toward a New Paradigm of Low Intensity Conflict.* Boulder, CO: Westview, 1991.

Mao Tse-tung. *Basic Tactics.* Trans. Stuart Schram. New York: Praeger, 1966.

———. *On the Protracted War.* Peking: Foreign Languages Press, 1954.

———. *Selected Military Writings.* Peking: Foreign Languages Press, 1966.

McKuen, John. *The Art of Counter-Revolutionary Warfare.* London: Faber and Faber, 1966.

Mockaitis, Thomas R. *British Counterinsurgency 1919–1960.* New York: St. Martin's 1990.

Nasution, Abdul H. *Fundamentals of Guerrilla Warfare.* New York: Praeger, 1965 [orig. 1953].

Ney, Virgil. "Guerrilla Warfare: Annotated Bibliography." *Military Review*, vol. 41 (November 1961).

O'Neill, Bard E. *Insurgency and Terrorism: Inside Modern Revolutionary Warfare.* Washington, DC: Brassey's, 1990.

O'Neill, Bard E., William Weston, and Donald Alberts, eds. *Insurgency in the Modern World.* Boulder, CO: Westview, 1980.

Orlov, Alexander. *Handbook of Intelligence and Guerrilla Warfare.* Ann Arbor: University of Michigan, 1963.

Osanka, Franklin Mark, ed. *Modern Guerrilla Warfare: Fighting Communist Guerrilla Movements, 1941–1961.* Glencoe, IL: Free Press, 1962.

O'Sullivan, N. K., ed. *Revolutionary Theory and Political Reality.* New York: St. Martin's, 1983.

O'Sullivan, Patrick, and Jesse W. Miller. *The Geography of Warfare.* New York: St. Martin's, 1983.

Paget, Julian. *Counter-Insurgency Campaigning.* London: Faber and Faber, 1967.

Paret, Peter, ed. *Makers of Modern Strategy: Machiavelli to the Modern Age.* Princeton, NJ: Princeton University, 1986.

Pauker, Guy. *Sources of Insurgency in Developing Countries.* Santa Monica, CA: RAND, 1973.

Pomeroy, W. J. *Guerrilla and Counter-Guerrilla Warfare.* New York: International Publishers, 1964.

Pustay, John S. *Counterinsurgency Warfare.* New York: Free Press, 1965.

Reigel, Corey Walter. *The First World War in East Africa.* Doctoral dissertation. Temple University, Philadelphia, 1990.

"Revolutionary War: Western Response." Special Issue of the *Journal of International Affairs*, vol. 25, no. 1 (1971).

Russell, D.E.H. *Rebellion, Revolution and Armed Force.* New York: Academic Press, 1974.

Sanger, Richard H. *Insurgent Era.* Washington, DC: Potomac Books, 1967.

Scott, Andrew M. *Insurgency.* Chapel Hill, NC: University of North Carolina, 1970.

Scott, Harriet, and William Scott. *The Soviet Art of War.* Boulder, CO: Westview, 1982.

Shafer, D. Michael. *Deadly Paradigms: The Failure of U.S. Counterinsurgency Policy.* Princeton, NJ: Princeton University, 1988.

Shultz, Richard. "Coercive Force and Military Strategy: Deterrence Logic and the Cost-

Benefit Model of Counterinsurgency Warfare." *Western Political Quarterly*, vol. 32 (December 1979).

———. "The Low-Intensity Conflict Environment of the 1990s."*Annals of the American Academy of Political and Social Science*, vol. 157 (September 1991).

Shy, John, and Thomas Collier. "Revolutionary Warfare," Peter Paret, ed. *Makers of Modern Strategy*. Princeton, NJ: Princeton University, 1986.

Singh, B., and Ko Wang Mei. *Theory and Practice of Modern Guerrilla Warfare*. New York: Asia Publishing House, 1971.

Skocpol, Theda. "What Makes Peasants Revolutionary?" *Comparative Politics*, vol. 14 (April 1982).

Standing, Percy Cross. *Guerrilla Leaders of the World*. Boston: Houghton Mifflin, 1913.

Staudenmaier, William C., and Alan Sabrossky. "A Strategy of Counter-Revolutionary War." *Military Review*, vol. 65 (February 1985).

"Subnational Conflict." Special Issue of *World Affairs*, vol. 146 (Winter 1983–84).

Summers, Harry G. "Principles of War and Low-Intensity Conflict." *Military Review*, vol. 65 (February 1985).

Sun Tzu. *The Art of War*. Trans. Samuel B. Griffith. New York: Oxford University, 1963.

Sutherland, C. H. V. *The Romans in Spain*. London: Methuen, 1939.

Teng, Ssu-Yu. *The Nien Army and Their Guerrilla Warfare, 1851–1868*. Paris: Mouton, 1961.

Thaxton, Ralph. "On Peasant Revolution and National Resistance: Towards a Theory of Peasant Mobilization and Revolutionary War with Special Reference to Modern China." *World Politics*, vol. 30, no. 1 (1977).

Thayer, C. W. *Guerrilla*. New York: Harper and Row, 1965.

Thompson, Loren B., ed. *Low-Intensity Conflict: The Pattern of Warfare in the Modern World*. Lexington, MA: Lexington, 1989.

U.S. Army Department. *Readings in Guerrilla Warfare*. Fort Bragg, NC: Special Warfare Center, 1960.

———. *Analytical Review of Low-Intensity Conflict*. Fort Monroe, VA: Joint Low-Intensity Conflict Project, 1986.

U.S. Department of Defense. *Casebook on Insurgency and Revolutionary Warfare: 23 Summary Accounts*. Washington, DC: American University, 1962.

U.S. Marine Corps. *Small Wars Manual*. Washington, DC: Government Printing Office, 1940.

U.S. Naval Institute. *Studies in Guerrilla Warfare*. Annapolis, MD: 1963.

Van Creveld, Martin. *Command in War*. Cambridge, MA: Harvard University, 1985.

———. *Technology and War: From 2000 BC to the Present*. New York: Free Press, 1989.

Walton, John. *Reluctant Rebels*. New York: Columbia University, 1984.

Ware, Lewis B., ed. *Low Intensity Conflict in the Third World*. Maxwell Air Force Base, AL: Air University Press, 1988.

Weigley, Russell E. *The American Way of War: A History of United States Military Strategy and Policy*. Bloomington, IN: Indiana University 1973;

Wickham-Crowley, Timothy P. *Guerrillas and Revolution in Latin America: A Comparative Study of Insurgents and Regimes since 1956*. Princeton, NJ: Princeton University, 1992.

Wolf, Charles., Jr. *Insurgency and Counterinsurgency: New Myths and Old Realities*. Santa Monica, CA: RAND, 1965.

Wolf, Eric. *Peasant Wars of the Twentieth Century*. New York: Harper and Row, 1969.

Woolley, Peter J. "Geography and the Limits of U.S. Military Intervention." *Conflict Quarterly*, vol. 11 (Fall 1991).

Zawodny, J. K. "Guerrillas and Sabotage: Organization, Operations, Motivation, Escalation." *Annals of the American Academy of Political and Social Science*, vol. 341 (May 1962).

THE AMERICAN REVOLUTION, THE VENDÉE, AND SPAIN

Two absolutely indispensable studies of the American Revolution as a whole are Piers Mackesy, *The War for America, 1775–1783*, from a British viewpoint, and Christopher Ward, *The War of the Revolution* (2 volumes). Other good military studies include Willard M. Wallace's brief introductory account, *Appeal to Arms: A Military History of the American Revolution*; John Shy, *A People Numerous and Armed*; Don Higginbotham, *The War of American Independence*; and Don Higginbotham, ed., *Military Analysis of the Revolutionary War*.

For studies of the campaign in the South and the political and military conditions there, see John Richard Alden, *The South in the Revolution, 1763–1789*; a solid and well-received work by John S. Pancake, *This Destructive War: The British Campaign in the Carolinas 1780–1782*; a small but immensely valuable volume by Russell F. Weigley, *The Partisan War: The South Carolina Campaign of 1780–1782*, analyzes the essence of the guerrilla situation from the perspectives of both sides; and an older work, Edward McCrady, *The History of South Carolina in the Revolution, 1780–1783*; and Ronald Hoffmann et al., eds., *An Uncivil War: The Southern Backcountry during the American Revolution*. See also Jac Weller, "Irregular but Effective: Partizan Weapons and Tactics in the American Revolution, Southern Theatre: An Interpretation"; Clyde R. Ferguson, "Functions of the Partisan Militia During the American Revolution: An Interpretation"; and the idiosyncratic but informative work by Henry ("Lighthorse Harry") Lee, *Memoirs of the War in the Southern Department of the United States*.

On particular American guerrilla leaders, good studies include Hugh F. Rankin, *Francis Marion: The Swamp Fox*, a very creditable job; Robert D. Bass, *The Swamp Fox*, a solid exposition of Marion and his exploits; Robert D. Bass, *Gamecock: The Life and Times of General Thomas Sumter*, filled with detailed analysis of the small battles of this campaign; Anne King Gregorie, *Thomas Sumter*; A. N. Waring, *The Fighting Elder: Andrew Pickens*; North Callahan, *Daniel Morgan: Ranger of the Revolution*; and Daniel E. Fitz-Simons, "Francis Marion the 'Swamp Fox': An Anatomy of a Low-Intensity Conflict." On the notorious British counterinsurgent leader Banastre Tarleton, see Robert D. Bass, *The Green Dragon*.

On General Nathanael Greene, the main architect of the American victory in the South, see the following: George Washington Greene, *The Life of Nathanael Greene*, (3 volumes); Elswyth Thane, *The Fighting Quaker: Nathanael Greene*;

Theodore Thayer, *Nathanael Greene: Strategist of the American Revolution*, not a traditional military history but rather a definitive personal biography; and M. F. Treacy, *Prelude to Yorktown: The Southern Campaign of Nathanael Greene*. For the commander of the disastrous encounter at Camden, South Carolina, see Paul David Nelson, *General Horatio Gates*. For George Washington's role in Carolina, see James Thomas Flexner, *George Washington in the American Revolution*. Specialized accounts of the American regular armies include E. Wayne Carp, *To Starve the Army at Pleasure: Continental Army Administration and American Political Culture 1775–1783*; and Charles Royster, *A Revolutionary People at War: The Continental Army and the American Character*, which examines the motives and aspirations of those who fought in the ranks of the Continental Army.

Two good essays on the American approach to the war are Russell F. Weigley, "American Strategy: A Call for a Critical Strategic History," and John Shy, "American Society and Its War for Independence," both in D. Higginbotham, ed., *Reconsiderations on the Revolutionary War*.

Useful studies of British strategy include, for the ill-fated Saratoga campaign that was defeated in large part by irregulars and that led directly to the invasion of the Carolinas, James P. Baxter, ed., *The British Invasion from the North* [The Journal of Lt. William Digby]; Harrison Bird, *The March of Saratoga*; Hoffman Nickerson, *The Turning Point of the Revolution*; and William L. Stone, *The Campaign of Lt. General John Burgoyne and Lt. Colonel Barry St. Leger*.

Ira D. Gruber, "Britain's Southern Strategy," should be read in conjunction with treatments of the British army and its peculiar problems fighting a war in North America; among the best of these are R. Arthur Bowler, *Logistics and the Failure of the British Army in America, 1775–1783*; and Edward F. Curtis, *The Organization of the British Army in the American Revolution*. On the Yorktown campaign, the direct result of the Cornwallis's Carolina fiasco, see Thomas J. Fleming, *Beat the Last Drum: The Siege of Yorktown*; and Henry P. Johnson, *The Yorktown Campaign of Cornwallis*.

For studies of individual British commanders, see Troyer Steven Anderson, *The Command of the Howe Brothers during the American Revolution*; Henry Clinton, *The American Rebellion: Sir Henry Clinton's Narrative of his Campaigns, 1775–1782*; William B. Willcox, *Portrait of a General: Sir Henry Clinton*; and Franklin and Mary Wickwire, *Cornwallis: The American Adventure*.

On the activities of the Loyalists and their fate, consult Robert O. Demond, *The Loyalists in North Carolina during the Revolution*; Robert Stansbury Lambert, *South Carolina Loyalists in the American Revolution*; William H. Nelson, *The American Tory*; and Paul H. Smith, *Loyalists and Redcoats: A Study in British Revolutionary Policy*.

On the all-important French alliance, see Samuel Flagg Bemis, *The Diplomacy of the American Revolution*; Orville Murphy, *Charles Gravier Comte de Vergennes: French Diplomacy in the Age of Revolution 1719–1787*; and James Breck Perkins, *France in the American Revolution*. On the epic struggle between

France and Britain for control of the North American continent, see Francis Parkman, *A Half-Century of Conflict*.

On the Vendée, William Doyle, *The Oxford History of the French Revolution*, is a first-class study which needs to be consulted by any student of the events; the same is true for Simon Schama's magisterial *Citizens*; both of these works take a very unromanticized view of the Revolution. A similar outstanding work is François Furet, *Interpreting the French Revolution*.

Older but still quite useful treatments include Alexis de Tocqueville's small classic, *The Old Regime and the French Revolution*; Louis Adolfe Thiers, *History of the French Revolution*; A. Aulard, *The French Revolution: A Political History, 1789–1804*, which celebrates the Revolution in all its aspects; Albert Mathiez, *The French Revolution*; Georges Lefebvre, *The French Revolution*; and Albert Soboul, *The French Revolution 1787–1799*.

On the French army before and after the Revolution, consult Samuel F. Scott, *The Response of the Royal Army to the French Revolution*; Jean-Paul Bertaud, *The Army of the French Revolution*; Richard Cobb, *The People's Armies*; and Ramsay Weston Phipps, *The Armies of the First French Republic*.

For the dreadful campaigns of extermination waged by the Revolutionary government against the peasants of the Vendée, see the concise but indispensable study by Peter Paret, *Internal War and Pacification: The Vendée 1789–1796*; L. A. Taylor, *The Tragedy of an Army: La Vendée in 1793*; see also Charles Tilly, *The Vendée*, and Michael Ross, *Banners of the King*. For a review of some of the older literature see Harvey Mitchell, ''The Vendée and Counter-revolution: A Review Essay,'' in *French Historical Studies*. On Brittany and the Chouans, two very valuable treatments are Maurice Hutt, *Chouannerie and Counter-Revolution*, and Donald Sutherland, *The Chouans: The Social Origins of Popular Counterrevolution in Upper Brittany 1770–1798*. For the religious dimensions of the Revolution and the uprisings in the Vendée and elsewhere, see the illuminating work by John McManners, *The French Church and the Revolution*. John M. Sherwig, *Guineas and Gunpowder: British Foreign Aid in the Wars with France 1793–1815*, sheds light on the general system of British alliances and the Vendean connection.

For good discussions of guerrilla and counterinsurgent tactics throughout history and to introduce the subject of the Spanish campaign, see Archer Jones, *The Art of War in the Western World*; C. E. Callwell, *Small Wars: Their History and Tactics*, always repays effort; and Antoine-Henri Jomini, *The Art of War*, has some excellent observations on Napoleon's Spanish troubles.

Raymond Carr, *Spain, 1808–1939*, is a concise overview of the Spanish picture, beginning with the Napoleonic invasion. Useful sources of general background material on the Napoleonic empire and its weaknesses include: Louis Adolphe Thiers, *History of the Consulate and the Empire under Napoleon*; Georges Lefebvre, *Napoleon*; A. G. Macdonell, *Napoleon and His Marshals*; and the Count de Las Cases, *Memoirs of the Life, Exile and Conversations of the Emperor Napoleon*.

Good general studies of Napoleon's invasion and effort to subdue Spain are: Owen Connelly, *Blundering to Glory: Napoleon's Military Campaigns*; David Gates, *The Spanish Ulcer: A History of the Peninsular War*; Gabriel H. Lovett, *Napoleon and the Birth of Modern Spain*; the profusely illustrated work by J. Tranie and J.-C. Carmigniani, *Napoleon's War in Spain*; Richard Humble, *Napoleon's Peninsular Marshals*. D. Chlapowski, *Memoirs of a Polish Lancer*, gives some insight into the appeal of the Napoleonic vision, which far transcended the boundaries of France.

For the relation between military affairs and politics in Napoleonic Spain, see two solid studies by Owen Connelly, *The Gentle Bonaparte: A Biography of Joseph, Napoleon's Elder Brother*, and *Napoleon's Satellite Kingdoms*.

Don W. Alexander, *Rod of Iron: French Counterinsurgency Policy in Aragon during the Peninsular War*, is an exhaustive treatment of the war in that key province; John L. Tone, *The Fatal Knot: The Guerrilla War in Navarre and the Defeat of Napoleon in Spain* is another very illuminating regional study. On guerrilla leadership, see William F. Lewis, *Francisco Xavier Mina: Guerrilla Warrior for Romantic Liberalism*, and the hard-to-find tract by Francisco Mina, *A Short Extract from the Life of General Mina Published by Himself*.

Focusing on the British effort in the Peninsular War are: J. W. Fortescue, *History of the British Army*, volumes 8 and 9; Charles Oman, *A History of the Peninsular War*; Michael Glover, *Wellington's Peninsular Victories*; Elizabeth Longford, *Wellington: The Years of the Sword*; W.F.P. Napier, *History of the War in the Peninsula and in the South of France*; and J.F.C. Fuller, *A Military History of the Western World*, volume 2.

Alden, John Richard. *The South in the Revolution, 1763–1789*. Baton Rouge, LA: Louisiana State University, 1957.

Alexander, Don W. *Rod of Iron: French Counterinsurgency Policy in Aragon during the Peninsular War*. Wilmington, DE: Scholarly Resources, 1985.

Anderson, Troyer Steven. *The Command of the Howe Brothers during the American Revolution*. New York: Oxford University, 1936.

Aulard, A. *The French Revolution: A Political History 1789–1804*. vol. 2. trans. Bernard Miali. New York: Scribner's, 1910.

Bass, Robert D. *Gamecock: The Life and Times of General Thomas Sumter*. New York: Holt, Rinehart and Winston, 1961.

———. *The Green Dragon*. New York: Henry Holt, 1957.

———. *Swamp Fox*. New York: Henry Holt, 1959.

Baxter, James P., ed. *The British Invasion from the North* [*Journal of Lt. William Digby*]. New York: Da Capo, 1970 [orig. 1887].

Bird, Harrison. *March to Saratoga*. New York: Oxford University, 1963.

Bemis, Samuel Flagg. *The Diplomacy of the American Revolution*. Bloomington, IN: Indiana University Press, 1935.

Bertaud, Jean-Paul. *The Army of the French Revolution*. Trans. R. R. Palmer. Princeton, NJ: Princeton University, 1988.

Bowler, R. Arthur. *Logistics and the Failure of the British Army in America, 1775–1783*. Princeton, NJ: Princeton University, 1975.

Callahan, North. *Daniel Morgan: Ranger of the Revolution*. New York: Holt, Rinehart and Winston, 1961.

Callwell, C. E. *Small Wars: Their Principles and Practice*. Wakefield, UK: EP Publishing, 1976 [orig. 1906].

Carp, E. Wayne. *To Starve the Army at Pleasure: Continental Army Administration and American Political Culture 1775–1783*. Chapel Hill, NC: University of North Carolina, 1984.

Carr, Raymond. *Spain 1808–1939*. Oxford, UK: Oxford University, 1966.

Chlapowski, Dezydery. *Memoirs of a Polish Lancer*. Chicago: Emperor's Press, 1992.

Clinton, Henry. *The American Rebellion: Sir Henry Clinton's Narrative of his Campaigns 1775–1782*. Ed. William B. Willcox. New Haven, CT: Yale University, 1954.

Cobb, Richard. *The People's Armies*. New Haven, CT: Yale University, 1987.

Connelly, Owen. *Blundering to Glory: Napoleon's Military Campaigns*. Wilmington, DE: Scholarly Resources, 1987.

———. *The Gentle Bonaparte: A Biography of Joseph, Napoleon's Elder Brother*. New York: Macmillan, 1968.

———. *Napoleon's Satellite Kingdoms*. New York: Free Press, 1965.

Curtis, Edward E. *The Organization of the British Army in the American Revolution*. New Haven, CT: Yale University, 1926.

DeMond, Robert O. *The Loyalists in North Carolina during the Revolution*. Hamden, CT: Archon Books, 1964 [orig. 1940].

Doyle, William. *The Oxford History of the French Revolution*. Oxford, UK: Oxford University, 1989.

Ferguson, Clyde R. "Functions of the Partisan Militia in the South during the American Revolution: An Interpretation," W. Robert Higgins, ed. *The Revolutionary War in the South: Power, Conflict and Leadership*. Durham, NC: Duke University, 1979.

Fitz-Simons, Daniel E. "Francis Marion the 'Swamp Fox': An Anatomy of a Low-Intensity Conflict." *Small Wars and Insurgencies*, vol. 6 (Spring 1995).

Fleming, Thomas J. *Beat the Last Drum: The Siege of Yorktown*. New York: St. Martin's, 1963.

Flexner, James Thomas. *George Washington in the American Revolution*. Boston: Little, Brown, 1968.

Fortescue, J. W. *History of the British Army*, vols. 8 and 9. London: Macmillan, 1919–1920.

Fuller, J.F.C. *Military History of the Western World*, vol. 2. New York: Da Capo, 1955.

Furet, François. *Interpreting the French Revolution*. Trans. Elborg Forster. Cambridge, UK: Cambridge University, 1981.

Gates, David. *The Spanish Ulcer: A History of the Peninsular War*. New York: Norton, 1986.

Glover, Michael. *Wellington's Peninsular Victories*. New York: Macmillan, 1963.

Greene, George Washington. *The Life of Nathanael Greene*. Cambridge, MA: Hurd and Houghton, 1871. 3 vols.

Gregorie, Anne King. *Thomas Sumter*. Columbia, SC: R. L. Bryan, 1931.

Gruber, Ira D. "Britain's Southern Strategy," W. Robert Higgins, ed. *The Revolutionary War in the South: Power, Conflict and Leadership*. Durham, NC: Duke University, 1979.

Higginbotham, Don.*The War of American Independence*. New York: Macmillan, 1971.

Higginbotham, Don, ed. *Military Analysis of the Revolutionary War.* Millwood, NY: KTO Press, 1977.

Hoffmann, Ronald, Thad W. Tate, and Peter J. Albert, eds. *An Uncivil War: The Southern Backcountry During the American Revolution.* Charlottesville, VA: University of Virginia, 1985.

Humble, Richard. *Napoleon's Peninsular Marshals.* New York: Taplinger, 1974.

Hutt, Maurice. *Chouannerie and Counter-Revolution.* Cambridge, UK: Cambridge University, 1983.

Johnson, Henry P. *The Yorktown Campaign of Cornwallis.* New York: Harper, 1981.

Jomini, Antoine-Henri. *The Art of War.* Trans. G. H. Mendell and W. P. Craighill. Westport, CT: *Greenwood*, n.d. [orig. trans. 1862].

Jones, Archer. *The Art of War in the Western World.* New York: Oxford University, 1987.

Lambert, Robert Stansbury. *South Carolina Loyalists in the American Revolution.* Columbia, SC: University of South Carolina, 1987.

Las Cases, Count de. *Memoirs of the Life, Exile and Conversations of the Emperor Napoleon.* New York: Armstrong, 1883.

Lee, Henry. *Memoirs of the War in the Southern Department of the United States.* ed. Robert E. Lee. New York: Arno Press, 1969 [orig. 1869].

Lefebvre, Georges. *The French Revolution.* New York: Columbia University. 2 vols. 1962–1964.

———. *Napoleon.* Trans. Henry F. Stockhold. New York: Columbia University, 1969 [orig. 1936]. 2 vols.

Lewis, William F. *Francisco Xavier Mina: Guerrilla Warrior for Romantic Liberalism.* Doctoral dissertation, University of California, Santa Barbara, 1968.

Longford, Elizabeth. *Wellington: The Years of the Sword.* New York: Harper and Row, 1969.

Lovett, Gabriel H. *Napoleon and the Birth of Modern Spain.* New York: New York University, 1965. 2 vols.

Macdonell, A. G. *Napoleon and His Marshals.* New York: Macmillan, 1934.

Mackesy, Piers. *The War for America, 1775–1783.* Cambridge, MA: Harvard University, 1965.

Mathiez, Albert. *The French Revolution.* Trans. Catherine A. Phillips. New York: Russell and Russell, 1962 [orig. 1928].

McCrady, Edward. *The History of South Carolina in the Revolution, 1780–1783.* New York: Paladin, 1969 [orig. 1902].

McManners, John. *The French Church and the Revolution.* Westport, CT: Greenwood, 1982.

Mina, Francisco. *A Short Extract from the Life of General Mina Published by Himself.* London, 1825.

Mitchell, Harvey. "The Vendée and Counterrevolution: A Review Essay." *French Historical Studies,* vol. 5, no. 4 (Fall 1968).

Murphy, Orville. *Charles Gravier Comte de Vergennes: French Diplomacy in the Age of Revolution, 1719–1787.* Albany, NY: State University of New York, 1982.

Napier, W.F.P. *History of the War in the Peninsula and in the South of France.* London: Frederick Warne, 1890–1892. 6 vols.

Nelson, Paul David. *General Horatio Gates.* Baton Rouge, LA: Louisiana State University, 1976.

Nelson, William H. *The American Tory*. Oxford, UK: Oxford University, 1961.

Nickerson, Hoffman. *The Turning Point of the Revolution*. Fort Washington, NY: Kennikat Press, 1928. 2 vols.

Oman, Charles. *A History of the Peninsular War*. Oxford, UK: Oxford University, 1902–1930. 7 vols.

Pancake, John S. *This Destructive War: The British Campaign in the Carolinas, 1780–1782*. University, AL: University of Alabama, 1985.

Paret, Peter. *Internal War and Pacification: The Vendée 1789–1796*. Princeton, NJ: Princeton University Center of International Studies, 1961.

Parkman, Francis. *A Half-Century of Conflict*. Boston: Little, Brown, 1910. 2 vols.

Perkins, James Breck. *France in the American Revolution*. Boston: Houghton Mifflin, 1911.

Phipps, Ramsay Weston. *The Armies of the First French Republic*. Westport, CT: Greenwood, 1980 [orig. 1931].

Rankin, Hugh F. *Francis Marion: The Swamp Fox*. New York: Crowell, 1973.

Ross, Michael. *Banners of the King*. New York: Hippocrene, 1975.

Royster, Charles. *A Revolutionary People at War: The Continental Army and American Character, 1775–1783*. Chapel Hill, NC: University of North Carolina, 1979.

Schama, Simon. *Citizens: A Chronicle of the French Revolution*. New York: Knopf, 1989.

Scott, Samuel F. *The Response of the Royal Army of the French Revolution*. Oxford, UK: Oxford University, 1978.

Sherwig, John M. *Guineas and Gunpowder: British Foreign Aid in the Wars with France, 1793–1815* Cambridge, MA: Harvard University, 1969.

Shy, John. "American Society and Its War for Independence." Don Higginbotham, ed. *Considerations on the Revolutionary War*. Westport, CT: Greenwood, 1978.

———. *A People Numerous and Armed*. Oxford, UK: Oxford University, 1976.

Smith, Paul H. *Loyalists and Redcoats: A Study in British Revolutionary Policy*. Chapel Hill, NC: University of North Carolina, 1964.

Soboul, Albert. *The French Revolution 1787–1799*. Trans. A. Forrest and C. Jones. New York: Random House, 1974 [orig. 1962].

Stone William L. *The Campaign of Lieut. Gen. John Burgoyne and the Expedition of Lieut. Col. Barry St. Leger*. New York: Da Capo, 1970 [orig. 1877].

Sutherland, Donald. *The Chouans: The Social Origins of Popular Counterrevolution in Upper Brittany 1770–1798*. Oxford UK: Oxford University, 1982.

Taylor, L. A. *The Tragedy of an Army: La Vendée in 1793*. London: Hutchinson, 1913,

Thane, Elswyth. *The Fighting Quaker: Nathanael Greene*. New York: Hawthorn, 1972.

Thayer, Theodore. *Nathanael Greene: Strategist of the American Revolution*. New York: Twayne, 1960.

Thiers, Louis Adolphe. *History of the Consulate and the Empire of France under Napoleon*, vol. 6. Philadelphia, PA: Lippincott, 1894.

———. *The History of the French Revolution*. Trans. Frederick Shoberl. Philadelphia, PA: Lippincott, 1894.

Tilly, Charles. *The Vendée*. Cambridge, MA: Harvard University, 1964.

Tocqueville, Alexis de. *The Old Regime and the French Revolution*. Garden City, NY: Doubleday Anchor, 1955 [orig. 1856].

Tone, John L. *The Fatal Knot: The Guerrilla War in Navarre and the Defeat of Napoleon in Spain*. Chapel Hill, NC: University of North Carolina, 1994.

Tranie, J., and J.-C. Carmigniani. *Napoleon's War in Spain*. Trans. Janet Mallender and
    J. Clements. London: Arms and Armour, 1982.
Treacy, M. F. *Prelude to Yorktown: The Southern Campaign of Nathanael Greene*.
    Chapel Hill, NC: University of North Carolina, 1963.
Wallace, Willard M. *Appeal to Arms: A Military History of the American Revolution*.
    New York: Harper, 1951.
Ward, Christopher. *The War of the Revolution*. New York: Macmillan, 1952. 2 vols.
Waring, A. N. *The Fighting Elder: Andrew Pickens*. Columbia, SC: University of South
    Carolina, 1962.
Weigley, Russell F. "American Strategy: A Call for a Critical Strategic History." Don
    Higginbotham, ed. *Reconsiderations on the Revolutionary War*. Westport, CT:
    Greenwood, 1978.
———. *The Partisan War: The South Carolina Campaign of 1780–1782*. Columbia, SC:
    University of South Carolina, 1970.
Weller, Jac. "Irregular But Effective: Partizan [*sic*] Weapons Tactics in the American
    Revolution, Southern Theatre." The Editors of Military Affairs. *Military Analy-
    sis: An Anthology*. Millwood, NY: KTO Press, 1977.
Wickwire, Franklin, and Mary Wickwire. *Cornwallis: The American Adventure*. Boston,
    MA: Houghton Mifflin, 1970.
Willcox, William B. *Portrait of a General: Sir Henry Clinton in the War of Indepen-
    dence*. New York: Knopf, 1964.

THE AMERICAN CIVIL WAR, THE BOERS, AGUINALDO, LAWRENCE, WORLD WAR I

There is of course a library-full of good background studies on the American
Civil War. Two of the best received and most durable of them are: the trilogies
by Bruce Catton, *The Centennial History of the Civil War* (*The Coming Fury*,
Terrible Swift Sword, *Never Call Retreat*) and *The Army of the Potomac* (*Mr.
Lincoln's Army*, *Glory Road*, and *A Stillness at Appomatox*). Vast in conception
and filled with illuminating detail is Allan Nevins, *The Ordeal of the Union: A
House Dividing 1852–1857*. Other outstandingly useful studies include Richard
E. Berringer, et al., *Why the South Lost the Civil War*; Herman Hattaway and
Archer Jones, *How the North Won*; James M. McPherson, *The Battle Cry of
Freedom*; Charles H. Wesley, *The Collapse of the Confederacy*; and Bell Irvin
Wiley, *The Road to Appomatox*. For a revealing portrait of the ordinary Con-
federate soldier in the ranks, see Bell Irvin Wiley's *Johnny Reb: The Common
Soldier of the Confederacy*; see also the two good collections of essays, David
Donald, ed., *Why the North Won the Civil War*, and Henry Steele Commager,
ed., *The Defeat of the Confederacy*. Last under this heading but hardly least,
Robert L. Kerby, "Why the Confederacy Lost," vigorously argues the arresting
thesis that the Confederacy's key mistake was opting for conventional war instead of massive guerrilla resistance from the beginning.

On Lincoln as a war leader and strategist, see T. Harry Williams, *Lincoln and
His Generals*, which makes a powerful case that Lincoln was the best Union

strategist; see also James M. McPherson, "Lincoln and the Strategy of Unconditional Surrender." For a wider context of these judgments, see Allan Nevins, *The Statesmanship of the Civil War*; and very rich rewards indeed, about insurgency and many other topics, await anyone who will patiently mine *The Collected Works of Abraham Lincoln*, edited by Roy P. Basler.

On the leadership of the Confederacy there is the magisterial multivolume work by Douglas Southall Freeman, *R. E. Lee*; A. L. Long wrote *Memoirs of Robert E. Lee*. Other useful works include Clifford Dowdey, *Lee*; two studies by Clement Eaton, *Jefferson Davis* and *A History of the Southern Confederacy*; Bell Irvin Wiley, *The Road to Appomatox*; and Paul D. Escott, *After Secession: Jefferson Davis and the Failure of Southern Nationalism*, along with which one should consult the brief but illuminating work by Drew Gilpin Faust, *The Creation of Confederate Nationalism*. Throughout the war the Confederacy was wracked by internal dissension and even internecine armed conflict; on this important subject consult the following outstanding works: Georgia Lee Tatum, *Disloyalty in the Confederacy*; Alfred Burton Moore, *Conscription and Conflict in the Confederacy*; Ella Lonn, *Desertion during the Civil War*; Thomas William Humes, *The Loyal Mountaineers of Tennessee* (originally published in 1888); and the excellent study by John G. Barrett, *The Civil War in North Carolina*. For a brief but revealing and disturbing look at Confederate counterinsurgency in North Carolina, see Phillip Shaw Paludan, *Victims: A True Story of the Civil War*.

Sherman's strategic conception that the war could be brought to an end through the exhaustion of the Confederacy is well-known because of his march through Georgia; but the sequel, at least equally destructive, to that famous campaign appears in John G. Barrett, *Sherman's March through the Carolinas*.

On Mosby and his famous Rangers, see John S. Mosby, *The Memoirs of Colonel John S. Mosby*; Virgil Carrington Jones, *Grey Ghosts and Rebel Raiders*; Kenin H. Siepel, *Rebel: The Life and Times of John Singleton Mosby*; and Jeffrey D. Wert, *Mosby's Rangers*. For Union counterinsurgency efforts, see Carl Brent Beamer, *Gray Ghostbusters: Eastern Theater Union Counterguerrilla Operations in the Civil War*.

For the war on the Kansas-Missouri frontier, one must read Michael Fellman's beautifully written but thoroughly chilling description of the fate of civilians caught in a counterinsurgency, *Inside War: The Guerrilla Conflict in Missouri during the American Civil War*. Consult also Jay Monaghan, *Civil War on the Western Border, 1854–1865*; Richard S. Brownlee, *Gray Ghosts of the Confederacy*; and Thomas Goodrich, *Black Flag: Guerrilla Warfare on the Western Border*. For studies of the most notorious character to come out of this border guerrilla strife, perhaps the most notorious character of the entire American Civil War, see Albert Castel, *William Clarke Quantrill: His Life and Times*, and William Elsey Connelley, *Quantrill and the Border Wars*. See also W. Wayne Smith, "An Experiment in Counterinsurgency: The Assessment of Confederate Sympathizers in Missouri." Finally, see Daniel E. Sutherland, "Guerrillas: The Real War in Arkansas."

On the problems attendant upon the generation of sufficient Unionist manpower to discourage any plans for continuing the war in the guerrilla style after Appomatox, see Eugene C. Murdock, *One Million Men: The Civil War Draft in the North*. Of increasing importance in the ever-growing Union appetite for men to fill the ranks of its armies were the blacks, both freemen and former slaves; two very good studies of black troops in the Union armies are Joseph T. Glaathaar, *Forged in Battle: The Civil War Alliance of Black Soldiers and White Officers*, and Dudley Taylor Cornish, *The Sable Arm*.

On the American conflict in the wake of the Spanish-American War with the followers of Emilio Aguinaldo, for background see Margaret Leech's much-praised *In the Days of McKinley*, along with Richard Welch, *Response to Imperialism: The United States in the Philippine-American War*, and Julius Pratt, *Expansionists of 1898*. On the politico-military aspects of the war, John Morgan Gates, *Schoolbooks and Krags: The United States Army in the Philippines, 1898–1902 is* essential; a very useful military analysis is Brian McAlister Linn, *The U.S. Army and Counterinsurgency in the Philippine War 1899–1902*, which stresses the contribution that decentralization of command made to the American victory. Other helpful studies are Glenn A. May, *Battle for Batangas: A Philippine Province at War*, John R. M. Taylor, *The Philippine Insurrection against the United States: A Compilation of Documents with Notes and Introduction* (5 volumes); Joseph L. Schott, *The Ordeal of Samar*; Stuart C. Miller, *"Benevolent Assimilation": The American Conquest of the Philippines*; and W. Sexton, *Soldiers in the Sun*. One should certainly consult Frederick Funston's vigorous *Memories of Two Wars: Cuban and Philippine Experiences*. (Funston actually captured Aguinaldo, by an elaborate ruse.) Additional works of merit include James H. Blount, *The American Occupation of the Philippines, 1898–1912*; Moorfield Storey, *Conquest of the Philippines by the United States, 1898–1925*; David Sturtevant, *Popular Uprising in the Philippines, 1840–1940*; Leon Wolff, *Little Brown Brother*; James A. Leroy, *The Americans in the Philippines*; Peter W. Stanley, ed., *Reappraising an Empire: New Perspectives on Philippine-American History*; U.S. Senate, *Hearings: Affairs in the Philippine Islands* [1902]; Glenn Anthony May, "Why the United States Won the Philippine-American War 1899–1902"; and Edward J. Filiberti, "The Roots of U.S. Counterinsurgency Doctrine." Interesting glimpses of American statesmanship of this era abound in H. W. Morgan, ed., *Making Peace with Spain: The Diary of Whitelaw Reid*. Finally, in his mature years Emilio Aguinaldo, the leader of the Filipino guerrillas of 1899, wrote *A Second Look at America*, in which he stated, among other things, that the American occupation and conquest of the Philippines was on balance a good thing for the latter.

On the conflict between the British Empire and the Boer republics, two outstanding and widely praised works are Thomas Packenham, *The Boer War*, and Byron Farwell, *The Great Anglo-Boer War*. Early studies of the South African conflict include L. Amery, ed., *The Times History of the War in South Africa 1899–1902*; F.H.E. Cunliffe, *History of the Boer War*; C. Doyle, *The Great

Boer War; and H. W. Wilson, *After Pretoria: The Guerrilla War*. For studies of some of the outstanding Boer chiefs, see P. J. Sampson, *The Capture of De Wet*, and Johannes Meintjes, *De La Rey, Lion of the West*; See also D. Reitz, *Commando: A Boer Journal of the Boer War*, a highly acclaimed work written by a twenty-one-year-old veteran; another indispensable memoir is Christian Rudolph De Wet, *The Three Years' War*; Paul Kruger's *Memoirs* vigorously presents the Boer position; and see also J. S. Marais, *The Fall of Kruger's Republic*. On one of the most controversial aspects of the struggle see A. C. Martin, *The Concentration Camps 1900–1902*. Other useful works are : D. Judd, *The Boer War*; Edgar Holt, *The Boer War* (pro-British); Peter Warwicke, ed., *The South African War*; Theodore Caldwell, ed., *The Anglo-Boer War*; and A. N. Porter, *The Origins of the South African War: Joseph Chamberlain and the Diplomacy of Imperialism*.

Regarding the exploits of Lawrence of Arabia, see his *Seven Pillars of Wisdom*, and his essay "Guerrilla Warfare" in the *Encyclopedia Brittanica* (reprinted 1957). The essay on Lawrence in Lewis Gann, *Guerrillas in History*, is incisive. An outstanding work is F. Armitage, *The Desert and the Stars: A Biography of Lawrence of Arabia*; relentlessly hostile to Lawrence and very controversial is Richard Aldington, *Lawrence of Arabia*; other interesting studies are Robert Graves, *Lawrence of Arabia*; L. Hart, *Colonel Lawrence: The Man behind the Legend*; B. H. Liddel Hart, *T. E. Lawrence*; Anthony Nutting, *Lawrence of Arabia*; and Desmond Stewart, *T. E. Lawrence*.

At least four other books deserve mention here. Still widely considered the premier study of the 1870–1871 conflict, Michael Howard's *The Franco-Prussian War* provides a dramatic look at French guerrilla activities, actual and potential, and the significant effect these exerted on Prussian planning and conduct. Finally, three works dealing with one of the most successful yet least-known guerrilla leaders of this century, Paul von Lettow-Vorbeck: see his *My Reminiscences of East Africa*, along with Leonard Mosley's well-crafted study, *Duel for Kilimanjaro*, and Corey Walter Reigel, *The First World War in East Africa*.

Aguinaldo, Emilio. *A Second Look at America*. New York: Robert Speller, 1957.

Aldington, Richard. *Lawrence of Arabia*. London: Collins, 1955.

Amery, L. S., ed., *The Times History of the War in South Africa 1899–1902*. London: Sampson, Low, Marston, 1900–1909. 3 vols.

Armitage, F. *The Desert and the Stars: A Biography of Lawrence of Arabia*. New York: Holt, 1955.

Barrett, John G. *The Civil War in North Carolina*. Chapel Hill, NC: University of North Carolina, 1963.

———. *Sherman's March through the Carolinas*. Chapel Hill, NC: University of North Carolina, 1956.

Basler, Roy P., ed. *The Collected Works of Abraham Lincoln*. New Brunswick, NJ: Rutgers University, 1953. 9 vols.

Beamer, Carl Brent. *Gray Ghostbusters: Eastern Theater Union Counterguerrilla Operations in the Civil War*. Doctoral dissertation, Ohio State University, 1988.

Berringer, Richard E., Herman Hattaway, Archer Jones, and William N. Still, Jr. *Why the South Lost the Civil War*. Athens, GA: University of Georgia, 1986.

Blount, James H. *The American Occupation of the Philippines 1898–1912*. New York: Putnam, 1913.

Brownlee Richard S. *Gray Ghosts of the Confederacy: Guerrilla Warfare in the West, 1861–1865*. Baton Rouge, LA: Louisiana State University, 1958.

Caldwell, Theodore, ed. *The Anglo-Boer War*. Boston: D. C. Heath, 1965.

Castel, Albert. *William Clarke Quantrill: His Life and Times*. New York: Frederick Fell, 1962.

Catton, Bruce. *The Army of the Potomac*. Garden City, NY: Doubleday, 1951–1953. 3 vols.

———. *The Centenniel History of the Civil War*. Garden City, NY: Doubleday, 1961–1965. 3 vols.

Commager, Henry Steele, ed. *The Defeat of the Confederacy*. New York: Van Nostrand, 1964.

Connelley, William Elsey. *Quantrill and the Border Wars*. New York: Pageant, 1956 [orig. 1909].

Cornish, Dudley Taylor. *The Sable Arm*. New York: Longmans, Green, 1956.

Cunliffe, F.H.E. *History of the Boer War*. London: Methuen, 1901–1904. 2 vols.

De Wet, Christian Rudolf. *The Three Years' War*. London: Constable, 1902.

Donald, David, ed. *Why the North Won the Civil War*. Baton Rouge, LA: Louisiana State University, 1960.

Dowdey, Clifford. *Lee*. Boston: Little, Brown, 1965.

Doyle, C. *The Great Boer War*. New York: McClure and Phillips, 1902.

Eaton, Clement. *A History of the Southern Confederacy*. New York: Free Press, 1954.

———. *Jefferson Davis*. New York: Free Press, 1977.

Escott, Paul D. *After Secession: Jefferson Davis and the Failure of Confederate Nationalism*. Baton Rouge, LA: Louisiana State University, 1978.

Farwell, Byron. *The Great Anglo-Boer War*. New York: Harper and Row, 1976.

Faust, Drew Gilpin. *The Creation of Confederate Nationalism: Ideology and Identity in the Confederate South*. Baton Rouge, LA: Louisiana State University, 1988.

Fellman, Michael. *Inside War: The Guerrilla Conflict in Missouri during the American Civil War*. New York: Oxford University, 1989.

Filiberti, Edward J. "The Roots of U.S. Counterinsurgency Doctrine." *Military Review*, vol. 68 (January 1988).

Freeman, Douglas Southall. *R. E. Lee*. New York: Scribner's, 1935–1936.

Funston, Frederick. *Memories of Two Wars: Cuban and Philippine Experiences*. New York: Scribner's, 1911.

Gates, John Morgan. *Schoolbooks and Krags: The United States Army in the Philippines 1898–1902*. Westport, CT: Greenwood, 1973.

Glatthaar, Joseph T. *Forged in Battle: The Civil War Alliance of Black Soldiers and White Officers*. New York: Meridian, 1991.

Goodrich, Thomas. *Black Flag: Guerrilla Warfare on the Western Border*. Bloomington, IN: Indiana University, 1995.

Graves, Robert. *Lawrence of Arabia*. London: Jonathan Cape, 1927.

Hart, L. *Colonel Lawrence: The Man behind the Legend*. New York: Dodd, Mead, 1934.

Hattaway, Herman, and Archer Jones. *How the North Won*. Urbana, IL: University of Illinois, 1991.

Holt, Edgar. *The Boer War*. London: Putnam, 1958.

Howard, Michael. *The Franco-Prussian War*. New York: Dorset, 1961.

Humes, Thomas William. *The Loyal Mountaineers of Tennessee*. Spartanburg, SC: Reprint Company, 1974 [orig. 1888].

Jones, Virgil Carrington. *Grey Ghosts and Rebel Raiders*. New York: Henry Holt, 1956.

Judd, D. *The Boer War*. London: Hart-Davis, MacGibbon, 1977.

Kerby, Robert L. "Why the Confederacy Lost." *Review of Politics*, vol. 35 (July 1973).

Kruger, Paul. *Memoirs*. Port Washington, NY: Kennikat, 1970 [orig. 1902]. 2 vols.

Lawrence, T. E. "Guerrilla Warfare," *Encyclopedia Britannica*, 1957, vol. 10.

———. *Seven Pillars of Wisdom: A Triumph*. Garden City, NY: Doubleday, 1936.

Leech, Margaret. *In the Days of McKinley*. New York: Harper and Row, 1959.

Leroy, James A. *The Americans in the Philippines*. New York: Houghton Mifflin, 1914.

Lettow-Vorbeck, Paul von. *My Reminiscences of East Africa*. London: Hurst and Blackett, 1920.

Liddel Hart, B. H. *T. E. Lawrence*. London: Jonathan Cape, 1934.

Linn, Brian McAlister. *The U.S. Army and Counterinsurgency in the Philippine War, 1899–1902*. Chapel Hill, NC: University of North Carolina, 1989.

Long, A. L. *Memoirs of Robert E. Lee*. Secaucus, NJ: Blue and Grey Press, 1983.

Lonn, Ella. *Desertion during the Civil War*. Gloucester, MA: Peter Smith, 1966 [orig. 1928].

Marais, J. S. *The Fall of Kruger's Republic*. London: Oxford University, 1961.

Martin, A. C. *The Concentration Camps 1900–1902*. Cape Town: Howard Timmins, 1957.

May, Glenn A. *Battle for Batangas: A Philippine Province at War*. New Haven, CT: Yale University, 1991.

May, Glenn Anthony. "Why the United States Won the Philippine-American War, 1899–1902." *Pacific Historical Review*, vol. 52 (November 1983).

McPherson, James M. *Battle Cry of Freedom*. New York: Oxford University, 1988.

———. "Lincoln and the Strategy of Unconditional Surrender." Gabor S. Boritt, ed. *Lincoln, the War President*. New York: Oxford University, 1992.

Meintjes, Johannes. *De La Rey: Lion of the West*. Johannesburg: Keartland, 1966.

Miller, Stuart Creighton. *"Benevolent Assimilation": The American Conquest of the Philippines, 1899–1903*. New Haven, CT: 1982.

Monaghan, Jay. *Civil War on the Western Border 1854–1865*. Boston, MA: Little, Brown, 1955.

Moore, Albert Burton. *Conscription and Conflict in the Confederacy*. New York: Hillary House, 1963 [orig. 1924].

Morgan, H. W., ed. *Making Peace with Spain: The Diary of Whitelaw Reid*. Austin, TX: University of Texas, 1965.

Mosby, John S. *The Memoirs of Colonel John S. Mosby*. New York: Kraus Reprint Co., 1969.

Mosley, Leonard. *Duel for Kilimanjaro*. London: Weidenfeld and Nicolson, 1963.

Murdock, Eugene C. *One Million Men: The Civil War Draft in the North*. Westport, CT: Greenwood, 1971.

Nevins, Allan. *Ordeal of the Union: A House Dividing, 1852–1857*. New York: Scribner's, 1947.

————. *The Statesmanship of the Civil War*. New York: Macmillan, 1953.

Nutting, Anthony. *Lawrence of Arabia*. London: Hollis and Carter, 1961.

Packenham, Thomas. *The Boer War*. New York: Random House, 1979.

Paludan, Phillip Shaw. *Victims: A True Story of the Civil War*. Knoxville, TN: University of Tennessee, 1981.

Porter, A. N. *The Origins of the South African War: Joseph Chamberlain and the Diplomacy of Imperialism*. New York: St. Martin's, 1980.

Pratt, Julius. *Expansionists of 1898*. Baltimore: Johns Hopkins University, 1951.

Reitz, D. *Commando: A Boer Journal of the Boer War*. London: Faber and Faber, 1929.

Sampson, P. J. *The Capture of De Wet*. London: Edward Arnold, 1915.

Schott, Joseph L. *The Ordeal of Samar*. Indianapolis IN: Bobbs-Merrill, 1965.

Sexton, W. *Soldiers in the Sun*. New York: Military Service, 1939.

Shy, John, and Thomas Collier. "Revolutionary Warfare." Peter Paret, ed. *Makers of Modern Strategy*. Princeton, NJ: Princeton University, 1986.

Siepel, Kenin H. *Rebel: The Life and Times of John Singleton Mosby*. New York: St. Martin's, 1983.

Smith, W. Wayne. "An Experiment in Counterinsurgency: The Assessment of Confederate Sympathizers in Missouri." *Journal of Southern History*, vol. 35 (August 1969).

Stanley, Peter W., ed. *Reappraising an Empire: New Perspectives on Philippine-American History*. Cambridge, MA: Harvard University, 1984.

Stewart, Desmond. *T. E. Lawrence*. New York: Harper and Row, 1977.

Storey, Moorfield. *Conquest of the Philippines by the United States, 1898–1925*. New York: G. P. Putnam's Sons, 1926.

Sturtevant, David R. *Popular Uprising in the Philippines, 1840–1940*. Ithaca, NY: Cornell University, 1976.

Sutherland, Daniel E. "Guerrillas: The Real War in Arkansas." *Arkansas Historical Quarterly*, vol. 52 (Fall 1993).

Tatum, Georgia Lee. *Disloyalty in the Confederacy*. Chapel Hill, NC: University of North Carolina, 1934.

Taylor, John R. M. *The Philippine Insurrection against the United States: A Compilation of Documents with Notes and Introduction*. Pasay City, RP: Eugenio Lopez, 1971–1973. 5 vols.

U.S. Senate, 57th Congress, Committee on the Philippines. *Hearings: Affairs in the Philippine Islands*. Washington, DC: Government Printing Office, 1902.

Warwick, Peter, ed. *The South African War*. Harlow, UK: Longman, 1986.

Welch, Richard E. *Response to Imperialism: The United States and the Philippine-American War*. Chapel Hill, NC: University of North Carolina, 1979.

Wert, Jeffrey D. *Mosby's Rangers*. New York: Simon and Schuster, 1990.

Wesley, Charles H. *The Collapse of the Confederacy*. New York: Russell and Russell, 1937.

Wiley, Bell Irvin. *Johnny Reb: The Common Soldier of the Confederacy*. Baton Rouge, LA: Louisiana State University, 1970 [orig. 1943].

————. *The Road to Appomatox*. New York: Atheneum, 1983 [orig. 1956].

Williams, T. Harry. *Lincoln and His Generals*. New York: Knopf, 1952.

Wilson, H. W. *After Pretoria: The Guerrilla War*. London: Amalgamated, 1902. 2 vols.

Wolff, Leon. *Littler Brown Brother: How the United States Purchased and Pacified the Philippine Islands at the Century's Turn*. New York: Doubleday, 1961.

EUROPE IN WORLD WAR II

Good comparative treatments of European underground and guerrilla resistance to the Nazis include: C.N.M. Blair, *Guerrilla Warfare*; M.R.D. Foot, *Resistance: European Resistance to Nazism 1939–1945*; J. Haestrup, *European Resistance Movements 1939–1945*; K. Macksey, *The Partisans of Europe in the Second World War*, Henri Michel, *The Shadow War: European Resistance 1939–1945*; the Department of the Army study *German Anti-Guerrilla Operations in the Balkans, 1941–1944*; and D. M. Condit, *Case Study in Guerrilla War: Greece during World War II*.

There is a very extensive literature on the Yugoslavian resistance. Vladimir Dedijer, a close comrade of Tito during and after the war, has written *Tito*, and *With Tito through the War: Partisan Diary 1941–1944*. Milovan Djilas, who later went to prison under Tito, produced the grim *Wartime*, which relates the negotiations between the Partisans and the Germans, as well as his classic *Conversations with Stalin*. Additional works produced during the war are A. Brown, *Mihailovich and Wartime Resistance*, and George Sava, *The Chetniks*. Fitzroy Maclean, a British soldier who saw the fighting in Yugoslavia at first hand, wrote the highly praised, adventurous account *Disputed Barricade*, and his *Eastern Approaches* contains some very good descriptions of the tactics of both guerrillas and Germans. F. W. Deakin, a British officer who served as liaison with Tito and was very critical of Mihailovich, wrote *The Embattled Mountain*. Jozo Tomasevich's *The Chetniks: War and Revolution in Yugoslavia 1941–1945*, as well as his essay "Yugoslavia during the Second World War," are also anti-Mihailovich. Additional views favorable to Tito are Walter Roberts, *Tito, Mihailovich and the Allies*, and Stephen Clissold's *Whirlwind: An Account of Marshal Tito's Rise to Power*. On the other side, an early postwar work unsympathetic to Tito is D. Martin, *Ally Betrayed: The Uncensored Story of Tito and Mihailovich*, while Matteo Milazzo, *The Chetnik Movement and the Yugoslav Resistance*, stresses the short-term nature of Mihailovich's tactical truces with the Axis.

A very large shadow has been thrown over many of the above-mentioned books by Michael Lees's uncompromisingly revisionist *The Rape of Serbia: The British Role in Tito's Grab for Power 1943–1944*; citing disturbing revelations from hitherto secret government documents, Lees argues that Soviet agents within the British government willfully misled Churchill into abandoning Mihailovich and shifting support to Tito, thus paving the war for the communist dictatorship at war's end.

For Poland, and especially the 1944 rising of the Polish Home Army in Warsaw, the memoirs of the Polish commander, General Komorowski (known by his codename Bor), *The Secret Army*, are invaluable. Jan Ciechanowski, who fought in the struggle as a young boy, produced an excellent account in *The Warsaw Uprising of 1944*. Irene Orska wrote an early treatment, *Silent Is the Vistula: The Story of the Warsaw Uprising*. Other illuminating studies of that tragedy are George Bruce, *The Warsaw Uprising*; Johanna Hanson, *The Civilian Population and the Warsaw Uprising of 1944*; and two solid works by Stefan Korbonski, who was a key leader of the Polish Underground, *Fighting Warsaw* and *The Polish Underground State*. J. K. Zawodny, a Polish academic who settled in America after the war, produced the well-written and impassioned *Nothing But Honor: The Story of the Warsaw Uprising 1944*.

On the terrible events in the Warsaw Ghetto in 1943, Shmuel Krakovski, *The War of the Doomed: Jewish Armed Resistance in Poland 1942–1944*, is valuable. Other useful studies are Israel Gutman, *The Jews of Warsaw, 1939–1943: Ghetto, Underground, Revolt*, and David Kurzman, *The Bravest Battle: The 28 Days of the Warsaw Ghetto Uprising*. Richard Lukas has produced the well-researched *The Forgotten Holocaust: The Poles under German Occupation*, in which he seeks to refute blanket charges that most Poles were fanatical anti-Semites.

For the almost-forgotten guerrilla struggles in Ukraine before and after the end of World War II, see the solid work, based on captured German documents, by John Armstrong, *Ukrainian Nationalism*. Other helpful works are Yaroslav Belinsky, *The Second Soviet Republic: The Ukraine after World War II*, and Alexander Buchsbajew, *Toward a Theory of Guerrilla Warfare: A Case Study of the Ukrainian Nationalist Underground in the Soviet Union and Communist Poland*.

For the Italian resistance, which emerged only after the landing of Allied forces in the country and the simultaneous fall of Mussolini, see Charles F. Delzell, *Mussolini's Enemies*; David W. Elwood, *Italy 1943–1945*; and Maria Di Blasio Wilhelm, *The Other Italy: Italian Resistance in World War II*. On France, in addition to the relevant chapters in the comparative works cited above, see Blake Ehrlich, *The French Resistance*.

Armstrong, John A. *Ukrainian Nationalism*. New York: Columbia University, 1955.

Bilinsky, Yaroslav. *The Second Soviet Republic: The Ukraine after World War II*. New Brunswick, NJ: Rutgers University, 1964.

Blair, C. N. M. *Guerrilla Warfare*. London: Ministry of Defense, 1957.

Bor [Komorowski, T.] *The Secret Army*. New York: Macmillan, 1951.

Brown, A. *Mahailovic and Yugoslav Resistance*. London: Lane, 1943.

Bruce, George. *The Warsaw Uprising*. London: Rupert Hart-Davis, 1972.

Buchsbajew, Alexander. *Toward A Theory of Guerrilla Warfare: A Case Study of the Ukrainian Nationalist Underground in the Soviet Union and Communist Poland*. Doctoral dissertation, City University of New York, 1984.

Ciechanowski, Jan. *The Warsaw Uprising of 1944*. Cambridge, UK: Cambridge University, 1974.

Clissold, Stephen. *Whirlwind: An Account of Marshal Tito's Rise to Power*. New York: Philosophical Library, 1949.

Condit, D. M. *Case Study in Guerrilla War: Greece during World War II*. Washington, DC: Department of the Army, 1961.

Davidson, Basil. *Partisan Picture*. Bedford, UK: Bedford, 1946.

Deakin, F. W. D. *The Embattled Mountain*. London: Oxford University, 1971.

Dedijer, Vladimir. *Tito*. New York: Simon and Schuster, 1953.

———. *With Tito through the War: Partisan Diary 1941–1944*. London: Alexander Hamilton, 1951.

Delzell, Charles F. *Mussolini's Enemies*. Princeton, NJ: Princeton University, 1961.

Djilas, Milovan. *Conversations with Stalin*. New York: Harcourt, Brace and World, 1962.

———. *Wartime*. Trans. Michael B. Petrovich. London: Secker and Warburg, 1977.

Ehrlich, Blake. *The French Resistance*. London: Chapman and Hall, 1966.

Ellwood, David W. *Italy 1943–1945*. New York: Holmes and Meier, 1985

Foot, M.R.D. *Resistance: European Resistance to Nazism 1939–1945*. New York: Mc-Graw-Hill, 1977.

Gutman, Israel. *The Jews of Warsaw 1939–1943: Ghetto, Underground, Revolt*. Bloomington, IN: Indiana University, 1982.

Haestrup, J. *European Resistance Movements, 1939–1945*. Westport, CT: Meckler, 1981.

Hanson, Joanna. *The Civilian Population and the Warsaw Uprising of 1944*. Cambridge, UK: Cambridge University, 1982.

Korbonski, Stefan. *Fighting Warsaw*. Trans. F. Czarnomski. New York: Funk and Wagnalls, 1968.

———. *The Polish Underground State*. Trans. M. Erdman. New York: Columbia University, 1978.

Krakowski, Shmuel. *The War of the Doomed: Jewish Armed Resistance in Poland, 1942–1944*. New York: Holmes and Meier, 1984.

Kurzman, Dan. *The Bravest Battle: The 28 Days of the Warsaw Ghetto Uprising*. Los Angeles: Pinnacle, 1976.

Lees, Michael, *The Rape of Serbia: The British Role in Tito's Grab for Power, 1943–1944*. New York: Harcourt, Brace, Jovanovich, 1990.

Lukas, Richard. *The Forgotten Holocaust: The Poles under German Occupation, 1939–1944*. Lexington, KY: University of Kentucky, 1986.

Macksey, K. *The Partisans of Europe in the Second World War*. New York: Stein and Day, 1975.

Maclean, Fitzroy. *Disputed Barricade*. London: Jonathan Cape, 1957.

———. *Eastern Approaches*. London: Jonathan Cape, 1949.

Martin, D. *Ally Betrayed: The Uncensored Story of Tito and Mihailovich*. New York: Prentice-Hall, 1946.

Michel, Henri. *The Shadow War: European Resistance 1939–1945*. Trans. Richard Barry. New York: Harper and Row, 1972.

Milazzo, Matteo. *The Chetnik Movement and the Yugoslav Resistance*. Baltimore, MD: Johns Hopkins University, 1975.

Orska, Irene. *Silent is the Vistula: The Story of the Warsaw Uprising*. Trans. E. Erdman. New York: Longmans Green, 1946.

Roberts, Walter R. *Tito, Mihailovic, and the Allies, 1941–1945*. New Brunswick, NJ: Rutgers University, 1973.

Sava, George. *The Chetniks*. London: Faber and Faber, 1942.

Tomasevich, Jozo. *The Chetniks: War and Revolution in Yugoslavia 1941–1945*. Stanford, CA: Stanford University, 1975.

———. "Yugoslavia During the Second World War." W. Vucinich, ed. *Contemporary Yugoslavia*. Berkeley, CA: University of California, 1969.

U.S. Department of the Army. *German Antiguerrilla Operations in the Balkans (1941–1944)*. Washington, DC: Government Printing Office, 1954.

Wilhelm, Maria de Blasio. *The Other Italy: Italian Resistance in World War II*. New York: Norton, 1988.

Zawodny, J. K. *Nothing But Honor: The Story of the Warsaw Uprising 1944*. Stanford, CA: The Hoover Institution, 1978.

THE COLD WAR

The Cold War: Political Background

Good studies of the political genesis of the Cold War include Dean Acheson, *Present at the Creation*; George F. Kennan, *Memoirs 1925–1950*; *Foreign Relations of the United States* (for individual years); Winston Churchill, *Triumph and Tragedy*, volume vi of his *History of the Second World War*; Harry S. Truman, *Memoirs*; Hugh Seton-Watson, *Eastern Europe between the Wars*; Franz Borkenau, *European Communism*; John Lewis Gaddis, *Strategies of Containment*; Thomas Greene, *Comparative Revolutionary Movements*; Chong-Sik Lee, *Revolutionary Struggle in Manchuria: Chinese Communism and Soviet Interest 1922–1945*; Bruce R. Kuniholm, *The Origins of the Cold War in the Near East: Great Power Conflict and Diplomacy in Iran, Turkey, and Greece*; Charles B. McLane, *Soviet Strategies in Southeast Asia: An Exploration of Eastern Policy under Lenin and Stalin*; J. H. Brimmell, *Communism in South East Asia: A Political Analysis*; Richard H. Shultz, Jr., et al., *Guerrilla Warfare and Counterinsurgency: U.S.-Soviet Policy in the Third World*; and Philip E. Moseley, "Soviet Policy and the Revolution in Asia."

The Cold War: Military Background

For background reading on the military aspects of the various Cold War struggles, see the venerable classic by C. E. Callwell, *Small Wars*, and the useful surveys by Walter Laqueur, *Guerrilla*, and Robert Asprey, *War in the Shadows*. Helpful comparative studies in a historical mold include Geoffrey Fairbairn, *Revolutionary Guerrilla War: The Countryside Version*, a valuable comparative analysis of Malaya, Cuba, and Viet Nam; David Galula, *Counterinsurgency Warfare: Theory and Practice*, by a retired French army officer; Anthony James Joes, *Modern Guerrilla Insurgency*, a comparative analysis of six conflicts; James Eliot Cross, *Conflict in the Shadows: The Nature and Politics of Guerrilla War*; Peter Paret and John Shy, *Guerrillas in the 1960s*; Otto Heilbrunn, *Partisan Warfare*; C. A. Dixon and Otto Heilbrunn, *Communist Guerrilla Warfare*; Ernesto Guevara, *Guerrilla Warfare*; Brian Crozier, *The Rebel: A Study of Postwar Insurrections*; Mark Katz, *The Third World in Soviet Military Thought*; Jac Weller, *Fire and Movement: Bargain-Basement Warfare in the Far East*; Michael Carver, *War since 1945*; Sir Robert Thompson, *Revolutionary War in*

World Strategy; Eric Wolf, *Peasant Wars of the Twentieth Century*; Anthony James Joes, *From the Barrel of a Gun: Armies and Revolutions*; Robert E. Harkavy and Stephanie Neumann, *The Lessons of Recent Wars in the Third World*, vol. 1; Donald Robinson, *The Dirty Wars*; Jay Mallin, *Strategy for Conquest: Communist Documents on Guerrilla Warfare*; Sam Sarkesian, *America's Forgotten Wars: The Counterrevolutionary Past and Lessons for the Future*; J.L.S. Girling, *People's War: Conditions and Consequences in China and South East Asia*; Kim Joo-Jock, ed., *Armed Communist Movements in Southeast Asia*, including Indonesia, Malaysia, Singapore, the Philippines, and Thailand; two older standard collections, Franklin Mark Osanka, ed., *Modern Guerrilla War*, and T. N. Greene, ed., *The Guerrilla—And How to Fight Him*; William J. Pomeroy, ed., *Guerrilla Warfare and Marxism*; The U.S. Naval Institute, *Studies in Guerrilla Warfare*; The U.S. Armed Services' Joint Low Intensity Conflict Project, *Analytical Review of Low Intensity Conflict*; Samuel P. Huntington, "Patterns of Intervention: America and the Soviets in the Third World"; Shee Poon Kim, "Insurgency in Southeast Asia"; and Thomas P. Thornton, "The Emergence of Communist Revolutionary Doctrine."

The Chinese Communists

On Chinese communist guerrilla warfare, in addition to works of Mao Tsetung and others previously cited, see the very useful book by F. F. Liu, *A Military History of Modern China, 1924–1949*; two first-rate studies by E. F. Carlson, *Twin Stars over China*, very good on military campaigns by a Marine major, and *The Chinese Army*; Chong-Sik Lee, *Counterinsurgency in Manchuria: The Japanese Experience 1931–1945*; Chalmers Johnson, *Peasant Nationalism and Communist Power*, a comparison of Chinese and Yugoslav communist guerrillas; Martin Eban, *Lin Piao*, and Thomas W. Robinson, *A Politico-Military Biography of Lin Piao*; Stuart Schram, *Mao Tse-tung*; Mark Selden, *The Yenan Way in Revolutionary China*; James F. Sheridan, *China in Disintegration: The Republican Era 1912–1949*; Lionel Chassin, *The Communist Conquest of China: A History of the Civil War 1945–1949*; W. W. Whitson, *The Chinese High Command: A History of Communist Military Politics 1927–1971*; a hagiographical work by Agnes Smedley, *The Great Road: The Life and Times of Chu Teh*; Samuel B. Griffith, *The Chinese People's Liberation Army*; Alexander George, *The Chinese Communist Army in Action*; Edward Katzenbach and Gene Hanrahan, "The Revolutionary Strategy of Mao Tse-tung"; and Howard L. and Scott Boorman, "Chinese Communist Insurgent Warfare." For information on communist figures, consult Donald Klein and Ann B. Clark, *Biographical Dictionary of Chinese Communism 1921–1965*. For an excellent illumination of the background to the civil war see Lucian Pye, *Warlord Politics*.

The Greek Civil War

For background reading on the Greek conflict, Elizabeth Barker's *Macedonia: Its Place in Balkan Power Politics*, is a classic work on this complex subject;

see as well Robert L. Wolff, *The Balkans in Our Times*. Good studies of the prelude to and events of the civil war include D. M. Condit, *Case Study in Guerrilla War: Greece during World War II*; Hugh Gardner, *Guerrilla and Counterguerrilla Warfare in Greece, 1941–1945*; D. George Kousoulas, *Modern Greece*; William H. McNeill, *Greece: American Aid in Action*; Floyd Spencer, *War and Postwar Greece*; Howard Jones, *"A New Kind of War": America's Global Strategy and the Truman Doctrine in Greece*; Peter J. Stavrakis, *Moscow and Greek Communism 1944–1949*. For the efforts of the communist-led Greek Democratic Army to take over the country, C. M. Woodhouse, *The Struggle for Greece*, is indispensable; so is D. George Kousoulas, *Revolution and Defeat: The Story of the Greek Communist Party*. Edgar O'Ballance, *The Greek Civil War* is also very valuable. See also Anthony James Joes, *Modern Guerrilla Insurgency*; Reginald Leeper, *When Greek Meets Greek*; Kenneth Young, *The Greek Passion*; Lawrence S. Wittner, *American Intervention in Greece, 1943–1949*; Constantine Tsoucalas, *The Greek Tragedy*; S. Zotos, *Greece: The Struggle for Freedom*; Alexander Papagos (commander of the Greek national forces during the last year of the civil war), "Guerrilla Warfare"; D. George Kousoulas, "Greece: The Guerrilla War the Communist Lost"; James A. Van Fleet, "How We Won in Greece"; E. R. Wainhouse, "Guerrilla War in Greece, 1946–1949: A Case Study"; R. V. Burks, "Statistical Profile of the Greek Communist"; and J. C. Murray, "The Anti-Bandit War."

The Malayan Emergency

There is truly first-class literature on the Malayan Emergency. See F. Spencer-Chapman, *The Jungle Is Neutral*, by an Englishman who lived with guerrillas in Japanese-occupied Malaya; Ruth McVey, *The Calcutta Conference and the Southeast Asia Uprising*; Richard Stubbs, *Hearts and Minds in Guerrilla Warfare: The Malayan Emergency of 1948–1960*; Richard L. Clutterbuck, *Riot and Revolution in Singapore and Malaya 1945–1953*; John Coates, *Suppressing Insurgency: An Analysis of the Malayan Emergency of 1948–1954*; Edgar O'Ballance, *Malaya: The Communist Insurgent War 1948–1960*; Anthony Short, *The Communist Insurrection in Malaya, 1948–1960*; Lucian Pye, *Guerrilla Communism in Malaya*, based on testimony of captured and surrendered guerrillas, is immensely helpful; see also Director of Operations, Malaya, *The Conduct of Anti-Terrorist Operations*; Gene Hanrahan, *The Communist Struggle in Malaya*; R. W. Komer, *The Malayan Emergency in Retrospect*; John Cloake, *Templer, Tiger of Malaya*, on the man who got the credit for the defeat of the guerrillas; Harry Miller, *The Communist Menace in Malaya* and *Jungle Warfare in Malaya: The Campaign against Communism 1948–1960*; and A. J. Stockwell, "Insurgency and Decolonization during the Malayan Emergency."

For explicit comparisons of Malaya and Viet Nam, see an illuminating work by a civilian who helped shape British counterinsurgency policy in Malaya, Sir Robert Thompson, *Defeating Communist Insurgency: The Lessons of Malaya and Viet Nam*; Richard L. Clutterbuck, *The Long, Long War: Counterinsurgency in Malaya and Viet Nam*; and Robert O. Tilman, "The Non-Lessons of the Emergency in Malaya," warning against automatic transfers of lessons and principles from Malaya to South Viet Nam.

The Philippines

On the communist efforts to subvert the Philippines, consult two works by the principal Huk military commander, Luis Taruc, *Born of the People*, a ferociously communist manifesto, and the much more chastened *He Who Rides the Tiger*; Carlos P. Romulo, *Crusade in Asia*, by a Filipino statesman with a long and impressive career; Lawrence M. Greenburg, *The Hukbalahap Insurrection: A Case Study of Successful Anti-Insurgency Operations in the Philippines, 1946–1955*; Benedict J. Kerkvliet, *The Huk Rebellion: A Study in Peasant Revolt in the Philippines*; Napoleon Valeriano and C.T.P. Bohannan, *Counter-Guerrilla Operations: The Philippine Experience*; Alvin Scaff, *The Philippine Answer to Communism*; Edward Lansdale, *In the Midst of Wars*, by a close American adviser to Ramon Magsaysay. See also Harvey Averch and John Koehler, *The Huk Rebellion in the Philippines*; John Koehler, *Explaining Dissident Success: The Huks in Central Luzon*; Leonard Davis, *Revolutionary Struggle in the Philippines*; Eduardo Lachia, *The Huks: Philippine Agrarian Society in Revolt*; William J. Pomeroy, "The Philippine Peasantry and the Huk Revolt," and James Richardson, "The Huk Revolt," both disagree with Kerkvliet's assessment of communist influence among the Huks; David Sturtevant, "Filipino Peasant Rebellions Examined: Lessons from the Past"; and Kenneth M. Hammer, "Huks in the Philippines." See also John A. Larkin, "Early Guerrilla Struggle in the Philippines."

For the New People's Army and related groups, see Greg Jones, *Red Revolution: Inside the Philippine Guerrilla Movement*, based on extensive interviews with NPA members; Richard J. Kessler, *Rebellion and Repression in the Philippines*, very sympathetic to NPA; William Chapman, *Inside the Philippine Revolution*, a primer on the Philippine extreme left; and Justus van der Kroef, *Aquino's Philippines: The Deepening Security Crisis*. Some helpful articles are Edgar O'Ballance, "The Communist New People's Army"; Gareth Porter, "Philippine Communism after Marcos"; Justus van der Kroef, "Aquino and the Communists: A Philippine Strategic Stalemate?"; and José Magno and A. J. Gregor, "Insurgency and Counterinsurgency in the Philippines."

The Viet Nam Wars

The amount of material on the Viet Nam struggles is enormous, and what follows represents only a careful selection. For the reader's convenience, I have arranged citations on Viet Nam according to the following categories: histories of Vietnamese communism; the French war in Indochina; general treatments of the American war; North Viet Nam (including Hanoi military doctrine and the

PAVN); the Viet Cong; South Viet Nam (including Diem, the internal politics of the South, ARVN, the Tet and Easter offensives, the last days of the Saigon government, and southern views on the outcome of the conflict); the Eisenhower administration and the Dien Bien Phu crisis; the U.S. Army in Viet Nam; "Lessons Learned"; U.S. counterinsurgency doctrine; the war on the province and village levels; critiques of the American war while it was going on; older but still useful studies; and a short list on the celebrated Edward Lansdale.

For general studies of Vietnamese communism, excellent treatments include Douglas Pike, *History of Vietnamese Communism 1925–1976*; Huynh Kim Khanh, *Vietnamese Communism 1925–1945*; Robert F. Turner, *Vietnamese Communism: Its Origins and Development*; William S. Turley, *Vietnamese Communism in Comparative Perspective*; John T. McAlister, *Viet Nam: The Origins of Revolution*; Hoang Van Chi, *From Colonialism to Communism: A Case History of North Viet Nam*; and P. J. Honey, *North Viet Nam Today*. David G. Marr, *The Viet Nam Tradition on Trial 1920–1945*, explains how the communists defeated other nationalist forces. See also Jean Lacouture, *Ho Chi Minh: A Political Biography*, and Ho Chi Minh, *Ho Chi Minh on Revolution*.

Concerning the French War in Viet Nam, consult Paul Ely, *Lessons of the War in Indochina*, a rich study by a French general with first-hand experience in the war; Vo Nguyen Giap, *People's War, People's Army*, by the Viet Minh commander; Peter M. Dunn, *The First Viet Nam War*, with good detail on the French reoccupation of Cochinchina after the Japanese surrender; Edgar O'Ballance, *The Indo-China War 1945–1954*; Bernard Fall, *Street without Joy*, on French military operations; Lucien Bodard, *The Quicksand War*, a condensation of two earlier books by a correspondent with many years of experience in Southeast Asia; Ellen J. Hammer, *The Struggle for Indochina 1944–1954*, a reliable account; and Donald Lancaster, *The Emancipation of French Indochina*. On the decisive battle of Dien Bien Phu, see Bernard Fall's classic description, *Hell in a Very Small Place*, as well as Jules Roy, *The Battle of Dien Bien Phu*, and Vo Nguyen Giap (the victor in that battle), *Dien Bien Phu*. Roger Trinquier, *Modern Warfare: A French View of Counterinsurgency*, is a chilling blueprint for military totalitarianism. See also Philippe Devillers and Jean Lacouture, *End of a War: Indochina 1954*, a French view of the evacuation of Viet Nam; Samuel B. Griffith, *Peking and People's War*; and Jean Larteguy, *Yellow Fever*, a novel about the French pullout from what became North Viet Nam. For deep background, see John Cady, *The Roots of French Imperialism in Asia*; William Duiker, *The Rise of Nationalism in Viet Nam, 1920–1941*, Bruce M. Lockhart; *The End of the Vietnamese Monarchy*; Anthony Short, *The Origins of the Viet Nam War*; and Archimedes Patti's naive *Why Viet Nam?* See also John Pimlott, "The French Army: From Indochina to Chad," and J. Kim Munholland, " 'Collaboration Strategy' and the French Pacification of Tonkin, 1885–1897."

For Washington's view of both the insurgency in French Indochina and the struggle in South Viet Nam, the beginning of wisdom is to be sought in a close study of *The Pentagon Papers* (Gravel edition), volume 1. Useful overall studies of the American phase of the conflict include Guenter Lewy, *America in Viet Nam*, a pioneering academic study and still of great value; William Duiker, *The Communist Road to Power in Viet Nam*, focusing on Hanoi's strategy; George C. Herring, *America's Longest War*; Anthony James Joes, *The War For South Viet Nam*, reevaluating South Vietnamese efforts; Timothy J. Lomperis, *The War Everyone Lost—And Won: America's Intervention in Viet Nam's Twin Struggles*, which makes the important point that Hanoi shifted to conventional war because the communists never won sufficient legitimacy among the South Vietnamese; Thomas C. Thayer, *War without Fronts: The American Experience in Viet Nam*, effectively using statistics to show how the Americans repeated many of the mistakes of the French; Gabriel Kolko, *Anatomy of a War*, an unabashed apologia for the communist side. Then there is Phillip B. Davidson, *Viet Nam at War: The History*, a massive and generally well-received study, highly critical, like Summers, of using U.S. forces for anti-guerrilla fighting; what Davidson does is done well, but, since he completely ignores ARVN and the Territorial Forces, his presentation is incomplete and therefore distorting.

Well-known studies by a competent historian sympathetic to the insurgent side are Joseph Buttinger's *The Smaller Dragon: A Political History of Viet Nam, Viet Nam: A Dragon Embattled, Viet Nam: A Political History*, and *A Dragon Defiant: A Short History of Viet Nam*.

For studies of North Vietnamese military doctrine, consult Patrick J. McGarvey, *Visions of Victory: Selected Vietnamese Communist Military Writings 1965–1968*; Melvin Gurtov, *Hanoi on Peace and War*, on the North's concept of "decisive victory"; Vo Nguyen Giap, *The Military Art of People's War*, and *How We Won the War*, by the famed commander of Hanoi's forces; and Hammond Rolph, "Vietnamese Communism and the Protracted War." On the North Vietnamese Army, see Douglas Pike, *PAVN*, one of several indispensable studies by that author; Konrad Kellen, *A Profile of the PAVN Soldier in Viet Nam*; and Robert O'Neill, *General Giap*, and *The Strategy of General Giap since 1964*. Peter Macdonald's *Giap: The Victor in Viet Nam*, is disappointingly naive, with distressing lacunae.

For the Viet Cong, see the handbooks by Truong Chinh (pseud.), *Primer for Revolt* and *The Resistance Will Win*; Douglas Pike's exhaustive study, *Viet Cong*; M. Anderson et al., *Insurgent Organization and Operations: A Case Study of the Viet Cong in the Delta 1964–1966*; Darryl Henderson, *Why the Viet Cong Fought: A Study of Motivation and Control in a Modern Army in Combat*; Konrad Kellen, *A View of the VC*; Michael Lee Lanning and Dan Gragg, *Inside the VC and the NVA* [North Vietnamese Army, also called PAVN], based on diaries and interrogations; George K. Tanham, *Communist Revolutionary Warfare: From the Viet Minh to the Viet Cong*; J. J. Zasloff, *Origins of the Insurgency in South Viet Nam, 1954–1960: The Role of the Southern Viet Minh Cadres*; Nathan Leites, *The Viet Cong Style of Politics*; John C. Donnell, *Viet Cong Recruitment: Why and How Men Join*; Douglas Pike, *The Viet Cong Strategy of Terror*; W. P. Davidson, *Some Observations on Viet Cong Operations in the Villages*; Truong Nhu Tang, *A Viet Cong Memoir*, by a high-ranking communist who came over to the Saigon side; James McCoy, *Secrets of the Viet Cong*; and George Carver, "The Faceless Viet Cong."

On Ngo Dinh Diem's administration and overthrow, consult the indispensable study by Ellen J. Hammer, *A Death in November: America in Viet Nam 1963*; see also Mieczyslaw Maneli, *War of the Vanquished*, by a disillusioned Polish diplomat in Viet Nam; Denis Warner's valuable *The Last Confucian*; and the first-rate study by Robert Scigliano, *South Viet Nam: Nation under Stress*.

On the internal politics of the state of South Viet Nam, see the classic study by Dennis J. Duncanson, *Government and Revolution in Viet Nam*. Other fine works include Bernard Fall's illuminating *The Two Viet Nams: A Political and Military History*; Charles Stuart Callison, *Land to the Tiller in the Mekong Delta*, a study of the massive land reform of the 1970s; Samuel Popkin, *The Rational Peasant*; Robert L. Sansom, *The Economics of Insurgency in the Mekong Delta of Viet Nam*; Allan E. Goodman, *Politics in War: The Bases of Political Community in South Viet Nam*, showing the brittleness of much Viet Cong support especially after the 1967 elections; Howard R. Penniman, *Elections in South Viet Nam*, making the case that the country was moving slowly but unmistakably toward electoral democracy; Robert Thompson, *No Exit from Viet Nam*, by a counterinsurgency expert who had high hopes for the survival of the South; Richard W. Lindholm, ed., *Viet Nam: The First Five Years*; the Michigan State University study, *Problems of Freedom: South Viet Nam since Independence*; Ellen Hammer, "South Viet Nam: The Limits of Political Action"; and J. A. C. Grant, "The Viet Nam Constitution of 1956."

For the South Vietnamese Army (ARVN), see James Lawton Collins, *The Development and Training of the South Vietnamese Army*; Ronald H. Spector, *Advice and Support: The Early Years 1941–1960*; Dong Van Khuyen, *The RVNAF*; Ngo Quangh Truong, *Territorial Forces*; Allan E. Goodman, *An Institutional Profile of the South Vietnamese Officer Corps*; Thomas R. Cantwell, *The Army of South Viet Nam: A Military and Political History*; Tran Van Don, *Our Endless War*, by one of the generals who helped overthrow Diem; Keith William Nolan, *Into Laos*; and Cao Van Vien et al., *The U.S. Advisor*.

On the last days of South Viet Nam, by which time the war had become almost totally a conventional one, see Cao Van Vien, *The Final Collapse*, an invaluable study by the ARVN's Chief of Staff; Arnold Isaacs, *Without Honor: Defeat in Viet Nam and Cambodia*, covering the time between the U.S. withdrawal and the fall of Saigon; William E. Le Gro, *Viet Nam from Ceasefire to Capitulation*; Alan Dawson, *55 Days: The Fall of South Viet Nam*, bitterly critical of U.S. Ambassador Graham Martin; Denis Warner, *Certain Victory: How Hanoi Won the War*; Olivier Todd, *Cruel April*; Larry Engelmann, *Tears before the Rain: An Oral History of the Fall of South Viet Nam*; and for Hanoi's official view of these days and events, Tran Van Tra, *Concluding the 30 Years' War*, and Van Tien Dung, *Our Great Spring Victory*.

For South Vietnamese views of the war and how it ended, see Cao Van Vien and Dong Van Khuyen, *Reflections on the Viet Nam War*; Bui Diem, *In the Jaws of History*, by the long-time Saigon ambassador to Washington, who criticizes the Americans for taking over the war and ignoring the needs of the South Vietnamese; Stephen Hosmer et al., *The Fall of South Viet Nam*, based on interviews with high-ranking South Vietnamese political and military figures; and Lam Quang Thi, *Autopsy: The Death of South Viet Nam*. On relations between Washington and Saigon, consult Nguyen Tien Hung and Jerrold Schechter, *The Palace File: Viet Nam Secret Documents*.

On the decisive Tet offensive of 1968, see the following outstanding studies: Don Oberdorfer, *Tet!*; Peter Braestrup, *Big Story*, by a veteran correspondent who highlights the distortions of television presentation of the Tet offensive; Hoang Ngoc Lung, *The General Offensives of 1968–1969*; and James J. Wirtz, *The Tet Offensive: Intelligence Failure in War*. On Hanoi's massive and unsuccessful Easter Offensive of 1972, see Ngo Quang Truong, *The Easter Offensive of 1972*, and G. H. Turley, *The Easter Offensive*.

Valuable studies of the Eisenhower administration and Viet Nam include Melanie Billings-Yun, *Decision against War: Eisenhower and Dien Bien Phu*, based on a comparison of French and U.S. original documents; Melvin Gurtov, *The First Viet Nam Crisis: Chinese Communist Strategy and United States Involvement 1953–1954*; see also George C. Herring and Richard H. Immerson, "Eisenhower, Dulles, and Dien Bien Phu." Larry Berman, *Planning a Tragedy: The Americanization of the War in Viet Nam*, focuses on the Johnson decision to commit large ground forces, as does Brian VanDeMark, *Into the Quagmire: Lyndon Johnson and the Escalation of the Viet Nam War*.

On the experiences of the U.S. Army in Viet Nam, see Andrew F. Krepinevich's highly critical *The Army and Viet Nam*; Dave Richard Palmer, *Summons of the Trumpet*; two interesting studies by Shelby Stanton, *Green Berets at War: U.S. Army Special Forces in Southeast Asia 1956–1975*, and *The Rise and Fall of an American Army: U.S. Ground Forces in Viet Nam 1965–1973*, largely a combat history; Bruce Palmer, *The Twenty-Five-Year War: America's Military Role in Viet Nam*, which, like Summers's book, argues that holding a line between the North and South would have been the best strategy for the Americans; Al Santoli, *Everything We Had*; Albert N. Garland, ed., *A Distant Challenge: The U.S. Infantryman in Viet Nam 1967–1972*; Cincinnatus (pseud.), *Self-Destruction: The Disintegration and Decay of the United States Army during the Viet Nam Era*; Peter M. Dunn, "The American Army: The Viet Nam War"; C. N. Barclay, "The Western Soldier versus the Communist Insurgent"; and Richard H. Shultz, "Breaking the Will of the Enemy in the Viet Nam War."

Under the rubric of "American Lessons Learned," consult the following collections, each of which contains valuable contributions: Richard A. Hunt and Richard Shultz, eds., *Lessons from an Unconventional War*; L. J. Matthews and D. E. Brown, eds., *Assessing the Viet Nam War*; and W. Scott Thompson and D. D. Frizzell, eds., *The Lessons of Viet Nam*. Chalmers Johnson, *Autopsy on*

People's War, is brief, incisive, and invaluable. The Royal United Services Institution, *Lessons from the Viet Nam War*, is somewhat disappointing because of its generality. For the views of the U.S. commander during the worst years of the war, see William Westmoreland, *A Soldier Reports*, along with Admiral U.S. Grant Sharp, *Strategy for Defeat: Viet Nam in Retrospect*. Other good studies include Robert W. Komer, head of pacification efforts, *Bureaucracy Does Its Thing: Institutional Constraints on US-GVN Performance in Viet Nam*; Robert L. Gallucci, *Neither Peace Nor War: The Politics of American Military Policy in Viet Nam*, which blames Army bureaucracy for the failure to develop a more effective strategy; Stuart A. Herrington, *Peace with Honor? An American Reports on Viet Nam*, a valuable contribution; Mark Clodfelter, *The Limits of Air Power: The American Bombing of North Viet Nam*; Leslie Gelb and R. K. Betts, *The Irony of Viet Nam*; Charles Wolf, *The Logic of Failure: A Viet Nam "Lesson"*; William Colby, *Lost Victory*, in which the former CIA Director identifies the assassination of Diem, Americanization of the war, and the abandonment of the South Vietnamese as the three major U.S. errors in Viet Nam; Robert Shaplen, *Bitter Victory*, written after the author had returned to Viet nam in 1984; John Pimlott, ed., *Viet Nam: The History and the Tactics*; Richard Nixon, *No More Viet Nams*; Robin Higham, *Intervention or Abstention*; and H. Heymann and W. Whitson, *Can and Should the United States Preserve a Military Capability for Revolutionary Conflict?* See also Allan E. Goodman, *The Lost Peace: America's Search for a Negotiated Settlement of the Viet Nam War*; and W. J. Thies, *When Governments Collide: Coercion and Diplomacy in the Viet Nam Conflict 1964–1968*. Finally, see the U.S. Army's *Low Intensity Conflict Field Manual*, FM 100–20.

Helpful articles under the "lessons learned" heading include Hung P. Nguyen, "Communist Offensive Strategy and the Defense of South Viet Nam"; George K. Tanham, "Some Insurgency Lessons from Southeast Asia"; Guenter Lewy, "Some Political-Military Lessons of the Viet Nam War"; Stephen Rosen, "Viet Nam and the American Theory of Limited War"; John Waghelstein, "Post–Viet Nam Counterinsurgency Doctrine"; Steven E. Daskal, "The Insurgency Threat and Ways to Defeat It"; Laurence E. Grintner, "How They Lost: Doctrines, Strategies and Outcomes of the Viet Nam War"; and William Zimmerman and Robert Axelrod, "The 'Lessons' of Viet Nam and Soviet Foreign Policy."

On the crucial subject of Laos and its role in the development and outcome of the war, the provocative and well-received study by Norman B. Hannah, *The Key to Failure: Laos and the Viet Nam War*, is indispensable. See also useful studies by Charles Stephenson, *The End of Nowhere: American Policy toward Laos since 1954*; Arthur Dommen, *Conflict in Laos*; Nina Adams and A. W. McCoy, *Laos: War and Revolution*; and Roland Paul, "Laos: Anatomy of an American Involvement."

For critical discussion of U.S. counterinsurgency doctrine as practiced in Viet

Nam, see the extremely influential study by Harry Summers, *On Strategy: A Critical Analysis of the Viet Nam War*, which rejects the large-scale use of U.S. forces for guerrilla-fighting; Douglas Blaufarb, *The Counterinsurgency Era: U.S. Doctrine and Performance*, which among other things suggests some of the moral dilemmas of counterinsurgency; Larry E. Cable, *Conflict of Myths: The Development of American Counterinsurgency Doctrine and the Viet Nam War*, which excoriates "gradual response"; D. Michael Shafer, *Deadly Paradigms: The Failure of U.S. Counterinsurgency Policy*, which claims that defeat of insurgents in Greece and the Philippines had little to do with American efforts, while Viet Nam showed all the flaws of the real American thinking about insurgency; Neil Sheehan, *A Bright Shining Lie: John Paul Vann and America in Viet Nam*; Tran Dinh Tho, *Pacification*, by a high-ranking ARVN officer; William A. Nighswonger, *Rural Pacification in Viet Nam*; Dale Andrade, *Ashes to Ashes: The Phoenix Program and the Viet Nam War*; and Stephen T. Hosmer, *The Army's Role in Counterinsurgency and Insurgency*. See also George K. Tanham and Denis J. Duncanson, "Some Dilemmas of Counterinsurgency"; Chalmers Johnson, "Civilian Loyalties and Guerrilla Conflict"; and R. W. Komer, "Impact of Pacification on Insurgency in South Viet Nam." Under the heading of "Might-Have-Been," see "A Program for the Pacification and Long-Term Development of South Viet Nam" (often referred to as PROVN), a vigorous 1966 attack by some younger American officers on "search-and-destroy" tactics.

Three excellent studies of the war at the province level are Jeffrey Race, *War Comes to Long An*; Eric M. Bergerud, *The Dynamics of Defeat: The Viet Nam War in Hua Nghia Province*; and William R. Andrews, *The Village War: Vietnamese Communist Revolutionary Activity in Dinh Truong Province*.

For enlightening studies of the Combined Action Program, or CAPS, and the American war at the grassroots level, see two books by F. J. West, *Small Unit Action in Viet Nam* and *The Village*; Michael E. Peterson, *The Combined Action Platoons*; and Stuart A. Herrington, *Silence Was a Weapon: The Viet Nam War in the Villages*. For a very critical view of American counterinsurgency at the village level, see Jonathan Schell, *The Village of Ben Suc*.

For attempts to evaluate the war while the fighting was still going on, see Sir Robert Thompson, *Peace Is Not at Hand*, all of whose writings are rewarding; see also Chester L. Cooper, *The Lost Crusade: America in Viet Nam*; and Robert Shaplen, *The Lost Revolution: The U.S. in Viet Nam 1946–1966*. For an assessment by the Marine Commandant, consult L. W. Walt, *Strange War, Strange Strategy*. For the views of one of Kennedy's ambassadors to Saigon, see Maxwell Taylor, *Swords and Ploughshares*. See also Melvin Gurtov and Konrad Kellen, *Viet Nam: Lessons and Mislessons*.

For earlier studies of the conflict from various American viewpoints, see Malcolme W. Browne, *The New Face of War*, by a Pulitzer Prize–winning correspondent friendly to the South's cause; Wesley Fishel, *Viet Nam: Anatomy of a Conflict*; Frank Trager, *Why Viet Nam?*; Roy Jumper and Majorie Weiner Normand, "Viet Nam," in George Kahin, ed., *Government and Politics in Southeast Asia*; and Boyd Bashore, "Dual Strategy for Limited War."

On the legendary Ed Lansdale, who played key advisory roles in both the Philippines and South Viet Nam, consult Cecil B. Curry, *Edward Lansdale, The Unquiet American*. See also Edward G. Lansdale, *In the Midst of Wars: An American's Mission to Southeast Asia*; and two articles by him in *Foreign Affairs*, "Viet Nam: Do We Understand Revolution?" and "Viet Nam: Still the Search for Goals." Jean Larteguy, *Yellow Fever*, has a main character modelled on Lansdale.

On Viet Nam after the conquest of the south, consult William J. Duiker, *Viet Nam since the Fall of Saigon*, and Nguyen Van Canh, *Viet Nam under Communism 1975–1982*.

On Cambodia's Khmer Rouge, see Michael Vickery, *Cambodia, 1975–1982*; P. Charnbhumidol, *The Kampuchean Conflict, 1975–1985*; Ben Kiernan, *How Pol Pot Came to Power: A History of Communism in Kampuchea 1930–1975*; and the collection of essays edited by Ben Kiernan, *Genocide and Democracy in Cambodia*.

Afghanistan

The best single volume on the Soviet invasion of Afghanistan and the nationwide resistance this provoked is probably Rosanne Klass, ed., *Afghanistan: The Great Game Revisited*. For background to the Soviet invasion of Afghanistan, see Louis Dupree's widely hailed *Afghanistan*; Arnold Fletcher, *Afghanistan: Highway of Conquest*; J. A. Norris, *The First Afghan War*; W. E. D. Allen and Paul Muratoff, *Caucasian Battlefields*; Michael Rywkin, *Russia in Central Asia*; Richard A. Pierce, *Russian Central Asia 1867–1917*; Geoffrey Wheeler, *The Modern History of Soviet Central Asia*; Alvin Z. Rubinstein, *The Great Game: Rivalry in the Persian Gulf and South Asia*; Alexandre Bennigsen, *The Soviet Union and Muslim Guerrilla Wars 1920–1981*; Stephen T. Hosmer and Thomas W. Wolfe, *Soviet Policy and Practice toward Third World Conflicts*; M. Nazif Sharani and Robert L. Canfield, eds., *Revolutions and Rebellions in Afghanistan*; Alexandre Bennigsen, "Muslim Guerrilla Warfare in the Caucusus 1918–1928"; and Leon B. Poullada, "Afghanistan and the United States: The Crucial Years."

On the Soviet invasion and the immediate aftermath, consult Anthony Arnold, *Afghanistan: The Soviet Invasion in Perspective*; Abdul Samad Ghaus, *The Fall of Afghanistan: An Insider's Account*; Joseph J. Collins, *The Soviet Invasion of Afghanistan: A Study in the Use of Force in Soviet Foreign Policy*; Thomas Hammond, *Red Flag over Afghanistan*; David Charters, "Coup and Consolidation: The Soviet Seizure of Afghanistan"; Joseph J. Collins, "The Soviet Invasion of Afghanistan: Methods, Motives and Ramifications"; Marie Broxup, "The Soviets in Afghanistan: The Anatomy of a Takeover"; and Yosef Bodansky, "The Bear on the Chessboard: Soviet Military Gains in Afghanistan."

For the destruction of Afghan society, see Eliza Van Hollen, *Afghanistan: Three Years of Occupation*; U.S. State Department, Bureau of Intelligence and Research, *Afghanistan: Four Years of Occupation*; J. Bruce Amstutz, *Afghanistan: The First Five Years of Soviet Occupation*; Paul Trottier and Craig Karp, *Afghanistan: Five Years of Occupation*. There are three reports by Craig Karp for the U.S. State Department: *Afghanistan: Six Years of Soviet Occupation*; *Afghanistan: Seven Years of Occupation*; and *Afghanistan: Eight Years of Soviet Occupation*. See also Barnett R. Rubin and Jeri Laber, *A Nation Is Dying: Afghanistan under the Soviets 1979–1987*; and Arthur Bonner, *Among the Afghans*, an excellent piece of journalism that identified the growing dependence of the resistance on sales of opium, and the deep and ominous political rifts among its various elements. In addition, see Michael Barry, ''Afghanistan: Another Cambodia?'', and Stuart Schwartzstein, ''Chemical Warfare in Afghanistan.'' Doris Lessing, a novelist, laments the outside world's indifference to the suffering of Afghanistan in *The Wind Blows Away Our Words*.

For descriptions and analyses of the fighting see Mark Galleotti, *Afghanistan: The Soviet Union's Last War*; Edward Girardet, *Afghanistan: The Soviet War*; James S. Robbins, *Soviet Counterinsurgency Strategy in Afghanistan 1979–1989*; Alexander Alexiev, *Inside the Soviet Army in Afghanistan*; S. E. Wimbush and A. Alexiev, *Soviet Central Asian Soldiers in Afghanistan*; David C. Isby, *War in a Distant Country*, by a first-hand and sympathetic observer of the mujahideen; Grant M. Farr, *Afghan Resistance: The Politics of Survival*; Mike Martin, *Afghanistan: Inside a Rebel Stronghold*; Michael Radu, *The New Insurgencies: Anticommunist Guerrillas in the Third World*; Olivier Roy, *Islam and Resistance in Afghanistan* and *The Lessons of the Soviet-Afghan War*; Barnett R. Rubin, *To Die in Afghanistan*; Nigel Ryan, *A Hitch or Two in Afghanistan*; Mark Urban, *War in Afghanistan*; André Brigot and Olivier Roy, *The War in Afghanistan*; Gerard Chaliand, *Report from Afghanistan*; and Anthony H. Cordesman and Abraham F. Wagner, *The Lessons of Modern War, vol. 2. The Afghan and Falkland Conflicts*; and Gennady Bocharov, *Russian Roulette: Afghanistan through Russian Eyes*. For a description, perhaps misleadingly named, by two former high-ranking Soviet officers, see Oleg Sarin and Lev Dvoretsky, *The Afghan Syndrome: The Soviet Union's Viet Nam*.

Useful articles and briefer studies include Douglas M. Hart, ''Low Intensity Conflict in Afghanistan: The Soviet View''; Karl Bernstein, ''Arms for Afghanistan''; Gerard Chaliand, ''The Bargain War in Afghanistan''; Joseph J. Collins, ''Soviet Military Performance in Afghanistan: A Preliminary Assessment''; Edward Girardet, ''Russia's War in Afghanistan''; Geoffrey Jukes, ''The Soviet Armed Forces and the Afghan War''; Mark Katz, ''Anti-Soviet Insurgencies: Growing Trend or Passing Phase?''; Ellie D. Krakowski, ''Afghanistan: The Forgotten War''; Claude Malhuret, ''Report from Afghanistan''; Barnett R. Rubin, ''The Fragmentation of Afghanistan''; R. Paschall, ''Marxist Counterinsurgencies''; William R. Bode, ''The Reagan Doctrine''; and Ali T. Sheikh, ''Not the Whole Truth: Media Coverage of the War in Afghanistan.''

For good discussions of some of the consequences of the invasion for the Soviet regime, see the highly praised study by Henry Bradsher, *Afghanistan and the Soviet Union*; Anthony Arnold, *The Fateful Pebble: Afghanistan's Role in the Fall of the Soviet Empire*; T. Daly, *Afghanistan and Gorbachev's Global Foreign Policy*; Amin Saikal and William Maley, eds., *The Soviet Withdrawal from Afghanistan*; and Graham E. Fuller, "The Emergence of Central Asia."

Thailand

On the low-level communist insurgency in Thailand, useful studies include Daniel D. Lovelace, *China and People's War in Thailand 1964–1968*; Donald P. Weatherbee offers a good history of the Thai Communist Party in *The United Front in Thailand: A Documentrary Analysis*. See also George K. Tanham, *Trial in Thailand*; Jeffrey Race, "War in Northern Thailand"; Stuart Slade, "Successful Counterinsurgency: How the Thais Burned the Books and Beat the Guerrillas"; Tom Marks, "Maoist Miscue: The Demise of the Communist Party of Thailand"; Justus van der Kroef, "Guerrilla Communism and Counterinsurgency in Thailand"; and the special issue of *World Affairs*, "Reflections on Counterinsurgency in Thailand." An older but still helpful study is Donald E. Nuechterlein, *Thailand and the Struggle for Southeast Asia*.

After the Cold War

For works about guerrilla insurgency looking toward the post–Cold War world, see two studies by the Regional Conflict Working Group, *Supporting U.S. Strategy for Third World Conflict*, and *Commitment to Freedom: Security Assistance as a U.S. Policy in the Third World*. Edward Rice, *Wars of the Third Kind*, raises many useful questions. Also worth consulting are John M. Collins, *America's Small Wars: Lessons for the Future*; Rod Paschall, *LIC 2010: Special Operations and Unconventional Warfare in the Next Century*; and Larry Cable, "Reinventing the Round Wheel: Insurgency, Counter-Insurgency and Peace-keeping Post Cold War." See also Bruce Russett and James S. Sutterlin, "The U.N. in a New World Order."

Acheson, Dean. *Present at the Creation*. New York: Norton, 1969.

Adams, Nina, and A. W. McCoy, eds. *Laos: War and Revolution*. New York: Harper and Row, 1970.

Alexiev, Alexander. *Inside the Soviet Army in Afghanistan*. Santa Monica, CA: RAND, 1988.

Allen, W.E.D., and Paul Muratoff. *Caucasian Battlefields*. Cambridge, UK: Cambridge University, 1953.

Amstutz, J. Bruce. *Afghanistan: The First Five Years of Soviet Occupation*. Washington, DC: National Defense University, 1986.

Anderson, M., M. Arnstein, and H. Averch. *Insurgent Organization and Operations: A*

Case Study of the Viet Cong in the Delta, 1964–1966. Santa Monica, CA: RAND, 1967.

Andrade, Dale. *Ashes to Ashes: The Phoenix Program and the Viet Nam War.* Lexington, MA: Lexington Books, 1990.

Andrews, William R. *The Village War: Vietnamese Communist Revolutionary Activity in Dinh Truong Province.* Columbia, MO: University of Missouri, 1973.

Arnold, Anthony. *Afghanistan: The Soviet Invasion in Perspective.* Stanford, CA: Hoover Institution, 1985 (revised).

———. *The Fateful Pebble: Afghanistan's Role in the Fall of the Soviet Empire.* Novato, CA: Presidio, 1993.

Averch, Harvey, and John Koehler. *The Huk Rebellion in the Philippines: Quantitative Approaches.* Santa Monica: RAND, 1970.

Barclay, C. N. "The Western Soldier versus the Communist Insurgent." *Military Review,* February 1969.

Barker, Elisabeth. *Macedonia: Its Place in Balkan Power Politics.* London: Royal Institute of International Affairs, 1950.

Barry, Michael. "Afghanistan: Another Cambodia?" *Commentary,* August 1982.

Bashore, Boyd. "Dual Strategy for Limited War." *Military Review,* vol. 40 (May 1960).

Bennigsen, Alexandre. "Muslim Guerrilla Warfare in the Caucasus, 1918–1928." *Central Asian Survey,* vol. 2, no. 1 (1983).

———. *The Soviet Union and Muslim Guerrilla Wars 1920–1981.* Santa Monica, CA: RAND, 1981.

Bergerud, Eric M. *The Dynamics of Defeat: The Viet Nam War in Hua Nghia Province.* Boulder, CO: Westview, 1991.

Berman, Larry. *Planning a Tragedy: The Americanization of the War in Viet Nam.* New York: Norton, 1982.

Bernstein, Carl. "Arms for Afghanistan." *The New Republic,* July 18, 1981.

Billings-Yun, Melanie. *Decision against War: Eisenhower and Dien Bien Phu.* New York: Columbia University, 1988.

Blaufarb, Douglas S. *The Counterinsurgency Era: U.S. Doctrine and Performance.* New York: Free Press, 1977.

Bocharov, Gennaday. *Russian Roulette: Afghanistan through Russian Eyes.* New York: HarperCollins, 1990.

Bodansky, Yosef. "The Bear on the Chessboard: Soviet Military Gains in Afghanistan." *World Affairs,* vol. 5, no. 3 (Winter 1982–83).

Bodard, Lucien. *The Quicksand War.* Trans. P. O'Brian. Boston: Little, Brown, 1967.

Bode, William R. "The Reagan Doctrine." *Strategic Review,* Winter 1986.

Bonner, Arthur. *Among the Afghans.* Durham, NC: Duke University, 1987.

Boorman, Howard L., and Scott Boorman. "Chinese Communist Insurgent Warfare." *Political Science Quarterly,* June 1966.

Borkenau, Franz. *European Communism.* New York: Harper, 1953.

Bradsher, Henry. *Afghanistan and the Soviet Union.* Durham, NC: Duke University, 1985.

Braestrup, Peter. *Big Story.* Boulder, CO: Westview, 1977.

Brigot, André, and Olivier Roy. *The War in Afghanistan.* New York: Harvester-Wheatsheaf, 1988.

Brimmell, J. H. *Communism in South East Asia: A Political Analysis.* London: Oxford University, 1959.

Browne, Malcolm W. *The New Face of War*. New York: Bobbs-Merrill, 1965.

Broxup, Marie. "The Soviets in Afghanistan: The Anatomy of a Takeover." *Central Asian Survey*, vol. 1, no. 4 (April 1983).

Bui Diem. *In the Jaws of History*. Boston: Houghton Mifflin, 1987.

Burks, R. V. "Statistical Profile of the Greek Communist." *Journal of Modern History*, vol. 27 (1955).

Buttinger, Joseph. *A Dragon Defiant: A Short History of Viet Nam*. New York: Praeger, 1972.

———. *The Smaller Dragon: A Political History of Viet Nam*. New York: Praeger, 1958.

———. *Viet Nam: A Dragon Embattled*. New York: Praeger, 1967. 2 vols.

———. *Viet Nam: A Political History*. New York: Praeger, 1968.

Cable, Larry. *Conflict of Myths: The Development of American Counterinsurgency Doctrine and the Viet Nam War*. New York: Free Press, 1986.

———. "Reinventing the Round Wheel: Insurgency, Counter-Insurgency and Peacekeeping Post Cold War." *Small Wars and Insurgencies*, Vol. 4 (Summer 1993).

———. *Unholy Grail: The U.S. and the Wars in Viet Nam*. London: Routledge, 1991.

Cady, John. *Roots of French Imperialism in Asia*. Ithaca, NY: Cornell University, 1954.

Callison, Charles Stuart. *Land to the Tiller in the Mekong Delta*. Lanham, MD: University Press of America, 1983.

Callwell, C. E. *Small Wars: Their Principles and Practice*. Wakefield, UK: EP Publishing, 1976 (original 1906).

Cantwell, Thomas R. *The Army of South Viet Nam: A Military and Political History, 1955–1975*. Doctoral dissertation, University of New South Wales, 1989.

Cao Van Vien. *The Final Collapse*. Washington, DC: U.S. Army Center of Military History, 1983.

Cao Van Vien and Dong Van Khuyen. *Reflections on the Viet Nam War*. Washington, DC: U.S. Army Center of Military History, 1980.

Cao Van Vien, et al., *The U.S. Advisor*. Washington, DC: U.S. Army Center of Military History, 1980.

Carlson, E. F. *The Chinese Army*. New York: Institute of Pacific Relations, 1940.

———. *Twin Stars over China*. New York: Dodd, Mead, 1940.

Carver, George. "The Faceless Viet Cong." *Foreign Affairs*, vol. 44 (April 1966).

Carver, Michael. *War since 1945*. New York: G. P. Putnam, 1981.

Chaliand, Gerard. "The Bargain War in Afghanistan." Gerard Chaliand, ed., *Guerrilla Strategies*. Berkeley, CA: University of California, 1982.

———. *Report from Afghanistan*. New York: Viking, 1982.

Chapman, William. *Inside the Philippine Revolution: The New People's Army and Its Struggle for Power*. New York: Norton, 1987.

Charnbhumidol, Pitchayaphant. *The Kampuchean Conflict, 1975–1985*. Doctoral dissertation, Claremont Graduate School, 1992.

Charters, David. "Coup and Consolidation: The Soviet Seizure of Afghanistan." *Conflict Quarterly*, Spring 1981.

Chassin, Lionel M. *The Communist Conquest of China: A History of the Civil War 1945–1949*. Cambridge, MA: Harvard University, 1965.

Churchill, Winston. *The Second World War*. vol. 6, *Triumph and Tragedy*. Boston: Houghton Mifflin, 1953.

Cincinnatus (pseud.). *Self-Destruction: The Disintegration and Decay of the United States Army during the Viet Nam Era*. New York: Norton, 1981.

Cloake, John. *Templer, Tiger of Malaya*. London: Harrap, 1985.

Clodfelter, Mark. *The Limits of Air Power: The American Bombing of North Viet Nam*. New York: Free Press, 1989.

Clutterbuck, Richard L. *The Long, Long War: Counterinsurgency in Malaya and Viet Nam*. New York: Praeger, 1966.

———. *Riot and Revolution in Singapore and Malaya 1945–1963*. London: Faber and Faber, 1973.

Coates, John. *Suppressing Insurgency: An Analysis of the Malayan Emergency, 1948–1954*. Boulder, CO: Westview, 1992.

Colby, William. *Lost Victory*. Chicago: Contemporary Books, 1989.

Collins, James Lawton. *The Development and Training of the South Vietnamese Army, 1950–1972*. Washington, DC: U.S. Department of the Army, 1975.

Collins, John M. *America's Small Wars: Lessons for the Future*. Washington, DC: Brassey's, 1991.

Collins, Joseph J. "The Soviet Invasion of Afghanistan: Methods, Motives and Ramifications." *Naval War College Review*, November 1980.

———. *The Soviet Invasion of Afghanistan: A Study in the Use of Force in Soviet Foreign Policy*. Lexington, MA: Lexington Books, 1985.

———. "Soviet Military Performance in Afghanistan: A Preliminary Assessment." *Comparative Strategy*, vol. 4 (Spring 1983).

Condit, D. M. *Case Study in Guerrilla War: Greece during World War II*. Washington, DC: U.S. Department of the Army, 1961.

Cooper, Chester L. *The Lost Crusade: America in Viet Nam*. New York: Dodd, Mead, 1970.

Cordesman, Anthony H., and Abraham F. Wagner. *The Lessons of Modern War*. vol. 2, *The Afghan and Falkland Conflicts*. Boulder, CO: Westview, 1990.

Cross, James Eliot. *Conflict in the Shadows: The Nature and Politics of Guerrilla War*. Garden City, NY: Doubleday, 1963.

Curry, Cecil B. *Edward Lansdale: The Unquiet American*. Boston: Houghton Mifflin, 1988.

Daley, T. "Afghanistan and Gorbachev's Global Foreign Policy." *Asian Survey*, vol. 29 (May 1989).

Daskal, Steven E. "The Insurgency Threat and Ways to Defeat It." *Military Review*, January 1986.

Davidson, Phillip B. *Viet Nam at War: The History, 1946–1975*. Novato, CA: Presidio Press, 1988.

Davidson, W. P. *Some Observations on Viet Cong Operations in the Villages*. Santa Monica, CA: RAND, 1968.

Davis, Leonard. *Revolutionary Struggle in the Philippines*. London: Macmillan, 1989.

Dawson, Alan. *55 Days: The Fall of South Viet Nam*. Englewood Cliffs, NJ: Prentice-Hall, 1977.

Devillers, Philippe, and Jean Lacouture. *End of a War: Indochina 1954*. Trans. A. Lieven and A. Roberts. New York: Praeger, 1969.

Director of Operations. *Malaya. The Conduct of Anti-Terrorist Operations*. Malaya: 1958 (3rd edition).

Dixon, C. A., and Otto Heilbrunn. *Communist Guerrilla Warfare*. New York: Praeger, 1962.

Dommen, Arthur. *Conflict in Laos*. New York: Praeger, 1964.

Dong Van Khuyen. *The RVNAF*. Washington, DC: U.S. Army Center of Military History, 1980.

Donnell, John C. *Viet Cong Recruitment: Why and How Men Join*. Santa Monica, CA: RAND Corporation, 1975.

Duiker, William J. *The Communist Road to Power in Viet Nam*. Boulder, CO: Westview, 1981.

————. *The Rise of Nationalism in Viet Nam, 1920–1941*. Ithaca, NY: Cornell University, 1976.

————. *Viet Nam since the Fall of Saigon*. Athens, OH: Ohio University, 1985.

Duncanson, Dennis J. *Government and Revolution in Viet Nam*. New York: Oxford University, 1968.

Dunn, Peter M. "The American Army: The Viet Nam War." Ian F. W. Beckett and John Pimlott, eds. *Armed Forces and Modern Counter-Insurgency*. New York: St. Martin's, 1985.

————. *The First Viet Nam War*. New York: St. Martin's, 1985.

Dupree, Louis. *Afghanistan*. Princeton, NJ: Princeton University, 1973.

Eban, Martin. *Lin Piao*. New York: Stein and Day, 1970.

Ely, Paul. *Lessons of the War in Indochina*, vol. 2 [translation]. Santa Monica, CA: RAND Corporation, 1967.

Englemann, Larry. *Tears before the Rain: An Oral History of the Fall of South Viet Nam*. New York: Oxford University, 1990.

Fairbairn, Geoffrey. *Revolutionary Guerrilla Warfare: The Countryside Version*. Harmondsworth, UK: Penguin, 1974.

Fall, Bernard. *Hell in a Very Small Place*. Philadelphia: Lippincott, 1967.

————. *Street without Joy*. Harrisburg, PA: Stackpole, 1964.

————. *The Two Viet Nams: A Political and Military Analysis*. New York: Praeger, 1967 (2nd ed., revised).

Farr, Grant M. *Afghan Resistance: The Politics of Survival*. Boulder, CO: Westview, 1987.

Fishel, Wesley. *Viet Nam: Anatomy of a Conflict*. Itasca, IL: Peacock, 1968.

Fletcher, Arnold. *Afghanistan: Highway of Conquest*. Ithaca, NY: Cornell University, 1965.

Foreign Relations of the United States [individual years]. Washington, DC: Government Printing Office, 1961–1977.

Fuller, Graham E. "The Emergence of Central Asia." *Foreign Affairs*, vol. 69, no. 2 (Spring 1990).

Gaddis, John Lewis. *Strategies of Containment*. New York: Oxford University, 1982.

Galeotti, Mark. *Afghanistan: The Soviet Union's Last War*. Portland, OR: Frank Cass, 1994.

Gallucci, Robert L. *Neither Peace Nor Honor: The Politics of American Military Policy in Viet Nam*. Baltimore: Johns Hopkins, 1975.

Galula, David. *Counter-Insurgency Warfare: Theory and Practice*. New York: Praeger, 1964.

Gardner, Hugh. *Guerrilla and Counterguerrilla Warfare in Greece 1941–1945*. Washington, DC: U.S. Department of the Army, 1962.

Garland, Albert N., ed. *A Distant Challenge: The U.S. Infantryman in Viet Nam, 1967–1972*. Nashville, TN: Battery Press, 1983. [Orig. 1969.]

Gelb, Leslie, and R. K. Betts. *The Irony of Viet Nam*. Washington, DC: Brookings Institute, 1979.

George, Alexander. *The Chinese Communist Army in Action*. New York: Columbia University, 1966.

Ghaus, Abdul Samad. *The Fall of Afghanistan: An Insider's Account*. London: Pergamon-Brassey's, 1988.

Giap, General. See Vo Nguyen Giap.

Girardet, Edward. *Afghanistan: The Soviet War*. New York: St. Martin's, 1985.

———. "Russia's War in Afghanistan." *Central Asian Survey*, vol. 2, no. 1 (July 1983).

Girling, J.L.S. *America and the Third World: Revolution and Intervention*. London: Routledge and Kegan Paul, 1980.

———. *People's War: Conditions and Consequences in China and South East Asia*. New York: Praeger, 1969.

Goodman, Allan E. *An Institutional Profile of the South Vietnamese Officer Corps*. Santa Monica, CA: RAND, 1970.

———. *The Lost Peace: America's Search for a Negotiated Settlement of the Viet Nam War*. Stanford, CA: Hoover Institution, 1978.

———. *Politics in War: The Bases of Political Community in South Viet Nam*. Cambridge, MA: Harvard University, 1973.

Grant, J.A.C. "The Viet Nam Constitution of 1956." *The American Political Science Review*, vol. 52 (June 1958).

Gravel Edition, The. *The Pentagon Papers*. Boston: Beacon, 1971. 5 vols.

Greenburg, Lawrence M. *The Hukbalahap Insurrection: A Case Study of a Successful Anti-Insurgency Operation in the Philippines, 1946–1955*. Washington, DC: U.S. Army Center of Military History, 1986.

Greene, Thomas. *Comparative Revolutionary Movements*. Englewood Cliffs, NJ: Prentice-Hall, 1984.

Greene, T. N., ed. *The Guerrilla—And How to Fight Him*. New York: Praeger, 1962.

Griffith, Samuel B. *The Chinese People's Liberation Army*. New York: McGraw-Hill, 1967.

———. *Peking and People's War*. New York: Praeger, 1966.

Grintner, Laurence E. "How They Lost: Doctrines, Strategies and Outcomes of the Viet Nam War." *Asian Survey*, vol. 15, no. 12 (December 1975).

Guevara, Ernesto. *Guerrilla Warfare*. New York: Vintage, 1960.

Gurtov, Melvin. *The First Viet Nam Crisis: Chinese Communist Strategy and United States Involvement, 1953–1954* New York: Greenwood, 1967.

———. *Hanoi on War and Peace*. Santa Monica, CA: RAND, 1967.

Gurtov, Melvin, and Konrad Kellen. *Viet Nam: Lessons and Mislessons*. Santa Monica, CA: RAND, 1969.

Halberstam, David. *The Making of a Quagmire*. New York: Random House, 1965.

Hammer, Ellen J. *A Death in November: America in Viet Nam 1963*. New York: Dutton, 1987.

———. "South Viet Nam: The Limits of Political Action." *Pacific Affairs*, 35 (Spring 1962).

———. *The Struggle for Indochina*. Stanford, CA.: Stanford University, 1954.

Hammer, Kenneth M. "Huks in the Philippines." Franklin Mark Osanka, ed. *Modern Guerrilla Warfare*. Glencoe, IL: Free Press, 1962.

Hammond, Thomas T. *Red Flag over Afghanistan*. Boulder, CO: Westview, 1984.

Hannah, Norman B. *The Key to Failure: Laos and the Viet Nam War*. Lanham, MD: Madison Books, 1987.

Hanrahan, Gene. *The Communist Struggle in Malaya*. New York: Institute of Pacific Relations, 1954.

Harkavy, Robert E., and Stephanie Neuman. *The Lessons of Recent Wars in the Third World*. vol. 1. Lexington, MA: Lexington Books, 1985.

Hart, Douglas M. "Low Intensity Conflict in Afghanistan: The Soviet View." *Survival*, vol. 24 (March/April 1982).

Heilbrunn, Otto. *Partisan Warfare*. New York: Praeger, 1962.

Henderson, Darryl. *Why the Viet Cong Fought: A Study of Motivation and Control in a Modern Army in Combat*. Westport, CT: Greenwood, 1979.

Herring, George C. *America's Longest War*. New York: Knopf, 1986. 2d ed.

Herring, George C., and Richard H. Immerson. "Eisenhower, Dulles, and Dien Bien Phu: 'The Day We Didn't Go to War' Revisited." *Journal of American History*, vol. 72 (September 1985).

Herrington, Stuart A. *Peace with Honor?* Novato, CA: Presidio, 1983.

———. *Silence Was a Weapon: The Viet Nam War in the Villages*. Novato, CA: Presidio, 1982.

Heymann, H. and W. Whitson. *Can and Should the United States Preserve a Military Capability for Revolutionary Conflict?* Santa Monica, CA: RAND, 1972.

Higham, Robin. *Intervention or Abstention: The Dilemma of American Foreign Policy*. Lexington, KY: University of Kentucky, 1975.

Ho Chi Minh. *Ho Chi Minh on Revolution*. New York: Praeger, 1967.

Hoang Ngoc Lung. *The General Offensives of 1968–1969*. Washington, DC: U.S. Army Center of Military History, 1981.

Hoang Van Chi. *From Colonialism to Communism. A Case History of North Viet Nam*. New York: Praeger, 1964.

Honey, P. J. *North Viet Nam Today: Profile of a Communist Satellite*. New York: Praeger, 1962.

Hosmer, Stephen T. *The Army's Role in Counterinsurgency and Insurgency*. Santa Monica, CA: RAND, 1990.

———. *Constraints on U.S. Strategy in Third World Conflicts*. New York: Crane, Russak, 1988.

Hosmer, Stephen T., Konrad Kellen, and Brian M. Jenkins. *The Fall of South of Viet Nam*. New York: Crane, Russak, 1980.

Hosmer, Stephen T., and Thomas W. Wolfe. *Soviet Policy and Practice toward Third World Conflicts*. Lexington, MA: Lexington Books, 1983.

Hung P. Nguyen. "Communist Offensive Strategy and the Defense of South Viet Nam." Lloyd J. Matthews and Dale E. Brown, eds. *Assessing the Viet Nam War*. McLean, VA: Pergamon-Brassey's, 1987.

Hunt, Richard A., and Richard H. Shultz, Jr., eds. *Lessons from an Unconventional War*. New York: Pergamon, 1982.

Huntington, Samuel P. "Patterns of Intervention: America and the Soviets in the Third World." *The National Interest*, vol. 7 (Spring 1987).

Huynh Kim Khanh. *Vietnamese Communism 1925–1945*. Ithaca, NY: Cornell University, 1982.

Isaacs, Arnold R. *Without Honor: Defeat in Viet Nam and Cambodia*. New York: Vintage, 1984.

Isby, David C. *War in a a Distant Country*. London: Arms and Armour, 1989.

Joes, Anthony James. *From the Barrel of a Gun*. Washington, DC: Pergamon-Brassey's, 1986

————. *Modern Guerrilla Insurgency*. New York: Praeger, 1992.

————. *The War for South Viet Nam*. New York: Praeger, 1989.

Johnson, Chalmers. *Autopsy on People's War*. Berkeley, CA: University of California, 1973.

————. "Civilian Loyalties and Guerrilla Conflict." *World Politics*, vol. 17 (1964).

————. *Peasant Nationalism and Communist Power*. Stanford, CA: Stanford University, 1961.

Joint Low Intensity Conflict Project. *Analytical Review of Low Intensity Conflict*. Washington, DC: Government Printing Office, 1986.

Jones, Gregg. *Red Revolution: Inside the Philippine Guerrilla Movement*. Boulder, CO: Westview, 1989.

Jones, Howard. *"A New Kind of War": America's Global Strategy and the Truman Doctrine in Greece*. New York: Oxford University, 1989.

Joo-Jock, Kim, ed. *Armed Communist Movements in Southeast Asia*. New York: St. Martin's, 1984.

Jukes, Geoffrey. "The Soviet Armed Forces and the Afghan War." Amin Saikal and William Maley, eds. *The Soviet Withdrawal from Afghanistan*. Cambridge, UK: Cambridge University, 1989.

Jumper, Roy, and Marjorie Weiner Normand. "Viet Nam." George Kahin, ed. *Government and Politics in Southeast Asia*. Ithaca, NY: Cornell University, 1964.

Karp, Craig. *Afghanistan: Eight Years of Soviet Occupation*. Washington, DC: U.S. Department of State, 1987.

————. *Afghanistan: Seven Years of Soviet Occupation*. Washington, DC: U.S. Department of State, 1986.

————. *Afghanistan: Six Years of Soviet Occupation*. Washington DC: U.S. Department of State, 1985.

Katz, Mark. "Anti-Soviet Insurgencies: Growing Trend or Passing Phase?" *Orbis*, vol. 30 (Summer 1986).

————. *The Third World and Soviet Military Thought*. Baltimore: Johns Hopkins, 1982.

Katzenbach, Edward L., and Gene Z. Hanrahan. "The Revolutionary Strategy of Mao Tse-tung." *Political Science Quarterly*, vol. 70 (September 1955).

Kellen, Konrad. *A Profile of the PAVN Soldier in Viet Nam*. Santa Monica, CA: RAND, 1966.

————. *A View of the VC*. Santa Monica, CA: RAND, 1969.

Kennan, George F. *Memoirs 1925–1950*. Boston: Little, Brown, 1967.

Kerkvliet, Benedict J. *The Huk Rebellion: A Study in Peasant Revolt in the Philippines*. Berkeley, CA: University of California, 1977.

Kessler, Richard J. *Rebellion and Repression in the Philippines*. New Haven, CT: Yale University 1989.

Kiernan, Ben. *How Pol Pot Came to Power: A History of Communism in Kampuchea 1930–1975*. London: Verso, 1985.

Kiernan, Ben, ed. *Genocide and Democracy in Cambodia: The Khmer Rouge, the United Nations, and the International Community*. New Haven, CT: Yale University, 1993.

Klass, Rosanne, ed. *Afghanistan: The Great Game Revisited*. New York: Freedom House, 1987.

Klein, Donald, and Ann B. Clark. *Biographical Dictionary of Chinese Communism, 1921–1965*. Cambridge, MA: Harvard University, 1970.

Koehler, John. *Explaining Dissident Success: The Huks in Central Luzon*. Santa Monica, CA: RAND, 1972.

Kolko, Gabriel. *Anatomy of a War: Viet Nam, the United States, and the Modern Historical Experience*. New York: Pantheon, 1985.

Komer, Robert W. *Bureaucracy Does Its Thing: Institutional Constraints on US-GVN Performance in Viet Nam*. Santa Monica, CA: RAND, 1972.

———. "Impact of Pacification on Insurgency in South Viet Nam." *Journal of International Affairs*, vol. 25, no. 1 (1971).

———. *The Malayan Emergency in Retrospect*. Santa Monica, CA: RAND, 1972.

Kousoulas, D. George. "The Guerrilla War the Communists Lost." U.S. Naval Institute Proceedings, vol. 89 (1963).

———. *Modern Greece*. New York: Scribner's, 1974.

———. *Revolution and Defeat: The Story of the Greek Communist Party*. London: Oxford University, 1965.

Krakowski, Ellie D. "Afghanistan: The Forgotten War." *Central Asian Survey*, vol. 4, no. 2 (October 1985).

Krepinevich, Andrew F., Jr. *The Army and Viet Nam*. Baltimore: Johns Hopkins University, 1986.

Kuniholm, Bruce R. *The Origins of the Cold War in the Near East: Great Power Conflict and Diplomacy in Iran, Turkey, and Greece*. Princeton, NJ: Princeton University, 1980.

Lachia, Eduardo. *The Huks: Philippine Agrarian Society in Revolt*. New York: Praeger, 1971.

Lacouture, Jean. *Ho Chi Minh: A Political Biography*. Trans. Peter Wiles. London: Penguin, 1968.

Lam Quang Thi. *Autopsy: The Death of South Viet Nam*. Phoenix, AZ: Sphinx, 1986.

Lancaster, Donald. *The Emancipation of French Indochina*. London: Oxford University, 1961.

Lanning, Michael Lee, and Dan Gragg. *Inside the VC and the NVA*. New York: Fawcett Columbine, 1992.

Lansdale, Edward G. *In the Midst of Wars: An American's Mission to Southeast Asia*. New York: Harper and Row, 1972.

———. "Viet Nam: Do We Understand Revolution?" *Foreign Affairs*, October 1964.

———. "Viet Nam—Still the Search for Goals." *Foreign Affairs*, October 1968.

Larkin, John A. "Early Guerrilla Struggle in the Philippines." *Peasant Studies*, vol. 19 (Fall 1991).

Larteguy, Jean. *Yellow Fever*. Trans. Xan Fielding. New York: Dutton, 1966.

Le Gro, William E. *Viet Nam from Ceasefire to Capitulation*. Washington, DC: U.S. Army Center of Military History, 1981.

Lee, Chong-Sik. *Counterinsurgency in Manchuria: The Japanese Experience 1931–1945*. Santa Monica, CA: RAND, 1967.

———. *Revolutionary Struggle in Manchuria: Chinese Communism and Soviet Interest 1922–1945*. Berkeley, CA: University of California, 1983.

Leeper, Reginald. *When Greek Meets Greek*. London: Chatto and Windus, 1950.

Leites, Nathan. *The Viet Cong Style of Politics*. Santa Monica, CA: RAND, 1969.

Lessing, Doris. *The Wind Blows away Our Words*. New York: Vintage, 1987.

Lessons from the Viet Nam War. London: Royal United Services Institution, 1969.

Lewy, Guenter. *America in Viet Nam*. New York: Oxford University, 1978.

————. "Some Political-Military Lessons of the Viet Nam War." Lloyd Matthews and Dale E. Brown, eds. *Assessing the Viet Nam War*. McLean, VA: Pergamon-Brassey's, 1989.

Lin Piao. *Long Live the Victory of People's War*. Peking, 1965.

Lindholm, Richard W., ed. *Viet Nam: The First Five Years*. East Lansing, MI.: Michigan State University, 1959.

Liu, F. F. *A Military History of Modern China, 1924–1949*. Princeton, NJ: Princeton University, 1956.

Lockhart, Bruce M. *The End of the Vietnamese Monarchy*. New Haven, CT: Yale University, 1993.

Lomperis, Timothy J. *The War Everyone Lost—And Won: America's Intervention in Viet Nam's Twin Struggles*. Baton Rouge, LA: Louisiana State University, 1984.

Lovelace, Daniel D. *China and "People's War" in Thailand, 1964–1969*. Berkeley, CA: University of California, 1971.

Low Intensity Conflict Field Manual 100–20. Washington DC: U.S. Department of the Army, 1981.

MacDonald, Peter. *Giap: The Victor in Viet Nam*. New York: Norton, 1993.

Magno, José, and A. J. Gregor. "Insurgency and Counterinsurgency in the Philippines." *Asian Survey*, vol. 26 (May 1986).

Malhuret, Claude. "Report from Afghanistan." *Foreign Affairs*, vol. 84 (Winter 1984).

Mallin, Jay. *Strategy for Conquest: Communist Documents on Guerrilla Warfare*. Coral Gables, FL: University of Miami, 1970.

Maneli, Mieczyslaw. *War of the Vanquished*. Trans. M. de Gorcey. New York: Harper and Row, 1971.

Marks, Tom. "Marxist Miscue: The Demise of the Communist Party of Thailand." *Small Wars and Insurgencies*, vol. 3 (Summer 1992).

Marr, David G. *The Viet Nam Tradition on Trial 1920–1945*. Berkeley, CA: University of California, 1981.

Martin, Mike. *Afghanistan: Inside a Rebel Stronghold*. Dorset, UK: Blandford, 1984.

Matthews, L. J., and D. E. Brown, eds. *Assessing the Viet Nam War*. Washington, DC: Pergamon-Brassey's, 1987.

McAlister, John T. *Viet Nam: The Origins of Revolution*. Garden City, NY: Doubleday Anchor, 1971.

McCoy, James. *Secrets of the Viet Cong*. New York: Hippocrene, 1992.

McGarvey, Patrick J. *Visions of Victory: Selected Vietnamese Communist Military Writings 1965–1968*. Stanford, CA: Hoover Institution, 1969.

McLane, Charles B. *Soviet Strategies in Southeast Asia: An Exploration of Eastern Policy under Lenin and Stalin*. Princeton, NJ: Princeton University, 1966.

McNeill, William H. *Greece: American Aid in Action*. New York: Twentieth Century Fund, 1957.

McVey, Ruth. *The Calcutta Conference and the South East Asian Uprising*. Ithaca, NY: Cornell University, 1958.

Miller, Harry. *The Communist Menace in Malaya*. New York: Praeger, 1954.

————. *Jungle Warfare in Malaya: The Campaign against Communism 1948–1960*. London: Arthur Barker, 1972.

Mosely, Philip E. "Soviet Policy and the Revolution in Asia." *Annals of the Academy of Political and Social Sciences*, vol. 276 (July 1951).

Munholland, J. Kim. " 'Collaboration Strategy' and the French Pacification of Tonkin, 1885–1897." *The Historical Journal*, vol. 24, no. 3 (1981).

Murray, J. C. "The Anti-Bandit War." Reprinted in *The Guerrilla—And How to Fight Him*. New York: Praeger, 1962.

Neuman, Stephania, and Robert Harkavy, eds. *The Lessons of Recent Wars in the Third World*. Lexington, MA: Lexington, 1987.

Ngo Quang Truong. *The Easter Offensive of 1972*. Washington, DC: U.S. Army Center of Military History, 1980.

————. *Territorial Forces*. Washington, DC: U.S. Army Center of Military History, 1981.

Nguyen Tien Hung, and Jerrold Schecter, *The Palace File: Viet Nam Secret Documents*. New York: Perenniel Library, 1989.

Nguyen Van Canh, *Viet Nam under Communism 1975–1982*. Stanford, CA: The Hoover Institution, 1983.

Nighswonger, William A. *Rural Pacification in Viet Nam*. New York: Praeger, 1966.

Nixon, Richard. *No More Viet Nams*. New York: Arbor House, 1985.

Nolan, Keith William. *Into Laos*. Novato, CA: Presidio, 1986.

Norris, J. A. *The First Afghan War*. Cambridge, UK: Cambridge University 1967.

Nuechterlein, Donald E. *Thailand and the Struggle for Southeast Asia*. Ithaca, NY: Cornell University, 1965.

O'Ballance, Edgar. "The Communist New People's Army." *Military Review*, vol. 68 (February 1988).

————. *The Greek Civil War*. London: Faber and Faber, 1966

————. *The Indo-China War 1945–1954*. London: Faber and Faber, 1964.

————. *Malaya: The Communist Insurgent War 1948–1960*. Hamden, CT: Archon, 1966.

Oberdorfer, Don. *Tet!* Garden City, NY: Doubleday, 1971.

O'Neill, Robert. *General Giap*. New York: Praeger, 1969.

————. *The Strategy of General Giap since 1964*. Canberra: Australian National University, 1969.

Osanka, Franklin Mark. *Modern Guerrilla Warfare*. New York: Free Press, 1962.

Palmer, Bruce, Jr. *The 25-Year War: America's Military Role in Viet Nam*. Lexington, KY: University of Kentucky, 1984.

Palmer, Dave Richard. *Summons of the Trumpet*. San Rafael, CA: Presidio, 1978.

Papagos, Alexander. "Guerrilla Warfare." F. M. Osanka, ed. *Modern Guerrilla Warfare*. New York: Free Press, 1962. [Also in *Foreign Affairs*, vol. 30 (January 1952).]

Paret, Peter, and John Shy. *Guerrillas in the 1960s*. New York: Praeger, 1962.

Paschall, Rod. *LIC 2010: Special Operations and Unconventional Warfare in the Next Century*. Washington, DC: Brassey's, 1990.

————. "Marxist Counterinsurgencies." *Parameters*, vol. 16, no. 2 (1986).

Patti, Archimedes. *Why Viet Nam?* Berkeley, CA: University of California, 1980.

Paul, Roland. "Laos: Anatomy of an American Involvement." *Foreign Affairs*, April 1971.

Penniman, Howard R. *Elections in South Viet Nam*. Washington, DC: American Enterprise Institute, 1972.

Peterson, Michael E. *The Combined Action Platoons: The U.S. Marines' Other War in Viet Nam*. New York: Praeger, 1989.

Pierce, Richard A. *Russian Central Asia 1867–1917: A Study in Colonial Rule*. Berkeley, CA: University of California, 1960.

Pike, Douglas. *History of Vietnamese Communism 1925–1976*. Stanford, CA: Hoover Institution, 1978.

———. *PAVN: People's Army of Viet Nam*. Novato, CA: Presidio, 1986.

———. *Viet Cong*. Cambridge, MA: MIT, 1966.

———. *The Viet Cong Strategy of Terror*. Cambridge, MA: MIT, 1970.

Pimlott, John. "The French Army: From Indochina to Chad." Ian F. W. Beckett and John Pimlott, ed. *Armed Forces and Modern Counter-Insurgency*. New York: St. Martin's, 1985.

Pimlott, John, ed. *Viet Nam: The History and the Tactics*. New York: Crescent, 1982.

Pomeroy, William J. "The Philippine Peasantry and the Huk Revolt." *Journal of Peasant Studies*, vol. 5, no. 4 (July 1978).

Pomeroy, William J., ed. *Guerrilla Warfare and Marxism*. New York: International Publishers, 1968.

Popkin, Samuel. *The Rational Peasant*. Berkeley, CA: University of California, 1979.

Porter, Gareth. "Philippine Communism After Marcos." *Problems of Communism*, vol. 6 (September–October 1987).

Poullada, Leon B. "Afghanistan and the United States: The Crucial Years." *Middle East Journal*, vol. 35, no. 2 (Spring 1981).

Pye, Lucian. *Guerrilla Communism in Malaya*. Princeton, NJ: Princeton University, 1956.

———. *Warlord Politics*. New York: Praeger, 1971.

Race, Jeffrey. *War Comes to Long An: Revolutionary Conflict in a Vietnamese Province*. Berkeley, CA: University of California, 1972.

———. "War in Northern Thailand." *Modern Asian Survey*, vol. 8 (January 1974).

Radu, Michael. *The New Insurgencies: Anticommunist Guerrillas in the Third World*. New Brunswick, NJ: Transaction, 1990.

"Reflections on Counterinsurgency in Thailand." Special issue of *World Affairs*, vol. 146 (Winter 1983/84).

Regional Conflict Working Group. *Commitment to Freedom: Security Assistance as a U.S. Policy Instrument in the Third World*. Washington, DC: Government Printing Office, 1988.

———. *Supporting U.S. Strategy for Third World Conflict*. Washington, DC: Government Printing Office, 1988.

Rice, Edward E. *Wars of the Third Kind: Conflict in Underdeveloped Countries*. Berkeley, CA: University of California, 1988.

Richardson, James. "The Huk Rebellion." *Journal of Contemporary Asia*, vol. 8, no. 2 (1978).

Robbins, James S. *Soviet Counterinsurgency Strategy in Afghanistan 1979–1989*. Doctoral Dissertation, Fletcher School of Law and Diplomacy, Tufts University, Medford, MA, 1991.

Robinson, Donald. *The Dirty Wars*. New York: Delacorte, 1968.

Robinson, Thomas W. *A Politico-Military Biography of Lin Piao*. Santa Monica, CA: RAND, 1971.

Rolph, Hammond. "Vietnamese Communism and the Protracted War." *Asian Survey*, vol. 12 (September 1972).

Romulo, Carlos P. *Crusade in Asia*. New York: John Day, 1955.

Rosen, Stephen. "Viet Nam and the American Theory of Limited War." *International Security*, vol. 7 (Fall 1982).

Roy, Jules. *The Battle of Dien Bien Phu*. New York: Harper and Row, 1965.

Roy, Olivier. *Islam and Resistance in Afghanistan*. Cambridge, UK: Cambridge University, 1986.

———. *The Lessons of the Soviet-Afghan War*. London: International Institute of Strategic Studies, 1991 [Adelphi Paper no. 259].

Rubin, Barnett R. *To Die in Afghanistan*. New York: Helsinki Watch and Asia Watch, 1985.

———. "The Fragmentation of Afghanistan." *Foreign Affairs*, vol. 68 (Winter 1989/90).

Rubin, Barnett R., and Jeri Laber. *A Nation Is Dying: Afghanistan under the Soviets 1979–1987*. Chicago: Northwestern University, 1988.

Rubinstein, Alvin Z. *The Great Game: Rivalry in the Persian Gulf and South Asia*. New York: Praeger, 1983.

Russett, Bruce, and James S. Sutterlin. "The U.N. in a New World Order." *Foreign Affairs*, vol. 70, no. 2 (Spring, 1991).

Ryan, Nigel. *A Hitch or Two in Afghanistan*. London: Weidenfeld and Nicolson, 1983.

Rywkin, Michael. *Russia in Central Asia*. New York: Collier, 1963.

Saikal, Amin, and William Maley, eds. *The Soviet Withdrawal from Afghanistan*. Cambridge, UK: Cambridge University, 1989.

Sansom, Robert L. *The Economics of Insurgency in the Mekong Delta of Viet Nam*. Cambridge, MA: MIT, 1970.

Santoli, Al. *Everything We Had: An Oral History of the Viet Nam War by Thirty-Three American Soldiers Who Fought It*. New York: Random House, 1981.

Sarin, Oleg, and Lev Dvoretsky. *The Afghan Syndrome: The Soviet Union's Viet Nam*. Novato, CA: Presidio, 1993.

Sarkesian, Sam. *America's Forgotten Wars: The Counterrevolutionary Past and Lessons for the Future*. Westport, CT: Greenwood, 1984.

Scaff, Alvin H. *The Philippine Answer to Communism*. Stanford, CA: Stanford University, 1955.

Schell, Jonathan. *The Village of Ben Suc*. New York: Random House, 1967.

Schram, Stuart. *Mao Tse-tung*. Harmondsworth, UK: Penguin, 1966.

Schwartzstein, Stuart J. D. "Chemical Warfare in Afghanistan." *World Affairs*, vol. 145, no. 3 (Winter 1982/83).

Scigliano, Robert. *South Viet Nam: Nation under Stress*. Boston: Houghton Mifflin, 1964.

Scott, Harriet, and William Scott. *The Soviet Art of War*. Boulder, CO: Westview, 1982.

Selden, Mark. *The Yenan Way in Revolutionary China*. Cambridge, UK: Cambridge University, 1971.

Seton-Watson, Hugh. *Eastern Europe between the Wars*. New York: Harper, 1967.

Shafer, D. Michael. *Deadly Paradigms: The Failure of U.S. Counterinsurgency Policy*. Princeton, NJ: Princeton University, 1988.

Shahrani, M. Nazif, and Robert L. Canfield, eds. *Revolutions and Rebellions in Afghan-istan*. Berkeley, CA: University of California, 1986.

Shaplen, Robert. *Bitter Victory*. New York: Harper and Row, 1986.

———. *The Lost Revolution: The U.S. in Viet Nam 1946–1966*. New York: Harper and Row, 1966.

Sharp, U. S. Grant. *Strategy for Defeat: Viet Nam in Retrospect*. San Rafael, CA: Presidio, 1978.

Shee Poon Kim. "Insurgency in Southeast Asia." *Problems of Communism*, vol. 32 (May-June, 1983).

Sheehan, Neil. *A Bright Shining Lie: John Paul Vann and America in Viet Nam*. New York: Random House, 1988.

Sheikh, Ali T. "Not the Whole Truth: Media Coverage of the Afghan Conflict." *Conflict Quarterly*, vol. 10, no. 4 (Fall 1990).

Sheridan, James E. *China in Disintegration: The Republican Era, 1912–1949*. New York: Free Press, 1975.

Short, Anthony. *The Communist Insurrection in Malaya, 1948–1960*. London: Frederick Muller, 1975.

———. *The Origins of the Viet Nam War*. London: Longman, 1989.

Shultz, Richard H., Jr. "Breaking the Will of the Enemy in the Viet Nam War." *Journal of Peace Research*, vol. 15, no. 2 (1978).

Shultz, Richard H., Jr., et al., eds. *Guerrilla Warfare and Counterinsurgency: U.S.-Soviet Policy in the Third World*. Lexington, MA: Lexington, 1989.

Slade, Stuart. "Successful Counterinsurgency: How the Thais Burned the Books and Beat the Guerrillas." *International Defense Review*, vol. 22, no. 10 (1989).

Smedley, Agnes. *The Great Road: The Life and Times of Chu Teh*. New York: Monthly Review, 1956.

Social Science Research Bureau of Michigan State University. *Problems of Freedom: South Viet Nam since Independence*. Glencoe, IL: Free Press of Glencoe, 1961.

Spector, Ronald H. *Advice and Support: The Early Years 1941–1960*. Washington, DC: U.S. Army Center of Military History, 1983.

Spencer, Floyd. *War and Postwar Greece*. Washington, DC: Library of Congress, 1952.

Spencer-Chapman, F. *The Jungle Is Neutral*. London: Chatto and Windus, 1949.

Stanton, Shelby. *Green Berets at War: U.S. Army Special Forces in Southeast Asia, 1956–1975*. Novato, CA: Presidio, 1985.

———. *The Rise and Fall of an American Army: U.S. Ground Forces in Viet Nam 1965–1973*. Novato, CA: Presidio, 1985.

Stavrakis, Peter J. *Moscow and Greek Communism 1944–1949*. Ithaca, NY: Cornell University, 1989.

Stephenson, Charles. *The End of Nowhere: American Policy toward Laos since 1954*. Boston: Beacon, 1973.

Stockwell, A. J. "Insurgency and Decolonization during the Malayan Emergency." *Journal of Commonwealth and Comparative Politics*, vol. 25 (March 1987).

Stubbs, Richard. *Hearts and Minds in Guerrilla Warfare: The Malayan Emergency of 1948–1960*. Singapore: Oxford University, 1989.

Sturtevant, David. "Filipino Peasant Rebellions Examined: Lessons from the Past." *CALC Report*, vol. 12, no. 3 (May-June 1986).

Summers, Harry. *On Strategy: A Critical Analysis of the Viet Nam War*. Novato, CA: Presidio, 1982.

Tanham, George K. *Communist Revolutionary Warfare: From the Viet Minh to the Viet Cong.* New York: Praeger, 1967 [revised].

———. "Some Insurgency Lessons from Southeast Asia." *Orbis*, vol. 16 (Fall 1972).

———. *Trial in Thailand.* New York: Crane, Russak, 1974.

Tanham, George K., and Dennis J. Duncanson. "Some Dilemmas of Counterinsurgency." *Foreign Affairs*, October 1969.

Taruc, Luis. *Born of the People.* Westport, CT: Greenwood, 1973 [original 1953].

———. *He Who Rides the Tiger.* New York: Praeger, 1967.

Taylor, Maxwell D. *Swords and Ploughshares.* New York: Norton, 1972.

Thayer, Thomas C. *War without Fronts: The American Experience in Viet Nam.* Boulder, CO: Westview, 1985.

Thies, W. J. *When Governments Collide: Coercion and Diplomacy in the Viet Nam Conflict 1964–1968.* Berkeley, CA: University of California, 1980.

Thompson, Sir Robert. *Defeating Communist Insurgency: The Lessons of Malaya and Viet Nam.* New York: Praeger, 1966.

———. *No Exit from Viet Nam.* New York: David McKay, 1969.

———. *Peace Is Not at Hand.* New York: David McKay, 1974.

———. *Revolutionary War in World Strategy.* New York: Taplinger, 1970.

Thompson, W. Scott, and Donaldson D. Frizzell, eds. *The Lessons of Viet Nam.* New York: Crane, Russak, 1977.

Thornton, Thomas P. "The Emergence of Communist Revolutionary Doctrine." C. E. Black and T. P. Thornton, eds. *Communism and Revolution: The Strategic Uses of Political Violence.* Princeton, NJ: Princeton University, 1964.

Tilman, Robert O. "The Non-Lessons of the Emergency in Malaya." *Asian Survey*, vol. 6, no. 8 (August 1966).

Todd, Olivier. *Cruel April: The Fall of Saigon.* New York: Norton, 1990.

Trager, Frank. *Why Viet Nam?* New York: Praeger, 1966.

Tran Dinh Tho. *Pacification.* Washington, DC: U.S. Army Center of Military History, 1980.

Tran Van Don. *Our Endless War.* San Rafael, CA: Presidio, 1978.

Tran Van Tra. *Concluding the 30-Years War.* Rosslyn, VA: Foreign Broadcast Information Service, 1983.

Trinquier, Roger. *Modern Warfare: A French View of Counterinsurgency.* New York: Praeger, 1964 [French publication 1961].

Trottier, Paul, and Craig Karp. *Afghanistan: Five Years of Occupation.* Washington, DC: U.S. State Department Special Report no. 120, 1984.

Truman, Harry S. *Memoirs.* New York: Doubleday, 1955 and 1956. 2 vols.

Truong Chinh (pseud.). *Primer for Revolt.* New York: Praeger, 1963.

———. *The Resistance Will Win.* Hanoi: Foreign Languages Publishing House, 1960.

Truong Nhu Tang. *A Viet Cong Memoir.* New York: Harcourt, 1987.

Tsoucalas, Constantine. *The Greek Tragedy.* Baltimore: Penguin, 1969.

Turley, G. H. *The Easter Offensive.* Novato, CA: Presidio, 1985.

Turley, William S. *Vietnamese Communism in Comparative Perspective.* Boulder, CO: Westview, 1980.

Turner, Robert F. *Vietnamese Communism: Its Origins and Development.* Stanford, CA: Hoover Institution, 1975.

Urban, Mark. *War in Afghanistan.* New York: St. Martin's, 1988.

U.S. Department of the Army. "A Program for the Pacification and Long-Term Development of South Viet Nam" [often called PROVN]. Washington, DC: 1966.

U.S. State Department, Bureau of Intelligence and Research. *Afghanistan: Four Years of Occupation*. Washington, DC: U.S. Department of State, 1983.

Valeriano, Napoleon, and C.T.P. Bohannan. *Counter-Guerrilla Operations: The Philippine Experience*. New York: Praeger, 1962.

Van der Kroef, Justus. "Aquino and the Communists: A Philippine Strategic Stalemate?" *World Affairs*, vol. 151 (Winter 1988/89).

———. *Aquino's Philippines: The Deepening Security Crisis*. London: Institute for the Study of Conflict, 1988.

———. "Guerrilla Communism and Counterinsurgency in Thailand." *Orbis*, vol. 18 (Spring, 1974).

Van Fleet, James A. "How We Won in Greece." *Balkan Studies*, vol. 8 (1967).

Van Hollen, Eliza. *Afghanistan: Three Years of Occupation*. Washington, DC: U.S. Department of State, 1982.

Van Tien Dung. *Our Great Spring Victory*. New York: Monthly Review, 1977.

VanDeMark, Brian. *Into the Quagmire: Lyndon Johnson and the Escalation of the Viet Nam War*. New York: Oxford University, 1991.

Vickery, Michael. *Cambodia, 1975–1982*. Boston: South End, 1984.

Vo Nguyen Giap. *Dien Bien Phu*. Hanoi: Foreign Languages Publishing House, 1964.

———. *How We Won the War*. Philadelphia: Recon, 1976.

———. *The Military Art of People's War*. New York: Monthly Review, 1970.

———. *People's War, People's Army*. New York: Praeger, 1962.

Waghelstein, John. "Post–Viet Nam Counterinsurgency Doctrine." *Military Review*, vol. 65 (May 1985).

Wainhouse, E. R. "Guerrilla War in Greece, 1946–1949: A Case Study." *Military Review*, June 1957.

Walt, L. W. *Strange War, Strange Strategy*. New York: Funk and Wagnalls, 1970.

Warner, Denis. *Certain Victory: How Hanoi Won the War*. Kansas City: Sheed, Andrews and McMeel, 1978

———. *The Last Confucian*. New York: Macmillan, 1963

Weatherbee, Donald P. *The United Front in Thailand: A Documentary Analysis*. Columbia, SC: University of South Carolina, 1970.

Weller, Jac. *Fire and Movement: Bargain-Basement War in the Far East*. New York: Crowell, 1967.

Weltz, Richard. "Moscow's Endgame in Afghanistan." *Conflict Quarterly*, vol. 12 (Winter 1992).

West, F. J., Jr. *Small Unit Action in Viet Nam*. Quantico, VA: U.S. Marine Corps, 1967.

———. *The Village*. New York: Harper and Row, 1972.

Westmoreland, William. *A Soldier Reports*. Garden City, NY: Doubleday, 1976.

Wheeler, Geoffrey. *The Modern History of Soviet Central Asia*. London: Weidenfeld and Nicolson, 1964.

Whitson, W. W. *The Chinese High Command: A History of Communist Military Politics, 1927–1971*. New York: Praeger, 1973.

Wimbush, S. E., and A. Alexiev. *Soviet Central Asian Soldiers in Afghanistan*. Santa Monica, CA: RAND Corp., 1984.

Wirtz, James J. *The Tet Offensive: Intelligence Failure in War*. Ithaca, NY: Cornell University, 1991.

Wittner, Lawrence S. *American Intervention in Greece 1943–1949*. New York: Columbia University, 1982.

Wolf, Charles, Jr. *The Logic of Failure: A Viet Nam "Lesson."* Santa Monica, CA: RAND, 1971.

Wolf, Eric. *Peasant Wars of the Twentieth Century*. New York: Harper and Row, 1969.

Wolff, Robert L. *The Balkans in Our Times*. Cambridge, MA: Harvard University, 1956.

Woodhouse, C. M. *The Struggle for Greece 1941–1949*. London: Hart-Davis, Mac-Gibbon, 1976.

Young, Kenneth. *The Greek Passion*. London: J. M. Dent, 1969.

Zasloff, J. J. *Origins of the Insurgency in South Viet Nam, 1954–1960: The Role of the Southern Viet Minh Cadres*. Santa Monica, CA: RAND, 1967.

Zimmerman, William, and Robert Axelrod. "The 'Lessons' of Viet Nam and Soviet Foreign Policy." *World Politics*, vol. 34, no. 1 (October, 1981).

Zotos, S. *Greece: The Struggle for Freedom*. New York: Crowell, 1967.

Latin America

Good comparative studies of Latin American guerrilla conflicts include: John J. Johnson, *The Military and Society in Latin America*, dated but still very useful for deep background; Alain Rouquie, *The Military and the State in Latin America*; John Lynch, *The Spanish American Revolutions*, provides much insight on the deeply conservative nature of Latin American societies; two good works by Timothy P. Wickham-Crowley, *Guerrillas and Revolution in Latin America: A Comparative Study of Insurgents and Regimes since 1956*, and *Exploring Revolution: Essays on Latin American Insurgency and Revolutionary Theory*; Max G. Manwaring, ed., *Uncomfortable Wars*, has several chapters on counterinsurgency in diverse Latin American states; Georges Fauriol, ed. *Latin American Insurgencies*; Alberto Bayo, *150 Questions for a Guerrilla*, by the man who helped train the Castro brothers in the rudiments of guerrilla war; Richard Gott, *Rural Guerrilla in Latin America*, extremely sympathetic to leftist guerrillas; Ernesto "Che" Guevara's very interesting little handbook, *Guerrilla Warfare*; Luis Mercier Vega, *Guerrillas in Latin America: The Technique of the Counter-State*, a wide-ranging and well-researched work that correctly predicted the failure of all or almost all Latin American guerrilla movements; Ernesto Betancourt, *Revolutionary Strategy: A Handbook for Practitioners*, a book that reaches some sound conclusions about the limitations of guerrilla war but whose highly schematic nature and academic tone make it somewhat inaccessible; Thomas A. Brown, *Statistical Indicators of the Effect of Military Programs on Latin America*; two works by Regis Debray, *Strategy for Revolution* (a series of essays) and *Revolution in the Revolution*, the most systematic exposition of the now totally discredited "foco" theory; Raymond Estep, *Guerrilla Warfare in Latin America 1963–1975*; Robert H. Dix, "Why Revolutions Succeed and Fail"; Gabriel Marcella, "The Latin American Military, Low Intensity Conflict, and Democracy"; Theda Skocpol, "What Makes Peasants Revolutionary?"; Richard Weitz, "Insurgency and Communism in Latin America 1960–1980"; Linda

Reif, "Women in Latin American Guerrilla Movements: A Comparative Perspective"; and Jean Larteguy, *The Guerrillas*.

Three useful studies of the Haitian revolution are: C. L. R. James, *The Black Jacobins: Toussaint L'Ouverture and the San Domingo Revolution*; Thomas Ott, *The Haitian Revolution*; and Martin Ros, *Night of Fire: The Black Napoleon and the Battle for Haiti*. On United States efforts to establish orderly government in Haiti from Woodrow Wilson to Franklin D. Roosevelt, see Robert and Nancy Heinl, *Written in Blood: The Story of the Haitian People 1492–1971*; Lester D. Langley, *The Banana Wars: United States Intervention in the Caribbean 1898–1934*; James H. McCrocklin, *Garde D'Haiti, 1915–1934*, the story of the national military force the U.S. Marines built in Haiti; Hans Schmidt, *The United States Occupation of Haiti 1915–1934*, a first-class study, very critical of American policies in that unhappy half-island; Selden Rodman, *Haiti: The Black Republic*; Ludwell Montague, *Haiti and the United States 1714–1938*; and for solid histories of the U.S. Marines, who had the responsibility for carrying out most of Washington's interventionist policy in Central America and the Caribbean, see Allan R. Millett, *Semper Fidelis: The History of the United States Marine Corps*, and Clyde Metcalf, *A History of the United States Marine Corps*.

On Castro and Cuba, for background see Samuel Farber, *Revolution and Reaction in Cuba, 1933–1960*; Louis A. Perez, *Army Politics in Cuba 1898–1958*; Ramon Ruiz, *Cuba: The Making of a Revolution*, a really excellent introduction; and the massive, impressively detailed work by Hugh Thomas, *Cuba: The Pursuit of Freedom*. On the Castroite insurrection per se, Theodore Draper's collection of essays, *Castro's Revolution: Myths and Realities*, punctured the myth of the peasant uprising. Other interesting studies include Ramon Bonachea and Marta San Martin, *The Cuban Insurrection, 1952–1959*; Carlos Franqui, *Diary of the Cuban Revolution*, an episodic account of the period 1952–1959 by a one-time close associate of Castro; Neill Macauley, *A Rebel in Cuba: An American's Memoir*, Robert Taber, *The War of the Flea*, a journalist asking for American support of Latin American revolutions; and the solid study by Boris Goldenberg, *The Cuban Revolution and Latin America*. See also Fidel Castro, *Selected Works*, vol. 1 *Revolutionary Struggle*; Ernesto Guevara, *Reminiscences of the Cuban Revolutionary War; Cuba Betrayed*, by Fulgencio Batista, the dictator whom Castro ousted, an interesting work that should be consulted; and two informative articles, Dickey Chapelle, "How Castro Won," and Neill Macauley, "The Cuban Rebel Army: A Numerical Survey."

Central America's guerrilla wars sparked the production of many works during the 1980s. For solid comparative studies of this troubled region consult Howard Wiarda, ed., *Rift and Revolution: The Central American Imbroglio*; James Dunkerley, *Power in the Isthmus: A Political History of Modern Central America*; Donald E. Schulz and Douglas Graham, *Revolution and Counterrevolution in Central America and the Caribbean*; Richard Allen White, *The Morass: United States Intervention in Central America* (deeply hostile to any U.S. intervention in Latin America). See also David C. Jordan, "U.S. Options—and illusions—in Central America''; Saul Landau, *The Guerrilla Wars of Central America*. See also the following collections: Robert Leiken, ed., *Central America: Anatomy of a Conflict*; Robert Leiken and Barry Rubin, eds., *The Central American Crisis Reader*; and Marlene Dixon and Suzanne Jonas, eds., *Revolution and Intervention in Central America*. Finally, see Henry Kissinger et al., *Report of the Bipartisan Commission on Central America*.

On Guatemala's long and intricate period of insurgency, consult Richard N. Adams, *Crucifixion by Power: Essays on Guatemalan National Social Structure 1944–1966*; Jonathan Fried et al., eds., *Guatemala in Rebellion: Unfinished History*; Peter Martin Stephenson, *Guerrilla Warfare, Population Growth and Economic Development: A Case Study of Guatemala*; Caesar D. Sereseres, "The Guatemalan Counterinsurgency Campaign of 1982–1985; A Strategy of Going it Alone," in Edwin G. Corr and Stephen Sloan, eds., *Low Intensity Conflicts: Old Threats in a New World*; Michael Sheehan, "Comparative Counterinsurgency Strategies: Guatemala and El Salvador"; and Mario Payeras, "Days of the Jungle: The Testimony of a Guatemalan Guerrillero, 1972–1976."

On the insurgency in El Salvador, perhaps the most useful studies are A. J. Bacevich et al., *American Military Policy in Small Wars: The Case of El Salvador*; John Waghelstein, *Observations and Experiences in Counterinsurgency*; Benjamin C. Schwarz, *American Counterinsurgency Doctrine and El Salvador: The Frustrations of Reform and the Illusions of Nationbuilding*; Max G. Manwaring and Court Prisk, eds., *El Salvador at War: An Oral History*; Edward G. Corr and Courtney Prisk, "El Salvador: Transforming Society to Win the Peace"; Max G. Manwaring, "Strategic Vision and Insurgency: Lessons from El Salvador and Peru" and "The Need for Strategic Perspective: Insights from El Salvador"; Victor M. Rosello, "Lessons from El Salvador"; Gabriel Marcella, "Concerning our Military Plans: The Military Strategy of the FMLN"; Enrique Baloyra, "Negotiating War in El Salvador: The Politics of Endgame"; James LeMoyne, "El Salvador's Forgotten War"; Samuel Dillon, "Dateline El Salvador: Crisis Renewed"; and Courtney Prisk, ed., *The Comandante Speaks*. Some earlier treatments are Alistair White, *El Salvador*; Robert Armstrong and Janet Shenk, *El Salvador: The Face of Revolution*; Cynthia Arnson, *El Salvador: A Revolution Confronts the United States*; Enrique Baloyra, *El Salvador in Transition*; R. Bruce McColm, *El Salvador: Peaceful Revolution or Armed Struggle*; Tommie Sue Montgomery, *Revolution in El Salvador* (which took the sensible and perceptive position that for a lasting peace guerrillas would have to accept participation in free elections); H. G. Hudson, "Are the Salvadoran Armed Forces Ready to Fold?"; and William Leogrande, "A Splendid Little War: Drawing the Line in El Salvador."

Regarding Nicaragua, the Sandinistas, and the Contras, one of the best studies is Shirley Christian, *Revolution in the Family*. On Sandinista ideology see David Nolan, *The Ideology of the Sandinistas and the Nicaraguan Revolution*, and Tomas Borge et al., *Sandinistas Speak*. Richard Millett has provided an excellent study of the Guardia Nacional under the Somozas in *Guardians of the Dynasty*;

in conjunction with Millett's book see Bernard Diederich, *Somoza and the Legacy of U.S. Involvement in Central America*. Other useful treatments are Samuel Dillon, *Commandos: The CIA and Nicaragua's Contra Rebels*; David Nolan, *FSLN*; Neill Macauley's *The Sandino Affair* is widely regarded as a classic study of U.S. interventionism in the Caribbean; John Booth, *The End and the Beginning: The Nicaraguan Revolution*; Omar Cabezas, *Fire from the Mountain: The Making of a Sandinista*; and Alfred Cuzzan and R. J. Heggen, "A Micropolitical Explanation of the 1979 Nicaraguan Revolution." For an unabashed celebration of the Sandinistas, see George Black, *The Triumph of a People: The Sandinista Revolution in Nicaragua*.

On the Sendero Luminoso and its antecedents in Peru, see the valuable book edited by David Scott Palmer, *The Shining Path of Peru*; Simon Strong, *Shining Path: The World's Deadliest Revolutionary Force*; U.S. House of Representatives, *The Shining Path after Guzman*; James Rudolph, *Peru: The Evolution of a Crisis*, which examines the failure of Peruvian democratic politics under Belaúnde and García; the excellent article by Cynthia McClintock, "Peru's Sendero Luminoso Rebellion: Origins and Trajectory," in Susan Eckstein, ed. *Power and Popular Protest: Latin American Social Movements*; Cynthia McClintock, "Why Peasants Rebel: The Case of Peru"; David Scott Palmer, "Rebellion in Rural Peru: Origins and Evolution of the Sendero Luminoso"; Ronald Berg, "Sendero Luminoso and the Peasantry of the Aduahuaylas"; Leon G. Campbell, "The Historiography of the Peruvian Guerrilla Movement"; and Orin Starn, "New Literature on Peru's Sendero Luminoso."

On the endemic violence in Colombia, valuable studies include Richard Maullin, *Soldiers, Guerrillas and Politics in Colombia*; Paul Oquist, *Violence, Conflict and Politics in Colombia*; Charles W. Bergquist et al., eds., *Violence in Colombia*; and J. Mark Ruhl, *Colombia: Armed Forces and Society*. Walter Broderick examines a peculiar episode in the country's recent history in *Camilo Torres: A Biography of the Priest-Guerrilla*. See also Jorge Osterling's article "Democracy in Colombia: Clientelist Politics and Guerrilla Warfare."

On Venezuela, see Daniel H. Levine, *Conflict and Political Change in Venezuela*; S. Ellner, "Political Party Dynamics in Venezuela and the Outbreak of Guerrilla War"; and numerous references and sub-chapters in Timothy Wickham-Crowley, *Guerrillas and Revolution in Latin America*.

On Ernesto Guevara's Bolivian fiasco, see Luis J. Gonzalez and G. Sanchez Salazar, *The Great Rebel: Che Guevara in Bolivia*; Donald C. Hodges, ed., *The Legacy of Che Guevara*; Daniel James, *Che Guevara: A Biography*, and *The Complete Bolivian Diaries of Che Guevara*, a very good translation; Robert F. Lamberg, "Che in Bolivia: The Revolution that Failed"; and Norman Gall, "The Legacy of Che Guevara."

Adams, Richard N. *Crucifixion by Power: Essays on Guatemalan National Social Structure, 1944–1966*. Austin, TX: University of Texas, 1970.

Armstrong, Robert, and Janet Shenk. *El Salvador: The Face of Revolution*. London: Pluto, 1982.

Arnson, Cynthia. *El Salvador: A Revolution Confronts the United States*. Washington, DC. Institute for Policy Studies, 1982.

Bacevich, A. J. et al. *American Military Policy in Small Wars: The Case of El Salvador*. Washington, DC: Brassey's, 1988.

Baloyra, Enrique. *El Salvador in Transition*. Chapel Hill. NC: University of North Carolina, 1982.

————. "Negotiating War in El Salvador: The Politics of Endgame." *Journal of Interamerican and World Affairs*, vol. 28, no. 1 (Spring 1986).

Batista, Fulgencio. *Cuba Betrayed*. New York: Vantage, 1962.

Bayo, Alberto. *150 Questions for a Guerrilla*. Boulder, CO: Pantheon, 1963.

Berg, Ronald. "Sendero Luminoso and the Peasantry of the Aduahuaylas." *Journal of Interamerican Studies and World Affairs*. vol. 28 (Winter 1986–1987).

Bergquist, Charles W., et al. *Violence in Colombia: The Contemporary Crisis in Historical Perspective*. Wilmington, DE: Scholarly Resources, 1992.

Betancourt, Ernesto F. *Revolutionary Strategy: A Handbook for Practitioners*. New Brunswick, NJ: Transaction, 1991.

Black, George. *Triumph of a People: The Sandinista Revolution in Nicaragua*. London: Zed, 1981.

Bonachea, Ramon and Marta San Martin. *The Cuban Insurrection, 1952–1959*. New Brunswick, NJ.: Transaction, 1974.

Booth, John. *The End and the Beginning: The Nicaraguan Revolution*. Boulder, CO: Westview, 1982.

Borge, Tomas, Carlos Fonseca, Daniel Ortega, Humberto Ortega, and Jaime Wheelock. *Sandinistas Speak*. New York: Pathfinder, 1982.

Broderick, Walter. *Camilo Torres: A Biography of the Priest-Guerrilla*. New York: Doubleday, 1975.

Brown, Thomas A. *Statistical Indications of the Effect of Military Programs on Latin America*. Santa Monica, CA: RAND, 1969.

Cabezas, Omar. *Fire from the Mountain: The Making of a Sandinista*. Trans. K. Weaver. New York: Crown, 1985.

Campbell, Leon G. "The Historiography of the Peruvian Guerrilla Movement." *Latin American Research Review*, vol. 8 (Spring 1973).

Castro, Fidel. *Selected Works*. vol. 1: *Revolutionary Struggle*. Cambridge, MA: MIT, 1971.

Chapelle, Dickey. "How Castro Won." Franklin Mark Osanka, ed. *Modern Guerrilla Warfare*. New York: Free Press, 1962.

Christian, Shirley. *Revolution in the Family*. New York: Vintage, 1986.

Corr, Edward G., and Courtney Prisk. "El Salvador: Transforming Society to Win the Peace." Edwin G. Corr and Stephen Sloan, ed. *Low-Intensity Conflict: Old Threats in a New World*. Boulder, CO: Westview, 1992.

Cuzan, Alfred G., and R. J. Heggen. "A Micropolitical Explanation of the 1979 Nicaraguan Revolution." *Latin American Research Review*, vol. 27 (1982).

Debray, Regis. *Revolution in the Revolution*. New York: Monthly Review, 1967.

————. *Strategy for Revolution*. London, Jonathan Cape, 1970.

Diederich, Bernard. *Somoza and the Legacy of U.S. Involvement in Central America*. New York: Dutton, 1981.

Dillon, Samuel. *Commandos: The CIA and Nicaragua's Contra Rebels*. New York: Holt, 1991.

———. "Dateline El Salvador: Crisis Renewed." *Foreign Policy*, no. 73 (Winter 1988–1989).

Dix, Robert H. "Why Revolutions Succeed and Fail." *Polity*, vol. 16 (Spring 1984).

Dixon, Marlene, and Suzanne Jonas, eds. *Revolution and Intervention in Central America*. San Francisco: Synthesis Publications, 1983.

Draper, Theodore. *Castro's Revolution—Myths and Realities*. London: Thames and Hudson, 1962.

Dunkerley, James. *Power in the Isthmus: A Political History of Modern Central America*. London: Verso, 1988.

Ellner, S. "Political Party Dynamics in Venezuela and the Outbreak of Guerrilla War." *Inter-American Economic Affairs*, vol. 34 (August 1980).

Estep, Raymond. *Guerrilla Warfare in Latin America, 1963–1975*. Maxwell Air Force Base, AL: Air University Press, 1975.

Farber, Samuel. *Revolution and Reaction in Cuba, 1933–1960*. Middletown, CT: Wesleyan University, 1976.

Fauriol, Georges, ed. *Latin American Insurgencies*. Washington, DC: Georgetown University, 1985.

Franqui, Carlos. *Diary of the Cuban Revolution*. Trans. Georgette Felix. New York: Viking, 1980.

Fried, Jonathan, et al., eds. *Guatemala in Rebellion: Unfinished History*. New York: Grove, 1983.

Gall, Norman. "The Legacy of Che Guevara." *Commentary*, vol. 44 (December 1967).

Goldenberg, Boris. *The Cuban Revolution and Latin America*. London: Allen and Unwin, 1965.

Gonzalez, Luis J., and G. Sanchez Salazar. *The Great Rebel: Che Guevara in Bolivia*. New York: Grove, 1969.

Gott, Richard. *Rural Guerrilla in Latin America*. Harmondsworth, UK: Penguin, 1973.

Guevara, Ernesto. *Guerrilla Warfare*. New York: Vintage, 1961.

———. *Reminiscences of the Cuban Revolutionary War*. New York: Grove, 1963.

Heinl, Robert, and Nancy Heinl. *Written in Blood: The Story of the Haitian People, 1492–1971*. Boston: Houghton Mifflin, 1978.

Hodges, Donald C., ed. *The Legacy of Che Guevara*. London: Thames and Hudson, 1977.

Hudson, H. G. "Are the Salvadoran Armed Forces Ready to Fold?" *World Affairs*, vol. 146 (Winter 1983/84).

James, C.L.R. *The Black Jacobins: Toussaint L'Ouverture and the San Domingo Revolution*. New York: Vintage, 1963.

James, Daniel. *Che Guevara—A Biography*. London: Allen and Unwin, 1970.

James, Daniel, ed. *The Complete Bolivian Diaries of Che Guevara*. London: Allen and Unwin, 1968.

Johnson, John J. *The Military and Society in Latin America*. Stanford, CA: Stanford University, 1964.

Jordan, David C. "U.S. Options—and Illusions—in Central America." *Strategic Review*, Spring 1982.

Kissinger, Henry, et al. *Report of the Bipartisan Commission on Central America*. Washington, DC: Government Printing Office, 1984.

Lamberg, Robert F. "Che in Bolivia: The 'Revolution' That Failed." *Problems of Communism*, vol. 19 (July–August 1970).

Landau, Saul. *The Guerrilla Wars of Central America*. New York: St. Martin's, 1993.

Langley, Lester D. *The Banana Wars: United States Intervention in the Caribbean, 1898–1934*. Chicago: Dorsey, 1985.

Larteguy, Jean. *The Guerrillas*. New York: World Press, 1970.

Leiken, Robert ed. *Central America: Anatomy of a Conflict*. New York: Pergamon, 1984.

Leiken, Robert S., and Barry Rubin, eds. *The Central American Crisis Reader*. New York: Summit, 1987.

LeMoyne, James. "El Salvador's Forgotten War." *Foreign Affairs*, Fall 1989.

LeoGrande, William. "A Splendid Little War: Drawing the Line in El Salvador." *International Security*, vol. 6, no. 1 (Summer 1981).

Levine, Daniel H. *Conflict and Political Change in Venezuela*. Princeton, NJ: Princeton University, 1973.

Lynch, John. *The Spanish American Revolutions, 1808–1826*. New York: Norton, 1973.

Macauley, Neill. *A Rebel in Cuba: An American's Memoir*. Chicago: Quadrangle, 1970.

———. "The Cuban Rebel Army: A Numerical Survey." *Hispanic American Historical Review*, vol. 58, no. 2 (May 1978).

———. *The Sandino Affair*. Durham, NC: Duke University, 1985.

Manwaring, Max G. "The Need for Strategic Perspective: Insights from El Salvador." Max G. Manwaring, ed. *Uncomfortable Wars: Toward a New Paradigm of Low Intensity Conflict*. Boulder, CO: Westview, 1991.

———. "Strategic Vision and Insurgency in El Salvador and Peru." Max G. Manwaring, ed. *Uncomfortable Wars: Toward a New Paradigm of Low Intensity Conflict*. Boulder, CO: Westview, 1991.

———. *Uncomfortable Wars: Toward a New Paradigm of Low Intensity Conflict*. Boulder, CO: Westview, 1991.

Manwaring, Max G., and Court Prisk, eds. *El Salvador at War: An Oral History*. Washington, D.C.: National Defense University, 1988.

Marcella, Gabriel. "The Latin American Military, Low Intensity Conflict, and Democracy." *Journal of Interamerican Studies and World Affairs*, vol. 32 (Spring 1990).

Marcella, Gabriel, trans. and ed. "Concerning Our Military Plans: The Military Strategy of the FMLN." Carlisle, PA: U.S. Army War College, 1986.

Maullin, Richard L. *Soldiers, Guerrillas and Politics in Colombia*. Toronto: Lexington, 1973.

McClintock, Cynthia. "Peru's Sendero Luminoso Rebellion: Origins and Trajectory." Susan Eckstein, ed. *Power and Popular Protest: Latin American Social Movements*. Berkeley, CA: University of California, 1989.

———. "Why Peasants Rebel: The Case of Peru." *World Politics*, vol. 37 (October 1985).

McColm, R. Bruce. *El Salvador: Peaceful Revolution or Armed Struggle*. New York: Freedom House, 1982.

McCrocklin, James H. *Garde D'Haiti, 1915–1934*. Annapolis, MD: United States Naval Institute, 1956.

Mercier Vega, Luis. *Guerrillas in Latin America: The Technique of the Counter-State*. Trans. D. Weissbort. New York: Praeger, 1969.

Metcalf, Clyde. *A History of the United States Marine Corps*. New York: Putnam, 1939.

Millett, Allen R. *Semper Fidelis: The History of the United States Marine Corps*. New York: Macmillan, 1980.

Millett, Richard. *Guardians of the Dynasty*. Maryknoll, NY: Orbis, 1977.

Millspaugh, Arthur C. *Haiti under American Control 1915–1930*. Boston: World Peace Foundation, 1931.

Montague, Ludwell. *Haiti and the United States, 1914–1938*. Durham, NC: Duke University, 1940.

Montgomery, Tommie Sue. *Revolution in El Salvador: Origins and Evolution*. Boulder, CO: Westview, 1982.

Nolan, David. *FSLN*. Miami, FL: University of Miami, 1984.

———. *The Ideology of the Sandinistas and the Nicaraguan Revolution*. Coral Gables, FL: University of Miami, 1984.

Oquist, Paul. *Violence, Conflict and Politics in Colombia*. New York: Academic, 1980.

Osterling, Jorge. "Democracy in Colombia: Clientelist Politics and Guerrilla Warfare." *Latin American Research Review*, vol. 27, no. 3 (1992).

Ott, Thomas. *The Haitian Revolution, 1789–1804*. Knoxville, TN: University of Tennessee, 1973.

Palmer, David Scott. "Rebellion in Rural Peru: Origins and Evolution of the Sendero Luminoso." *Comparative Politics*, vol. 18 (Spring 1986).

Palmer, David Scott, ed. *The Shining Path of Peru*. New York: St. Martin's, 1992.

Payeras, Mario. "Days of the Jungle: The Testimony of a Guatemalan Guerrillero, 1972–1976." *Monthly Review*, vol. 35, no. 3 (July–August 1983).

Perez, Louis A. *Army Politics in Cuba, 1898–1958*. Pittsburgh, PA: University of Pittsburgh, 1976.

Prisk, Courtney E., ed. *The Comandante Speaks*. Boulder, CO: Westview, 1991.

Reif, Linda L. "Women in Latin American Guerrilla Movements: A Comparative Perspective." *Comparative Politics*, vol. 18, no. 2 (January 1986).

Rodman, Selden. *Haiti: The Black Republic*. New York: Devin-Adair, 1961.

Ros, Martin. *Night of Fire: The Black Napoleon and the Battle for Haiti*. Trans. Karen Ford. New York: Sarpedon, 1994.

Rosello, Victor M. "Lessons from El Salvador." *Parameters*, vol. 23, no. 4 (Winter 1993–1994).

Rouquie, Alain. *The Military and the State in Latin America*. Trans. Paul Sigmund. Berkeley, CA: University of California, 1987.

Rudolph, James. *Peru: The Evolution of a Crisis*. New York: Praeger, 1992.

Ruhl, J. Mark. *Colombia: Armed Forces and Society*. New York: Syracuse University, 1980.

Ruiz, Ramon. *Cuba: The Making of a Revolution*. New York: Norton, 1968.

Schmidt, Hans. *The United States Occupation of Haiti 1915–1934*. New Brunswick, NJ: Rutgers University, 1971.

Schulz, Donald E., and Douglas Graham. *Revolution and Counterrevolution in Central America and the Caribbean*. Boulder, CO: Westview, 1984.

Schwarz, Benjamin C. *American Counterinsurgency Doctrine and El Salvador: The Frustrations of Reform and the Illusions of Nation Building*. Santa Monica, CA: RAND, 1991.

Sereseres, Caesar D. "The Guatemalan Counterinsurgency Campaign of 1982–1985: A Strategy of Going It Alone." Edwin G. Corr and Stephen Sloan, eds. *Low-Intensity Conflict: Old Threats in a New World*. Boulder, CO: Westview, 1992.

Sheehan, Michael. "Comparative Counterinsurgency Strategies: Guatemala and El Salvador." *Conflict*, vol. 9, no. 2 (1989).

Skocpol, Theda. "What Makes Peasants Revolutionary?" *Comparative Politics*, vol. 14 (April 1982).

Starn, Orin. "New Literature on Peru's Sendero Luminoso." *Latin American Research Review*, vol. 27 (Spring 1992).

Stephenson, Peter Martin. *Guerrilla Warfare, Population Growth and Economic Development: A Case Study of Guatemala*. Doctoral dissertation, MIT, 1973.

Strong, Simon. *Shining Path: The World's Deadliest Revolutionary Force*. London: HarperCollins 1992.

Taber, Robert. *The War of the Flea*. New York: L. Stuart, 1965.

Thomas, Hugh. *Cuba: The Pursuit of Freedom*. New York: Harper and Row, 1971.

United States Congress, Senate. *Inquiry into Occupation and Administration of Haiti and Santo Domingo*. Washington, DC: Government Printing Office, 1922.

United States House of Representatives. *The Shining Path after Guzman*. Washington, DC: Government Printing Office, 1992.

Waghelstein, John. *El Salvador: Observations and Experiences in Counterinsurgency*. Carlisle, PA: US. Army War College, 1985.

Walker, Thomas W., ed. *Reagan vs. the Sandinistas: The Undeclared War on Nicaragua*. Boulder, CO: Westview, 1987.

Weitz, Richard. "Insurgency and Communism in Latin America, 1960–1980." *Political Science* Quarterly, vol. 101, no. 3 (1986).

White, Alistair. *El Salvador*. New York: Praeger, 1973.

White, Richard Allen. *The Morass: United States Intervention in Central America*. New York: Harper and Row, 1984.

Wiarda, Howard, ed. *Rift and Revolution: The Central American Imbroglio*. Washington, DC: American Enterprise Institute, 1984.

Wickham-Crowley, Timothy. *Exploring Revolution: Essays on Latin American Insurgency and Revolutionary Theory*. Armonk, NY: M. E. Sharpe, 1991.

———. *Guerrillas and Revolution in Latin America: A Comparative Study of Insurgents and Regimes since 1956*. Princeton, NJ: Princeton University, 1992.

Wars of Decolonization

For a comparative focus on colonial and postcolonial conflicts, consult the work by the former Chief of the General Staff, Michael Carver, *War since 1945*; Joyce Lebra, *Japanese-Trained Armies in Southeast Asia*, an interesting work on a very neglected subject, focuses on India, Indonesia, and Burma; and there is always good ore to be mined from Eric Wolfe's wide-ranging *Peasant Wars of the Twentieth Century*.

The war in French Algeria, which offers so many lessons in counterinsurgency and had such explosive political consequences, has of course produced many excellent studies. See the solid account by a reliable student of many conflicts, Edgar O'Ballance, *The Algerian Insurrection, 1954–1962*; a well-received work written at the height of the struggle by an experienced journalist, Edward Behr, *The Algerian Problem*; a good academic treatment by David C.

Gordon, *The Passing of French Algeria*; Alf A. Heggoy, *Insurgency and Counterinsurgency in Algeria*, focuses on guerrilla terrorism and outside political forces working upon the French political system. Other worthwhile studies are John Talbott's concise and well-written *The War without a Name: France in Algeria 1954–1962*; the popular and panoramic book by Alistaire Horne, *A Savage War of Peace: Algeria 1954–1962*; Joseph Kraft, *The Struggle for Algeria*; Jules Roy, *The War in Algeria*; Tony Smith, *The French Stake in Algeria, 1954–1962*; Irwin M. Wall, "The French Communists and the Algerian War"; and Jean Larteguy's, *The Centurions*, a controversial novel about paratroop veterans of the Viet Nam struggle serving in Algeria. On the French army per se see two fine works, John Ambler, *Soldiers against the State: The French Army in Politics*; and George Kelly, *Lost Soldiers: The French Army and Empire in Crisis*, which is sympathetic to the army and severely critical of the politicians in Paris; an overall treatment of the history of the modern French army with good chapters on the Algerian conflict is Paul-Marie de la Gorce, *The French Army: A Political-Military History*.

For accounts of the life and counterinsurgency techniques of the famed French General Lyautey, see André Maurois, *Lyautey*; Sonia Howe, *Lyautey of Morocco*; and Douglas Porch, *The Conquest of Morocco*. The conjunction of French involvement in bitter counterinsurgency, first in Viet Nam and then immediately afterward in Algeria, gave rise to the concepts sometimes called "French Revolutionary Warfare." These ideas found expression in Roger Trinquier's *Modern Warfare: A French View of Counterinsurgency*, a French officer's truly chilling blueprint for military totalitarianism; and the interesting commentary on these concepts by Peter Paret, *French Revolutionary Warfare from Indochina to Algeria: An Analysis of a Political and Military Doctrine*.

Concerning the diverse struggles in Portuguese Africa, which continued for many years after decolonization, see (regarding Portuguese Guinea) the collection by the leader of the revolt there, Amilcar Cabral, *Revolution in Guinea*; Patrick Chabal, *Amilcar Cabral: Revolutionary Leadership and People's War*, the first full biography of Cabral based on his papers; Ronald H. Chilcote, "The Political Thought of Amilcar Cabral"; Gerald Chaliand, *Armed Struggle in Africa: With the Guerrillas in "Portuguese Guinea"* (the author sees armed revolution as the only way to change the existing social order); Fred Bridgland, *Jonas Savimbi: A Key to Africa*; Elaine Windrick, *Cold War Guerrilla: Jonas Savimbi, the U.S. Media and the Angolan War*; Basil Davidson, *The Liberation of Guinea*, with a foreword by Cabral. On Angola, see the two well-received volumes by John A. Marcum, *The Angolan Revolution* and *In the Eye of the Storm: Angola's People*; Basil Davidson, *The Angolan Revolution*; W. Martin James, *The Unita Insurgency in Angola*; and Jim Hooper, "Being There: Unita Guerrillas Attack with Impunity." For the wars in Mozambique, see William Finnegan, *A Complicated War: The Harrowing of Mozambique*; a highly praised work by Thomas H. Henrikson, *Revolution and Counterrevolution: Mozambique's War of Independence 1964–1974*; Allen and Barbara Isaacman, *Mozam-*

bique: From Colonialism to Revolution; E. Mondlane, *The Struggle for Mozambique*; Barry Munslow, *Mozambique: The Revolution and Its Origins*; and Alex Vines, *Renamo Terrorism in Mozambique*. For the broader context of these conflicts, consult Richard Gibson, *African Liberation Movements*; K. W. Grundy, *Guerrilla Struggle in Africa*; Douglas Porch, *The Portuguese Armed Forces and the Revolution*; and William LeoGrande, ed., *Cuba in Africa*.

On the Eritrean war, see Roy Pateman, *Eritrea: Even the Stones Are Burning*, and "The Eritrean War"; Richard F. Sherman, *Eritrea in Revolution*; and J. Bowyer Bell, "Endemic Insurgency and International Order: The Eritrean Experience."

Regarding the Tibetan resistance to Chinese occupation, for background see the highly detailed work by Melvin Goldstein, *A History of Modern Tibet 1913–1951*, as well as H. E. Richardson, *A Short History of Tibet*, and two older but still useful titles by Sir Charles Bell, *The People of Tibet* and *Tibet Past and Present*. For the guerrilla struggle, see Michel Peissel, *The Secret War in Tibet*; Frank Moraes, *The Revolt in Tibet*; John F. Avedon, *In Exile from the Land of the Snows*; George Patterson's truly engrossing *Requiem for Tibet* and *Tibet in Revolt*, as well as his article "The 'Fish' and the 'Sea' of Tibet: Fifteen Years of Guerrilla Warfare and Popular Unrest." On the Indian involvement in the struggle, see the work by the former head of Indian intelligence, B. N. Mullik, *My Years with Nehru*, as well as Michael Carver, *War since 1945*, and Neville Maxwell's very valuable *India's China War*. For a juridical evaluation of the Chinese invasion, see two works by the International Commission of Jurists, *The Question of Tibet and the Rule of Law*, and *Tibet and the Chinese People's Republic*. For a pro-Chinese view, see A. Tom Grunfeldt, *The Making of Modern Tibet*.

Concerning the protracted struggles in the Sudan, for background see P. M. Holt, *The Mahdist State in the Sudan* and *A Modern History of Sudan*, and P. M. Holt and M. W. Daly, *The History of the Sudan*. On the first insurgency, consult Edgar O'Ballance, *The Secret War in the Sudan*; Oliver Albino, *The Sudan: The Southern Viewpoint*; Cecil Eprile, *War and Peace in the Sudan*; Gabriel Warburg, *Islam, Nationalism and Communism in a Traditional Society: The Case of the Sudan*; and Keith Kyle, "The Southern Problem in the Sudan." For more recent developments, *Civil War in the Sudan*, edited by M. W. Daly and A. A. Sikainga, has some really valuable chapters; Peter Woodward, *Sudan 1898–1989: The Unstable State*, and J. Millard Burr and Robert O. Collins, *Requiem for the Sudan*, can also be consulted with profit. Amnesty International has published *Sudan: Human Rights Violations in the Context of Civil War*. Also the following articles are all useful: A. El-Affendi, "Discovering the South: Sudanese Dilemmas for Islam in Africa"; Carolyn Fluehr-Lobban, "Islamization in Sudan: A Critical Assessment"; N. A. L. Mohammed, "Militarization in the Sudan: Trends and Determinants"; Peter K. Bechtold, "More Turbulence in Sudan: A New Politics This Time?"; Francis Mading Deng, "War of Visions for the Nation"; Roger C. Glickson, "Counterinsurgency in Sudan: The Means to Win?''; and Milton Viorst, "Sudan's Islamic Experiment." Also consult *The World Today*, December 1984 and April 1992.

The conflict in Cyprus, which many would characterize as a terrorist campaign rather than a true guerrilla struggle, is another example of a very small war that manages to generate a rather large literature. See two works (with misleading names) by the rebellion's military leader, George Grivas, *Guerrilla Warfare and EOKA's Struggle,* and *General Grivas on Guerrilla Warfare*; the useful and revealing work edited by Charles Foley, *The Memoirs of General Grivas*; Dorros Alastros, *Cyprus Guerrilla—Grivas, Makarios and the British*; Dudley Barker, *Grivas: Portrait of a Terrorist*; W. Byford-Jones, *Grivas and the Story of EOKA*; and Charles Foley and W. Scobie, *The Struggle for Cyprus.*

As an introduction to guerrilla fighting in the Japanese-occupied Philippines, see Ira Wolfert, *American Guerrilla in the Philippines*, and Y. Panlilio, *The Crucible*. A very unusual and illuminating view of this period is presented by Mrs. L. R. Spencer, a Canadian married to an American engineer on Panay, in *Guerrilla Wife*.

The less-covered guerrilla conflicts often have valuable lessons to offer. On the fighting in East Timor, which has attracted little scholarly attention, see Carmel Budiardjo and Lieu Soei Liong, *The War against East Timor*, a work very sympathetic to the rebels and which reprints captured Indonesian Army documents. Another good study is John G. Taylor, *Indonesia's Forgotten War: The Hidden History of East Timor*. For Zimbabwe/Rhodesia, see Norma J. Kriger, *Zimbabwe's Guerrilla War: Peasant Voices*; on the various Burmese struggles, see Martin Smith's big, wide-ranging, and scholarly *Burma: Insurgency and the Politics of Ethnicity*. For a good treatment of the struggle between the Indonesians and the Dutch (very sympathetic to the former), see George McT. Kahin, *Nationalism and Revolution in Indonesia*, as well as the classic work of Nasution, *Fundamentals of Guerrilla Warfare*. Also worth consulting are N. Notosusanto, *The National Struggle and the Armed Forces in Indonesia*, and Lucian Ashworth, "The 1945–1949 Dutch-Indonesian Conflict: Lessons and Perspectives in the Study of Insurgency."

For the 1970s roots of many trends and events in the Middle East of the 1990s, see two solid works by Edgar O'Ballance: *The Kurdish Revolt, 1961–1970* and *Arab Guerrilla Power, 1967–1972.*

Alastos, Dorros. *Cyprus Guerrilla—Grivas, Makarios, and the British*. London: Heinemann, 1960.

Albino, Oliver. *The Sudan: The Southern Viewpoint*. Oxford, UK: Oxford University, 1970.

Ambler, John. *Soldiers against the State: The French Army in Politics*. New York: Doubleday, 1968.

Amnesty International. *Sudan: Human Rights Violations in the Context of Civil War*. New York: Amnesty International 1989.

Avedon, John F. *In Exile from the Land of the Snows*. New York: Knopf, 1984.

Barker, Dudley. *Grivas—Portrait of a Terrorist*. London: Cresset, 1959.

Bechtold, Peter K. "More Turbulence in Sudan: A New Politics This Time?" *Middle East Journal*, vol. 44 (Autumn 1990).

Behr, Edward. *The Algerian Problem*. New York: Norton, 1962.

Bell, J. Bowyer. "Endemic Insurgency and International order: The Eritrean Experience." *Orbis*, Summer 1974.

Bell, Sir Charles. *The People of Tibet*. London: Oxford University, 1928.

———. *Tibet Past and Present*. London: Oxford University, 1927.

Bridgland, Fred. *Jonas Savimbi: A Key to Africa*. Edinburgh: Mainstream, 1986.

Budiardjo, Carmel, and Lieu Soei Liong. *The War against East Timor*. London: Zed, 1984.

Burr, J. Millard, and Robert O. Collins. *Requiem for the Sudan*. Boulder, CO: Westview, 1995.

Byford-Jones, W. *Grivas and the Story of EOKA*. London: Robert Hale, 1959.

Cabral, Amilcar. *Revolution in Guinea*. Trans. R. Handeyside. London: Stage 1, 1969.

Carver, Michael. *War since 1945*. New York: G. P. Putnam's Sons, 1981.

Chabal, Patrick. *Amilcar Cabral: Revolutionary Leadership and People's War*. Cambridge, UK: Cambridge University, 1983.

Chaliand, Gerard. *Armed Struggle in Africa: With the Guerrillas in "Portuguese" Guinea* Trans. D. Rattray and R. Leonhardt. New York: Monthly Review, 1969 [French edition 1967].

Chilcote, Ronald H. "The Political Thought of Amilcar Cabral." *Journal of Modern African Studies*, vol. 3 (1968).

Daly, M. W. "Broken Bridges and Empty Basket: The Political and Economic Background of the Sudanese Civil War." M. W. Daly and A. A. Sikainga, eds. *Civil War in the Sudan*. New York: British Academic Press, 1993.

Daly, M. W., and A. A. Sikainga, eds. *Civil War in the Sudan*. New York: British Academic Press, 1993.

Davidson, Basil. *The Angolan Revolution*. Cambridge, MA: MIT, 1969.

———. *The Liberation of Guinea*. Harmondsworth, UK: Penguin, 1969.

De la Gorce, Paul-Marie. *The French Army: A Military-Political History*. New York: George Braziller, 1963.

Deng, Francis Mading. "War of Visions for the Nation." *Middle East Journal*, vol. 44 (Autumn 1990).

El-Affendi, Abdelwahab. "Discovering the South: Sudanese Dilemmas for Islam in Africa." *African Affairs*, vol. 89 (July 1990).

Eprile, Cecil. *War and Peace in the Sudan*. London: Hurst, 1968.

Finnegan, William. *A Complicated War: The Harrowing of Mozambique*. Berkeley, CA: University of California, 1992.

Fluehr-Lobban, Carolyn. "Islamization in Sudan: A Critical Assessment." *Middle East Journal*, vol. 44 (Autumn 1990).

Foley, Charles, ed. *Memoirs of General Grivas*. New York: Praeger, 1964.

Foley, Charles, and W. Scobie. *The Struggle for Cyprus*. Stanford, CA: Hoover Institution, 1975.

Gibson, Richard. *African Liberation Movements*. London: Oxford University, 1972.

Glickson, Roger C. "Counterinsurgency in Southern Sudan: The Means to Win?" *Journal of Conflict Studies*, vol. 15 (Spring 1995).

Goldstein, Melvin C. *A History of Modern Tibet, 1913–1951*. Berkeley, CA: University of California, 1989.

Gordon, David C. *The Passing of French Algeria*. New York: Oxford University, 1966.

Grivas, George. *General Grivas on Guerrilla Warfare*. Trans. A. Pallis. New York: Praeger, 1965.

———. *Guerrilla Warfare and EOKA's Struggle*. New York: Praeger, 1964.

Grundy, K. W. *Guerrilla Struggle in Africa*. New York: Grossman, 1971.

Grunfeldt, A. Tom. *The Making of Modern Tibet*. London: Zed, 1987.

Heggoy, Alf A. *Insurgency and Counterinsurgency in Algeria*. Bloomington, IN: Indiana University, 1972.

Henriksen, Thomas H. *Revolution and Counterrevolution: Mozambique's War of Independence 1964–1974*. Westport, CT: Greenwood, 1983.

Holt P. M. *A Modern History of the Sudan*. London: Weidenfeld and Nicolson, 1961.

———. *The Mahdist State in the Sudan*. Oxford, UK: Oxford University, 1958.

Holt, P. M., and M. W. Daly. *The History of the Sudan*. London: Longman, 1988, 4th ed.

Hooper, Jim. "Being There: Unita Guerrillas Attack with Impunity." *International Defense Review*, vol. 22, no. 6 (1989).

Horne, Alistair. *A Savage War of Peace: Algeria, 1954–1962*. New York: Viking, 1977.

Howe, Sonia. *Lyautey of Morocco*. London: Hodder and Stoughton, 1931.

Isaacman, Allen, and Barbara Isaacman. *Mozambique: From Colonialism to Revolution*. Boulder, CO: Westview, 1983.

James, W. Martin. *The Unita Insurgency in Angola*. Doctoral dissertation, Catholic University of America, 1987.

Johnson, Douglas H., and Gerard Prunier. "The Foundations and Expansion of the Sudan People's Liberation Army." M. W. Daly and A. A. Sikainga, eds. *Civil War in the Sudan*. New York: British Academic Press, 1993.

Kahin, George McT. *Nationalism and Revolution in Indonesia*. Ithaca, NY: Cornell University, 1952.

Kelly, George. *Lost Soldiers: The French Army and Empire in Crisis*. Cambridge, MA: MIT, 1965.

Khalid, M., ed. *John Garang Speaks*. London: KPI, 1987.

Kraft, Joseph. *The Struggle for Algeria*. Garden City, NY: Doubleday, 1961.

Kriger, Norma J. *Zimbabwe's Guerrilla War: Peasant Voices*. Cambridge, UK: Cambridge University, 1992.

Kyle, Keith. "The Southern Problem in Sudan. *The World Today*, vol. 22 (December 1966).

Larteguy, Jean. *The Centurions*. Trans. Xan [sic] Fielding. London: Hutchinson, 1961.

Lebra, Joyce C. *Japanese-Trained Armies in Southeast Asia*. New York: Columbia University, 1977.

Legal Enquiry Committee. *Tibet and the Chinese People's Republic*. Geneva: International Commission of Jurists, 1960.

———. *The Question of Tibet and the Rule of Law*. Geneva: International Commission of Jurists, 1959.

LeoGrande, William, et al. *Cuba in Africa*. Pittsburgh, PA: University of Pittsburgh, 1980.

Marcum, John. *In the Eye of the Storm: Angola's People*. London: Longman, 1972.

Marcum, John A. *The Angolan Revolution*. Cambridge, MA: MIT, 1969, 1978. 2 vols.

Maurois, André. *Lyautey*. Trans. H. Miles. New York: Appleton, 1931.

Maxwell, Neville. *India's China War*. New York: Anchor, 1972.

Mohammed, N.A.L. "Militarization in the Sudan: Trends and Determinants." *Armed Forces and Society*, vol. 19 (Spring 1993).

Mondlane, E. *The Struggle for Mozambique*. Harmondsworth, UK: Penguin, 1969.

Moraes, Frank. *The Revolt in Tibet*. New York: Macmillan, 1960.

Mullik, B. N. *My Years with Nehru: The Chinese Betrayal*. Bombay: Allied Publishers, 1971.

Munslow, Barry. *Mozambique: The Revolution and Its Origins*. London: Longman, 1983.

Nasution, Abdul. *Fundamentals of Guerrilla Warfare*. New York: Praeger, 1965 [orig. 1953].

O'Ballance, Edgar. *The Algerian Insurrection 1954–1962*. Hamden, CT: Archon, 1967.

———. *Arab Guerrilla Power, 1967–1972*. Hamden, CT: Archon, 1973.

———. *The Kurdish Revolt, 1961–1970*. London: Faber and Faber, 1973.

———. *The Secret War in the Sudan*. Hamden, CT: Archon, 1977.

Panlilio, Y. *The Crucible*. New York: Macmillan, 1950.

Paret, Peter. *French Revolutionary Warfare from Indochina to Algeria: An Analysis of a Political and Military Doctrine*. New York: Praeger, 1964.

Pateman, Roy. *Eritrea: Even the Stones Are Burning*. Trenton, NJ: Red Sea Press, 1990.

———. "The Eritrean War." *Armed Forces and Society*, vol. 17, no. 1 (Fall 1990).

Patterson, George. "The 'Fish' and the 'Sea' of Tibet: Fifteen Years of Guerrilla Warfare and Popular Unrest." *Current Scene* (Hong Kong), vol. 3 (1963).

———. *Requiem for Tibet*. London: Aurum, 1990.

———. *Tibet in Revolt*. London: Faber and Faber, 1960.

Peissel, Michel. *The Secret War in Tibet*. Boston: Little, Brown, 1973.

Porch, Douglas. *The Conquest of Morocco*. New York: Knopf, 1982.

———. *The Portuguese Armed Force and the Revolution*. London: Croom Helm, 1977.

Richardson, H. E. *A Short History of Tibet*. New York: E. P. Dutton, 1962.

Roy, Jules. *The War in Algeria*. New York: Grove, 1961.

Sherman, Richard F. *Eritrea in Revolution*. Doctoral dissertation, Brandeis University, 1980.

Smith, Martin. *Burma: Insurgency and the Politics of Ethnicity*. Atlantic Highlands, NJ: Zed, 1991.

Smith, Tony. *The French Stake in Algeria, 1945–1962*. Ithaca, NY: Cornell University, 1978.

Spencer, L. R. *Guerrilla Wife*. New York: Crowell, 1945.

Talbott, John. *The War without a Name: France in Algeria 1954–1962*. New York: Knopf, 1980.

Taylor, John G. *Indonesia's Forgotten War: The Hidden History of East Timor*. London: Zed, 1991.

Trinquier, Roger. *Modern Warfare: A French View of Counterinsurgency*. Trans. Daniel Lee. New York: Praeger, 1964 [French publication 1961].

Vines, Alex. *Renamo: Terrorism in Mozambique*. Bloomington, IN: Indiana University, 1991.

Viorst, Milton. "Sudan's Islamic Experiment." *Foreign Affairs*, vol. 74 (May–June 1995).

Waal, Alex de. "Some Comments on Militia in the Contemporary Sudan." M. W. Daly and A. A. Sikainga, *Civil War in the Sudan*. New York: British Academic Press, 1993.

Wall, Irwin M. "The French Communists and the Algerian War." *Journal of Contemporary History*, vol. 12 (1977).

Warburg, Gabriel. *Islam, Nationalism and Communism in a Traditional Society: The Case of the Sudan*. London: Frank Cass, 1978.

Windrick, Elaine. *The Cold War Guerrilla: Jonas Savimbi, the U.S. Media, and the Angolan War*. New York: Greenwood, 1992.

Wolf, Eric. *Peasant Wars of the Twentieth Century*. New York: Harper and Row, 1969.

Wolfert, Ira. *American Guerrilla in the Philippines*. New York: Avon, 1945.

Woodward, Peter. *Sudan, 1898–1989: The Unstable State*. Boulder, CO: L. Rienner, 1990.

Index

About the Author

ANTHONY JAMES JOES is Professor of International Politics and Director of
the International Relations Program at Saint Joseph's University. He is the author of *The War for South Viet Nam, 1954–1975* (Praeger, 1989), *Modern Guerrilla Insurgency* (Praeger, 1992), and *Guerrilla Conflict Before the Cold War*
(Praeger, 1996).

ISBN 0-313-29252-3

HARDCOVER BAR CODE